Supercharged Coding with GenAI

From vibe coding to best practices using GitHub Copilot, ChatGPT, and OpenAI

Hila Paz Herszfang

Peter V. Henstock

Supercharged Coding with GenAI

Portfolio Director: Gebin George
Relationship Lead: Sonia Chauhan
Project Manager: Prajakta Naik
Content Engineer: Aditi Chatterjee
Technical Editor: Irfa Ansari
Copy Editor: Safis Editing
Indexer: Pratik Shirodkar
Proofreader: Aditi Chatterjee
Production Designer: Vijay Kamble
Growth Lead: Nimisha Dua

First published: August 2025
Production reference: 3040925

Published by Packt Publishing Ltd.
Grosvenor House
11 St Paul's Square
Birmingham
B3 1RB, UK.

ISBN 978-1-83664-529-0
www.packtpub.com

To my husband, Dvir, my mother, Yifat, my father, Amos, my brother, Roy, and my dog, Panda— thank you for your support and encouragement throughout this journey.

– Hila

To my father, with special thanks to my mother, brother, and especially my wife for their support.

– Peter

Foreword

When Hila told me she was working on a book about GenAI-powered software development, I smiled. Of course, she was. We've collaborated on papers where AI meets cybersecurity, so I've seen her thinking firsthand—rigorous, curious, never satisfied with surface-level insights. If anyone was going to map the future of coding with AI, it was Hila.

This book is not just another tour of ChatGPT or Copilot. It's a builder's manual for the age of AI-augmented engineering. It's part workflow, part playbook, and part philosophical reflection on what it means to code when the machine is your collaborator. It goes from prompt engineering to system design, from small refactors to architectural guidance, from GitHub Copilot to OpenAI APIs, without losing the plot or pandering to hype. What I appreciate most is how grounded it is. Hila and Peter don't romanticize GenAI, and they don't fear it either. They approach it as engineers: curious, skeptical, and practical. How do you evaluate GenAI output? How do you keep it reliable? When should you override it, or better yet, teach it? These aren't abstract questions. They're daily challenges, and this book meets them with clarity and grit. For those of us who live at the intersection of AI, code, and security, this book feels like home. It speaks to the real problems developers face when integrating these tools into production environments, where correctness matters, hallucinations can be dangerous, and productivity means more than autocomplete. If you're looking for a book that teaches you how to code faster, sure, you'll get that. But if you're looking for a book that teaches you how to think more clearly about coding in a world where machines also write code, then this is your book.

Congratulations, Hila and Peter. You've created something timely, honest, and actually useful.

Mike Erlihson, PhD

Head of AI, Stealth Cyber Startup

The book *Supercharged Coding with GenAI* is an essential guide for Python practitioners who want to work better and faster with LLM tools. While many resources stop at simple prompt-engineering tips, this book goes further by setting out frameworks for working with generated code. While using generative AI tools requires new ways of structuring workflows and validating output, this book provides a systematic approach to turning generative AI into a true collaborator and ensuring that systems remain trustworthy in production.

Supercharged Coding with GenAI strikes a rare balance between technical precision and engineering pragmatism, which is exactly what the fast-moving conversation around generative AI in software development needs. Instead of showing you how to prompt ChatGPT to optimize code, Hila and Peter explain the types of optimizations available, such as memory and runtime, how to use LLMs to detect bottlenecks, and how these tools can then be applied to handle larger inputs. They also demonstrate how prompts for GitHub Copilot can be adapted for ChatGPT to add flexibility, or for the OpenAI API to address pragmatic use cases, discussing the advantages and limitations of each tool. With practical examples and clear scenarios, they show how you can apply generative AI in everyday work, from updating documentation to identifying unit tests mismatches.

For developers and teams navigating this new era, this is a must-have book. It is practical, rigorous, and will train you to be a supercharged coder.

Congratulations to Hila and Peter for creating a book that is not only timely but also lays a foundation for the future of engineering with AI.

Alice Fridberg

Data Science Team Lead, Arpeely

Contributors

About the authors

Hila Paz Herszfang, with seven years of building machine learning (ML) services and leading teams, holds a master's degree in information management systems and is completing a second master's in data science, both from Harvard Extension School. She developed a *Python for MLOps* Udemy course and runs a math and tech TikTok channel boasting 15K followers and 300K+ likes.

Peter V. Henstock is an AI expert with 25+ years of experience at Pfizer, Incyte, and MIT LL. He teaches graduate software engineering and AI/ML courses at Harvard Extension School. He holds a PhD in AI from Purdue and seven Master's degrees. Recognized as a top AI leader by DKA, Peter guides professionals in AI/ML, software, visualization, and statistics.

About the reviewers

Mike Erlihson is a seasoned AI professional, leveraging his PhD in mathematics and extensive expertise in deep learning and data science. As a prolific scientific content creator and lecturer, he has reviewed approximately 500 deep learning papers and hosted more than 50 recorded podcasts in the field, building a substantial following of over 60,000 on LinkedIn. In addition to his professional work, Mike is committed to education and knowledge sharing in the AI community, making complex topics accessible through his various content platforms.

Alice Fridberg is a data science team lead with a master's in applied statistics from Tel Aviv University. She specializes in innovative ML and deep learning methods for marketing optimization, forecasting, and user modelling. Her work earned her the *Top Women in Media & Ad Tech – Data Demystifiers* award. Alice in an active public speaker, delivering talks such as *A Brief History of Data Science* with the *Women on Stage* community. She also mentors students and early-career professionals through programs with DataHack, Women in Data Science, and Tel Aviv University.

Subscribe for a free eBook

New frameworks, evolving architectures, research drops, production breakdowns—AI_Distilled filters the noise into a weekly briefing for engineers and researchers working hands-on with LLMs and GenAI systems. Subscribe now and receive a free eBook, along with weekly insights that help you stay focused and informed.

Subscribe at https://packt.link/TRO5B or scan the QR code below:

Table of Contents

Chapter 5: Best Practices for Prompting with OpenAI API and GitHub Copilot 103

Chapter 9: Advanced Prompt Engineering for Coding-Related Tasks   209

Chapter 11: Fine-Tuning Models with OpenAI   265

Chapter 14: GenAI for Runtime and Memory Management   335

Preface

Supercharged Coding with GenAI aims to train software developers to achieve increased productivity throughout the **software development life cycle (SDLC)**. It covers not only the programming aspect but also how to write tests, documentation, and other aspects required for putting software into production using GenAI methods. The book introduces the *five S's* framework, a standardized approach for consistently producing high-quality output that many GenAI users face.

It guides you on how and when to use the three most common GenAI software tools that currently dominate the marketplace: ChatGPT, OpenAI API, and GitHub Copilot. Each of these tools offers a different interface for generating code, each with different strengths and weaknesses. Learning how to effectively use these tools is an empowering skill set in the quickly evolving field of software engineering.

This book is a hands-on approach, with many labs introduced throughout the different chapters, since GenAI coding tools require practice. The labs provide the necessary practice to challenge the knowledge and explore the key skills introduced. The book also dives deeper into the concepts behind how to use instructions, making sure that you not only learn *how* to do something but also understand *why* the GenAI is producing particular outputs.

The book is structured into three parts:

- *Part 1, Foundations for Coding with GenAI,* provides a quick start tutorial for the three different GenAI tools you can use for code completion and surrounding tasks. We will start with OpenAI API framework to harness the **large language models (LLMs)** as a software developer. We built a program for code completion so we can better understand the design of GenAI tools. Next, we will get started with GitHub Copilot and ChatGPT using three different interaction modes: chat, completion, and analysis. By then, we will also understand the design differences among the different interaction modes. Finally, we will introduce the five S's framework, a structured approach to crafting precise prompts that lead to predictable and more desirable outputs.

- *Part 2, Basics to Advanced LLM Prompting for GenAI Coding,* takes the next step toward becoming supercharged coders. We will dive deeper into the foundations of LLMs. The goal is to gain a better understanding of why these models work so much better than the many tools that came before them. We will then start developing the mindset of a supercharged coder by learning which tasks are native to the models, which require advanced prompting techniques, and which tasks are better handled without the assistance of GenAI altogether. We will also learn about applying advanced prompting techniques to coding-related tasks, how to evaluate the goodness of our output with evaluation techniques, and how to fine-tune a model to specialize it for a specific task.

- *Part 3, From Code to Production with GenAI,* is dedicated to the advanced SDLC approach, where we will be able to use our newly obtained skillset and mindset to work with GenAI tools. We will talk about logging, monitoring, debugging, unit testing, and documenting our code efficiently and quickly with GenAI tools. We will also apply prompt engineering techniques to both space and memory optimizations. We will close this chapter with talks about design, architecture, and the future.

Who this book is for

If you are a Python developer curious about GenAI and are looking to elevate your software engineering productivity, this book will transform your approach to software. We include many structured examples of varying problem complexity that will demonstrate the use of advanced prompting techniques, suitable for early intermediate through advanced developers.

To get the most out of this book, you should have at least one year of hands-on Python development experience and be somewhat familiar with the SDLC.

What this book covers

Chapter 1, From Automation to Full Software Development Life Cycle: The Current Opportunity for GenAI, describes the recent convergence of software development tools and the AI transformation with LLMs. It makes a case that now is the best time to improve skills in GenAI to produce quality code faster.

Chapter 2, Your Quickstart Guide to OpenAI API, introduces everything you need to know to begin using OpenAI. By the end of the chapter, you will be able to start using it to write code.

Chapter 3, A Guide to GitHub Copilot with PyCharm, VS Code, and Jupyter Notebook, provides setup instructions for GitHub Copilot, the pair programming GenAI tool. It then shows how to integrate GitHub Copilot with the two most popular IDEs. With this background, you will be able to prompt with GenAI.

Chapter 4, Best Practices for Prompting with ChatGPT, dives into prompting, which is a core skill for GenAI coding. This chapter introduces the five S's framework for consistent outputs.

Chapter 5, Best Practices for Prompting with OpenAI API and GitHub Copilot, completes *Part 1* of the book by extending the prompting methods to functions, classes, and methods. The methods are applied to not just writing code but also fixing bugs and providing documentation.

Chapter 6, Behind the Scenes: How ChatGPT, GitHub Copilot, and Other LLMs Work, sheds light on how LLMs work under the hood since such an understanding can help understand the strengths and limitations. The chapter begins with a statistical example as a motivation and continues through general LLMs. The chapter concludes with the extension to code-specific LLMs that are at the heart of GitHub Copilot.

Chapter 7, Reading and Understanding Code Bases with GenAI, showcases the effectiveness of the different GenAI tools in working with full code bases. The chapter shows how GenAI can explain how code works and help debug issues using the code and support documentation.

Chapter 8, An Introduction to Prompt Engineering, applies this recent field to code development and introduces few-shot learning. Prompt engineering methods are applied through OpenAI API and GitHub Copilot for code refactoring to support a consistent coding style.

Chapter 9, Advanced Prompt Engineering for Coding-Related Tasks, extends the few-shot approaches from *Chapter 8* into reasoning models. Iterative prompting, chain-of-thought prompting, and chaining can effectively deliver highly predictable code that implements key functionality, including code and comments.

Chapter 10, Refactoring Code with GenAI, revisits and extends the chain-of-thought prompting technique to improve code. The chapter covers examples of refactoring code for improved quality and performance.

Chapter 11, Fine-Tuning Models with OpenAI, compares and contrasts the few-shot learning approach with fine-tuning, a standard approach for customizing LLMs. The chapter uses the OpenAI Playground to compare the effectiveness and costs of the two approaches.

Chapter 12, Documenting Code with GenAI, begins *Part 3*, which focuses on SDLC components beyond coding. The chapter is a how-to guide for effectively writing docstrings, the standard documentation for Python. It also provides solutions to the problem of out-of-date comments within the code.

Chapter 13, Writing and Maintaining Unit Tests, demonstrates multiple methods for leveraging GenAI to accelerate the creation of tests. The chapter also covers the test-driven development (TDD) process of writing test cases first and automatically generating the functional code to pass the tests.

Chapter 14, GenAI for Runtime and Memory Management, delves into performance optimization, which is rarely discussed in GenAI code literature. Its examples show how to assess performance trade-offs and, using a combination of prompting with chaining prompts, how to estimate runtime capacities and optimize code to run at scale.

Chapter 15, Going Live with GenAI: Logging, Monitoring, and Errors, provides guidance on the use of GenAI for key late-stage components for putting code into production. The chapter brings together past concepts such as enforcing style, few-shot learning, and fine-tuning as applied to monitoring and logging methods.

Chapter 16, Architecture, Design, and the Future, discusses the rise of GenAI, software economics, and the changing landscape of software engineering. It provides a perspective on the future of software engineering from vibe coding to long-term expectations, including risks and governance.

To get the most out of this book

Following along will be easier if you bear the following in mind:

- **Examples:** Begin with the hands-on examples provided in each chapter to make sure that you can effectively use all the tools, rather than focus on just one
- **Labs:** Use the labs to test your knowledge of how you approach the challenges, and use the questions at the end of each chapter to make sure you grasp the fundamentals
- **GenAI approach:** Experiment with the different techniques from each chapter on your own code and examples to see how GenAI can change your approach to software engineering
- **Think beyond:** Reflect on how the practical knowledge of the introduced GenAI tools relates to the fundamentals of how LLMs work, and how they can enhance multiple aspects of your organization's software development practices

Here is a list of things you need to have:

Software/hardware covered in the book	System requirements
Python 3.11 or higher	Windows, macOS, or Linux.
LLM chat and embedding models	Windows, macOS, or Linux. You can decide to leverage your LLM of choice. Throughout the book, we will be using a variety of GPT models from ChatGPT, OpenAI API, and GitHub Copilot.

Download the example code files

The code bundle for the book is hosted on GitHub at `https://github.com/PacktPublishing/Supercharged-Coding-with-Gen-AI`. We also have other code bundles from our rich catalog of books and videos available at `https://github.com/PacktPublishing`. Check them out!

Download the color images

We also provide a PDF file that has color images of the screenshots/diagrams used in this book. You can download it here: `https://packt.link/gbp/9781836645290`.

Conventions used

There are a number of text conventions used throughout this book.

`CodeInText`: Indicates code words in text, database table names, folder names, filenames, file extensions, pathnames, dummy URLs, user input, and X handles. For example, "The edits window supports the slash commands such as `/fix`, `/explain`, and `/test`, as well as tailored instructions to modify your code."

A block of code is set as follows:

```
def get_geometric_mean_of_two_numbers(
    a: float,
    b: float,
) -> float:
    return pow(a * b, 1 / 2)



num1: float = 5.0
num2: float = 20.0
print(get_geometric_mean_of_two_numbers(num1, num2))
```

Any command-line input or output is written as follows:

```
(.venv) $ pip install openai
```

Bold: Indicates a new term, an important word, or words that you see on the screen, for example, in menus or dialog boxes. For example: "In this chapter, we will introduce the practice of **prompt engineering**, a field of study that started in 2020, which offers advanced techniques for refining prompts to achieve more reliable, predictable, and desirable outcomes in **large language model (LLM)**-based applications."

> Warnings or important notes appear like this.

> Tips and tricks appear like this.

Disclaimer on AI usage

The authors acknowledge the use of cutting-edge AI, such as ChatGPT, OpenAI API, and GitHub Copilot, with the sole aim of enhancing the language and clarity within the book, thereby ensuring a smooth reading experience for readers. It is important to note that the content itself has been crafted by the authors and edited by a professional publishing team.

Get in touch

Feedback from our readers is always welcome!

General feedback: Email feedback@packtpub.com and mention the book's title in the subject of your message. If you have questions about any aspect of this book, please email us at questions@packtpub.com.

Errata: Although we have taken every care to ensure the accuracy of our content, mistakes do happen. If you have found a mistake in this book, we would be grateful if you could report this to us. Please visit http://www.packtpub.com/submit-errata, click **Submit Errata**, and fill in the form.

Piracy: If you come across any illegal copies of our works in any form on the internet, we would be grateful if you would provide us with the location address or website name. Please contact us at copyright@packtpub.com with a link to the material.

If you are interested in becoming an author: If there is a topic that you have expertise in and you are interested in either writing or contributing to a book, please visit http://authors.packtpub.com/.

Join our Discord and Reddit spaces

You're not the only one navigating fragmented tools, constant updates, and unclear best practices. Join a growing community of professionals exchanging insights that don't make it into documentation.

Stay informed with updates, discussions, and behind-the-scenes insights from our authors. Join our Discord space at https://packt.link/z8ivB or scan the QR code below: 	Connect with peers, share ideas, and discuss real-world GenAI challenges. Follow us on Reddit at https://packt.link/0rExL or scan the QR code below: 

Share your thoughts

Once you've read *Supercharged Coding with GenAI*, we'd love to hear your thoughts! Scan the QR code below to go straight to the Amazon review page for this book and share your feedback.

https://packt.link/r/1836645295

Your review is important to us and the tech community and will help us make sure we're delivering excellent quality content.

Your Book Comes with Exclusive Perks — Here's How to Unlock Them

Unlock this book's exclusive benefits now

UNLOCK NOW

Scan this QR code or go to packtpub.com/
unlock, then search this book by name.
Ensure it's the correct edition.

*Note: Keep your purchase invoice ready before you
start.*

Enhanced reading experience with our Next-gen Reader:

> ☁ **Multi-device progress sync**: Learn from any device with seamless progress sync.

> 📑 **Highlighting and notetaking**: Turn your reading into lasting knowledge.

> 🔖 **Bookmarking**: Revisit your most important learnings anytime.

> ☀ **Dark mode**: Focus with minimal eye strain by switching to dark or sepia mode.

Learn smarter using our AI assistant (Beta):

> ✦ **Summarize it**: Summarize key sections or an entire chapter.

> ✦ **AI code explainers**: In the next-gen Packt Reader, click the **Explain** button above each code block for AI-powered code explanations.

Note: The AI assistant is part of next-gen Packt Reader and is still in beta.

Learn anytime, anywhere:

Access your content offline with DRM-free PDF and ePub versions—compatible with your favorite e-readers.

Unlock Your Book's Exclusive Benefits

Your copy of this book comes with the following exclusive benefits:

Next-gen Packt Reader

AI assistant (beta)

DRM-free PDF/ePub downloads

Use the following guide to unlock them if you haven't already. The process takes just a few minutes and needs to be done only once.

How to unlock these benefits in three easy steps

Step 1

Keep your purchase invoice for this book ready, as you'll need it in *Step 3*. If you received a physical invoice, scan it on your phone and have it ready as either a PDF, JPG, or PNG.

For more help on finding your invoice, visit https://www.packtpub.com/unlock-benefits/help.

Note: Did you buy this book directly from Packt? You don't need an invoice. After completing Step 2, you can jump straight to your exclusive content.

Step 2

Scan this QR code or go to packtpub.com/unlock.

On the page that opens (which will look similar to *Figure 0.1* if you're on desktop), search for this book by name. Make sure you select the correct edition.

⟨packt⟩	Q Search...							Subscription	🛒⁰	👤

Explore Products   Best Sellers   New Releases   Books   Videos   Audiobooks   Learning Hub   Newsletter Hub   Free Learning

Discover and unlock your book's exclusive benefits

Bought a Packt book? Your purchase may come with free bonus benefits designed to maximise your learning. Discover and unlock them here

● Discover Benefits   ○ Sign Up/In   ○ Upload Invoice

Need Help?

✦ **1. Discover your book's exclusive benefits**   ∧

Q   Search by title or ISBN

CONTINUE TO STEP 2

👤 **2. Login or sign up for free**   ∨

☁ **3. Upload your invoice and unlock**   ∨

Figure 0.1: Packt unlock landing page on desktop

Step 3

Sign in to your Packt account or create a new one for free. Once you're logged in, upload your invoice. It can be in PDF, PNG, or JPG format and must be no larger than 10 MB. Follow the rest of the instructions on the screen to complete the process.

Need help?

If you get stuck and need help, visit https://www.packtpub.com/unlock-benefits/help for a detailed FAQ on how to find your invoices and more. The following QR code will take you to the help page directly:

Note: If you are still facing issues, reach out to customercare@packt.com.

Part 1

Foundations for Coding with GenAI

In *Part 1* of this book, we introduce the fundamentals of GenAI for coding and get you started with both OpenAI API and GitHub Copilot. The part begins with a discussion of how GenAI for coding has recently emerged from the intersection of a long evolution in software development tools and the recent **large language models (LLMs)** from the AI space. This recent fusion of technologies has completely changed the programming landscape. Now is the perfect time to begin the journey since applying them across software engineering tasks requires both training and practice.

The remainder of *Part 1* provides hands-on guidance to start using OpenAI API and GitHub Copilot. After setting up these tools, the part introduces best practices for prompting.

This part contains the following chapters:

- *Chapter 1, From Automation to Full Software Development Life Cycle: The Current Opportunity for GenAI*
- *Chapter 2, Your Quickstart Guide to OpenAI API*
- *Chapter 3, A Guide to GitHub Copilot with PyCharm, VS Code, and Jupyter Notebook*
- *Chapter 4, Best Practices for Prompting with ChatGPT*
- *Chapter 5, Best Practices for Prompting with OpenAI API and GitHub Copilot*

1

From Automation to Full Software Development Life Cycle: The Current Opportunity for GenAI

If you are reading this book, you have probably heard some of the excitement, hype, concerns, and reality of **Generative Artificial Intelligence (GenAI)** for coding. You may have checked out some tutorials online and perhaps even explored using this technology for your own coding.

Learning to apply GenAI to software coding takes both practice and time. While there are many online demonstrations of the capabilities, there has not been a systematic approach for achieving functional, quality code with any consistency. There also aren't many resources that guide developers to use GenAI beyond simple code completion or perhaps testing. GenAI can be particularly useful in expediting tasks such as standardizing coding style to improve readability, debugging, optimizing performance, and the many other tasks performed by software engineers.

In this chapter, we will explore the following topics:

- Changing the software engineering field
- Introducing the rise of large language models
- Exploring the software development lifecycle
- Embracing a GenAI toolkit

- Is GenAI worth learning for software engineering?
- What you will get from this book

Changing the software engineering field

Computer programming and software engineering, in general, contribute not only to the tech industry, but to many different sectors of the economy, including commerce, finance, health, transportation, and energy. Software drives the creation of many new products. It increases the productivity of companies through the automation and optimization of processes and enables cost reductions.

As software continues to deliver economic value, new paradigms and tools for software developers have increased the ability to write quality software at a faster pace. Over the last couple of years, GenAI has become one of these tools.

In software engineering, GenAI has suddenly advanced to reach an inflection point and is fundamentally changing the field. This recent technology allows everyone from novices to expert software developers to supercharge their productivity not only in coding but, more generally, the full **software development lifecycle (SDLC)**.

Advanced technologies, including artificial intelligence, seem to be in the news every day lately. Despite this, many software engineers seem somewhat surprised that AI has progressed to the point that it can support their field and specific software development work. The current state of software engineering tools has resulted from the convergence of two separate trends. First, software development tools are not new but have progressed continuously over many decades. Second, GenAI technology has crossed over from the rapid emergence of **large language models (LLMs)**, which trace back to neural networks and the origins of artificial intelligence.

The evolution of tools for software development

The application of GenAI to software engineering is quite a recent development. Although AI has been discussed for many years as a promising set of tools for enhancing code development, the emergence of GenAI has ushered in a new era of capabilities.

Software development has experienced many new tools over the past decades that have transformed the field. It is easy to argue that software development is constantly evolving, with new tools that have streamlined the processes and enhanced productivity. This section provides an overview of some major technology revolutions that have aided software developers.

In the 1970s and 1980s, the *Maestro I* was developed as the first **integrated development environment (IDE)**, although it would hardly be recognized as such by today's standards. Its successors, such as *Borland's Turbo Pascal* and *Visual Studio*, provided an easy integration of coding, file management, debugging, compilation, and execution. Today's IDEs for Python, such as *Visual Studio Code*, *PyCharm*, and *Spyder*, facilitate global changes to variables, code highlighting, syntax checkers, and access to multiple tools.

Version control systems were a critical step in software engineering, enabling many developers to work on a single project. With a single code base, different versions of code can be tracked and managed. IBM's *IEBUPDTE* in the 1960s was a forerunner of the technology, followed by the *Revision Control System* in 1982 and the *Concurrent Versions System (CVS)* in 1986. It wasn't until 2005 that the now ubiquitous *Git* was developed, which enabled a distributed version control system.

Build tools and **continuous integration and continuous deployment (CI/CD)** systems speed the delivery process of software. Build tools such as Jenkins and Maven transform source code into executable code. CI/CD tools are often triggered by the build, but continue further to automate the testing, execute **linters** or other code tools, and often deploy the updated version to users. The full deployment pipeline frees the developers from the many manual steps and enables both a rapid and consistent way of providing users with the latest functionality.

Significant research has been poured into **software testing**. Apart from many specialized tools for different forms of testing, testing frameworks are now a standard part of virtually all software development suites. IDEs already speed up the process of creating skeleton tests from existing code by using method signatures and standard test naming conventions. The `unittest` frameworks run all the tests and report failures, significantly speeding up the process.

Code analysis and **refactoring** tools identify issues with code and can improve the overall quality. *SonarQube* is an example of a code analysis tool that performs static code analysis. It identifies potential problems with code, often referred to as **code smell**, but can also check for a range of potential issues, such as deviations in code style and poor security handling.

Some more advanced tools have been able to not only recognize coding problems but also fix them. For example, *ReSharper* actually refactors the code to improve its quality. Such tools save developers time and achieve this result through a combination of **pattern matching** and AI.

With continual changes in coding sources and packages, software development always seems to require new packages, platforms, or even languages. As a result, software developers require access to the latest manuals or other documentation. Some refer to searching for code examples in *Stack Overflow* or *Reddit*. Innovations in this space included *Kite*, AI-powered software that provided automated code completion and instant code documentation. Kite proved to reduce keyboard clicks and improved code development speed, gaining a user base of an estimated 500,000 programmers. Unfortunately, the company ceased to exist in 2021 and donated its multi-language code tools to the open source community.

Next, we will introduce the turning point in AI research that has driven significant adoption across a variety of domains, including software engineering.

Introducing the rise of LLMs

Over the past few short years, LLMs have emerged as the dominant AI resource for writing, research, and inference. They are currently transforming the tech industry, and their applications have a far-reaching impact across all fields. This section provides a brief overview of their unprecedented ascent.

Artificial Intelligence was formally started in 1956 at a famous Dartmouth College workshop of computer science experts. They coined the term **artificial intelligence (AI)** and set ambitious goals ranging from automated reasoning to **natural language processing (NLP)**. Although the participants expected a rapid progression to these goals, the compute and technology limitations thwarted their success. A publication in 1969 denounced the key technology and allegedly started the first well-documented **AI winter**, an extended period of no funding or research.

In the 1980s, **expert systems** emerged as a workable solution where rules could be crafted by technologists to reproduce human-like reasoning over limited domains for a specific problem. Despite some early successes with the approach, it proved difficult to craft and manage the ordering for sets of rules. This hindered its adoption and eventually led to the second AI winter.

Machine learning (ML), a sub-field of AI, emerged as the only viable solution. Unlike the hand-crafted rules of expert systems, ML systems could learn to make predictions or decisions directly from data. Research has led to dozens of techniques within the sub-field, but **neural networks** have become the dominant approach over the past dozen years. Mildly inspired by biological neurons, neural networks have proven to be a powerful system for learning and modeling data. Researchers have shown that neural networks can generalize well and approximate any function. **Deep learning**, any neural network with multiple layers of **neurons**, overcomes the limitations of more traditional machine learning techniques. Specifically, it can continue to learn when provided with ever larger training sets.

NLP is the application of machine learning to human language data. It applies to any texts, such as articles, blogs, emails, or books. The field draws from computer science, AI, and linguistics. Earlier methods drew extensively from statistical methods and later traditional ML techniques. In recent years, deep learning methods have revolutionized the NLP field by introducing **language models (LMs)**, which predict and generate text based on existing language data. LLMs are expanded versions of LMs, trained on massive datasets and billions of parameters, which are internal weights tuned to reflect the patterns in the training data. We will discuss LLMs extensively in later chapters of the book.

Over the past several years, deep learning models have been trained on ever-increasing volumes of text and, with new techniques, can understand how words within each sentence are related to each other. This class of LLMs includes OpenAI's *GPT*, Meta's *Llama*, Google's *Gemini*, Anthropic's *Claude*, and newer models continue to be developed. These LLMs were initially designed to accurately predict the next word of a phrase. At scale and with recent technologies, they have enabled **natural language generation (NLG)** solutions that can write full texts to enable report writing, question-answering, chatbots, and much more.

LLMs are typically trained on large sets of available online text sources, but the same models can also be trained on software code. These LLMs use publicly available code in Python, Java, and other programming languages that are mostly available from GitHub repositories. The result is that the LLMs can predict the next block of code, can generate comments, write tests, and even refactor code. These are all parts of the overall SDLC that we will describe in the next section.

Exploring the software development lifecycle

To deliver quality software, most software teams progress through a series of stages known as the **software development lifecycle (SDLC)**. As shown in *Figure 1.1*, these steps are designed to be an efficient approach that minimizes the risk of failure. The process usually begins with the recognition of an unmet business need, and cycles through many stages to meet the need with a software system. Projects progress from analyzing the existing state to gathering requirements, designing the system, implementing and testing the code, delivering the solution, and often maintaining the software.

While most people associate software development with coding, actual programming makes up only 25-35% of the overall effort, depending on the type of software and its requirements. The remaining steps are needed to gather requirements, test and document the code, deploy the software, and support its continued functionality, as shown in *Figure 1.1*.

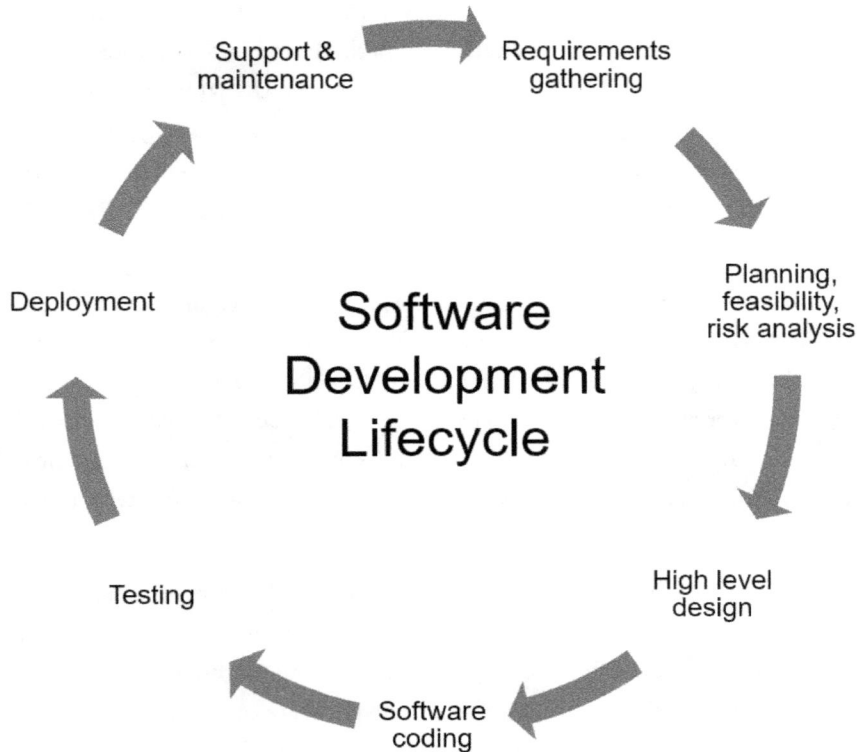

Figure 1.1: The SDLC – the continual process of developing or improving software systems from requirements through maintenance

The SDLC process begins with gathering requirements, followed by planning, feasibility, and risk analysis. A successful analysis leads to the creation of a high-level system design, and only after this step does an engineer continue on to software coding. The form will be formally tested before it is deployed, resulting in a live or **production** system. As the environment or business needs change, support and maintenance are always needed, and that can trigger the next development cycle.

> **Important note**
>
> While the SDLC is an industry-standard approach, individual organizations often introduce variations to tailor it for their software development processes. For instance, some organizations may choose to implement tests before writing the code, a practice known as **test-driven development (TDD)**. Others may create a prototype system or introduce a **proof of concept (POC)** before conducting a feasibility analysis, a step that has become easier to perform with the help of LLMs.

There are an increasing number of books and videos that describe the use of GenAI for coding, but the technology can supercharge the entire process, not just the actual coding implementation. This book will explore several of these aspects, including testing, documenting, and monitoring software. These are critical for the success of software projects.

Next, we will see how we can embrace a comprehensive GenAI toolkit in our technological stack as software developers.

Embracing a GenAI toolkit

This book focuses on three separate tools for software development: ChatGPT, OpenAI API, and GitHub Copilot. In 2024, these three tools had roughly a $35 million combined market size for software engineering applications. The market is expected to grow 25% per year throughout the rest of the decade, according to a *Research and Markets* report. The following chapters of the book will provide instructions on how to subscribe to these services and how to get started. These tools provide distinct kinds of functionality, and knowing when to use which tool is part of the learning curve. Later chapters will highlight the features and use cases for each of the tools.

ChatGPT

OpenAI has been a leader in LLMs since 2015. Led by CEO Sam Altman, the company has produced multiple versions of its **Generative Pretrained Transformer (GPT)** LLM. While these were well received, the release of ChatGPT in December 2022 transformed the perspectives of AI worldwide.

ChatGPT is an AI-driven chatbot, an application that is designed for text conversations using natural language. Its release spurred widespread use, reaching 100 million users the following month. It continues to be one of the most visited websites across the world.

While natural language conversations with ChatGPT often succeed in eliciting answers to questions, **prompt engineering** has proven a more robust technique. It is the art of crafting an instruction to produce a more desirable output. The prompt typically consists of context, instructions, a history of the dialog, and sometimes examples of desired output. This book will provide structured formats that guide the reader to effectively perform prompt engineering for producing code, comments, tests, and other outputs.

OpenAI API

ChatGPT is among the most popular tools for interacting with LLMs. However, in many cases, prompt engineering lacks the simple structures found in software, such as loops and conditions. OpenAI provides a developer platform for coding directly against the same OpenAI LLM used by ChatGPT. Through its **Application Programming Interface (API)**, OpenAI enables developers to combine software and prompt engineering. The API also provides specific added functionality that is useful for solving software engineering problems.

GitHub Copilot

While GitHub is one of the most popular platforms for sharing code using Git distributed version control, the company released GitHub Copilot in 2021. Originally powered by OpenAI's LLM, it provides intelligent code completion using GenAI's programming capability. The functionality has been integrated into many IDEs, including Visual Studio Code and PyCharm—two of the most popular IDEs for Python.

Unlike the other OpenAI models, Copilot functions as a **pair programmer**. This concept comes from the **Extreme Programming (XP)** agile methodology, where two developers work together to write code with a single keyboard. Although not yet a fully functioning pair programmer, Copilot can quickly find and display references for code syntax and even provide annotated examples or full code as requested by the user. It interprets the intention from the function and variable names used. Together with the surrounding code as context, it can predict and suggest the next block of code.

Next, we will review recent studies that assess the use of GenAI for software development.

Improving software development with GenAI

A number of studies have assessed whether GenAI provides increased productivity in coding tasks. *McKinsey* reported increases ranging from minimal to 50%, depending on the complexity of the task. For code documentation and generation, the gains were much higher than for difficult tasks. They found it was particularly good for routine tasks and repetitive work, as well as initial dives into new code projects. Refactoring code to make changes and tackling new challenges were also improved through GenAI technology. Perhaps as important, their study showed that users of GenAI for software felt happier, were able to focus more on meaningful work, and achieved *flow* much more frequently. The study details can be found at `https://www.mckinsey.com/capabilities/mckinsey-digital/our-insights/unleashing-developer-productivity-with-generative-ai`.

A similar study by *Exadel* reported that half of the developers in their study used GitHub Copilot at least 50% of the time. Two-thirds of these developers completed tasks more quickly, saving 10-30% of their development time. Copilot made them more productive and fulfilled. See `https://exadel.com/news/measuring-generative-ai-software-development/` for more details on the study.

Research by *Colombatto and Rivadulla* (`https://aws.amazon.com/blogs/apn/transforming-the-software-development-lifecycle-sdlc-with-generative-ai/`) found benefits of applying GenAI across the full SDLC. Examining data from AWS and IBM, they found that the benefits begin in the analysis phase with requirements engineering. Even in this early phase of the SDLC, the researchers observed up to a 60% reduction in time from using GenAI. They found a 30% reduction in development time and a 25% reduction in time for generating unit tests and test plans. Even though less time was spent, the code quality improved by 25%, which contributes to fewer bugs and lower software maintenance costs.

A study conducted by *BlueOptima* from 2022 to 2024 used code repositories to analyze productivity, quality, and cost across 77,338 developers. In contrast with the other studies that reported significant savings, the findings were much more modest. They found only a 3.99% increase in productivity for those with access to GenAI and a 5.12% decrease for those without. Quality still improved slightly, which is important since it proves that the productivity gains do not compromise quality, but the gains were not as significant. However, the study used access to these tools as an input variable without characterizing the training, familiarity, or integration of GenAI into their workflows. In addition, productivity is likely to increase as the predictive accuracy and overall performance of GenAI tools continue to rapidly improve. The details of the study can be found through this link: `https://www.blueoptima.com/resource/llm-paper-1/`.

Next, we will discuss our perspective on the benefits and downsides of using GenAI in software development.

Is GenAI worth learning for software engineering?

We have been using code completion tools for over a decade, but current GenAI tools are different. We have used the full range of tools, such as keyboard shortcuts, Stack Overflow searches for help, code API search tools, and all the latest refactoring tools and templates available in the IDE. All these strategies have helped us be more efficient in our work, but there has always been a lot of mundane, repetitive work that has limited our coding speed and enjoyment.

The benefits of coding with GenAI

GenAI tools have transformed our output. Within three months of using an earlier version of GitHub Copilot, we were writing code 15% faster. Now, after two years, the combination of GitHub Copilot, ChatGPT, and OpenAI API has supercharged our coding output more than anything else that we have used. We complete twice as much work as we did previously with multiple tools. The improvements in productivity were a combination of advances in the tools themselves as well as familiarity with how to use them, both of which are covered throughout this book.

Beyond the productivity in merely writing code, GenAI contributes to other aspects of software development. GenAI can help refactor code automatically, which helps make it more readable and hence maintainable. As shown in later chapters, code can also be improved by selecting better algorithms that execute faster. GenAI can also help write documentation of code and automate the creation of tests. With GitHub Copilot, the pair programming approach to efficient coding includes providing help, which is useful for senior developers, but invaluable to developers learning a new language or framework.

The downsides of coding with GenAI

The technology behind GenAI for software development is still quite new. Early studies from 2022 showed that GitHub Copilot's accuracy in producing correct code was below 50%. While advances and new versions of the underlying models continue to be released every few months, they are certainly not perfect.

In fact, GenAI has produced some of the worst fatal development mistakes we have ever seen. To put that in perspective, we have seen a data scientist pushing their entire environment file to the corporate repository, which exposed secret tokens that had to be replaced. One software developer crashed a microservice after renaming a file pandas. One data engineer spent two weeks learning *Cython* to handle a Python DataFrame memory issue instead of just switching to Dask or PySpark. GenAI may not only supercharge your strengths, but may also supercharge your weaknesses. After all, it is still a developing technology, but continues to improve arguably faster than anyone expected.

AI coding has made the headlines, but it may not be clear why it would fail. The underlying coding models are trained on available GitHub repository data and other code that is publicly available in various languages. For problems that are widely documented, such as the Fibonacci sequence calculation or the many code snippets used to pass *LeetCode* interviewing questions, the answers are nearly perfect. For this reason, YouTube is full of videos showing how GitHub Copilot can program a React web page in 3 minutes.

GenAI has far more difficulty solving more obscure coding tasks where there is far less training data. Even if the most famous *LeetCode's Two Sum Problem* were changed slightly to include Python Threads, for example, the solution would be unpredictable.

A well-documented problem with LLMs for generating text is that they tend to hallucinate or fabricate information when the answers are not apparent. Significant research is ongoing to counter this poorly understood problem. However, hallucinations and other LLM issues do occur when GenAI is applied to software engineering.

Some developers worry that GenAI coding tools will turn them into less capable developers. They fear that relying on automatic code completion, suggestions, and examples will cause them to lose their programming edge or familiarity with the functions.

Recent research by Michael Gerlick (https://doi.org/10.3390/soc15010006) suggests that AI tools might decrease our critical thinking capability through a process known as cognitive off-loading. However, similar arguments have been made about automated spelling checkers that produce better documents but perhaps reinforce our spelling crimes. It is true that it may take a bit longer to remember the exact syntax of adding tick marks to a matplotlib plot when the internet is down. However, if you can double your output with fewer keystrokes, you can focus on the more important problems that GenAI has yet to solve.

Takeaways

Recent blogs describe a new trend called **vibe coding**, where developers and even non-developers design and build full applications extensively using GenAI over a weekend that would probably take months. It is remarkable that the technology has advanced to the point where rapid proto-typing is effective. However, prototypes are not production code.

In many tutorials where GenAI fails, the common wisdom is *You should verify the output you get*, yet none offers a pragmatic way or even a guided mindset of how to effectively evaluate the outputs and improve the code.

It is considered good practice to apply unit and other testing approaches for all code. However, using GenAI is neither about blindly trusting nor fact-checking everything. GenAI failures do not mean we have to go overboard with fact-checking any piece of code it produces. Similarly, evidence of GenAI success does not imply you should push every memory optimization suggestion into production.

Leveraging GenAI is about developing a new set of skills to formalize the inputs and outputs obtained from LLMs. This will enable you to truly supercharge your coding tasks throughout the SDLC. It enables you to own the code whether you wrote it from scratch yourself or utilized LLMs. When you can assess the quality and risk of the output these tools generate, you will be able to transform your approach to software engineering.

Summary

This chapter highlighted that GenAI for coding emerged from the combination of software tool advancements with LLMs. This nascent technology applies not only to coding but can enhance many aspects of the SDLC. The combination of ChatGPT, OpenAI API, and GitHub Copilot provides a complementary set of tools that have been shown to not only improve productivity and enhance code quality but can even bring happiness to programmers.

Although the technology is new and still evolving, GenAI is already changing the software engineering field. This book was developed to provide a structured approach to effectively leverage the tools and achieve the best results across many aspects of the SDLC.

In the next chapter, we will introduce a quick-start guide to OpenAI API and use the **chat service** for coding tasks. We will build our own code completion program that takes a function's signature as input and returns its implementation as output.

Further reading

To learn more about the topics that were covered in this chapter, take a look at the following resources:

- VS Code Plugin: `https://github.com/kiteco/vscode-plugin`

- Begum Karaci Deniz, Chandra Gnanasambandam, Martin Harrysson, Alharith Hussin, Shivam Srivastava. *Unleashing developer productivity with Generative AI*: `https://www.mckinsey.com/capabilities/mckinsey-digital/our-insights/unleashing-developer-productivity-with-generative-ai`.

- Alexey Girzhadovich. *Scientifically Measuring the True Impact of Generative AI Software Development*: `https://exadel.com/news/measuring-generative-ai-software-development/`.

- Diego Colombatto and Jose Manual Pose Rivadulla. *Transforming the software development lifecycle (SDLC) with Generative AI*: `https://aws.amazon.com/blogs/apn/transforming-the-software-development-lifecycle-sdlc-with-generative-ai/`

- Research and Markets Report: Generative Artificial Intelligence (AI) in Coding Market - Forecasts from 2024 to 2029: `https://www.researchandmarkets.com/reports/6014321/generative-artificial-intelligence-ai-in?utm_source=GNE&utm_medium=PressRelease&utm_code=8xz7cm&utm_campaign=2014387+-+Generative+Artificial+Intelligence+(AI)+in+Coding+Market+Research+2024-2029%2c+Profiles+of+Codecademy%2c+CodiumAI%2c+Google%2c+IBM%2c+Microsoft%2c+NVIDIA%2c+OpenAI%2c+and+Tabnine&utm_exec=chdomspi`

- Michael Gerlick. *AI Tools in Society: Impacts on Cognitive Offloading and the Future of Critical Thinking:* `https://doi.org/10.3390/soc15010006`

Unlock this book's exclusive benefits now

Scan this QR code or go to packtpub.com/ unlock, then search for this book by name.

Note: Keep your purchase invoice ready before you start.

2

Your Quickstart Guide to OpenAI API

Generative artificial intelligence (GenAI) platforms such as OpenAI are transforming entire industries by empowering everyday users to generate custom answers to questions, reports, and images. You do not have to be an AI expert to leverage OpenAI to supercharge your software development. This chapter focuses on setting up OpenAI and using its **application programming interface (API)** calls to generate quality code.

OpenAI offers numerous services such as chat, image generation, and text-to-speech. These are available through a **RESTful HTTP** request, which is a standard way for applications to communicate over the web, or through a programmatic interface of the openai Python package.

In our first quickstart guide of the book, we will walk through three interactive labs and three sets of requests, working with the OpenAI Chat service. We will dive into the different models available through OpenAI API, and how to impact the AI-generated output.

We will obtain our project API keys, analyze the services' limits, and learn how to compute each request's costs. The costs are computed from the number of **tokens** or subword fragments of the model's input and output.

We will wrap up this chapter by creating a basic code completion program that can generate a Python code implementation based on a function signature.

In this chapter, we will explore the following topics:

- Introducing OpenAI API
- Obtaining your project API keys from OpenAI
- Sending your first OpenAI API request using the openai Python package
- Learning how request costs are calculated
- Understanding rate limits and usage restrictions for free and paid OpenAI accounts
- Analyzing request parameters
- Using OpenAI API to generate code

Technical requirements

To get the most out of this chapter, ensure you have the following:

- Your personal OpenAI account credentials
- Access to the book's GitHub repository, which is available at `https://github.com/PacktPublishing/Supercharged-Coding-with-Gen-AI`
- A virtual environment set up in your **integrated development environment** (IDE), either VS Code or PyCharm

If you require additional assistance in setting up your OpenAI account or a virtual environment in your IDE, refer to the *Appendix* for detailed instructions.

Introducing OpenAI API

The OpenAI platform offers a variety of **natural language processing** (NLP) services, powering many AI applications. At its core, the platform leverages **large language models** (LLMs) that are trained on a massive amount of data, with a complex architecture and billions of learnable parameters to produce AI-generated responses. Developers can interact with the platform through its API with text-based requests that are often called **prompts**. The prompts are processed, enriched, and transformed before being passed into the LLM model. The model's output is further refined and delivered as a response to the API request.

The Chat service by OpenAI is designed for conversational interactions with the LLM where the conversation uses three types of prompt roles – user, system, and assistant:

- **User prompts** represent an end user of the system such as a ChatGPT user, and resemble prompts we feed into ChatGPT, such as `Tell me about the Fibonacci sequence`.

- **Assistant prompts** represent the model output through the conversation and resemble answers we will get back from ChatGPT, such as The Fibonacci sequence is a series of numbers where each number is the sum of the two preceding ones.

- **System prompts** define the guidelines of the assistant behavior through the conversation, such as You are a helpful programming instructor.

Like many other GenAI tools in the industry, the OpenAI API calls are primarily a paid service. It does offer some limited free usage such as three requests per minute to a restricted selection of models, excluding *GPT-4o*. With just $5 in OpenAI credits, you can fully engage with the examples and labs presented in this book. We will instruct you how to do this right after our initial *Lab 2.1*.

OpenAI API through a RESTful HTTP request

The OpenAI API services are accessed via **RESTful HTTP requests**, a communication protocol based on the principles of **Representational State Transfer (REST)** architecture, and using the **HyperText Transfer Protocol (HTTP)**. RESTful HTTP provides a standardized way to send and retrieve data from servers over the internet. A request to OpenAI API includes four key components:

- **Endpoint**: The URL specifying the service you are accessing, such as https://api.openai.com/v1/chat/completions for the Chat service

- **HTTP method**: The action to perform, such as POST for OpenAI Chat service requests, which sends data to the server

- **Headers**: Metadata about the request, including your API token, to authenticate and provide context for the request

- **Body**: The data payload containing details such as the LLM to use and the input prompts

Here is an example of a request to the OpenAI API Chat service using the requests package in Python. It demonstrates how to make a POST request to the service, including a header with your API key for authentication and a body containing the data payload, such as the model and a prompt:

```python
import requests
import json
api_key = "your-key-here"
headers = {
    "Authorization": f"Bearer {api_key}",
    "Content-Type": "application/json"
}
payload = {
    "model": "your model's name here",
```

```
    "messages": "your message here"}
response = requests.post("https://api.openai.com/v1/chat/completions",
    headers=headers,
    data=json.dumps(payload))
chat_response = response.json()["choices"][0]["message"]["content"]
```

> 💡 **Quick tip:** Enhance your coding experience with the **AI Code Explainer** and **Quick Copy** features. Open this book in the next-gen Packt Reader. Click the **Copy** button
> (**1**) to quickly copy code into your coding environment, or click the **Explain** button
> (**2**) to get the AI assistant to explain a block of code to you.

```
                                                          Copy      Explain
function calculate(a, b) {                                 1          2
    return {sum: a + b};
};
```

> 📕 **The next-gen Packt Reader** is included for free with the purchase of this book. Scan the QR code OR visit packtpub.com/unlock, then use the search bar to find this book by name. Double-check the edition shown to make sure you get the right one.

Note that this code sample can also be found at the book's repository path, *ch2/code_samples/ openai_request.py*.

In this example, the payload is submitted in JSON format. If the request is successfully accepted and the server responds, the OpenAI API Chat service's output can be retrieved from `response. json()["choices"][0]["message"]["content"]`.

For Python developers, a more efficient approach to accessing the OpenAI Chat service is available. Rather than dealing with the complexities of crafting and sending RESTful HTTP requests, such as constructing the correct endpoint URL, setting authentication tokens in headers, formatting payloads in JSON, and handling potential response errors, we can leverage the dedicated openai package.

OpenAI API Python package installation

The openai Python package simplifies the process by abstracting complexities such as URL paths, retries, error handling, and authentication. This allows us to interact directly with Python objects, instead of manually constructing RESTful HTTP requests.

To install the openai package, run the following command in your terminal within your virtual environment:

```
(.venv) $ pip install openai
```

To verify that the openai package is installed correctly on your virtual environment, run the following command, which specifies the information of the package:

```
(.venv) $ pip show openai
```

Your console will output information about the package version, author, and support email.

With the openai package installed, we can simplify our interactions with the OpenAI platform using a programmatic framework. Instead of making direct RESTful HTTP requests, we will utilize Python classes. This results in fewer boilerplates, such as handling authentication and error management, and a more maintainable code.

Important note

If you are already working with the book repository, you do not need to install the openai package separately. It is already specified in the requirements.txt file and should be installed in your virtual environment. If you require additional assistance in setting up your virtual environments, refer to the *Appendix* for detailed instructions.

Obtaining your project API keys from OpenAI

All requests to OpenAI API require an authentication token, and we must obtain one prior to submitting any request.

Navigate to `https://platform.openai.com` and log in with the same credentials as you use for ChatGPT at `https://chat.openai.com/`.

Once logged in, click on **Dashboard** in the upper-right menu, then select **API keys** from the left menu.

Recently, OpenAI replaced personal API keys with the option to create a project API key. This new key serves two purposes. First, it allows personal use, as required for the work throughout this book. Second, it supports service API keys intended for non-human identities such as microservices running in production.

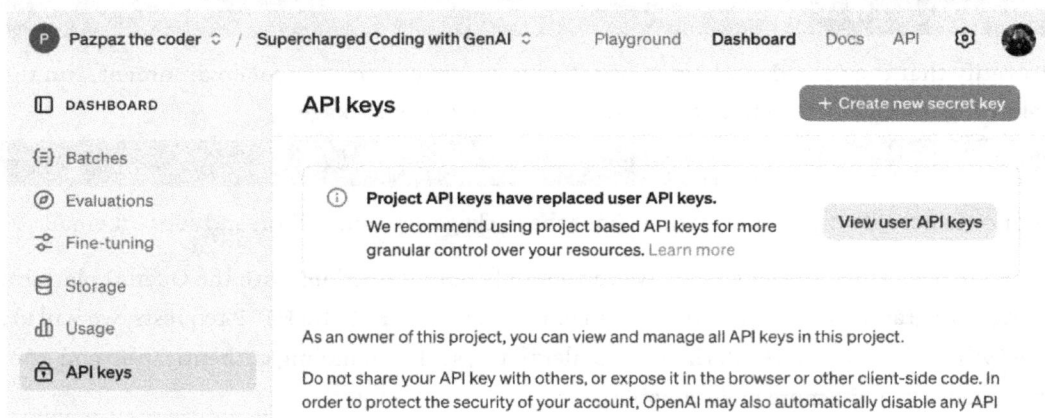

Figure 2.1: Project API keys dashboard

To generate your first API key, click on **Create new secret key** under your account icon at the upper left. Choose an API key that is owned by **You**, as we will use this key rather than assign it to a service account. You can assign a name for future reference, and it should be associated with a project (named *default project* if you have not changed the project name yet).

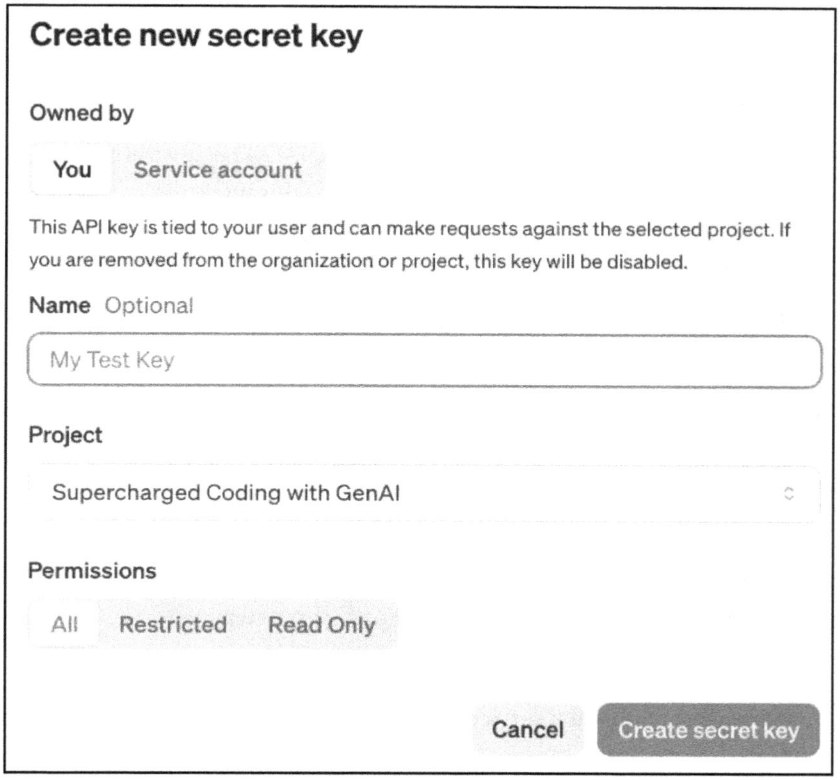

Create new secret key

Owned by

| You | Service account |

This API key is tied to your user and can make requests against the selected project. If you are removed from the organization or project, this key will be disabled.

Name Optional

```
My Test Key
```

Project

```
Supercharged Coding with GenAI                                        ○
```

Permissions

| All | Restricted | Read Only |

Cancel | Create secret key

Figure 2.2: Creating a new secret key for personal use

Once you click on **Create secret key**, the platform will generate a new secret key for you.

Return to your IDE, either VS Code or PyCharm, and export it as an environment variable from your terminal by running the following:

```
$ export OPENAI_API_KEY="your-key-here"
```

Alternatively, for a reproducible environment, you can use the *.env* file template provided with this book's repository:

```
≡ .env  ×

1    OPENAI_API_KEY="your-key-here"
```

Figure 2.3: The .env file template, placed at the root of the repository

If you choose to work with *.env* for your environment variables management, you should verify that your running configurations are set to work with this file. Refer to the *Appendix* if you need additional assistance.

Next, we will learn how to submit our first request to OpenAI API using the openai Python package, following a template that will be utilized throughout this book.

Lab 2.1 – sending your first OpenAI API request using the openai Python package

With the installed Python package and the API Keys, we are all set to execute our first OpenAI API request. Note that you do not need OpenAI platform credits to complete this lab, and we will instruct you how to load credits to your account later in this chapter. If you have previously loaded credits to the OpenAI platform, this example should cost no more than a fraction of a cent to execute.

In this lab, we will start with a simple template for executing OpenAI API requests to the Chat service and printing the response output. We will have three steps:

1. Create an openai.OpenAI class instance.
2. Submit a request to the Chat service with a single user prompt and a model selection such as *GPT-4o-mini* or *GPT-3.5-turbo*.
3. Print the response output.

These steps are in place in our starter code, and we will walk you through completing it, running it, and analyzing the results we get:

```python
import openai
from openai import OpenAI
if __name__ == "__main__":
    client: OpenAI = OpenAI()
    completion: openai.ChatCompletion = (
        client.chat.completions.create(
            model="", # Your model's name here
            messages=[] # Your messages here
        ))
    print("your print here")
```

In this lab walk-through, we will build on this starter code to complete the model and messages arguments, enabling us to receive an AI-generated response to our request from the OpenAI platform.

Lab 2.1 guided walk-through

Open *Lab 2.1* in the book's repository located at *ch2/labs/lab21.py*. First, we will instantiate a new instance of the openai.OpenAI class:

```
client: OpenAI = OpenAI()
```

We do not specify any authentication parameters directly in the code. The OpenAI client automatically retrieves the API key from the OPENAI_API_KEY environment variable. While it is possible to pass the API key using the api_key argument during instantiation, we strongly advise against hardcoding credentials in scripts for security reasons.

The next step is to send a request using the OpenAI client. We will initiate a call to the Chat service by accessing chat.completion, where we will define the necessary RESTful HTTP request parameters. This includes at least two parts: the model and messages keyword arguments. The model argument represents the name of the LLM you are querying, and the messages argument represents the input prompts sent to the model:

```
completion = client.chat.completions.create(
    model="", # Your model's name here
    messages=[] # Your messages here
)
```

If you have loaded credits onto your OpenAI platform account, enter the model value between the double quotes:

```
gpt-4o-mini
```

Otherwise, use the following model instead:

```
gpt-3.5-turbo
```

Next, add a single user prompt to the messages argument:

```
messages = [{"role": "user", "content": "What is the FizzBuzz problem?"}]
```

The last step is to print the response output of the Chat service. On the last line, replace the print statement with the following:

```
print(completion.choices[0].message.content)
```

At this point, your *Lab 2.1* code should look as follows:

```python
import openai
from openai import OpenAI
if __name__ == "__main__":
    client: OpenAI = OpenAI()
    completion: openai.ChatCompletion = client.chat.completions.create(
        model="gpt-4o-mini",
        messages=[{"role": "user", "content": "What is the FizzBuzz
problem?"}]
    )
    print(completion.choices[0].message.content)
```

Lab 2.1 is now ready to run and will print the Chat completion in response to the following user prompt: `What is the FizzBuzz problem?`.

> **Note**
>
> When working on your lab code, you can always find the full lab solutions in the `ch2/solutions` folder.

Lab 2.1 analysis

Run the script and check the output in the terminal if you are using VS Code, or the run console if you are using PyCharm. The output of the program should be the Chat service's response to the user prompt `What is the FizzBuzz problem?`, a problem we will revisit in later chapters.

Depending on the model you chose to work with (either *GPT-3.5-turbo* or the more advanced *GPT-4o-mini*), you might get quite a different output from the Chat service. For your reference, here is a response from the *GPT-3.5-turbo* model, which includes a context and problem description:

```
FizzBuzz is a common programming problem often used in job interviews
to test a candidate's ability to write simple code. The problem is as
follows:
Write a program that prints the numbers from 1 to 100. But for multiples
of three, print "Fizz" instead of the number, and for the multiples of
five, print "Buzz For numbers which are multiples of both three and five,
print "FizzBuzz"
```

Here is a response from the *GPT-4o-mini* model, which, in addition to the context and description, included a detailed explanation of the coding task stages, an example output, and the task's challenges:

```
The FizzBuzz problem is a classic programming task often used in
coding interviews and educational settings to test a developer's basic
understanding of control structures, loops, and conditional statements.
The problem is simple:
1. Write a program that prints the numbers from 1 to a specified number,
typically 100.
2. For multiples of three, print "Fizz" instead of the number.
3. For multiples of five, print "Buzz" instead of the number.
4. For numbers that are multiples of both three and five, print
"FizzBuzz."
The output would look something like this:
```
1, 2, Fizz, 4, Buzz, Fizz, 7, 8, Fizz, Buzz, 11, Fizz, 13, 14, FizzBuzz,
...
```

This task helps demonstrate an understanding of loops and conditionals,
often revealing both logical reasoning and code clarity.
```

In *Chapter 6*, we will explore the underlying differences between *GPT-4o* and *GPT-3.5* in greater detail.

Important note

As discussed in *Chapter 1*, applications built on top of LLMs rarely output deterministic results, and responses for similar prompts may differ due to prompt construction, user customization, and randomness. Moving forward in this book, we will discuss further how to control all three to achieve the desired outputs from the model.

Next, we will explore how to anticipate the costs associated with each API call and understand how tokens, as fragments of words, are used to calculate the request charges.

Learning how request costs are calculated

Since OpenAI API is primarily a paid service, it is essential to understand and anticipate the costs associated with each request.

Before proceeding with the lab exercises, it is strongly recommended that you add credits to your OpenAI platform account. An initial charge of $5 in credits should be more than enough to complete all the labs in this book. Loading credits will also upgrade your account from Free tier usage (with no prior credits) to a Tier 1 account, significantly increasing your rate and usage limits, as we will discuss later in this chapter.

To load credits, open the OpenAI **Billing Overview** page at `https://platform.openai.com/settings/organization/billing/overview` and add a payment method with a minimum charge of $5.

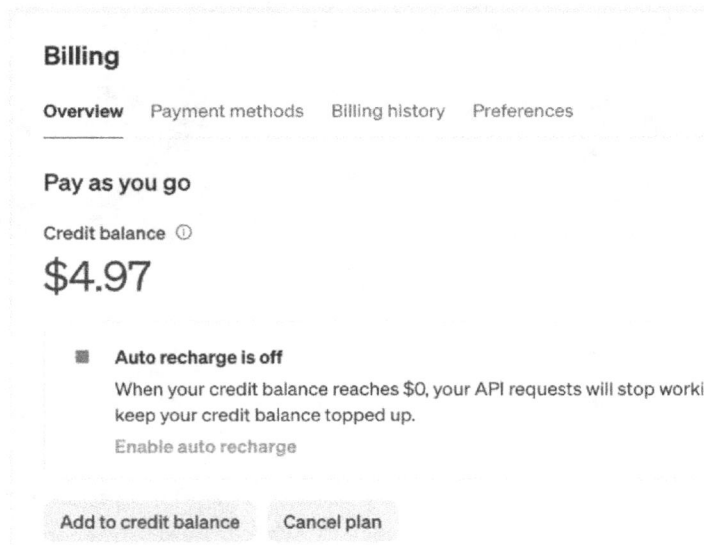

Billing

Overview   Payment methods   Billing history   Preferences

Pay as you go

Credit balance ⓘ

$4.97

▣   **Auto recharge is off**
     When your credit balance reaches $0, your API requests will stop workin
     keep your credit balance topped up.
     Enable auto recharge

Add to credit balance   Cancel plan

Figure 2.4: Remaining credit balance

You can also check your remaining balance at any time by visiting the same link.

Understanding tokens

The OpenAI platform calculates request costs based on **tokens**, which are small segments of text (often subwords, words, or characters) averaging about 0.75 words or 4 characters each. Text is divided into tokens by elements such as punctuation, root words, and word endings. We will discuss tokens in detail in *Chapter 6*.

Each API request consists of both input and output tokens, and OpenAI charges for both. For example, in *Lab 2.1*, the message {"role": "user", "content": "What is the FizzBuzz problem?"} contains 15 tokens. You can access the exact count from the prompt_token attribute as in the following code:

```
>> completion.usage.prompt_tokens
>> 15
```

Alternatively, we can estimate our total input token consumption using tools such as the OpenAI Tokenizer, available at https://platform.openai.com/tokenizer. The Tokenizer also color-codes the different tokens in the text, identifying words such as role and user as a single token, punctuation marks such as commas and question marks as a single token each, and FizzBuzz as three tokens.

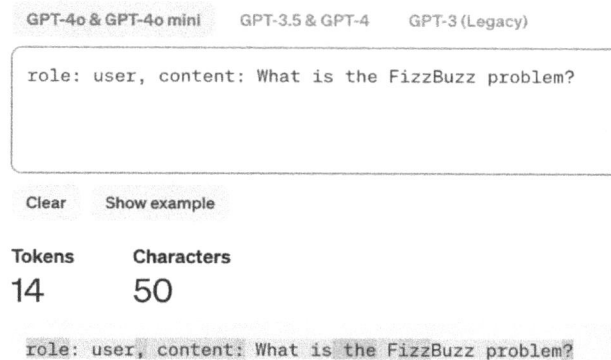

Figure 2.5: OpenAI Tokenizer simulation

Output tokens are also billed. For example, in *Lab 2.1*, the output response from the *GPT-4o-mini* model contains 292 tokens. You can access the completion_tokens attribute by calling the following:

```
>> completion.usage.completion_tokens
>> 292
```

This brings the total billable tokens to 307. You can access the total_tokens attributes by calling the following:

```
>> completion.usage.total_tokens
>> 307
```

How billing is computed

OpenAI charges for both input and output tokens, with costs varying by model. Newer, more advanced models typically have higher costs, while optimized versions, such as models with the *-mini* or *-turbo* postfix, are more affordable. You can find the full pricing details at `https://openai.com/api/pricing/`.

As of January 2025, input tokens for the *GPT-4o* model are priced at $2.50 per million tokens (or $1 for every 400,000 input tokens), while output tokens are priced at $10 per million tokens (or $1 for every 100,000 output tokens).

In *Lab 2.1*, we used the more affordable *GPT-4o-mini* model. Input tokens for this model cost $0.15 per million tokens (or $1 for every 6.6 million input tokens), and output tokens are priced at $0.60 per million tokens (or $1 for every 1.6 million output tokens). These costs are approximately 1/16 of the *GPT-4o* model's pricing.

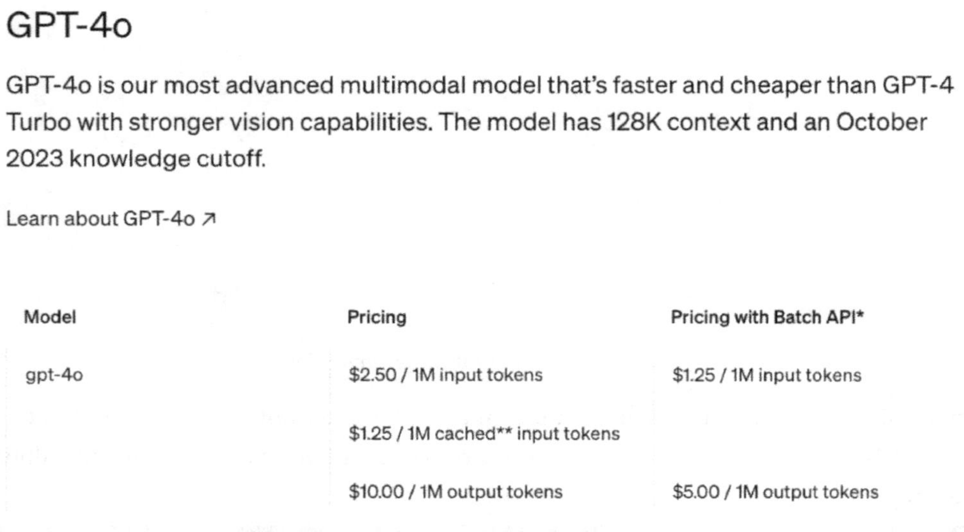

GPT-4o

GPT-4o is our most advanced multimodal model that's faster and cheaper than GPT-4 Turbo with stronger vision capabilities. The model has 128K context and an October 2023 knowledge cutoff.

Learn about GPT-4o ↗

Model	Pricing	Pricing with Batch API*
gpt-4o	$2.50 / 1M input tokens	$1.25 / 1M input tokens
	$1.25 / 1M cached** input tokens	
	$10.00 / 1M output tokens	$5.00 / 1M output tokens

Figure 2.6: Costs of GPT-4o input and output tokens

For example, we can calculate the cost of running *Lab 2.1*, which uses 15 input tokens and 292 output tokens. Based on the pricing for the *GPT-4o-mini* model, the cost is as follows:

```
>> (15 * 0.15 + 292 * 0.6) / 1000000
>> 0.00018
```

This is approximately 1/55 of a cent.

If we run *Lab 2.1* with the larger *GPT-4o* model instead, the cost would be as follows:

```
>> (15 * 2.5 + 292 * 10) / 1000000
>> 0.002
```

This amounts to 1/5 of a cent.

Keep these cost differences in mind when designing your own applications, especially when deciding between using more advanced models and their smaller, more affordable versions. Model prices have historically declined as newer models are introduced, so it is a good idea to periodically review the **Pricing** page at `https://openai.com/api/pricing/`.

With a clear understanding of cost calculations, we can now move on to discussing the limitations and restrictions associated with different tiers of OpenAI accounts.

Understanding rate limits and usage restrictions for free and paid OpenAI accounts

OpenAI usage is limited by three factors: **requests per minute (RPM)**, **requests per day (RPD)**, and **tokens per minute (TPM)**. The limits of each vary based on both the model and the type of account you have. For Free tier accounts with no credits added, the limit is three RPM, and only certain models are available, excluding *GPT-4o*. Token limits tend to be more restrictive for advanced models such as *GPT-4o* to all account tiers, whereas older or mini models, such as *GPT-4o-mini*, have more relaxed limits.

For reference, here are the rate limits for Free tier accounts as of January 2025:

Free tier rate limits

This is a high level summary and there are per-model exceptions to these limits (e.g. some legacy models or models with larger context windows have different rate limits). To view the exact rate limits per model for your account, visit the limits section of your account settings.

MODEL	RPM	RPD	TPM	BATCH QUEUE LIMIT
gpt-3.5-turbo	3	200	40,000	200,000
text-embedding-3-large	3,000	200	1,000,000	3,000,000
text-embedding-3-small	3,000	200	1,000,000	3,000,000

Figure 2.7: Rate limits example for Free tier accounts

And here are the rate limits for Tier 1 accounts as of January 2025:

Tier 1 rate limits

This is a high level summary and there are per-model exceptions to these limits (e.g. some legacy models or models with larger context windows have different rate limits). To view the exact rate limits per model for your account, visit the limits section of your account settings.

MODEL	RPM	RPD	TPM	BATCH QUEUE LIMIT
gpt-4o	500	-	30,000	90,000
gpt-4o-mini	500	10,000	200,000	2,000,000
gpt-4o-realtime-preview	100	100	20,000	-
gpt-4-turbo	500	-	30,000	90,000

Figure 2.8: Rate limits example for Tier 1 accounts

We encourage you to learn about your account's API limits by navigating to the **Settings** section in the upper-left corner of your organization: `https://platform.openai.com/settings/organization/limits`.

With Tier 1's increased RPM and TPM limits in place, we're now ready to move forward to the next lab, where we will explore additional parameters for OpenAI API.

Lab 2.2 — analyzing request parameters

In *Lab 2.2*, we will expand on our basic OpenAI API request to the Chat service by adding additional parameters to customize the model's response. This time, we will ask the Chat service to explain the *Two Sum problem*, a topic we will explore further in later chapters.

We will use a similar starter code from *Lab 2.1*, which includes setting up an OpenAI client and print statements:

```
client: OpenAI = OpenAI()
completion: openai.ChatCompletion = (
    client.chat.completions.create())
print("Completion Tokens: ")
print("Output: ")
```

In this lab's guided walk-through, we will add the following payload parameters:

n: Specifies the number of response variations

temperature: Controls the level of randomness in the model's output ranging from 0 to 2

max_tokens: Limits the number of tokens in each response

Applications such as code completion services often offer users multiple suggestions from a language model, so we may want to retrieve more than one response. Additionally, in some cases, such as generating a creative prompt (for example, Give me a marketing slogan for a book about GenAI for coding), we might prefer a higher degree of randomness in the output that can be obtained by setting the temperature parameter closer to its maximum value of 2.

The max_tokens parameter limits the number of tokens in the response, though it does not guarantee the output will be fully complete within that limit. When using max_tokens, OpenAI charges for the specified token limit rather than the actual number of tokens used, so it is best to set it close to the expected length of the response.

Lab 2.2 guided walk-through

This walk-through consists of two steps: updating the payload with additional parameters and adding a print statement to display the extra responses.

Open *Lab 2.2* in the book repository at *ch2/labs/lab22.py* and ensure that you have either set the OPENAI_API_KEY environment variable or configured your run settings to point to the *.env* file.

As the first step, update the arguments for the .create method on line 7 as follows:

1. Set the model to gpt-4o-mini:

   ```
   model = "gpt-4o-mini"
   ```

   If you have not added credits to your OpenAI platform account yet, your access may be limited to certain models, excluding gpt-4o-mini. In that case, use the gpt-3.5-turbo model instead.

2. Set a low temperature argument to reduce the randomness of the output:

   ```
   temperature=0.2
   ```

3. Set the max_tokens argument to restrict the model's output to a maximum of 100 tokens:

   ```
   max_tokens=100
   ```

4. Set the n argument to instruct the model to return a single response for the request:

```
n=1
```

5. Add a system prompt to the messages argument to give the agent the tone of a tech company hiring manager:

```
{"role": "system", "content": "You are a hiring manager at a tech
company."}
```

6. Add an additional user prompt to the messages argument asking about the Two Sum problem:

```
{"role": "user", "content": "What is the Two Sum problem?"}
```

7. For the second step, update the print statements to display the output token count and the model output.

8. Modify the first print statement to indicate the output count:

```
print("Completion Tokens: ", completion.usage.completion_tokens)
```

9. To display the output response, update the second print statement as follows:

```
print("Output: ", completion.choices[0].message.content)
```

If you followed all the steps correctly, your code should look like this:

```
import openai
from openai import OpenAI


if __name__ == "__main__":
    client: OpenAI = OpenAI()
    completion: openai.ChatCompletion = (
        client.chat.completions.create(
            model="gpt-4o-mini",
            temperature=0.2,
            max_tokens=100,
            n=1,
            messages=[{"role": "system", "content": "You are a hiring
manager at a tech company."},
            {"role": "user", "content": "What is the Two Sum problem?"}],
        ))
```

```
print("Completion Tokens: ", completion.usage.completion_tokens)
print("Output: ", completion.choices[0].message.content)
```

Lab 2.2 is now ready to run and will print the output token count along with the response to the user prompt What is the Two Sum problem?

Lab 2.2 analysis

Run the script and check the output. If you are using VS Code, look in the terminal, and if you are using PyCharm, check the run console. Ensure that the output token count does not exceed 100 and that the Chat service begins explaining the Two Sum problem, a topic we will revisit in future chapters.

Keep in mind that setting a max_tokens limit does not guarantee a complete explanation and may truncate responses.

The following is a sample output, limited to 100 tokens, obtained from running the lab. The completion was truncated at 100 tokens, equivalent to 84 words:

```
"The Two Sum problem is a classic algorithmic problem often encountered in
coding interviews and competitive programming. The problem can be stated
as follows:
Given an array of integers `nums` and an integer `target`, you need to
determine if there are two distinct indices `i` and `j` in the array such
that the sum of the elements at these indices equals the target value. In
other words, you need to find two numbers in the array that add up to the
specified target.
### Problem Statement"
```

Although this output is truncated, it may still provide sufficient information to understand the Two Sum problem.

> **Note**
>
> Question: Can you compute the cost of the *lab22.py* request?

Answer:

```
>> (28 * 0.15 + 100 * 0.6) / 1000000>>  0.000064
```

This is approximately 1/150 of a cent.

Multiple service responses with Lab 2.2

Reflecting on *Lab 2.2*, we can now better understand the impact that payload request parameters have on the initial output from the Chat service.

In that lab, we set the n parameter to 1, which is also the default value. However, in some GenAI applications, it may be beneficial to generate more than one response. For example, in tools such as GitHub Copilot or other code completion services, displaying multiple suggestions can enhance user experience. In such cases, increasing the number of responses with the n argument allows the model to provide multiple outputs. Keep in mind that the billing will include all generated outputs along with the input tokens.

In *Lab 2.2*, modify the n argument to request three different responses, and increase the temperature parameter to encourage more randomness and variety in the output:

```
n=3
temperature = 2
```

Now, update the print statements to include the additional outputs from the Chat service:

```
print("Output 1: ", completion.choices[0].message.content)
print("Output 2: ", completion.choices[1].message.content)
print("Output 3: ", completion.choices[2].message.content)
```

Run the lab again to view the three different responses from the Chat service explaining the Two Sum problem. Feel free to experiment with the parameters further to see how they affect the output.

Next, we will explore how to utilize OpenAI API for coding-related tasks, such as generating a Python code implementation based on a function's signature.

Lab 2.3 – using OpenAI API to generate code

Now that we have learned how to execute OpenAI API calls and configure various parameters, we can use them to create our own basic code completion program. Previously, developers could select models such as code-davinci-002, which were specifically trained for code completion. These models have since been deprecated and now chat services can effectively handle code completion tasks.

Routing chat capabilities to code completion

In this lab, we will create a code completion program by following five steps:

1. Define the input to function signatures only.

2. Add system prompts to guide the model in generating the complete code.

3. Wrap the function signature with a specific instruction for the model to complete the code.

4. Get the Chat service response for our request.

5. Extract only the code from the model's output to present to the end user.

These steps demonstrate that applications built on top of LLM models require a tailored approach such as using wrapping designs and specific prompts to align the model's output with the business problem at hand. We will cover that in depth later in the book.

Our starter code consists of all five steps, which we will complete in the guided walk-through:

```python
import openai
from openai import OpenAI


USER_PROMPT = """
user prompt here
"""
SYSTEM_PROMPT = "system prompt here"


def get_code_with_instructions(code: str) -> str:
    """

    Add a comment to the code for specific code completion instruction
    :param code: Python code as string
    :return: The code with additional instruction - "Complete this code"
    """


    return code + "your wrapping instructions here"


if __name__ == "__main__":
    client: OpenAI = OpenAI()

    completion: openai.ChatCompletion = (
        client.chat.completions.create())
```

```
for i in range(2):
    output = completion.choices[i].message.content
    print(f"Output {i + 1}:")
    try:
        suggested_code = output.split("```")[1]
        print(suggested_code)
    except IndexError:
        print(output)
```

In this lab walk-through, we will learn how to complete the system prompt, wrapping instructions for the get_code_with_instructions function, and payload arguments for client.chat.completions.create. Combined with a function signature as the user prompt, these elements will channel OpenAI's Chat service capabilities toward a targeted code completion program.

Lab 2.3 guided walk-through

Open *Lab 2.3* in the book repository at *ch2/labs/lab23.py* and ensure that you have either set the OPENAI_API_KEY environment variable or configured your run settings to point to the *.env* file.

First, set the user prompt to be a function signature for printing the Fibonacci sequence:

```
USER_PROMPT="""
def print_fibonacci_sequence(n: int) -> None:
"""
```

Next, include a system prompt to set guidelines for the assistant to act as an AI pair programmer:

```
SYSTEM_PROMPT = "You will be provided with a Python function signature.
Your task is to implement the function. Return code only. "
```

We will also wrap the function signature to include a specific instruction for code completion. Update the get_code_with_instructions function to wrap the given code with an extended comment that instructs the model to complete the function signature:

```
return code + "\n# Complete this code"
```

Next, configure the payload arguments by specifying the appropriate model, the desired number of responses, and the level of randomness:

1. Set the model to gpt-4o-mini:

    ```
    model = "gpt-4o-mini"
    ```

    If you have not loaded credits to your OpenAI platform account yet, your access may be limited to certain models, excluding gpt-4o-mini. In that case, use the gpt-3.5-turbo model instead.

2. Set a medium temperature argument to increase the randomness of the outputs:

    ```
    temperature=1
    ```

3. Set the n argument to instruct the model to return two different coding suggestions:

    ```
    n=2
    ```

4. Finally, set up the request arguments to include the wrapped function signature as the user prompt, along with a system prompt:

    ```
    model = "gpt-4o-mini"
    temperature=1
    n=2
    messages = [
        {"role": "system",
         "content": SYSTEM_PROMPT},
        {"role": "user",
         "content": get_code_with_instructions(USER_PROMPT)}
    ]
    ```

If you followed all the steps correctly, your lab's code should be implemented as follows:

```
import openai
from openai import OpenAI

USER_PROMPT = """
def print_fibonacci_sequence(n: int) -> None:
"""

SYSTEM_PROMPT = "You will be provided with a Python function signature.
```

```
Your task is to implement the function. Return code only."

def get_code_with_instructions(code: str) -> str:
    """
    Add a comment to the code for specific code completion instruction
    :param code: Python code as string
    :return: The code with additional instruction - "Complete this code"
    """
    return code + "\n# Complete this code"

if __name__ == "__main__":
    client: OpenAI = OpenAI()
    completion: openai.ChatCompletion = (
        client.chat.completions.create(
            model="gpt-4o-mini",
            temperature=1,
            n=2,
            messages=[
                {"role": "system", "content": SYSTEM_PROMPT},
                {"role": "user", "content": get_code_with_
instructions(USER_PROMPT)}
            ],
        )
    )
    ...
```

Lab 2.3 is now ready to run and will print two coding suggestions for the Fibonacci sequence.

Lab 2.3 analysis

In this lab, we wrapped the user prompt and added a supporting system prompt to explicitly define the task for the Chat service: to complete a function that prints the Fibonacci sequence based solely on its signature. The following is a sample output generated when running this lab with two outputs. The first response provides a shorter solution without type checking, printing the Fibonacci numbers one by one. The second response includes input validation, creates the sequence up to the n limit, and then prints the entire sequence:

```
Output 1:
def print_fibonacci_sequence(n: int) -> None:
```

```
    a, b = 0, 1
    for _ in range(n):
        print(a, end=' ')
        a, b = b, a + b
    print()   # for a new line after the sequence

Output 2:
def print_fibonacci_sequence(n: int) -> None:
    if n <= 0:
        print("Please enter a positive integer.")
        return

    sequence = []
    a, b = 0, 1
    count = 0

    while count < n:
        sequence.append(a)
        a, b = b, a + b
        count += 1

    print(sequence)
```

To further explore code completion, try adding additional system prompts such as add a docstring or add type hints and observe the results. You can also increase the number of returned outputs or modify the instructions in the wrapped user prompt to see how these changes affect the generated code.

Important note

In this lab, the system prompt includes specific instructions for the desired output: Return code only. In later chapters, we will explore how to craft more effective instructions to guide the model toward the desired output structure using best practices and prompt engineering techniques.

Summary

In the first quickstart guide, we used the openai Python package to build three different programs based on AI-generated output. We experimented with various models, including *GPT-4o* and *GPT-3.5*, explored different request parameters, and combined user prompts with system prompts.

We also loaded credits to the OpenAI platform, which increased our rate limits and allowed us to use a broader range of models. We learned how request costs are calculated based on the number of input and output tokens.

Finally, we developed a basic code completion program that wrapped a function signature, guiding the model to generate the rest of the function's implementation.

With these foundations in place, we can progress to the next chapter, *Quickstart Guide to GitHub Copilot*, and better understand how Copilot generates coding suggestions and how to tailor them to fit our unique preferences when necessary.

Quiz time

Before you proceed to the next chapter, make sure that you can confidently answer the following questions:

Question 1: What is the difference between a system prompt and a user prompt in a Chat service request?

Answer: User prompts are the inputs provided by the end user, such as the questions or commands given to ChatGPT. They represent the direct interaction with the AI-generated content, such as the following:

```
Explain the Two Sum problem
```

Here is another example:

```
def print_fibonacci_sequence(n): # complete this code
```

System prompts, however, define the guidelines and tone for the Chat interaction. They instruct the assistant on how to behave during the conversation with the end user, as in this example:

```
You are a technical interviewer for a software engineering internship
```

Here is another example:

```
You will be provided with a Python function signature. Your task is to
implement the function. Return code only.
```

Question 2: What are tokens, and how do they impact the cost of an OpenAI API request?

Answer: Tokens are small segments of text, typically averaging around 0.75 words or 4 characters each when the text is split into tokens based on elements such as punctuation, root words, and word endings. The cost of an OpenAI API request is calculated based on the number of input tokens, output tokens, and the max_tokens argument, with different models having varying token costs.

Further reading

To learn more about the topics that were covered in this chapter, take a look at the following resources:

- OpenAI Platform home page: https://platform.openai.com
- OpenAI API official documentation: https://platform.openai.com/docs/overview
- OpenAI Pricing: https://openai.com/api/pricing/
- OpenAI Rate Limits (General): https://platform.openai.com/docs/guides/rate-limits
- OpenAI available models: https://platform.openai.com/docs/models/model-endpoint-compatibility
- OpenAI individual rate limits: https://platform.openai.com/settings/organization/limits
- The FizzBuzz wiki page: https://en.wikipedia.org/wiki/Fizz_buzz
- The Two Sum Leet Code page: https://leetcode.com/problems/two-sum/description/

Subscribe for a free eBook

New frameworks, evolving architectures, research drops, production breakdowns—AI_Distilled filters the noise into a weekly briefing for engineers and researchers working hands-on with LLMs and GenAI systems. Subscribe now and receive a free eBook, along with weekly insights that help you stay focused and informed.

Subscribe at `https://packt.link/TR05B` or scan the QR code below.

3

A Guide to GitHub Copilot with PyCharm, VS Code, and Jupyter Notebook

GitHub Copilot, an **AI pair programmer**, is enabling developers to supercharge their coding abilities and write code more efficiently. The application uses an underlying **large language model (LLM)** designed specifically for code completion tasks, code analysis, and chat for coding-related tasks.

Since we built our own code completion program capable of completing a Python function based on its signature alone in *Chapter 2*, we can better understand the role of LLMs in Copilot's implementation, as well as what other preprocessing and postprocessing work is required.

This chapter is dedicated to working with GitHub Copilot in our **integrated development environment (IDE)**. First, we will set up a GitHub Copilot account and determine who is eligible for a free account. Then, we will connect our account to our IDE (either VS Code or PyCharm) and explore the three interaction modes of the tool: chat, completion, and analysis. We will also work with Copilot in a Jupyter Notebook using VS Code. PyCharm cannot run Jupyter notebooks yet with Copilot.

Through three interactive labs, we will implement a geometric mean calculator using all three GitHub Copilot interaction modes: chat, completion, and analysis. Additionally, we will experiment with keyboard shortcuts for core Copilot functionality to help streamline our workflow and boost productivity.

In this chapter, we will cover the following key topics:

- Introducing GitHub Copilot – our AI pair programmer
- Understanding GitHub Copilot's free account limits, costs, and policies
- Setting up Copilot in PyCharm and VS Code
- Using Copilot chat
- Introducing completion and keyboard shortcuts for geometric mean calculations
- Analyzing code with Copilot
- Working with Copilot in VS Code's Jupyter Notebook for code analysis

Technical requirements

To get the most out of this chapter, ensure you have the following:

- GitHub account
- Access to IDE – either VS Code or PyCharm
- Access to the book's repository, which is available at `https://github.com/PacktPublishing/Supercharged-Coding-with-Gen-AI`
- Virtual environment set up in your preferred IDE, VS Code or PyCharm

If you require additional assistance in setting up your OpenAI account or a virtual environment in your IDE, refer to the *Appendix* for detailed instructions.

Introducing GitHub Copilot – our AI pair programmer

GitHub Copilot is an AI-powered tool that uses LLMs trained on vast and diverse datasets containing a significant amount of open source code from public repositories across various programming languages, including Python. By combining the model's extensive knowledge with your code's context, GitHub Copilot provides tailored coding suggestions, as well as chat and code analysis features, to assist in your development process.

Code completion design overview

To provide meaningful code completions, Copilot processes the input and output of the LLM, like the code completion program developed in *Lab 2.3*. For the input, Copilot structures a prompt based on the lines surrounding the cursor, function signatures, and additional context, such as recent edits, Git details, file names and open files. The LLM's output is further processed, including validation to ensure it compiles successfully.

We can visualize Copilot's code completion process as a flowchart, as shown in *Figure 3.1*.

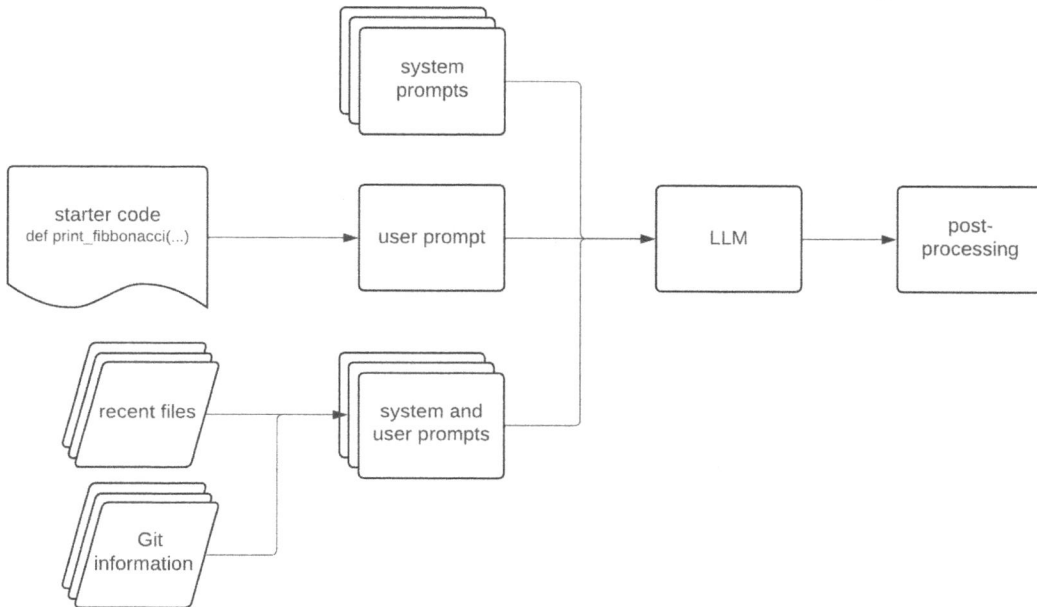

Figure 3.1: An overview of GitHub Copilot's suggestion process

In addition to code completion, GitHub Copilot offers two other modes of interaction: chat (available inline or through the chat window) and code analysis. Both modes are based on the underlying code and comments but differ in their final output and the postprocessing steps involved. We will discuss these extensively later in this chapter.

Important note

Some developers may think that GitHub Copilot sends the entire Git repository code they are working on to the LLM. This is very unlikely given two reasons: the cost of input tokens and the relevance of the entire code to the specific code completion task. It is far more likely that only relevant code is preprocessed by Copilot first. Then, only the necessary information including coding style preferences or relevant classes, code, and variables, is added to the prompt in addition to the cursor's surrounding context.

Understanding GitHub Copilot's free account limits, costs, and policies

To enable GitHub Copilot in your IDE, you first need to subscribe to the service through GitHub's platform. Like many other GenAI services, GitHub Copilot is primarily a paid service, though some exceptions allow free access.

Who is eligible for a free account?

There are three ways to qualify for GitHub Copilot at no cost:

- Free account available to anyone, which includes up to 2,000 code completions and 50 chat requests per month.
- Free pro account for students and educators with a valid university email
- Free pro account for maintainers of popular open source repositories

If you are a student or educator with a university email and the required documentation, you can apply for GitHub's Student Pack at https://education.github.com/pack.

If you are a leading maintainer of a popular open source repository, you may have free access to Copilot. GitHub determines eligibility based on internal criteria, without requiring an application process. If eligible, upon clicking your profile icon and selecting **Your Copilot,** you will be directed to a page titled *GitHub Copilot Individual* instead of a payment page, as detailed later in this chapter.

Some organizations and enterprises cover the cost of GitHub Copilot access for their users. If you belong to such an organization or enterprise, you will find a **request access** button next to the organization's name at https://github.com/settings/copilot. In these cases, you will not be charged for using Copilot, as the organization or enterprise will handle the licensing fees on your behalf.

Compared to individual accounts, GitHub Copilot for business and enterprises offers additional features, such as pull request summaries, a knowledge base, and the ability to fine-tune a custom LLM for enterprise versions. These options come at a higher cost than individual memberships.

Pricing

For individual users, the service is priced at $10 per month or $100 annually. For Copilot business, the rate is $19 per user per month, while the enterprise version increases to $39 per user per month.

Code completion policies

All GitHub Copilot users are governed by specific policies that define the scope of code suggestions, privacy, and access points, including your IDE and github.com.

A notable policy is *suggestions matching public code*. Since the GitHub Copilot model is primarily trained on open source and publicly available code repositories, some of its suggestions may be subject to copyright protection. To mitigate potential issues, GitHub provides users with an option to exclude coding suggestions that replicate such code.

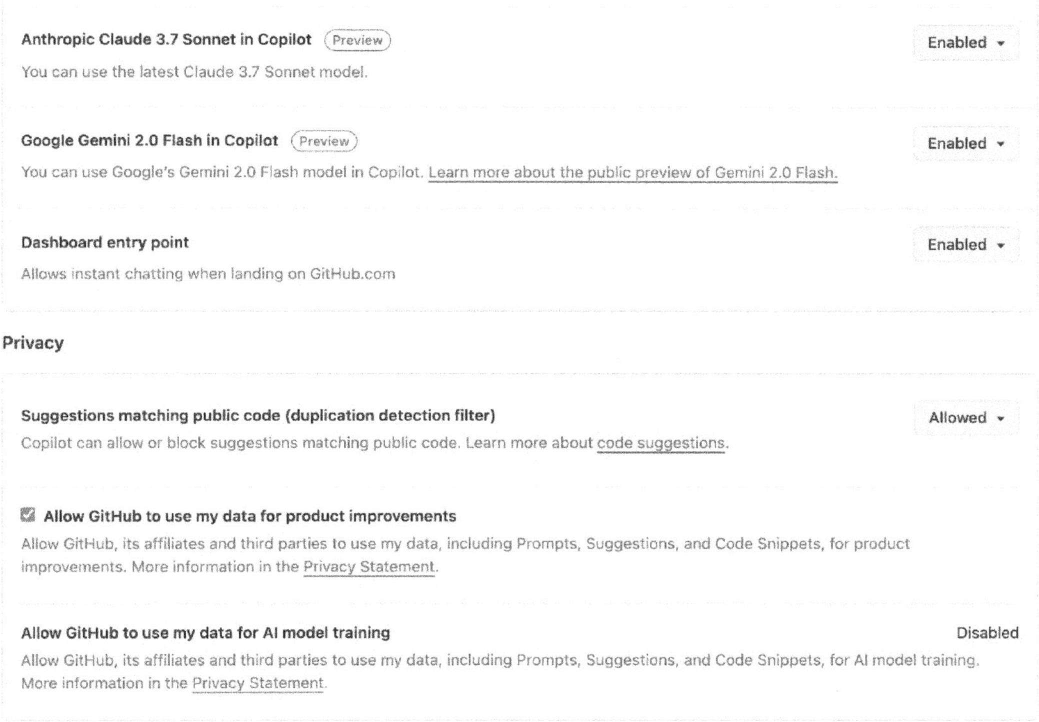

Anthropic Claude 3.7 Sonnet in Copilot (Preview)   Enabled ▾
You can use the latest Claude 3.7 Sonnet model.

Google Gemini 2.0 Flash in Copilot (Preview)   Enabled ▾
You can use Google's Gemini 2.0 Flash model in Copilot. Learn more about the public preview of Gemini 2.0 Flash.

Dashboard entry point   Enabled ▾
Allows instant chatting when landing on GitHub.com

Privacy

Suggestions matching public code (duplication detection filter)   Allowed ▾
Copilot can allow or block suggestions matching public code. Learn more about code suggestions.

☑ **Allow GitHub to use my data for product improvements**
Allow GitHub, its affiliates and third parties to use my data, including Prompts, Suggestions, and Code Snippets, for product improvements. More information in the Privacy Statement.

Allow GitHub to use my data for AI model training   Disabled
Allow GitHub, its affiliates and third parties to use my data, including Prompts, Suggestions, and Code Snippets, for AI model training. More information in the Privacy Statement.

Figure 3.2: Privacy and ownership options in Copilot

> 🔍 **Quick tip:** Need to see a high-resolution version of this image? Open this book in the next-gen Packt Reader or view it in the PDF/ePub copy.
>
> 🔒 **The next-gen Packt Reader** is included for free with the purchase of this book. Scan the QR code OR go to packtpub.com/unlock, then use the search bar to find this book by name. Double-check the edition shown to make sure you get the right one.

Here, suggestions that match public code are allowed. We also recommend enabling additional underlying models such as Anthropic Claude and Google Gemini alongside to support further experimentation.

For business or enterprise accounts, the policies are pre-determined by the administrator of the organization or enterprise. Individual account users, however, can set their own policies during account setup or through the Copilot settings page: `https://github.com/settings/copilot`.

Activating your GitHub Copilot account

To participate in the labs and hands-on exercises in this book, you will need either a free, pro, business, or enterprise GitHub Copilot account. If you wish to set up an individual account, go to `https://www.github.com`, click on your profile icon, and select **Your Copilot**.

Figure 3.3: Copilot access in the GitHub account

If you are a leading maintainer of a popular open source repository and qualify for free access to Copilot, you will be directed to a page titled *GitHub Copilot Individual* page. Otherwise, you will be directed to the payment page, where you can select a free trial option or a paid plan.

Select the plan that suits you, adjust settings to align with your individual or company policies (e.g., enable or disable public code matches), and enter your payment details.

Once completed, you will have access to Copilot services at `https://github.com/settings/copilot` as shown in *Figure 3.4*:

GitHub Copilot

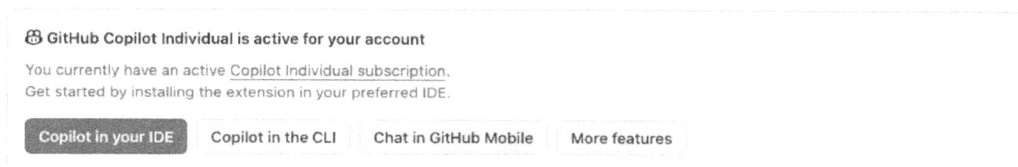

Figure 3.4: GitHub Copilot settings header

This page shows your access level, provides links to resources for setting up Copilot in your IDE, and outlines Copilot's privacy and ownership policies.

With our account now activated, we are ready to proceed and connect Copilot to our IDE.

Setting up Copilot in PyCharm and VS Code

GitHub Copilot is available via a PyCharm plugin or a VS Code extension. The core features of GitHub Copilot in both IDEs are similar, offering the three interaction modes we will cover in this book: chat, completion, and analysis.

However, Copilot is more tightly integrated with VS Code, meaning new features, such as Jupyter Notebook support or switching to newer LLMs, are often released in VS Code before they are available in the PyCharm extension.

Since your GitHub Copilot subscription can be used across multiple IDEs, we encourage PyCharm users to try VS Code to explore Jupyter Notebook support. However, the labs in this book are tailored for both PyCharm and VS Code.

GitHub Copilot plugin for PyCharm

To install the GitHub Copilot plugin in PyCharm, go to **PyCharm | Settings | Plugins**, then search `GitHub Copilot` in the marketplace. After installation, you will be prompted to restart your IDE.

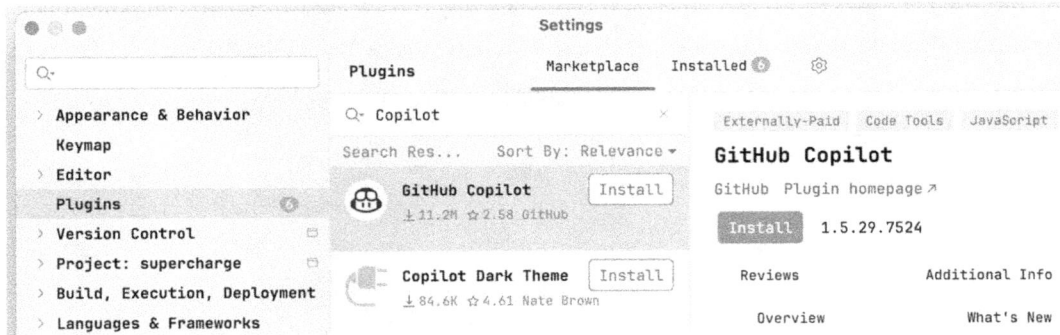

Figure 3.5: GitHub Copilot Plugin in PyCharm

When your IDE restarts, you will be prompted to log in to your GitHub account.

To check whether the service is available, look for the Copilot icon at the bottom of the IDE. Hovering over it should display **Ready**.

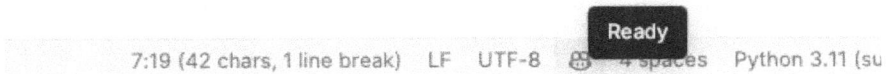

Figure 3.6: GitHub Copilot plugin icon health check in PyCharm

This confirms that the plugin is set up correctly, allowing us to start using Copilot.

GitHub Copilot extension for VS Code

To install the Copilot extension, navigate to **Code | Extensions**, search `GitHub Copilot`, and install it. When you do this, the GitHub Copilot Chat extension will also be automatically installed.

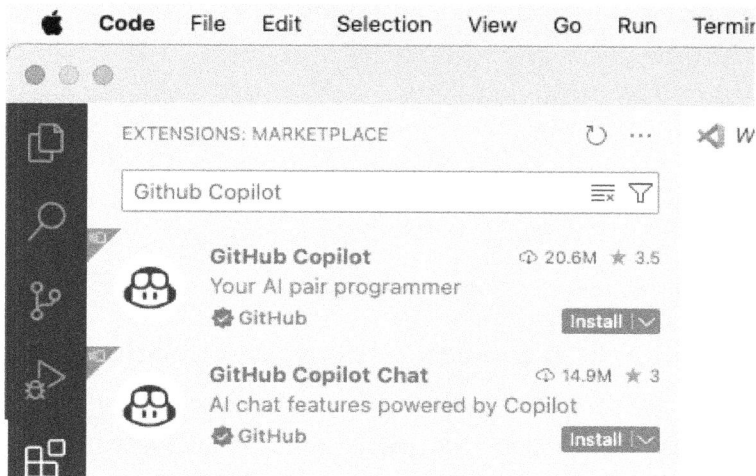

Figure 3.7: GitHub Copilot and Copilot Chat extension in VS Code

After the installation, the GitHub Copilot extension window will open, prompting you to authenticate or sign up for a GitHub Copilot account.

To check whether the extension is working properly after authentication, click on the GitHub Copilot icon in the bottom-right corner to open **GitHub Copilot Menu**.

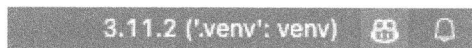

Figure 3.8: GitHub Copilot icon in the bottom right window

A drop-down list will appear, and if you are logged into your GitHub account with a stable internet connection, the status should display **Ready**.

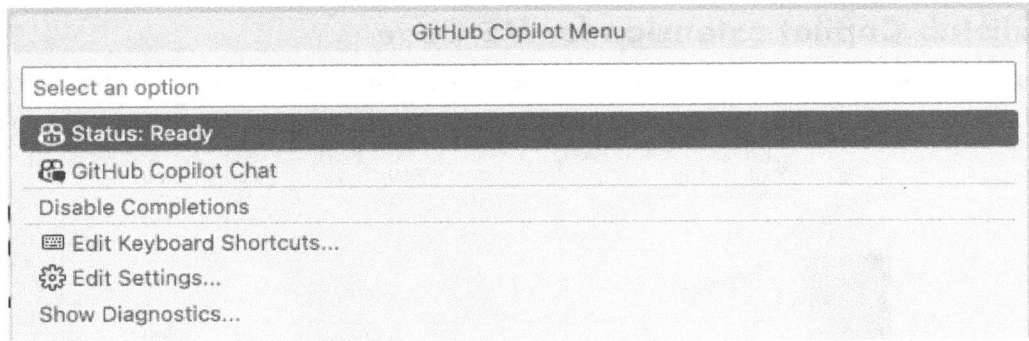

Figure 3.9: Verifying GitHub Copilot extension status in VS Code

This confirms that the extension is set up correctly, allowing us to start using Copilot.

The three interaction modes — chat, completion, and analysis

Originally designed to provide tailored code completion suggestions, GitHub Copilot now offers three key interaction modes powered by LLMs: chat, completion, and analysis:

1. **Chat** is accessible via a chat window resembling the ChatGPT interface or through an inline compact view. We will use this mode when we want contextual assistance with coding-related questions.

2. **Completion** is available automatically in our files. As we type, Copilot will suggest code completions based on the code we write. We will use this mode when implementing new code.

3. **Analysis** includes features such as *explain*, *fix*, and *tests*, which are available through the chat window, the inline chat, and the edits window in VS Code. We will use this mode when interacting with existing code.

In the next three labs, we will experiment with each of these interaction modes.

Using Copilot chat

The chat feature complements GitHub Copilot's code completion capabilities. The chat window can assist with questions related to your code, external topics, terminal commands, and even the VS Code IDE itself.

In VS Code, you can open the Copilot chat window using *Ctrl + Alt + I* (or *cmd + control + I* on Mac). Alternatively, click on the Copilot icon next to the top search bar of the screen.

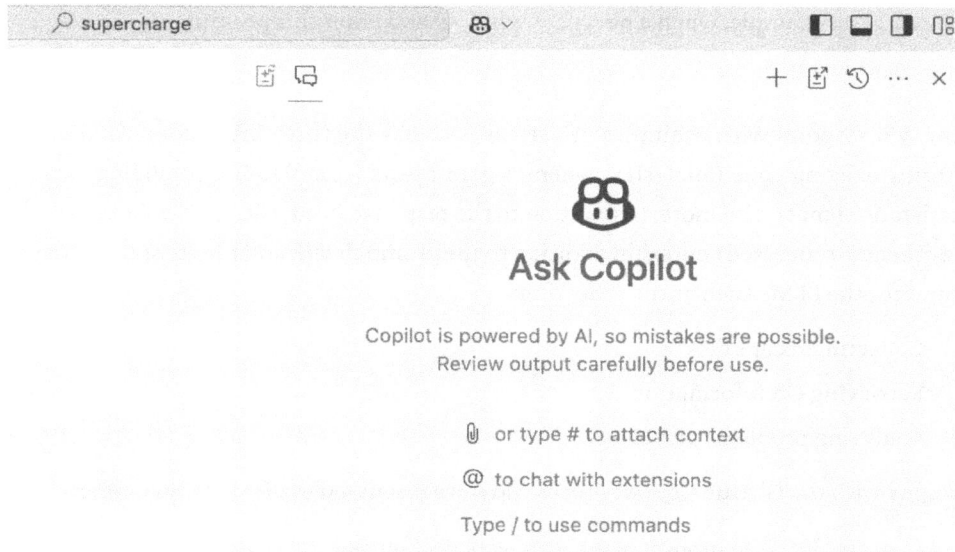

Figure 3.10: GitHub Copilot chat window in VS Code

In PyCharm, you can open the Copilot chat window using *Ctrl + Shift + C* or by selecting the **GitHub Copilot Chat** tab in the left-hand menu.

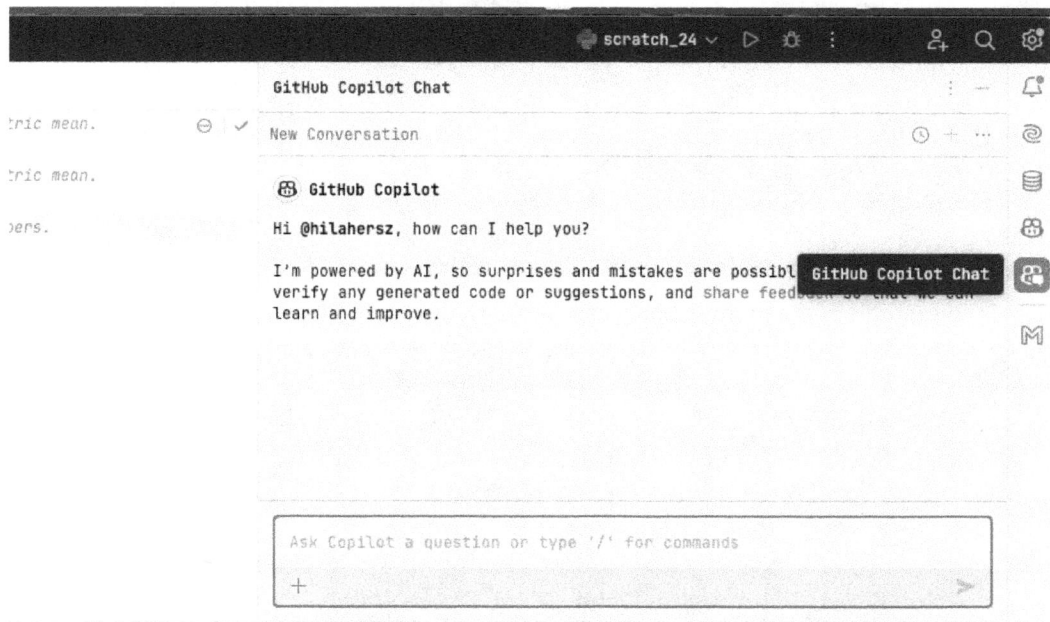

Figure 3.11: GitHub Copilot chat window in PyCharm

Let us look at an example. Open a new chat window and enter this prompt:

```
What can you do?
```

Copilot will respond with examples of use cases across the three interaction modes, such as refactoring existing code (analysis), generating unit tests (completion), providing version control assistance (chat), and more. In addition to the response itself, GitHub Copilot chat will also display the pre-processed context in addition to the prompt itself, and the steps taken to prepare the input for the LLMs such as the following:

- Collecting recent files
- Retrieving Git information
- Analyzing problems and errors

This aligns with the GitHub Copilot process flow we discussed earlier in this chapter.

Here is an example of the prompt, What can you do?, output in PyCharm:

```
I can assist you with various programming tasks, such as:

- Writing and debugging code
- Explaining code snippets and concepts
- Providing code examples and templates
- Assisting with version control (e.g., Git)
- Helping with configuration and setup of development environments
- Offering best practices and optimization tips

If you have a specific question or need help with a particular piece of
code, feel free to ask!
```

Here is an example of the prompt, What can you do?, output in VS Code:

```
I can assist with various programming tasks, including:
* Answering general programming questions
* Explaining how the code in your active editor works
* Reviewing the selected code in your active editor
* Generating unit tests for the selected code
* Proposing fixes for problems in the selected code
* Scaffolding code for a new file or project in your workspace
* Creating a new Jupyter Notebook
* Finding relevant code to your query
```

```
* Proposing fixes for test failures
* Answering questions about VS Code
* Generating query parameters for workspace search
Running commands
* Explaining terminal outputs
* Providing step-by-step guidance for terminal tasks

How can I assist you today?
```

The PyCharm plugin and the VS Code extension may produce different outputs for the same prompt. This occurs because the GitHub Copilot application handles files in PyCharm and VS Code slightly differently, offers distinct features in each, and incorporates an element of randomness. Keep in mind that, like any GenAI output, suggestions may not always be accurate or complete, as we will observe later in this chapter.

Next, we will explore how the chat window can enhance code completion tasks within our IDE, even when further exploration of a topic is needed (such as an explanation of the geometric mean).

Lab 3.1 – calculating geometric mean with chat completion

In *Lab 3.1*, we will explore the geometric mean through the chat interaction mode. The geometric mean is a way of averaging numbers that are multiplicative in nature, such as financial portfolio growth rates, population growth rates, or drug concentrations that vary exponentially over time. Unlike the arithmetic mean, which calculates the sum of a sequence of numbers divided by its length, the geometric mean is the n-th root of the product of the numbers:

$$\text{Arithematic Mean} = \frac{1}{n}\sum_{i=1}^{n} x_i$$

$$\text{Geometric Mean} = \left(\prod_{i=1}^{n} x_i\right)^{\frac{1}{n}}$$

For example, the geometric mean of 5 and 20 is 10, because of the following:

$$(20.5)^{\frac{1}{2}} = (100)^{\frac{1}{2}} = \sqrt{100} = 10$$

Similarly, the geometric mean of 5, 20, and 10 is also 10, because of the following:

$$(20 \cdot 5 \cdot 10)^{\frac{1}{3}} = (1000)^{\frac{1}{3}} = \sqrt[3]{1000} = 10$$

In this lab, we will use the chat window along with code completion. First, we will obtain an explanation of the geometric mean using the chat window. Next, we will utilize Copilot to complete an implementation based on a function signature, including the name, parameters, type hints, and return values. Finally, we will print the function's output by defining sample call parameters.

Lab 3.1 guided walk-through

Open *Lab 3.1* in the book's repository at *ch3/labs/lab31.py* and ensure that you have a stable internet connection, and that GitHub Copilot is ready.

The starter code consists of three parts:

```
# Part 1: Open the chat window and ask to explain the geometric mean.


# Part 2: Implement the geometric mean function for two floating-point
numbers.


# Part 3: Call
```

Part 1 is for practice only, Part 2 requires specifying the function signature for code completion, and Part 3 involves adding sample parameters and printing their response.

For Part 1, delete the comment, open the Copilot chat window and enter the following prompt:

```
Explain the geometric mean.
```

This prompt will provide an explanation of the geometric mean. Note that the explanation may be truncated due to the max_tokens limit of Copilot, which we have no control over, or contain raw mathematical formatting, such as LaTeX code instead of compiled equations. Despite this, it should still provide enough information for us to understand the topic.

For Part 2, delete the comment and type the function signature to calculate the geometric mean of two floating-point numbers:

```
def get_geometric_mean_of_two_numbers(
    a: float,
    b: float,
) -> float:
```

This function signature, with its name, parameters, type hints, and return type, is considered a complete prompt to Copilot that should yield a desirable implementation.

In `Part 3`, delete the comment and add a sample call that tests the implementation. Enter the following prompt:

```
num1: float = 5.0
num2: float = 20.0
print
```

The `print` statement acts as the cue for Copilot, which will likely suggest a call to the `get_geometric_mean` function using `num1` and `num2` as arguments.

If you followed all the steps correctly, your code should look like this:

```
def get_geometric_mean_of_two_numbers(
        a: float,
        b: float,
) -> float:
    return pow(a * b, 1 / 2)


num1: float = 5.0
num2: float = 20.0
print(get_geometric_mean_of_two_numbers(num1, num2))
```

Lab 3.1 is now ready to run and will print the geometric mean of 5 and 20, which is as follows:

```
10.0
```

Lab 3.1 analysis

In this lab, we used Copilot chat to learn about the geometric mean. We also leveraged code completion based on either a function signature as a starter code or a print call as a cue.

For your reference, here is the Copilot chat response to the prompt, `Explain the geometric mean`. We generated it using the VS Code chat window with the *GPT-4o* model. The response includes raw LaTeX code and is truncated before the full output:

```
>> The geometric mean is a measure of central tendency that is
particularly useful for sets of numbers whose values are meant to be
multiplied together or are exponential in nature. It is defined as the nth
root of the product of n numbers.
Formula
```

```
For a set of ( n ) positive numbers ( x_1, x_2, \ldots, x_n ), the
geometric mean ( G ) is given by:
[ G = \left( \prod_{i=1}^{n} x_i \right)^{\frac{1}{n}} ]
Steps to Calculate
Multiply all the numbers together to get the product.
Take the nth root of the product, where ( n ) is the total number of
values.
Example
Consider the numbers 2, 8, and 4:
Multiply the numbers: ( 2 \times 8 \times 4 = 64 )
Since there are 3 numbers, take the cube root: ( \sqrt[3]{64} =
```

Choosing the underlying models to power the chat is available in the bottom-right corner of the chat window.

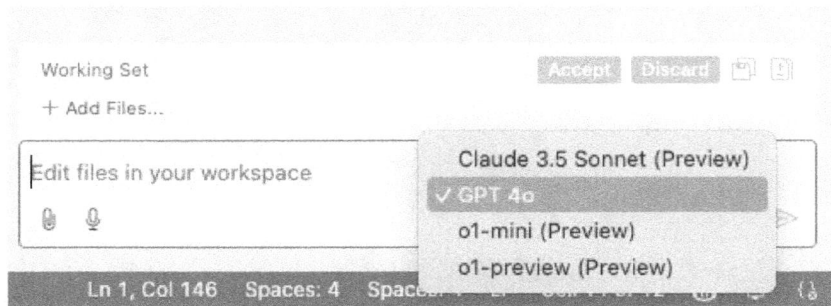

Figure 3.12: Model selection for the Copilot chat window

We found this response lacking due to the truncation of the example, as Copilot imposes a max_ tokens limit on model outputs, and the formatting of mathematics as raw LaTeX code. However, for topics we are already familiar with, the chat window saves considerable time and eliminates the need to use external tools, such as Google or ChatGPT.

Next, we will further explore GitHub Copilot's code completion capabilities using a variety of keyboard shortcuts to make our experience even smoother.

Lab 3.2 — introducing completion and keyboard shortcuts for geometric mean calculations

Keyboard shortcuts are vital for enhancing a programmer's efficiency, especially when working with Copilot, which provides a wide range of options to accept or reject suggestions partially or fully. This lab will focus on implementing the geometric mean using code completion, incorporating keyboard shortcuts to do the following:

- Reject a suggestion
- Regenerate a rejected suggestion
- Accept a full suggestion or parts of it
- Switch between different code options.

In this lab, we will implement the geometric mean for a sequence of floating-point numbers using a function signature and an instructive prompt to validate the input arguments. We will explore various implementation suggestions, selectively accepting or rejecting parts of them.

> **Important note**
>
> This lab includes standard keyboard shortcuts for working with Copilot. If any of these are missing or you would prefer different shortcuts, you can customize them by editing your keymap. In PyCharm, navigate to **Settings | Keymap**, and in VS Code, go to **Settings | Keyboard Shortcuts**. For further assistance with keyboard shortcuts, refer to the *Appendix*.

Lab 3.2 guided walk-through

Open *Lab 3.2* in the book repository at *ch3/labs/lab32.py* and ensure that you have a stable internet connection, and that GitHub Copilot is ready.

There is no starter code for this lab. Our task is to begin by typing an instructive function signature to calculate the geometric mean of a sequence of floating-point numbers.

Add the following code to the file. If you type it rather than copy and paste it, Copilot may offer early completion suggestions. Ignore these until you complete the prompt:

```
def get_geometric_mean(*nums):
```

At this point, you should already see completion suggestions by Copilot. Use the following instructions for both PyCharm and VS Code to explore these suggestions:

```
ch3 > solutions > 🐍 lab32.py > 🔶 get_geometric_mean
1   def get_geometric_mean(
2   |        *nums: float,
3   ) -> float:
        if not nums:
            return 0
        product = 1
        for num in nums:
            product *= num
        return product ** (1 / len(nums))
```

Figure 3.13: Copilot code completion example in VS Code

To experiment with Copilot's keyboard shortcuts, follow these steps. If any of the keyboard shortcuts are different or missing in your interface, make sure to find the alternate shortcuts:

1. Accept the entire code completion by pressing *Tab*.
2. Then, undo it by *Ctrl + Z / cmd + Z*.
3. In PyCharm, accept a single line from the suggestion by pressing *Ctrl + Alt +* the right arrow (*cmd + control +* right if you are a Mac user).
4. In VS Code, there is no default keyboard shortcut for this. Instead, hover over the suggested text, click on the ellipsis (**...**), and select **Accept Line**.
5. Then, undo it by pressing *Ctrl + Z / cmd + Z*.
6. Accept a single word from the suggestion by pressing *Ctrl +* the right arrow (*cmd +* the right arrow if you are a Mac user).
7. Then, undo it by pressing *Ctrl + Z / cmd + Z*.
8. Hide the suggestion by pressing *Esc*.
9. Retrigger the Copilot suggestion by pressing *Alt + * (*option + * if you are a Mac user).
10. Toggle to the next suggestion by pressing *Alt +]* (*option +]* if you are a Mac user). Go back to previous suggestions by pressing *Alt + [* (*option + [* if you are a Mac user).
11. In PyCharm, access the code completion pane by right-clicking on Copilot's suggestions and selecting **Copilot: Open Completion**.
12. In VS Code, access it by pressing *Ctrl + Enter*.

Next, we encourage you to modify the prompt by adjusting the function name, arguments, type hints, or return type. Keep practicing with the keyboard shortcuts and observe how the completions evolve with each change.

Lab 3.2 analysis

In this lab, we practiced keyboard shortcuts in PyCharm and VS Code to streamline pairing with Copilot, making it easier to accept, reject, or switch between completion suggestions smoothly.

For your reference, a sample completion for the get_geometric_mean implementation in PyCharm is shown in *Figure 3.14*.

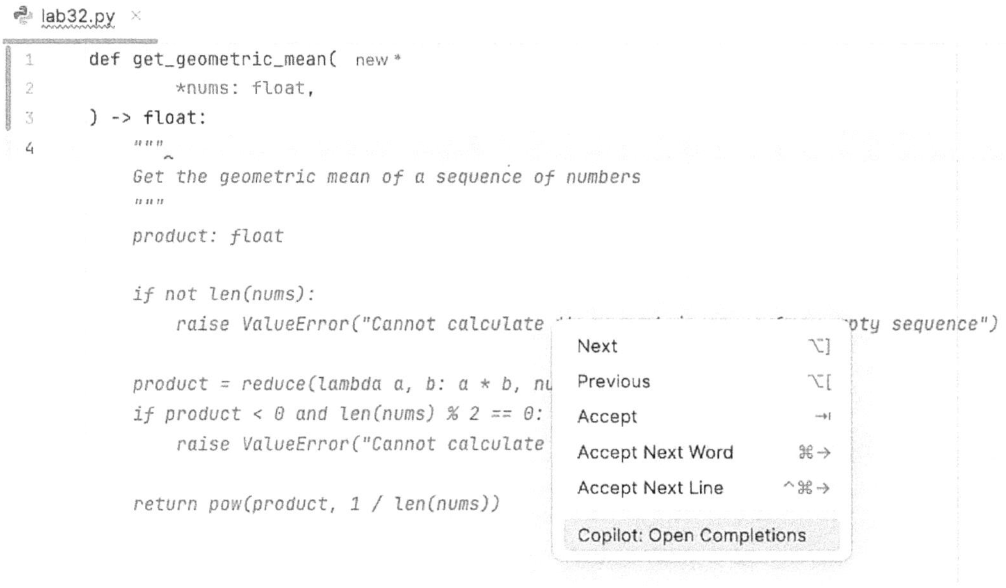

Figure 3.14: Copilot inline menu in PyCharm

When right-clicking on the completion and selecting **Copilot: Open Completion**, the completion pane displays various suggestions provided by Copilot.

GitHub Copilot

Accept solution

```
"""Calculate the geometric mean of the input numbers."""
    return (len(nums) * (math.prod(nums))) ** (1 / len(nums))
```

Accept solution

```
return (prod(nums)) ** (1 / len(nums))
```

y sequence")

Accept solution

```
"""Calculate the geometric mean of a list of numbers.

    Args:
        nums: A list of numbers.

    Returns:
        The geometric mean of the numbers.
    """
```

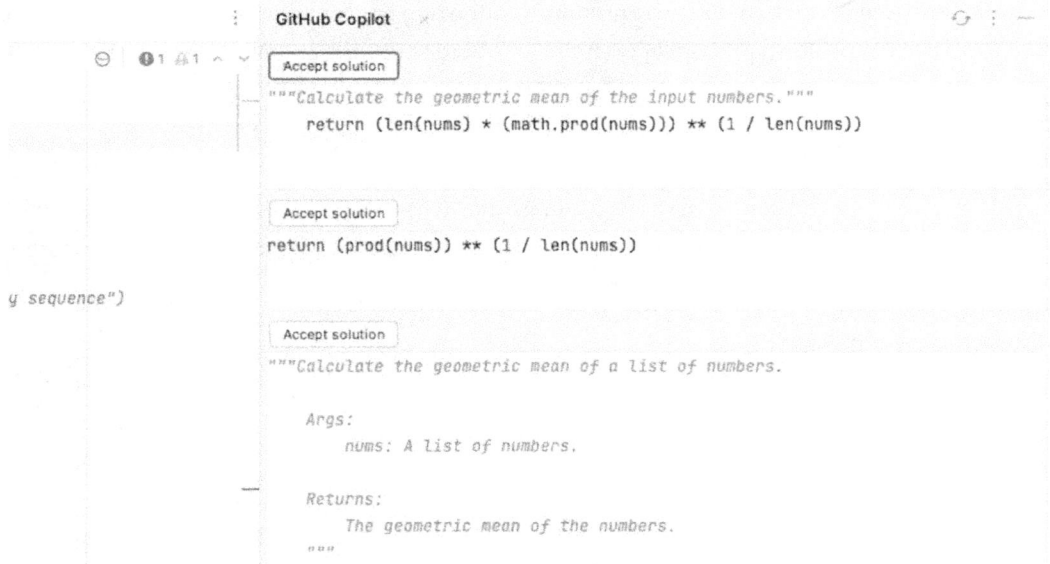

Figure 3.15: Copilot code completion pane in PyCharm

We can then choose to accept any of these suggested solutions.

Similarly, VS Code will also display a variety of different completion suggestions.

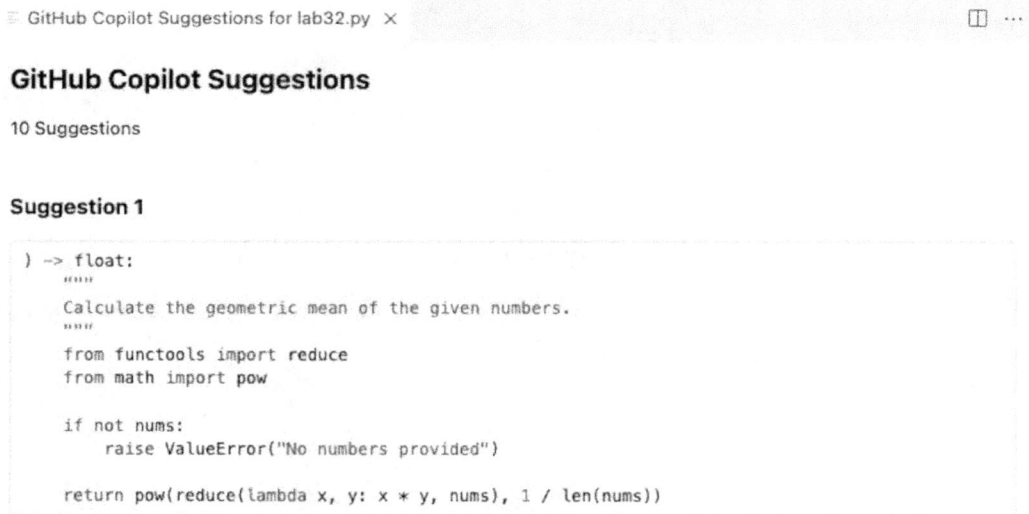

GitHub Copilot Suggestions for lab32.py ✕

GitHub Copilot Suggestions

10 Suggestions

Suggestion 1

```
) -> float:
    """
    Calculate the geometric mean of the given numbers.
    """
    from functools import reduce
    from math import pow

    if not nums:
        raise ValueError("No numbers provided")

    return pow(reduce(lambda x, y: x * y, nums), 1 / len(nums))
```

Figure 3.16: VS Code Copilot code completion pane

Here too, we can then choose to accept any of these suggested solutions.

> **Important Note**
>
> In later chapters, we will explore best practices for prompt precision and prompt engineering techniques. These will help us better structure a function's content by covering aspects like input validation, formatting with type hints, and handling side effects such as monitoring and logging.

Next, we will explore Copilot's code analysis options, demonstrating how they complement code completion when working with existing code.

Analyzing code with Copilot

The recently introduced code analysis features in both PyCharm and VS Code complement GitHub Copilot's code completion capabilities. It can be accessed via the Copilot menu or the inline chat window using commands such as /fix /explain and /test

To use these features, right-click on your code, select **Copilot**, and you will see the available options. This menu is accessible in both PyCharm and VS Code.

Here is how the menu appears in PyCharm:

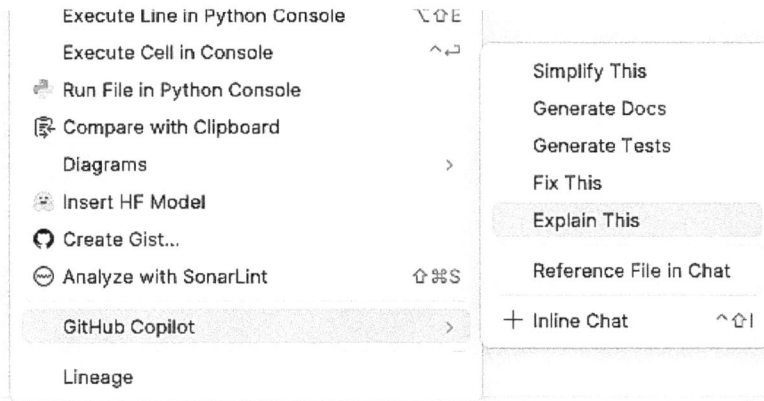

Figure 3.17: Copilot code analysis in PyCharm

Here is how the menu appears in VS Code:

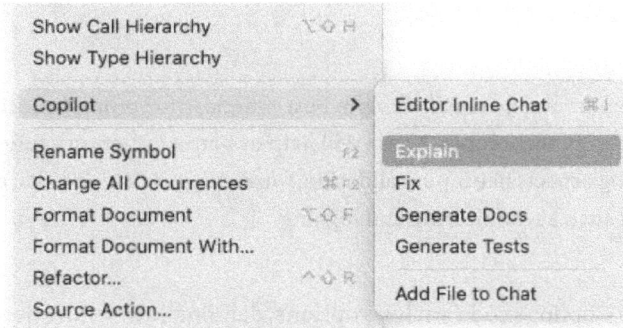

Show Call Hierarchy   ⌥⇧H
Show Type Hierarchy

Copilot   >   Editor Inline Chat   ⌘I

Rename Symbol   F2   Explain
Change All Occurrences   ⌘F2   Fix
Format Document   ⌥⇧F   Generate Docs
Format Document With...   Generate Tests
Refactor...   ⌃⇧R
Source Action...   Add File to Chat

Figure 3.18: Copilot code analysis in VS Code

For quicker access, you can use Copilot inline chat commands. In VS Code, press *Ctrl + I* (*cmd + I* for Mac).

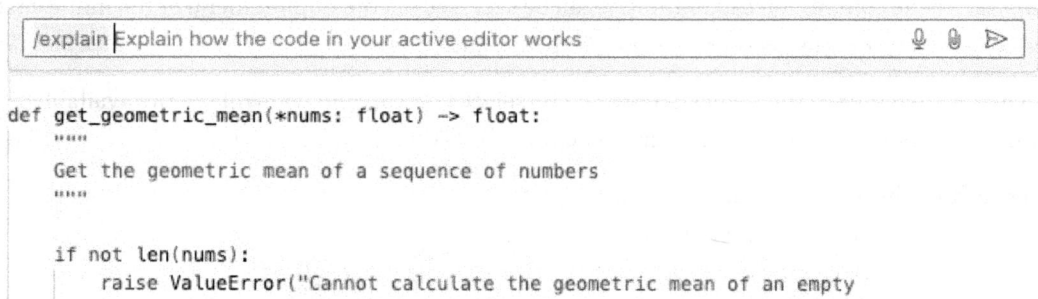

```
/explain Explain how the code in your active editor works

def get_geometric_mean(*nums: float) -> float:
    """
    Get the geometric mean of a sequence of numbers
    """

    if not len(nums):
        raise ValueError("Cannot calculate the geometric mean of an empty
```

Figure 3.19: Copilot editor inline chat in VS Code

In PyCharm, press *Ctrl + Shift + I* (*cmd + shift + I* for older Mac versions of PyCharm).

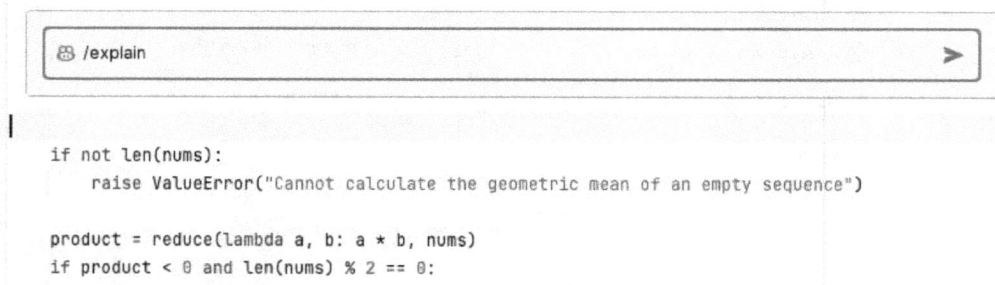

```
/explain

    if not len(nums):
        raise ValueError("Cannot calculate the geometric mean of an empty sequence")

    product = reduce(lambda a, b: a * b, nums)
    if product < 0 and len(nums) % 2 == 0:
```

Figure 3.20: Copilot inline chat in PyCharm

In the inline chat window, type your code analysis command, such as /fix or /explain.

Analyzing code with Copilot editor window in VS Code

GitHub Copilot has recently introduced a dedicated editor window to enhance editing tasks and streamline working across multiple files simultaneously. To access the window, open the chat window and select **Edit**, as shown in *Figure 3.21*:

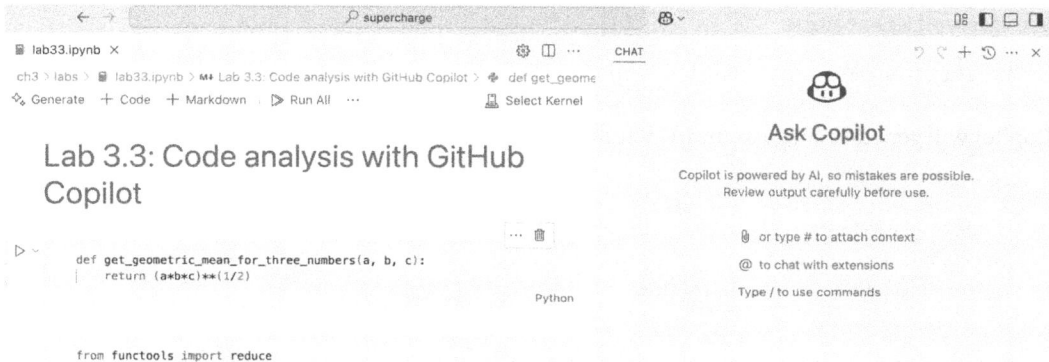

Figure 3.21: Accessing Copilot's edits window

In this editor window, you can add files you want to work on or target specific sections using the annotation #selection, as shown in *Figure 3.22*:

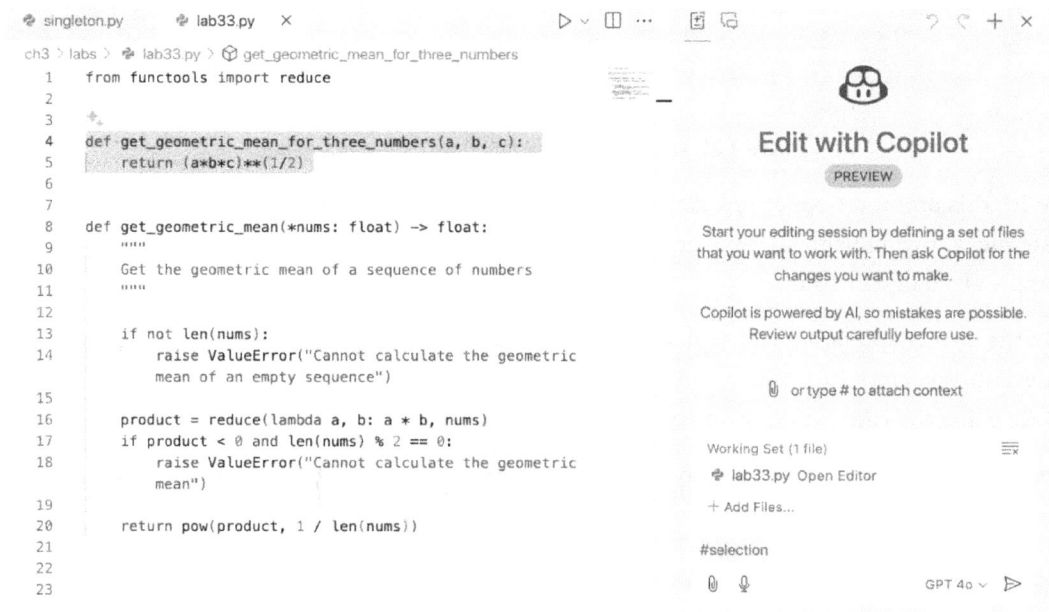

Figure 3.22: Working with #selection in Copilot edits window

The edits window supports the slash commands such as `/fix`, `/explain`, and `/test`, as well as tailored instructions to modify your code. For instance, to add input validation for `float` inputs to the following function:

```
def get_geometric_mean_for_three_numbers(a, b, c):
```

We can type the prompt:

```
#selection add input validation for float inputs.
```

Copilot will generate suggestions to include input validation for float types, as shown in *Figure 3.23*:

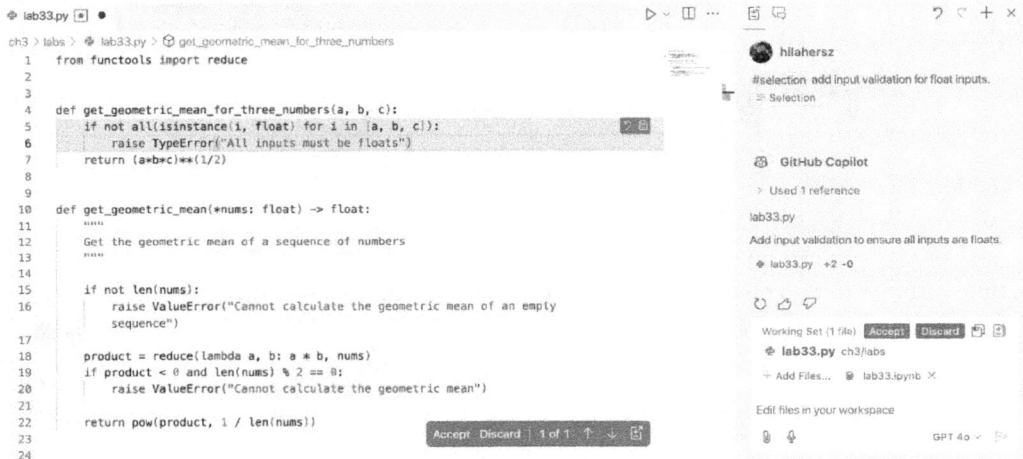

Figure 3.23: Adding input validation with the edits window

With this prompt, Copilot presents suggestions in a version control format within the working set file, allowing us to approve or revert each change individually. We can also click **Accept** to apply all changes at once.

In the next chapters, we will explore best practices for crafting precise prompts to achieve more desirable results with Copilot, including its edits window. Later in the book, we will delve deeper into using the edits window for prompt engineering techniques and refactoring code.

Now that we have explored how to analyze and edit code with Copilot, we can practice addressing and fixing a faulty implementation of the geometric mean, using both VS Code and PyCharm.

Lab 3.3 – working with Copilot in VS Code's Jupyter Notebook for Code Analysis

The following lab focuses on code analysis. We will use the /fix command to fix an incorrect implementation of the geometric mean for three floating-point numbers. We will then use the /explain command to get a brief explanation of an implementation for the geometric mean of a sequence of numbers.

The lab is available in two formats: a Jupyter Notebook or a Python script. If you are using VS Code, choose the Jupyter Notebook version to explore Copilot's features for notebooks. Since Jupyter Notebook support is not yet available in PyCharm, a Python script version is also provided. In *Lab 3.3 guided walk-through*, we will cover both formats and use Copilot's code analysis features to fix and understand code more efficiently.

Lab 3.3 guided walk-through

Open *Lab 3.3* from the book repository: If you are using VS Code, go to *ch3/labs/lab33.ipynb*, and if you are using PyCharm, go to *ch3/labs/lab33.py*. Make sure you have a stable internet connection, and that GitHub Copilot is ready.

Our starter code includes two functions that we will apply code analysis to. The first function, get_geometric_mean_for_three_numbers, incorrectly implements the geometric mean for three floating-point numbers, as it takes the square root of their product instead of the cube root.

The second function, get_geometric_mean, calculates the geometric mean for a sequence of numbers of any length. It first validates that there is at least one item in the sequence. Then, it computes the product of all the numbers using a reduce operation. It also checks that the root results in a real number, which occurs if either the product is positive, or the required root is odd. Finally, after validation, it returns the n-th root of the product for a sequence of length n:

```
from functools import reduce

def get_geometric_mean_for_three_numbers(a, b, c):
    return (a*b*c)**(1/2)

def get_geometric_mean(*nums: float) -> float:
    """
    Get the geometric mean of a sequence of numbers
    """
```

```
    if not len(nums):
        raise ValueError("Cannot calculate the geometric mean of an empty
sequence")

    product = reduce(lambda a, b: a * b, nums)
    if product < 0 and len(nums) % 2 == 0:
        raise ValueError("Cannot calculate the geometric mean")
    return pow(product, 1 / len(nums))
```

The calculation in get_geometric_mean_for_three_numbers is incorrect, as it takes the square root of the product of the numbers instead of the cube root.

To fix this code, choose the fix option or type /fix in the inline chat.

Copilot should suggest replacing the incorrect square root with the cube root:

```
    return (a*b*c)**(1/3)
```

For your reference, here is a sample output in VS Code with the proposed fix (note that this fix could be implemented in your code using the **Accept** button):

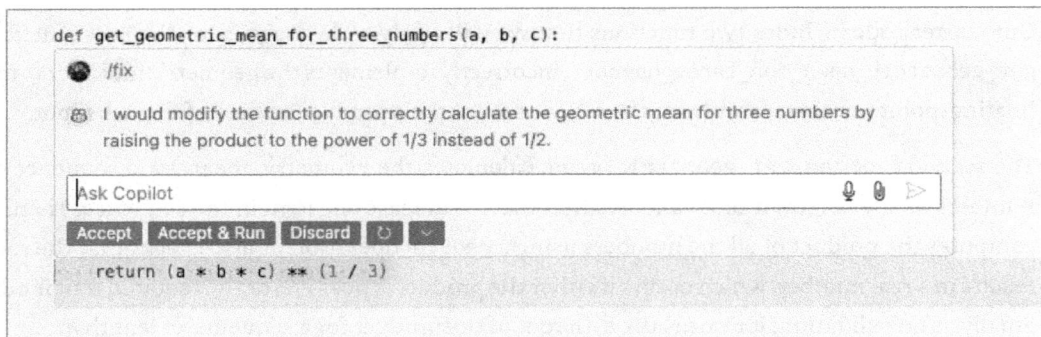

Figure 3.24: Copilot fix suggestion in VS Code

In PyCharm, here is a sample output with the proposed fix. To accept it, click the **Preview** button and then **Accept**.

```
def get_geometric_mean_for_three_numbers(a, b, c):    Hila Paz Herszfang
```

> 3 steps completed successfully

The problem in the selected line is that the exponent should be (1/3) instead of (1/2) to correctly calculate the geometric mean of three numbers.

```
return (a * b * c) ** (1 / 3)
```

> Using 1 Reference

```
return (a*b*c)**(1/2)
```

Figure 3.25: Copilot fix suggestion in PyCharm

In the top-left corner, the preview icon is the first on the left. Click it to open the preview mode:

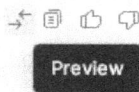

Figure 3.26: The Preview button for accepting Copilot changes in PyCharm

The preview window displays the original code on the left and the proposed fix on the right, with an **Accept** button to confirm the changes.

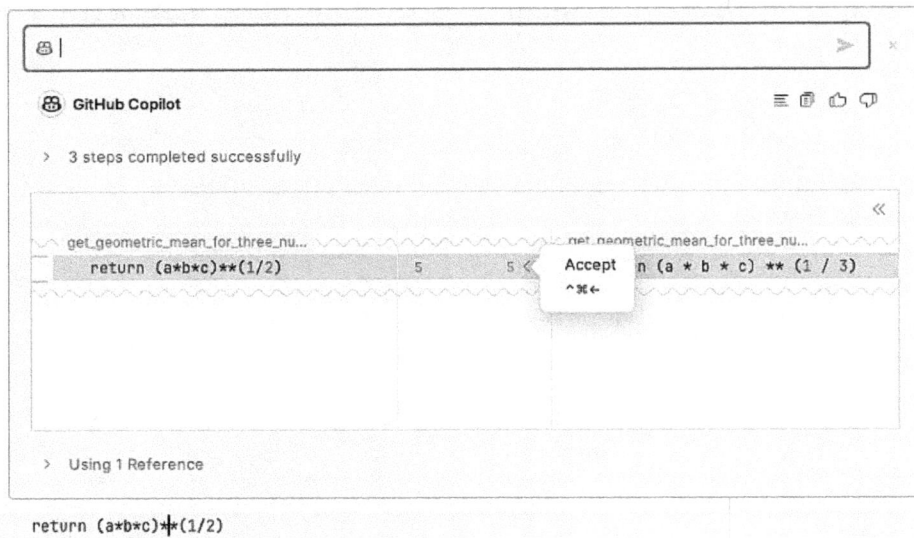

Figure 3.27: Accepting Copilot fix suggestions in PyCharm

Accept this proposed implementation.

Next, move your cursor to the get_geometric_mean function and examine how Copilot explains its four parts: validating the input length, computing the product, verifying that the geometric mean is real, and returning the n-th root of the product.

Right-click on the code, select **Copilot | explain**, or use the keyboard shortcuts to open the inline chat and type /explain. Copilot should cover all four steps of the function.

Lab 3.3 analysis

In this lab, we used the code analysis mode to efficiently review existing code. Since a sizable portion of our work as software developers involves maintaining code rather than generating new code, these extended capabilities are invaluable for enhancing our productivity.

For reference, here is the code explanation we obtained in VS Code, covering the four steps of the function:

```
The provided code defines a function get_geometric_mean that calculates
the geometric mean of a sequence of numbers. The function accepts a
variable number of floating-point arguments (*nums) and returns a
floating-point result.

The function begins by checking if the sequence of numbers is empty using
if not len(nums). If the sequence is empty, it raises a ValueError with
the message "Cannot calculate the geometric mean of an empty sequence".
This ensures that the function does not proceed with an invalid input.

Next, the function calculates the product of all the numbers in the
sequence using the reduce function combined with a lambda function (lambda
a, b: a * b). The reduce function applies the lambda function cumulatively
to the items of the sequence, effectively multiplying all the numbers
together.

After calculating the product, the function checks if the product is
negative and if the number of elements in the sequence is even (if product
< 0 and len(nums) % 2 == 0). If both conditions are true, it raises a
ValueError with the message "Cannot calculate the geometric mean". This
check is necessary because the geometric mean of a set of numbers that
includes an even number of negative values is not defined in the real
number system.

Finally, the function returns the geometric mean by taking the nth
root of the product, where n is the number of elements in the sequence
(pow(product, 1 / len(nums))). The pow function is used to compute the
nth root, which is equivalent to raising the product to the power of the
reciprocal of the number of elements.

Overall, the function is designed to handle various edge cases and ensure
that the geometric mean is calculated correctly for valid inputs.
```

Overall, Copilot explains all four steps of the function well and addresses its input. However, the interpretation of the real geometric mean output is missing from Copilot's explanation, as shown in the highlighted part of the output:

```
After calculating the product, the function checks if the product is
negative and if the number of elements in the sequence is even...
```

Rather than being a limitation of the tool, this suggests that our implementation could be improved. We will explore this further in *Chapter 4*.

Summary

In this chapter, we took our first steps with the GitHub Copilot by setting up subscriptions and enabling Copilot in our IDE. Through three labs, we explored its three interaction modes: chat, completion, and analysis.

After implementing a basic code completion program in *Chapter 2*, we were able to better understand how GitHub Copilot is designed. Copilot enhances the code to be completed with contextual information, such as recent edits, coding preferences, and Git logs. This information is processed into user and system prompts, which are then fed to an LLM. The model's output is further processed before being presented to the user.

Throughout the three labs, we utilized the three interaction modes to implement and refine several calculators of the geometric mean. We saw how a function signatures can be used as a prompt to Copilot. We also experimented with various completion options using keyboard shortcuts. While mastering these techniques requires some practice, they can significantly boost productivity when working with Copilot.

In the next chapter, we will discuss the three pillars of good model output: model mastery, evaluation metrics, and precise prompts. We will also learn about the best practices in making our prompt precise with the five S's: having a structured prompt, providing surrounding context, focusing on a single task, and having specific and short instructions.

Quiz time

Before you proceed to the next chapter, make sure that you can confidently answer the following questions.

Question 1: Is Copilot a paid service?

Answer: Copilot is primarily a paid service, with a few exceptions including free limited access. Students, educators, and maintainers of leading open-source repositories are also eligible for a free subscription.

Question 2: What are the three interaction modes for GitHub Copilot?

Answer: Copilot's original task of code completion is complemented by two additional features: chat, which is available inline or through the chat window, and code analysis, which is accessible via the Copilot right-click menu, using slash commands, such as /fix and /explain, or in the edits window within VS Code.

Further reading

To learn more about the topics that were covered in this chapter, look at the following resources:

- GitHub Copilot documentation: https://docs.github.com/en/copilot/quickstart
- Copilot subscription plans: https://docs.github.com/en/copilot/about-github-copilot/subscription-plans-for-github-copilot
- Copilot setup in your IDE: https://docs.github.com/en/copilot/setting-up-github-copilot/setting-up-github-copilot-for-yourself
- Copilot best practices: https://docs.github.com/en/copilot/using-github-copilot/best-practices-for-using-github-copilot

4

Best Practices for Prompting with ChatGPT

GenAI applications excel in certain aspects of coding and often achieve high scores in coding assignment tests. Ongoing improvements to these models continue to push the boundaries, as they begin to master a wide range of coding-related tasks and supercharge the way we develop and refine code.

To achieve good results from GenAI applications, we will focus on three pillars: **model mastery** of the specific task at hand, **evaluation metrics** to critically assess the output, and crafting **precise prompts** to clearly achieve the desired outcome.

This chapter focuses on best practices for crafting prompts in coding-related tasks, guided by the **five S's: structured** prompt, including **surrounding** context, focusing on a **single** task, providing **specific** instructions, and keeping the prompt as **short** as possible. Later in the book, we will delve into advanced prompt engineering techniques, methods to construct manual and automatic evaluation metrics, and strategies for improving the model's mastery of specific tasks.

Through two interactive labs, we will explore how following best practices for crafting prompts for coding-related tasks leads to reusable prompt structures. We will apply these principles to refine a prompt for translating **Graphical User Interface (GUI)** actions into **Command-Line Interface (CLI)** commands. We will also review a sample prompt published by OpenAI and analyze it through the lens of the five S's for crafting prompts. This analysis will help us understand how these examples yield desirable outcomes and highlight potential improvements, which we will explore further in later chapters of the book.

In this chapter, we will cover the following topics:

- Can we trust GenAI for coding tasks?
- Best practices for crafting prompts for coding tasks
- Crafting prompts for ChatGPT
- Prompt samples by OpenAI

Technical requirements

To get the most out of this chapter, ensure you have the following:

- OpenAI account with access to ChatGPT
- Access to the book's repository available at `https://github.com/PacktPublishing/Supercharged-Coding-with-Gen-AI`

If you need help creating an OpenAI account, refer to the *Appendix* for detailed guidance.

Can we trust GenAI for coding tasks?

Large language models (**LLMs**) are continuously improving their capabilities in mathematics and coding, achieving impressive results in both areas. For instance, internal research by OpenAI showed that the *GPT-o1* model scored correctly on 11 out of 15 questions in the **American Invitational Mathematics Examination** (**AIME**). This performance not only exceeds the threshold required to qualify for the **USA Mathematical Olympiad** (**USAMO**) or the **USA Junior Mathematical Olympiad** (**USAJMO**) but also places the model in the top percentile of participants. Similarly, when evaluated on coding problems from the *Codeforces* competition website, the internal research showed that the model performed at the 89th percentile, highlighting its proficiency in tackling challenging coding tasks.

Yet, the web is filled with screenshots, videos, and examples of highly undesirable outputs from certain prompts. Not long ago, the author encountered a **pull request** (**PR**) containing a file named new.env that exposed seven secret keys. A post-mortem meeting dedicated to that issue revealed that the data scientist who committed the file had used the following prompt:

```
How can I commit my files to GitHub from the PyCharm terminal?
```

The output included the following instruction:

```
git add .
```

The data scientist, who typically utilized PyCharm's **Git tool window** and was used to choosing the files to commit manually, failed to notice that the file named new.env with the secret keys had been included in the commit. This incident highlights that following GenAI-generated instructions can sometimes lead to risky outcomes.

This example does not imply that we should distrust all GenAI output or validate every detail. The fault did not occur because of the model's hindsight about exposing secret keys through a .env file. Instead, it stemmed from a poorly crafted prompt combined with the model's bias toward suggesting CLI commands such as git add ., which frequently appear in online manuals.

We argue that crafting a better prompt, such as the following, would lead to a more desirable model output:

```
CONTEXT: You will be provided with PyCharm GUI steps enclosed with {{{
STEPS }}} to execute a process enclosed with {{{ PROCESS }}}.
TASK: Convert the steps to CLI commands.
PROCESS: {{{ Commit and push files to a remote git branch }}}
STEPS: {{{
1. Review changed files
2. Stage the desired files
3. Add a commit message
4. Commit the files
5. Validate branch name
6. Push the changes to the remote branch
}}}
CLI COMMANDS:
```

This prompt, which follows the best practices for crafting effective prompts, is structured, provides surrounding context for the problem, focuses on a single task, is specific, and is short enough. In this chapter, we will explore how to create such prompts and understand why following these practices leads to better GenAI outputs.

The three pillars of good outputs

To achieve good results from GenAI applications, we will focus on the three pillars: model mastery, evaluation metrics, and crafting precise prompts.

Model mastery refers to an LLM's ability to handle a specific task described in a prompt. For instance, GPT models are extensively trained in Python code and problems such as those found on *LeetCode*, a platform for coding interview preparation. However, when the task deviates from mainstream topics, such as integrating Python **threading** to parallelize code execution across cores and virtual cores, there is significantly less training material available online, leading to outputs that may not match the quality of those for well-covered topics. Keep in mind that for such topics, LLM outputs may be suboptimal. However, we can enhance model mastery using techniques such as fine-tuning to achieve more desirable outputs. This will be covered in greater detail later in the book.

Evaluation metrics refer to the manual and automatic methods we use to assess the quality of GenAI outputs. Effective prompting always involves evaluating the GenAI output, as it is not guaranteed that good results will be achieved on the first attempt. Manual evaluations involve tasks we can personally verify, such as the following:

- Reading code in a language we recognize, such as Python
- Asking for CLI commands we can identify as incorrect
- Evaluating visual outputs such as plots to see whether they align with our expectations
- Verifying straightforward outputs, such as ensuring a requested CSS color matches light pink

Automatic evaluations rely on computational checks, such as:

- Compiling suggested code to ensure it runs without errors.
- Running unit tests to validate functional correctness.
- Using frameworks such as *OpenAI Evals* to systematically assess outputs.

These evaluations help detect faulty outputs and guide iterative improvements toward better suggestions.

OpenAI Evals in brief

Evals is a system designed to assess the performance of LLM applications by using a collection of prompts and expected outputs. These can include prompts and outputs provided by the system itself or custom examples that we create. Accessible via both Python package installers and a CLI, it compares the application's outputs against the expected results and assigns a performance score to the full set. In later chapters, we will delve into strategies for improving evaluation metrics and explore how to effectively leverage the OpenAI Evals system for evaluating GenAI outputs.

Precise prompts refer to how closely the instructions given to the model align with the actual task we want it to perform. When prompts are ambiguous, the model is likely to fill in gaps with assumptions based on its training data, which may not always align with the task at hand.

For example, the prompt `How can I commit my files to GitHub from the PyCharm terminal?` is less precise than a prompt providing specific steps performed in the PyCharm GUI and a request to convert these steps to CLI commands.

Next, we will explore best practices for designing prompts for coding tasks and learn how to refine these prompts into precise inputs that produce high-quality outputs.

Best practices for crafting prompts for coding tasks

When working with GenAI applications for coding-related tasks, the best practices for crafting precise prompts can be summarized by the five S's:

- **Structured** prompts with a clear separation between the instructions and provided data
- **Surrounding** information that provides context for the problem, such as the code language for the provided code and whether it compiles
- **Single-task** focus to ensure each prompt addresses only one objective
- **Specific** instructions detailing how the coding task should be performed, rather than using generic requests
- **Short** and minimal prompts that avoid fluff, redundant, or overly verbose instructions

Let us dive into each of these practices.

Structured

Just as well-written, functional Python code separates logic from data, a good prompt should also distinguish instructions from provided data. When including elements such as steps, code snippets, or code drafts, ensure they are separated from the main instructions and aliased appropriately for clarity and reusability.

Replace unstructured prompts that mix supporting data with instructions, such as the following:

```
Convert the COBOL code
IDENTIFICATION DIVISION.
PROGRAM-ID.
...
to Python.
```

Use a structured approach that separates the instructions from the data:

```
CONTEXT: You will be provided with a COBOL code enclosed with {{{ COBOL
CODE }}}.
TASK: Your task is to convert it to Python, with the following guidelines:
...
COBOL CODE: {{{
}}}
Python Code:
```

This structured prompt is simple to reuse with other COBOL snippets.

Surrounding information

When specifying the surrounding context, include information about the data relevant to the problem. Here are three examples of three different prompt pieces that could be used for different tasks:

- `You are provided with Python code / a function / a function signature.`
- `You are provided with a Python function that contains a bug.`
- `You are provided with GUI steps.`

These instructions are general and avoid specific details, making them reusable:

- The first and second examples do not specify any function
- The third example does not describe specific GUI steps

As a result, these prompt pieces are reusable across various tasks.

Single task per prompt

Always aim for a single task in your prompts. This approach not only improves your ability to evaluate the model's output by focusing on a single task but also increases the likelihood that the model has encountered similar tasks during its training, enhancing its mastery of the topic.

For example, in refactoring tasks, refrain from combining multiple objectives, as follows:

```
Explain the following function and fix compilation bugs.
```

While LLMs are well trained on both individual tasks, combining them into a single prompt may be less common, reducing the model's mastery of the topic. Instead, focus on either explaining the function or fixing its compilation bugs.

Specific instructions

As software developers, it is tempting to use keywords such as *optimize, improve, refactor*, or *scale*. However, these are broad and ambiguous, often leaving room for interpretation by the model.

To achieve better results, use specific instructions, such as the following:

- Use list comprehensions instead of for loops.
- Use np.array to vectorize for loop computations.
- Convert hard-coded integers to global constants.
- Cache function results using lru_cache.

Specific instructions eliminate ambiguity, ensuring the model understands exactly what changes or actions are expected, and increase the likelihood of producing the desired outcome.

Short prompts

Focus on including only relevant information, leaving fluff out, and avoiding ambiguity in your language. Note that this does not mean that you should avoid valuable and relevant information. With the GPT-o1 model supporting over 65,000 tokens (about 164 pages), it can handle longer prompts if its content is minimal and relevant.

For example, avoid phrases such as the following:

```
I think that the following function has a bug [...]
```

Prefer instructions such as the following:

```
find the compilation error in [...]
```

Additionally, avoid vague phrases such as the following:

```
It looks like this for loop could be converted to a list comprehension.
```

Prefer instead the following instruction:

```
Convert the for loop to a list comprehension.
```

Keeping your prompts minimal and relevant and avoiding fluff and ambiguity allows the model to focus on the specific instructions at hand.

Next, we will see how to adapt these best practices to crafting prompts for ChatGPT.

Crafting prompts for ChatGPT

When crafting prompts for ChatGPT, we can apply the structured approach suggested earlier:

```
CONTEXT: ...
TASK: ...
SUPPORTING_DATA: {{{
}}}
COMPLETION:
```

Replace `SUPPORTING_DATA` with terms such as `CODE`, `STEPS`, `OLD_CODE`, or any other appropriate label for the provided data. Replace `COMPLETION` with terms such as `SOLUTION`, `CLI COMMANDS`, `NEW_CODE`, or another label that matches the desired model output.

When working with the *GPT-4o* model with the integrated *canvas editor*, apply the following structure:

```
CONTEXT: ...
TASK: ...
SUPPORTING_DATA: {{{ }}}
```

To access it, start a new GPT-4o chat and type the following to launch the canvas editor:

```
Open Python editor
```

Then, add your supporting code to the Python editor as you would in any IDE, as shown in *Figure 4.1*:

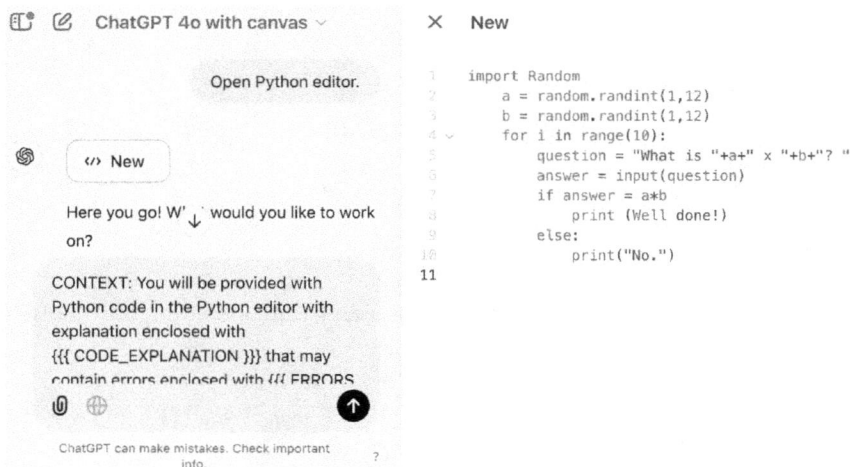

Figure 4.1: GPT-4o with canvas editor for Python

ChatGPT will edit your code based on your request and provide additional output in the chat window, as shown in *Figure 4.2*:

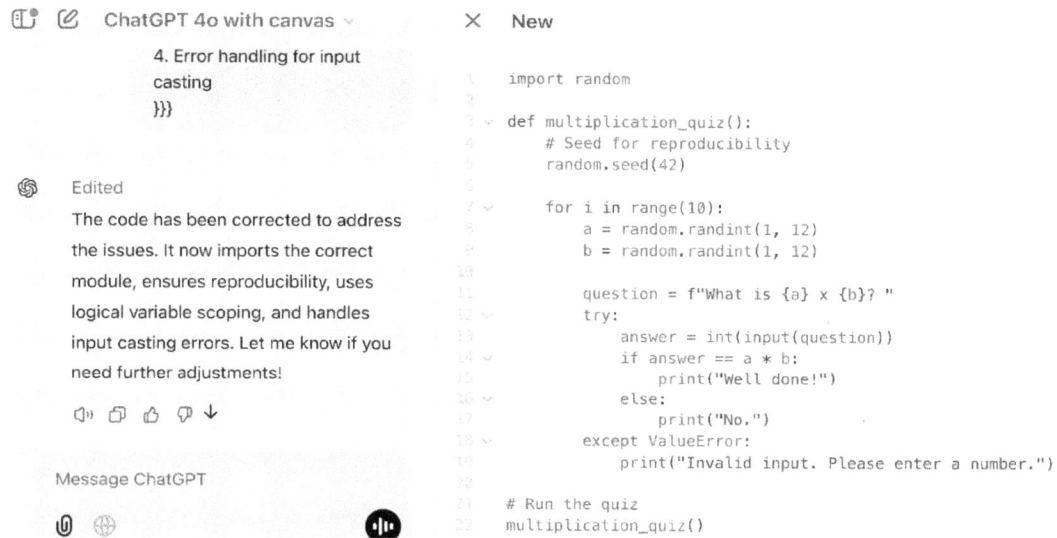

Figure 4.2: Sample edited code from canvas editor

Later in this chapter, we will use the canvas editor in ChatGPT to fix errors in a function.

In the upcoming lab, we will follow these practices to refine a ChatGPT prompt for converting PyCharm GUI steps into Git CLI commands. We will also evaluate how these improvements improve the model output.

Lab 4.1 – converting PyCharm GUI steps to CLI

When transitioning from GUI steps to working directly with the CLI for Git operations, we can use ChatGPT to construct the steps required for committing and pushing staged files to a remote repository. A critical part of this process involves manually reviewing the staged files to ensure that only the desired ones are committed to our remote branch.

By applying the best practices for prompt precision, we will refine the following initial prompt into a prompt that produces a more reliable output:

```
How can I commit my files to GitHub from the PyCharm terminal?
```

For reference, using this initial prompt alone may result in a response such as the one shown in the following figure when entering it into the GitHub Copilot chat window:

```
Ask   Edit                                                      ⋮  —

Committing to a New GitHub Branch                            🕐  +  ⋯

Here's how to commit files to a new branch on GitHub using
the PyCharm terminal:

  1. Create and switch to a new branch
  2. Add files to staging
  3. Commit changes
  4. Push the new branch to GitHub


  # Create and switch to new branch
  git checkout -b feature-branch

  # Add all modified files to staging
  git add .

  # Commit changes with a message
  git commit -m "Your commit message"

  # Push new branch to GitHub
  git push -u origin feature-branch


    ⋄⋄  Can you explain how to resolve merge conflicts when
         pushing to GitHub?

  Ask Copilot a question or type '/' for commands

    +                              Claude Sonnet 3.5   ⌄    ➤
```

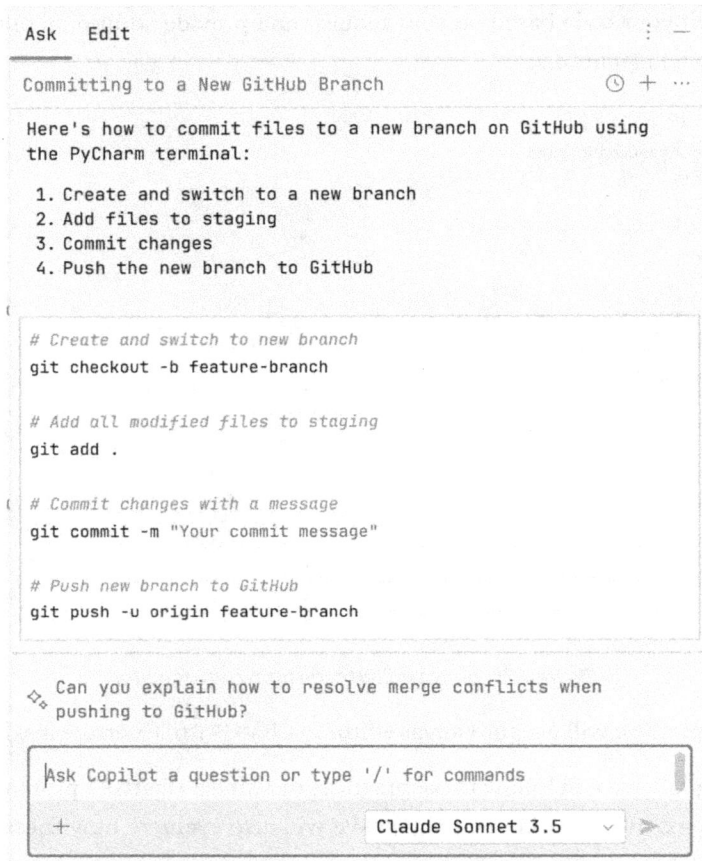

Figure 4.3: Copilot chat suggestion

🔍 **Quick tip**: Need to see a high-resolution version of this image? Open this book in the next-gen Packt Reader or view it in the PDF/ePub copy.

🔒 **The next-gen Packt Reader** is included for free with the purchase of this book. Scan the QR code OR go to packtpub.com/unlock, then use the search bar to find this book by name. Double-check the edition shown to make sure you get the right one.

In our guided walk-through, we will apply the following best practices to craft a more effective prompt:

- **Structured format**: Separate the logic of the task from the actual steps to be converted and the desired GUI process
- **Surrounding context**: Provide the context of the data and structure
- **Single-task focus**: Narrow the task to converting GUI steps into CLI commands
- **Specific instructions**: Clearly indicate all steps previously executed from the GUI, avoiding a generic request
- **Short prompt**: Eliminate redundant details such as PyCharm terminal

We will then feed this refined prompt to ChatGPT and observe how applying these best practices enhances the trustworthiness and reliability of the model's output.

Lab 4.1 guided walk-through

Navigate to https://chatgpt.com/ and start a new chat with the *GPT-o1-mini* model. This model has high proficiency in **science, technology, engineering, and mathematics (STEM)** tasks, particularly coding and mathematics. As of November 2024, it achieves the highest performance among available GPT models on the *Codeforces* coding exam.

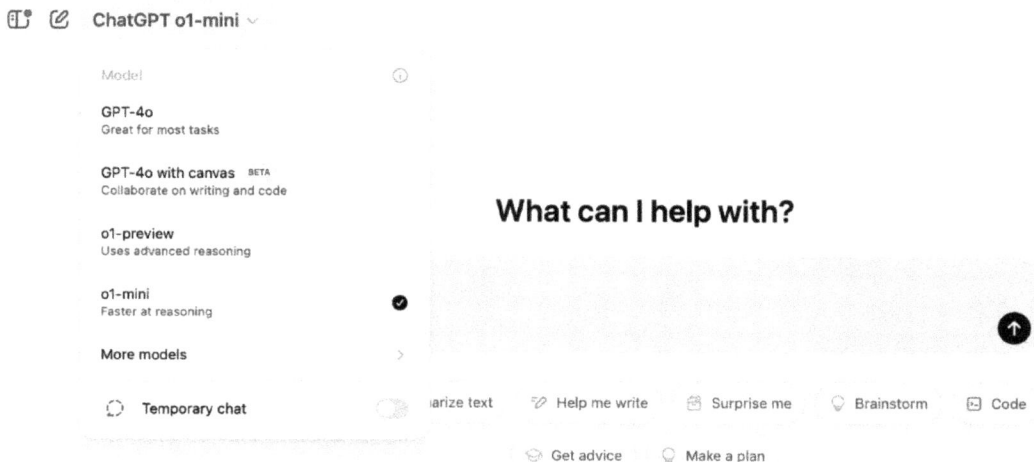

Figure 4.4: ChatGPT model menu

Our starter information consists of the following:

- **Scenario**: A data scientist aims to work with the terminal instead of the PyCharm GUI to push changes into a desired branch

- **Initial prompt**:

```
How can I commit my files to GitHub from the PyCharm
terminal?
```

We will now address each of the five S's best practices for coding-related prompts following these four guidelines:

- Structure the prompt
- Add surrounding context
- Focus on a specific task
- Include specific instructions

Throughout the steps, we will follow the fifth best practice of keeping prompts short, ensuring they remain minimal and free of unnecessary details and fluff.

Step 1 – structure the prompt

A well-structured prompt separates the instructions from the data, ensuring clarity and allowing for simple adjustments. In this case, the instructions outline the task, while the data contains the specific steps required to push the files to the remote branch. For ChatGPT, one strategy is to alias the data by enclosing it within delimiters such as {{{ DATA }}} for easy reference:

```
Instructions with reference to data enclosed with {{{ DATA }}}
...
DATA: {{{
...
}}}
Solution:
```

Important note

We recommend using {{ DATA }} as an alias because the {{ }} delimiter is rare in both code and other types of data. However, choosing alternative separators is also acceptable if they do not commonly appear in your code. For example, enclosers such as """ """ are used in Python for multi-line strings and could cause confusion for the model if used as delimiters.

Step 2 – add surrounding context

A precise prompt should include information about the surrounding context of the problem and the provided data. When converting GUI commands into terminal commands, a clear and relevant surrounding context might look like this:

```
CONTEXT: You will be provided with PyCharm GUI steps enclosed with {{{
STEPS }}} to execute a process enclosed with {{{ PROCESS }}}.
```

By avoiding references to specific processes, such as committing and pushing files to a remote Git branch, this context remains flexible and can be reused for similar tasks in the future.

Add this context at the beginning of your ChatGPT prompt to establish the context of the task.

Step 3 – single task

Our single task in this lab is to translate GUI steps into CLI commands. A clear phrasing of this task could be as follows:

```
TASK: Convert the steps to CLI commands.
```

This prompt piece specifies that the GUI step needs to be converted into corresponding CLI commands.

Add this prompt piece directly below the surrounding context information. Then, complete the structured prompt with the following line at the end:

```
CLI COMMANDS:
```

This signals to the model that the output should be the list of CLI commands to execute.

Step 4 – specific instructions

In this lab, we aim to provide detailed and accurate instructions reflecting what is typically done when pushing changed files to a remote branch. In PyCharm, the first step of reviewing changed files can be performed by navigating to the Git tool window icon in the left menu:

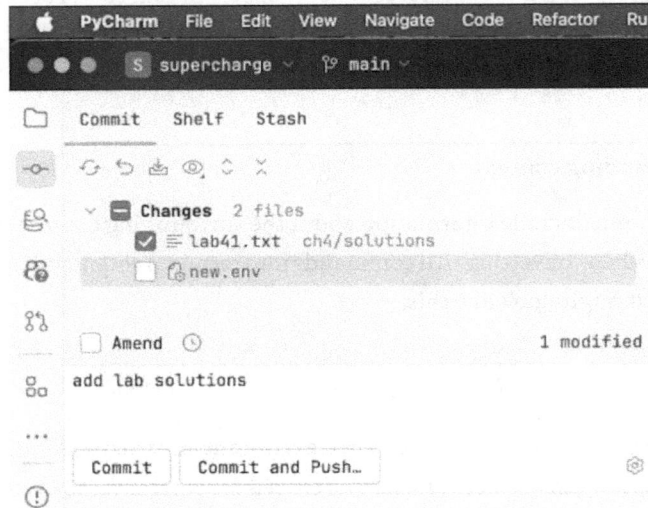

Figure 4.5: Git tool window

It is good practice to manually review your staged files in the working directory, ensuring that files such as new.env, which should be ignored by Git, are not included in the commit.

After adding a commit message and clicking on **Commit and Push**, PyCharm pops up the push window, indicating that the selected files are about to be pushed to the remote branch.

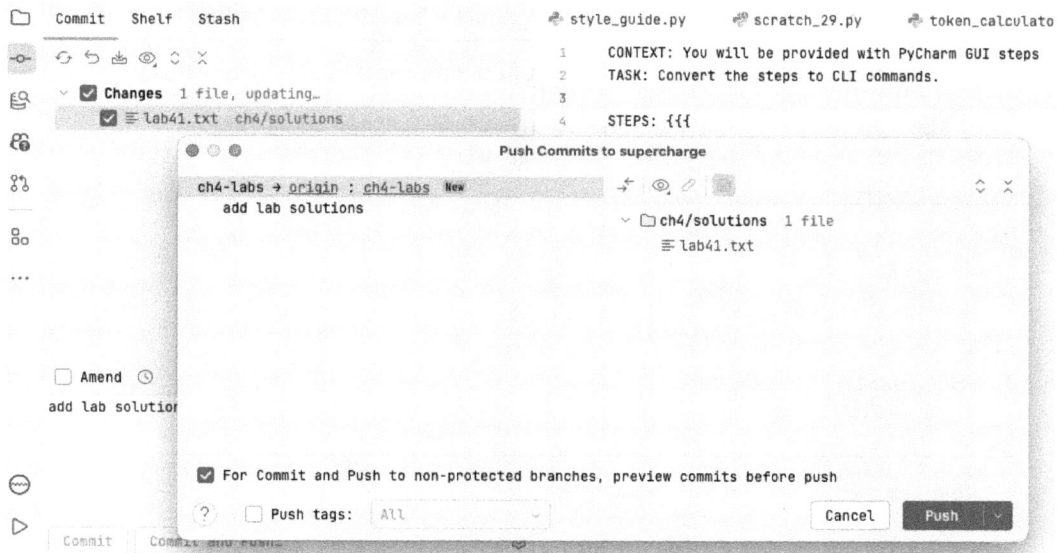

Figure 4.6: Pushing a commit to a remote branch from PyCharm

In this figure, we can see that a single file, the solution to *Lab 4.1*, is being pushed to a new remote branch called ch4-labs.

Describing these steps may look like this:

```
STEPS: {{{
1. Review changed files
2. Stage the desired files
3. Add a commit message
4. Commit the files
5. Validate branch name
6. Push the changes to the remote branch
}}}
```

Include these steps in the prompt, placing them directly beneath the TASK line.

If you have followed all the steps correctly, your final prompt should look like this:

```
CONTEXT: You will be provided with PyCharm GUI steps enclosed with {{{
STEPS }}} to execute a process enclosed with {{{ PROCESS }}}.
TASK: Convert the steps to CLI commands.
PROCESS: {{{ Commit and push files to a remote Git branch }}}
STEPS: {{{
1. Review changed files
2. Stage the desired files
3. Add a commit message
4. Commit the files
5. Validate branch name
6. Push the changes to the remote branch
}}}

CLI COMMANDS:
```

Your prompt is now ready to use in ChatGPT. Execute it and refer to the lab analysis for a sample output generated by the model.

Lab 4.1 analysis

In this lab, we crafted a precise prompt by applying the five S's best practices. When we ran the prompt in ChatGPT using the *GPT-o1-mini* model, the output provided a set of CLI commands for committing and pushing the desired files to a remote branch. The generated commands were as follows:

6. Push the changes to the remote branch
}}}

CLI COMMANDS:

```bash
# Step 1: Review changed files
git status

# Step 2: Stage the desired files
git add <file_name>  # Replace <file_name> with the specific file(s) you want to s
# OR to stage all changes
git add .

# Step 3: Add a commit message
git commit -m "Your commit message here"

# Step 4: Commit the files (already combined with Step 3)

# Step 5: Validate branch name
git branch  # This shows the current branch

# Step 6: Push the changes to the remote branch
git push origin <branch_name>  # Replace <branch_name> with your current branch nar
```

Figure 4.7: ChatGPT's response to the Lab 4.1 prompt

This output is more desirable than the initial prompt because it directly references each of the six steps we would perform using the GUI, providing explanations for each corresponding command. Additionally, the output aligns with the prompt's specificity, offering only the CLI commands with minimal surrounding explanation.

Important note

Refining prompts using the five S's best practices may seem like a lot of work initially. However, over time, seasoned prompters develop their own reusable prompt templates, making the process more efficient. Well-structured prompts are reproducible across different tasks and adapting them with varied data can often be done at scale. In the next chapters, we will reuse prompts crafted with these best practices for a variety of tasks.

Having introduced and implemented the best practices for crafting precise prompts, we can now observe how applying the five S's can further enhance outputs, even from prompts already considered strong. Next, we will delve into OpenAI's examples of good prompts, analyze them through the lens of the five S's, and refine a prompt further to achieve a more desirable output.

Prompt samples by OpenAI

OpenAI occasionally updates a collection of sample prompts tailored to various tasks, including coding, content generation, translations, and grammar corrections. These prompts display the core capabilities where the underlying models exhibit strong mastery. They have been carefully crafted and have demonstrated consistent success across these use cases.

You can explore the full list of prompts and filter the samples by category at `https://platform.openai.com/docs/examples`.

Prompt examples

Explore what's possible with some example prompts

Q Search...			Extract ⌄

▶▶	**Summarize for a 2nd grader** Simplify text to a level appropriate for a second-grade student.	⊞	**Parse uns** Create tabl
			All categories
			Extract
			Generate
			Transform
#	**Explain code** Explain a complicated piece of code.	🔑	**Keywords** Extract key Code Natural Language Structured Data
#	**Tweet classifier** Detect sentiment in a tweet.	☑	**Mood to color** Turn a text description into a color.
☑	**Meeting notes summarizer** Summarize meeting notes including overall discussion, action items, and future topics.	🏷	**Review classifier** Classify user reviews based on a set of tags.

Figure 4.8: OpenAI sample prompts

When clicking on a prompt sample from this page, we can observe the prompt itself, divided into a system prompt and a user prompt, a sample response, and a code snippet demonstrating how to implement the prompt using OpenAI API.

Improve code efficiency

Transform   Code

Provide ideas for efficiency improvements to Python code.

Prompt

SYSTEM   You will be provided with a piece of Python code, and your task is to provide ideas for efficiency improvements.

USER   from typing import List

```python
def has_sum_k(nums: List[int], k: int) -> bool:
    """
    Returns True if there are two distinct elements in nums such that their sum
    is equal to k, and otherwise returns False.
    """
    n = len(nums)
    for i in range(n):
        for j in range(i+1, n):
            if nums[i] + nums[j] == k:
                return True
    return False
```

Sample response

Figure 4.9: Improve code efficiency prompt example

In this example, the system prompt contains general instructions describing the task to be performed, while the user prompt includes the import statement and a function that could benefit from efficiency improvements.

Next, we will critically analyze a sample prompt to assess how well it aligns with the five S's.

Lab 4.2 – code debugging

In this lab, we will examine a Python bug fixer use case through the lens of our best practices.

Navigate to https://platform.openai.com/docs/examples and search for *Python bug fixer*. This should yield the following prompt example to instruct the model to find a bug in a Python program that quizzes a user on multiplication problems:

Python bug fixer

Transform   Code

Find and fix bugs in source code.

Prompt

SYSTEM	You will be provided with a piece of Python code, and your task is to find and fix bugs in it.

USER	```python
	import Random
	a = random.randint(1,12)
	b = random.randint(1,12)
	for i in range(10):
	    question = "What is "+a+" x "+b+"? "
	    answer = input(question)
	    if answer = a*b
	        print (Well done!)
	    else:
	        print("No.")
	``

Sample response

There are several bugs in the provided code:

1. The import statement is incorrect. Python is case-sensitive, so "Random" should be "random".
2. Variables `a` and `b` are defined outside the loop, so they will not change for each iteration. They should be inside the loop if you want to generate different questions.

Figure 4.10: Sample prompt for Python bug fixer

This prompt, like the code efficiency improvement prompt example by OpenAI, separates the system and user prompts while providing a sample response. Scrolling further down the window reveals the code necessary to implement this prompt with OpenAI API.

In the guided walk-through, we will identify the errors in the provided code, so we can better evaluate the output of the model. In the analysis, we will analyze the usage of the five S's and see how we can improve the prompt even further.

Lab 4.2 guided walk-through

Before we can analyze the output of the model, here are the errors in the user-provided functions:

- **Compilation errors:**

    - **Typo in import statement:** `import Random` should be corrected to `import random`.

    - **Type error:** The `question` variable cannot concatenate integers a and b with strings directly. This needs to be resolved by converting integers to strings.

    - **Missing colon:** The `if` statement is missing a `:` character at the end, leading to `SyntaxError`.

    - **Invalid assignment:** The `answer = a*b` statement attempts to assign a value within the `if` condition. Modern Python compilers will raise `SyntaxError` as this is an invalid syntax.

    - **Invalid print statement:** The string `Well done!` is not enclosed with quotes and therefore is an invalid syntax.

- **Logical errors:**

    - The a and b variables are generated once before the loop and remain constant through all 10 iterations. This is not desirable.

    - The output from the user is a string, while the comparison is made against integers. As a result, `answer` of type `str` can never be equal to a `*` b, which is of type `int`.

- **Reproducibility issue:**

    - The code with random numbers is not reproducible across runs due to the absence of a `random` seed set. Without this, the output will vary unpredictably between executions.

Considering the output published on the OpenAI website, here is a summary of identified and fixed code errors and issues:

Error type	Problem	Error	Found	Fixed
Compilation	Invalid case	import Random	Yes	Yes
Compilation	Concatenate `int` and `str`	a + " x " + b	Yes	Yes
Compilation	Missing colon in `if` statement	if statement ...	**No**	Yes

Error type	Problem	Error	Found	Fixed
Compilation	Assignment in `if` statement	`if answer = a * b`	**Yes**	**Yes**
Compilation	Missing quotes for `str`	`print(Well done!)`	**Yes**	**Yes**
Logic	Random numbers generated once	`a, b` outside the `for` loop	**No**	**No**
Logic	`str` compared to `int`	`answer = a * b`	**Yes**	**Yes**
Reproduce	No seed set	Missing `random.seed(...)`, or equivalent initialization	**No**	**No**

Table 4.1: OpenAI API's performance in detecting and fixing errors

The proposed solution also introduced a new issue related to casting the input to an integer; there is no proper error handling if an input such as `hello` cannot be cast.

The following is the full model response, as published on the OpenAI website:

```
There are several bugs in the provided code:
1. The import statement is incorrect. Python is case-sensitive, so
"Random" should be "random".
2. Variables `a` and `b` are defined outside the loop, so they will not
change for each iteration. They should be inside the loop if you want to
generate different questions.
3. In the question string, `a` and `b` are integers, so you need to
convert them to strings using the `str()` function to concatenate them.
4. In the if statement, you are using a single equals sign `=` which is
an assignment operator. You should use the double equals sign `==` for
comparison.
5. The print statement "Well done!" is not enclosed in quotes. In Python,
strings must be enclosed in quotes.
6. The input from the user is a string, so you need to convert it to an
integer using the `int()` function before comparing it with the product of
`a` and `b`.


Here is the corrected code:
```

```python
import random
for i in range(10):
    a = random.randint(1,12)
    b = random.randint(1,12)
    question = "What is "+ str(a) +" x "+ str(b) +"? "
    answer = int(input(question))
    if answer == a*b:
        print ("Well done!")
    else:
        print("No.")
```

Next, we will analyze the prompt through the lens of the five S's, evaluate the quality of the output based on the errors identified, fixed, and introduced, and propose improvements to achieve a better outcome.

Lab 4.2 analysis

The prompt introduced in this example mostly aligns with the five S's guidelines:

- **Good structure**: The instructions are clearly separated from the code, making the prompt reusable and adaptable for other tasks.

- **Sufficient surrounding context**: The prompt provides context by mentioning Python code as the supporting data.

- **No single task**: The prompt combines two related tasks, identifying and fixing errors in the code. While these tasks are interconnected, focusing solely on fixing the errors could improve the model's response and responsibility.

- **Specific**: The task specifies that the model should identify and fix the errors in the code. However, the instructions could be improved by explicitly stating the types of errors to address, such as compilation, logical scoping, reproducibility, or error handling.

- **Short**: The prompt is concise and avoids unnecessary or irrelevant details.

Overall, following most of the guidelines resulted in a decent output. Since we have strong evaluation capabilities and are aware of all the errors the model should address, we can continue iterating to resolve all remaining issues in the code.

Alternatively, we could better align the best practices with the following prompt:

```
CONTEXT: You will be provided with Python code in the Python editor with
explanation enclosed with
{{{ CODE_EXPLANATION }}} that may contain errors enclosed with {{{ ERRORS
}}}.

TASK: Fix the errors in the code.

CODE_EXPLANATION: {{{
Run 10 random multiplication quizzes and provide feedback about each to
the user
}}}

ERRORS: {{{
1. Compilation
2. Reproducibility of random number generation
3. Logical scoping of variable assignments
4. Error handling for input casting
}}}
```

Using this prompt with *GPT-4o with canvas* resulted in an output that addressed all the required fixes.

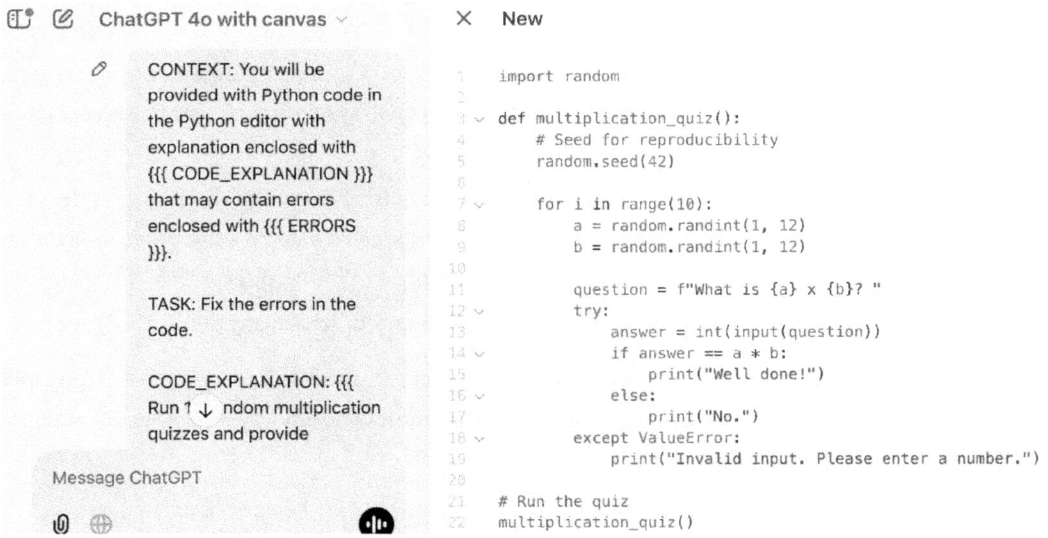

Figure 4.11: Better output

All compilation, logic, reproducibility, and error handling are addressed in the fixes.

Even better prompts

In the next chapters, we will explore advanced prompt engineering techniques such as **iterative prompting** for creating a feedback loop with LLMs and **chain-of-thought prompting** for guiding model reasoning. These techniques will enable us to refine prompts that yield decent results for manual use and scale them effectively for broader applications.

Summary

In this chapter, we explored how to achieve high-quality GenAI outputs by focusing on the three pillars: model mastery for handling a specific topic, evaluation metrics, and precise prompts. We examined how imprecise prompts can lead to risky outcomes, such as CLI commands exposing secret keys, and demonstrated how following best practices can produce far better and more reliable model outputs.

We also learned about the five S's of prompt precision best practices for coding-related tasks: keeping a structured prompt, providing surrounding context, maintaining a single task per prompt to best leverage model mastery and evaluation capabilities, ensuring that prompts are specific rather than general and vague, and keeping the input as short as possible by removing irrelevant information and fluff.

With two interactive labs, we explored how to implement those best practices in ChatGPT. With an OpenAI example of a good prompt to a bug fix, we saw that even good prompts can be improved to achieve more desirable results.

In the next chapter, we will explore how to apply the five S's using OpenAI API and GitHub Copilot. In later chapters, we will delve into advanced prompt engineering techniques to further refine prompts and meet specific engineering needs in the **Software Development Life Cycle (SDLC)**.

Quiz time

Before you proceed to the next chapter, make sure that you can confidently answer the following questions:

Question 1: What are the three factors that determine the quality of output of an LLM?

Answer: Model mastery, evaluation capabilities, and prompt precision. Model mastery means how much the LLM trained on this specific task, evaluation capabilities means how much we can assess the desirability of the outcome, and prompt precision means to what extent the prompt is crafted to tell the model what exactly we need.

Question 2: What are the best practices for a coding-related task prompt?

Answer: The best practices are the five S's, structuring the prompt to accommodate supporting data such as code and steps, including surrounding context on the task, focusing on a single task per prompt, and keeping specific and short instructions.

Question 3: Which parts of a prompt can be reproducible?

Answer: When following the best practices of precise prompts, we can reuse the surrounding context and the single task. These can be leveraged to many prompts and reused with a change of the details, such as the function attached, steps to be converted to CLI commands, or improvements required to a given function. This is highly efficient for large-scope refactoring tasks, repetitive tasks, and many more examples we will see in the book.

Further reading

To learn more about the topics that were covered in this chapter, look at the following resources:

- OpenAI on GPT-o1 performances: `https://openai.com/index/openai-o1-mini-advancing-cost-efficient-reasoning/`

- American Invitational Mathematics Examination: `https://en.wikipedia.org/wiki/American_Invitational_Mathematics_Examination`

- Codeforces: `https://codeforces.com/`

- Prompt best practices in OpenAI: `https://help.openai.com/en/articles/6654000-best-practices-for-prompt-engineering-with-the-openai-api`

- Prompt examples in OpenAI: `https://platform.openai.com/docs/examples`

Subscribe for a free eBook

New frameworks, evolving architectures, research drops, production breakdowns—AI_Distilled filters the noise into a weekly briefing for engineers and researchers working hands-on with LLMs and GenAI systems. Subscribe now and receive a free eBook, along with weekly insights that help you stay focused and informed.

Subscribe at `https://packt.link/TR05B` or scan the QR code below.

5

Best Practices for Prompting with OpenAI API and GitHub Copilot

In the concluding chapter of *Part 1*, we will explore how to apply best practices for crafting prompts tailored to OpenAI API and GitHub Copilot. These practices are encapsulated in the **five S's**: **structuring** the prompt, providing **surrounding** context, focusing on a **single** task, including **specific** instructions, and keeping prompts **short** and fluff-free. While the core principles remain consistent, their application varies slightly across different GenAI tools.

We will delve into working with Python objects such as functions, classes, and methods for coding-related tasks. We will leverage the built-in `inspect` package to extract key details about objects, such as their source code, docstrings, and filenames. We will also learn how to integrate this information into the system and user prompts offered by OpenAI API, combining context, task focus, and concise, structured instructions.

Additionally, we will examine how GitHub Copilot inherently provides structure, context, and single-task focus while generating short, specific prompts for us. We will learn techniques to extend Copilot's capabilities by incorporating additional structure and precision, ensuring minimal fluff and redundant comments.

Through two interactive labs, we will implement these practices using a real-world example: a **Singleton design pattern** to enforce single-instance creation per class. Using OpenAI API, we will craft a docstring for the Singleton `__call__` method, which controls the instantiation process of a new class instance. Then, with Copilot, we will generate a unit test to validate the functionality and fix a faulty implementation.

In this chapter, we will cover the following topics:

- Extracting properties from Python objects for OpenAI API
- Crafting precise prompts for OpenAI API
- Generating docstrings with OpenAI API
- Crafting precise prompts for GitHub Copilot
- Fixing faulty implementation with GitHub Copilot

Technical requirements

To get the most out of this chapter, ensure you have the following:

- GitHub Copilot account
- **Integrated development environment (IDE)** – either VS Code or PyCharm
- OpenAI account with access to OpenAI API
- Access to the book's repository, which is available at `https://github.com/PacktPublishing/Supercharged-Coding-with-Gen-AI`
- Virtual environment set up in VS Code or PyCharm
- OpenAI API token

For assistance setting up a GitHub Copilot account, refer to *Chapter 2*. For instructions on setting up OpenAI API access and token generation, see *Chapter 3*. If you need help creating an OpenAI account or setting up a virtual environment in your IDE, refer to the *Appendix* for detailed guidance.

Extracting properties from Python objects for OpenAI API

When using OpenAI for coding tasks, we often include details about Python objects such as variables, functions, and classes in our prompts. This helps with various tasks such as debugging, generating docstrings, creating unit test suites, or improving code. The information provided may include the object name, arguments, return type, filename, docstring, and source code.

Throughout this book, we frequently use the built-in `inspect` package to extract relevant details from Python objects. Additionally, we leverage some special attributes, identified by a **double underscore (dunder)**, such as `obj.__attribute__`, which store metadata about the object or class. Here are some more examples:

- `obj.__name__` retrieves the name of the object
- `obj.__class__.__name__` retrieves the class name of an instance or function or the metaclass name of a class
- `obj.__doc__` retrieves the docstring of the object

To extract the source code and filename of an object, we typically use Python's built-in `inspect` library:

- `inspect.getsource(obj)` retrieves the source code of the object
- `inspect.getfile(obj)` retrieves the file name of the object

For example, we can use `inspect.getsource(obj)` to retrieve the source code for the faulty implementation of the `multiplication_quiz` function discussed in *Lab 4.2* in *Chapter 4*. This function is intended to execute 10 different multiplication quizzes, as outlined in its docstring, but contains implementation bugs that we need to address:

```python
def multiplication_quiz() -> None:
    """

    This function generates a multiplication quiz of ten different random
multiplication questions between 1 and 12.
    The user is prompted to answer each question. If the user answers
correctly, the function prints "Well done!".
    If the user answers incorrectly, the function prints "No.".
    """

    a = random.randint(1, 12)
    b = random.randint(1, 12)
    score = 0
    for _ in range(10):
        question = "What is " + a + " x " + b + "? "
        answer = input(question)
        if answer == a * b:
            print("Well done!")
            score += 1
```

```
    else:
        print("No.")
print(f"Your score is {score} out of 10.")
```

💡 **Quick tip**: Enhance your coding experience with the **AI Code Explainer** and **Quick Copy** features. Open this book in the next-gen Packt Reader. Click the **Copy** button

(1) to quickly copy code into your coding environment, or click the **Explain** button

(2) to get the AI assistant to explain a block of code to you.

```
                                                      Copy      Explain

                                                       1          2
function calculate(a, b) {
  return {sum: a + b};
};
```

🔒 **The next-gen Packt Reader** is included for free with the purchase of this book. Scan the QR code OR visit packtpub.com/unlock, then use the search bar to find this book by name. Double-check the edition shown to make sure you get the right one.

The code for the function can be extracted using the getsource function:

```
inspect.getsource(multiplication_quiz)
```

The returned value will be a string containing the function's code as text, as shown here:

```
'def multiplication_quiz() -> None:\n    """\n    This function generates
a multiplication quiz of ten different random multiplication questions
between 1 and 12. ... the rest of the code is omitted for brevity ...'
```

This format is easily interpreted by GenAI applications and **large language models** (LLMs), and we will use it to include Python objects and code blocks in our prompts, enclosed within {{ }}}.

Next, we will explore how these objects are integrated into OpenAI prompts using the five S's best practices for crafting precise and effective prompts.

Crafting precise prompts for OpenAI API

Applying best practices for building a precise prompt with OpenAI API enables us to automate and scale the prompting process while ensuring quality outputs from the underlying LLMs.

We will revisit the five S's best practices, beginning with structuring OpenAI API prompts. We will craft system prompts that incorporate the surrounding context and focus on a single task, enabling the development of reproducible and adaptable templates. Additionally, we will explore how incorporating specific and short instructions helps transform diverse inputs into concise user prompts.

Structured prompts

To structure prompts for OpenAI API, we use **system prompts** and **user prompts** to separate the surrounding context and single task objective from specific details such as steps, source code, and data. System prompts define the context and task, allowing for reuse across varying details such as different source codes. In later chapters of the book, we will also explore how to integrate **assistant prompts** to achieve even more refined results from our prompts.

In Python, this prompt structure usually includes a variable called SURROUND to provide the surrounding context and a variable called SINGLE_TASK to specify the task for the model. It may be structured as follows:

```python
SURROUND = " Your surrounding context here "
SINGLE_TASK = " Your task here "


def get_user_prompt(*args, **kwargs) -> str:
    return """
    # your code here
    COMPLETION:
    """


system_prompt = f"{SURROUND} {SINGLE_TASK}"
user_prompt = get_user_prompt(...)


messages = [
```

```
        {"role": "system", "content": "system_prompt"
        {"role": "user", "content": user_prompt},
    ]
```

In this structure, the `messages` parameter combines both `system_prompt` and `user_prompt` to form a precise prompt for OpenAI API. `system_prompt` integrates SURROUND and SINGLE_TASK, while the `get_user_prompt` function provides details such as steps, source code, and object information, concluding with a lead-in cue such as COMPLETION to align with SINGLE_TASK, as we will discuss in depth throughout this chapter.

Now that we have examined the structure that combines both system prompts and user prompts, let us dive deeper into each, starting with system prompts.

System prompts with the surrounding context and single task

In OpenAI API, system prompts are used to define the surrounding context and specify a single task. These prompts are designed to be reproducible, accommodating varying supporting data.

For instance, a system prompt might state that the model is provided with a code snippet and tasked with identifying the programming language:

```
SURROUND = "You will be provided with a code snippet enclosed with {{{
CODE }}}."
SINGLE_TASK = "Your task is to identify the programming language of the
provided code snippet."


system_prompt = f"{SURROUND} {SINGLE_TASK}"
```

The SURROUND context specifies that the provided data is a code snippet in an unidentified language, while SINGLE_TASK clarifies that the expected output should identify the programming language of the code.

In another scenario, the task might involve generating documentation for a Python function where the programming language (Python) and object type (function) are already known. In such cases, this information should be included in the surrounding context to help the model focus on generating the docstring rather than determining the language or object type:

```
SURROUND = "You will be provided with a Python function enclosed with {{{
FUNCTION }}}."
SINGLE_TASK = "Your task is to generate a Google Style docstring for it."


system_prompt = f"{SURROUND} {SINGLE_TASK}"
```

In this case, SURROUND provides context about the Python function, enabling the model to concentrate on the task of generating docstrings, as specified in SINGLE_TASK.

User prompts with specific instructions

To create an effective user prompt for OpenAI API call, we typically define a get_user_prompt function that encapsulates the necessary task details along with a lead-in cue to align with the system prompt.

For example, if the task is to identify the programming language from the source code, the function implementation might look like this:

```python
def get_user_prompt(code_source: str) -> str:
    return f"""
    CODE: {{{{{{ {code_source} }}}}}}
    PROGRAMMING LANGUAGE:
    """
```

In the preceding implementation, {{ in f-strings are used to represent a literal {. As a result, {{{{{{ is required to represent {{{. Also, the source code is retrieved as a string, requiring no further conversion.

In a different scenario involving Python objects, such as extracting the docstring for a class method, the source code can be directly obtained from the object. The implementation of get_user_prompt in this case might look like this:

```python
def get_user_prompt(func: callable) -> str:
    return f"""
    FUNCTION: {{{{{{ {inspect.getsource(func)} }}}}}}
    DOCSTRING:
    """
```

In this implementation, the inspect.getsource function is used to extract the source code from the function.

Next, we will combine system prompts and user prompts to observe how they work together to produce high-quality outputs.

Lab 5.1 – Generating docstrings with OpenAI API

In this lab, we will utilize OpenAI API to generate a docstring for the __call__ method in a Singleton design pattern, as outlined in the following steps. The __call__ method defines the **instantiation process**, which involves creating or managing a new instance of the class.

Singleton design pattern

As Python developers, we often use design patterns to define and control the behavior of Python objects, such as functions and classes. One such pattern is the **Singleton pattern**, which ensures that only one instance of a class is created and used throughout the program's execution.

Regular classes create a new instance from scratch with each instantiation, using either provided arguments or default parameters. For example, consider the following program with an Environment class that defaults to the name Production:

```python
class Environment:
    def __init__(self, name: str = "Production"):
        self.name = name


env1 = Environment("Development")
env2 = Environment()
print("env1 name: ", env1.name)
print("env2 name: ", env2.name)
```

In this case, env1 and env2 are two separate instances of the Environment class. For instance, the name attribute of env1 is set to Development, while the name of env2 is set to Production based on the provided default argument.

The output of this program is as follows:

```
env1 name:  Development
env2 name:  Production
```

The Singleton design pattern ensures that only one instance of a class is created and maintained throughout the program's runtime. It is typically implemented using a **metaclass**, which acts as a **class of classes**, defining how other classes are structured and behave.

A typical Singleton implementation maintains a **registry** dictionary of instantiated classes. For each class defined with metaclass=Singleton, whenever a new instance is requested, the Singleton checks its registry for an existing instance of that class. If an instance is found, it is returned; otherwise, a new instance is created and added to the registry. Here is an example of such an implementation:

```python
class Singleton(type):
    _instances = {}

    def __call__(cls, *args, **kwargs):
        if cls not in cls._instances:
            cls._instances[cls] = super(Singleton, cls).__call__(*args,
**kwargs)
        return cls._instances[cls]
```

In this implementation, the __call__ method is invoked whenever a class of the Singleton type, referred to as cls (a common name for a class argument), attempts to instantiate a new instance. If an instance of the class already exists, it is stored in the _instances attribute with the class's hash as the key, and the existing instance is returned. Otherwise, a new instance of cls is created as usual and added to the _instances registry for future use.

To use classes of the Singleton type, such as Environment, we specify that the metaclass for the class is Singleton, as shown here:

```python
class Environment(metaclass=Singleton):
    def __init__(self, name: str = "Production"):
        self.name = name
```

Assigning the Singleton metaclass ensures that all instances of the class refer to the same object. When two instances are created, one with the Development name and the other without any parameters, both Environment instances will share the name Development:

```python
env1 = Environment("Development")
env2 = Environment()
print("env1 name: ", env1.name)
print("env2 name: ", env2.name)
```

In this case, env1 and env2 are the same instance and env2.name is also expected to be Development. The program output confirms this, as shown here:

```
env1 name:  Development
env2 name:  Development
```

Next, we will see how to leverage OpenAI API to generate a docstring for the Singleton __call__ method.

Generating a docstring

A **docstring** is a special string literal in Python that provides a clear description of an object's purpose, behavior, arguments, and return values, typically for functions or classes, and would be followed by the code implementation. For instance, here is a **Google-style docstring** for a function that calculates the *n*th Fibonacci number:

```
def fibonacci(n):
    """
    Calculate the n-th Fibonacci number.
    The Fibonacci sequence is a series of numbers where each number is the
sum
    of the two preceding ones, starting from 0 and 1. This implementation
uses
    an iterative approach for better performance with large values of n.

    Args:
        n (int): The position in the Fibonacci sequence (0-indexed).

    Returns:
        int: The n-th Fibonacci number.

    Raises:
        ValueError: If n is a negative integer.

    Examples:
        >>> fibonacci(0)
        0
        >>> fibonacci(1)
        1
        >>> fibonacci(5)
```

```
        5
    """

    ...
```

We will explore how to effectively create and utilize high-quality docstrings for Python objects in greater detail in *Chapter 18*.

In this lab, we will focus on crafting a simple Google-style docstring for the __call__ method of the Singleton class, incorporating information about the source code of the Python object.

Lab 5.1 guided walk-through

Open *Lab 5.1* in the book repository at ch5/labs/lab51.py and ensure that you have either set the OPENAI_API_KEY environment variable or configured your run settings to point to the .env file.

The starter code includes the implementation of the Singleton metaclass, along with placeholders for the SURROUND and SINGLE_TASK strings, the get_user_prompt function, and the messages parameter for OpenAI API:

```python
import inspect
from openai import OpenAI
from openai.types.chat import ChatCompletion


SURROUND = ""
SINGLE_TASK = ""

class Singleton(type):
    _instances = {}

    def __call__(cls, *args, **kwargs):
        if cls not in cls._instances:
            cls._instances[cls] = super(Singleton, cls).__call__(*args,
**kwargs)
        return cls._instances[cls]

def get_user_prompt(func: callable) -> str:
    ...
```

```python
if __name__ == "__main__":

    client: OpenAI = OpenAI()
    completion: ChatCompletion = client.chat.completions.create(
        model="gpt-4o-mini",
        messages=[],
    )
    print("Docstring:", completion.choices[0].message.content)
```

In the guided walk-through, we will complete the SURROUND and SINGLE_TASK strings, the get_ user_prompt function, and the messages parameter.

First, we will define the surrounding context and single task for the reusable system prompt. Update the SURROUND and SINGLE_TASK strings as follows:

```python
SURROUND = "You will be provided with a Python function enclosed with {{{
Function }}}."
SINGLE_TASK = "Your task is to generate Google Style docstring for it."
```

These strings inform the model that the provided source code is a Python function and specify that the generated docstring should follow Google-style conventions.

Next, we will integrate specific and short instructions into the user prompt. Implement the get_ user_prompt function to encapsulate the source code of a provided function, along with a lead-in cue to generate a Google-style docstring:

```python
def get_user_prompt(func: callable) -> str:
    return f"""
    FUNCTION: {{{{{{ {inspect.getsource(func)} }}}}}}

    GOOGLE STYLE DOCSTRING:
    """
```

Finally, complete the messages argument for OpenAI API call by including the system prompt with the SURROUND and SINGLE_TASK strings, along with the output of get_user_prompt encapsulating the __call__ method of the Singleton class:

```python
messages=[
    {"role": "system", "content": f"{SURROUND} {SINGLE_TASK}"},
    {"role": "user", "content": get_user_prompt(Singleton.__call__)},
],
```

If you have completed all the steps correctly, your lab code should appear as follows:

```python
import inspect
from openai import OpenAI
from openai.types.chat import ChatCompletion


SURROUND = "You will be provide with a Python function enclosed with {{{
Function }}}."
SINGLE_TASK = "Your task is to generate Google Style docstring for it"

class Singleton(type):
    _instances = {}

    def __call__(cls, *args, **kwargs):
        if cls not in cls._instances:
            cls._instances[cls] = super(Singleton, cls).__call__(*args,
**kwargs)
        return cls._instances[cls]

def get_user_prompt(func: callable) -> str:
    return f"""
Function: {{{{{{ {inspect.getsource(func)} }}}}}}
GOOGLE STYLE DOCSTRING:
"""

if __name__ == "__main__":

    client: OpenAI = OpenAI()
    completion: ChatCompletion = client.chat.completions.create(
        model="gpt-4o-mini",
        messages=[
            {"role": "system", "content": f"{SURROUND} {SINGLE_TASK}"},
            {"role": "user", "content": get_user_prompt(Singleton.__
call__)},
        ],
    )
    print("Docstring:", completion.choices[0].message.content)
```

Your lab is now ready to execute and generate a Google-style docstring. Stay tuned for the lab analysis, where we will review a sample output from the run.

Lab 5.1 analysis

In this lab, we demonstrated how applying the five S's best practices for precise prompts can yield good results with just a few lines of code. Using OpenAI API, we successfully generated a Google-style docstring for the __call__ method of the Singleton class.

For reference, here is a sample output from the lab, which produced a Google-style docstring that clearly explains the method's general purpose, its arguments, and its return value, ensuring that the same single instance of the class is returned for every instantiation:

```python
Docstring: ```python
def __call__(cls, *args, **kwargs):
    """Overrides the default behavior of instance creation to ensure that
only one instance of
    the class is created (Singleton Pattern).

    This method checks if the class has already been instantiated. If not,
it creates a new instance
    and stores it in the class's `_instances` dictionary. Subsequent calls
will return the existing
    instance.

    Args:
        cls: The class that is being instantiated.
        *args: Variable length argument list for the class constructor.
        **kwargs: Arbitrary keyword arguments for the class constructor.

    Returns:
        The single instance of the class.
    """
```

This docstring accurately describes the _instances attribute of the Singleton metaclass, which stores the single instances of the class, as well as the arguments of the __call__ method and its return value.

Having explored how to craft prompts for OpenAI API using the five S's, including system and user prompts that integrate information about Python objects for coding tasks, identifying the programming language of a code snippet, and generating a Google-style docstring, we will now turn to implementing the five S's best practices for prompt precision when crafting prompts for GitHub Copilot.

Crafting precise prompts for GitHub Copilot

When working with GitHub Copilot's three interaction modes, code completion, chat, and code analysis, many best practices are already built in. Copilot structures the prompt automatically, providing surrounding context for these modes, each with a clearly defined single task, whether it is completing code, engaging in a chat, or analyzing code. The prompts are also designed to be specific and short.

However, we can use the five S's more precisely and achieve even better results. In this section, we will use the Singleton design pattern as an example to explore how Copilot supports code completion, code analysis, and chat.

With an understanding of this pattern and its applications, let us examine how the five S's are implemented and can be extended within Copilot's three interaction modes.

Structuring with a lead-in cue

Copilot automatically structures prompts for its three interaction modes while considering surrounding context such as the filename, open files, code before and after the cursor, and Git history to generate a prompt on your behalf.

To improve Copilot's structured prompts, you can provide lead-in cues such as def func_name, the start of a variable declaration, env1 =, or the beginning of a return statement for an f-string, such as return """. These lead-ins, like the closing cues used in ChatGPT and OpenAI prompts, help clarify the starting point for Copilot's generation and ensure it proceeds as intended.

For example, consider a prompt such as the following:

```
class Singleton
```

This is more effective than a comment such as the following:

```
# Implement a Singleton meta-class that ensures only one instance of a
class is created.
```

The first option provides a clear lead-in cue indicating the class to be implemented, while the latter is likely to result in another comment instead of initiating the actual implementation.

For reference, here is a sample completion generated by Copilot, which includes an additional comment on the next line:

```
copilot_samples.py  ×

1    # Implement a Singleton meta-class that ensures only one instance of a class is created.
2    # The Singleton class should be used to store the total cost of all prompts.
     💡
```

Figure 5.1: Comment completion with a code comment instead of an implementation

Copilot interprets the request as an opportunity to elaborate further on the Singleton implementation as a comment rather than starting the actual implementation.

Here is a sample completion based on the lead-in cue, `class Singleton`:

```
copilot_samples.py  ×

1    # Implement a Singleton meta-class that ensures only one instance of a class is created.
2    💡
3    class Singleton(type):  new *
         _instances = {}

         def __call__(cls, *args, **kwargs):
             if cls not in cls._instances:
                 cls._instances[cls] = super(Singleton, cls).__call__(*args, **kwargs)
             return cls._instances[cls]
```

Figure 5.2: Lead-in code for Copilot to implement the Singleton metaclass

In this case, Copilot correctly inferred that it should generate the metaclass implementation even before the `Singleton` class name was fully specified.

Surrounding with imports and hashtags

GitHub Copilot already supplies the underlying LLM with extensive context across its three interaction modes. This includes information such as the filename, analysis of open files for coding preferences and customization, `import` statements, code before and after the cursor, the programming language being used, and preferred styling guidelines.

When writing new code, we can enhance the surrounding context by explicitly including cues about the import statements we plan to use. For instance, if we plan to use the built-in @dataclass decorator, which simplifies data-focused classes by automatically generating boilerplate code such as the __init__ method, adding an import statement such as from dataclasses import dataclass helps Copilot understand the decorators we want to work with:

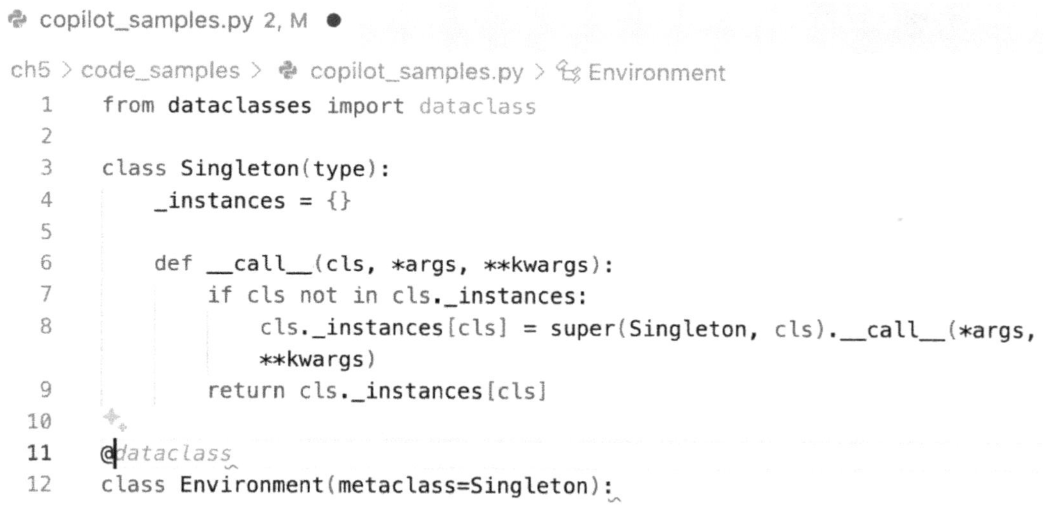

```
🐍 copilot_samples.py 2, M ●

ch5 > code_samples > 🐍 copilot_samples.py > ⚘ Environment
 1    from dataclasses import dataclass
 2
 3    class Singleton(type):
 4        _instances = {}
 5
 6        def __call__(cls, *args, **kwargs):
 7            if cls not in cls._instances:
 8                cls._instances[cls] = super(Singleton, cls).__call__(*args,
                   **kwargs)
 9            return cls._instances[cls]
10
11    @dataclass
12    class Environment(metaclass=Singleton):
```

Figure 5.3: Import cues for dataclass decorators

In this example, Copilot autocompletes the @ cue with the appropriate @dataclass decorator. See the *Further reading* section for additional resources on data classes.

When using Copilot in VS Code, you can enhance the surrounding context in the chat by referencing elements such as @workspace or @terminal. These annotations, while beginning with @, do not refer to decorators but rather specify the environment the chat should consider.

Additionally, specific files or code selections can be referenced using the hashtag, #.

For example, to request an explanation of the __call__ method in the Singleton metaclass, you can select the method, type #selection in the chat, and then use the /explain command, as shown in *Figure 5.4*.

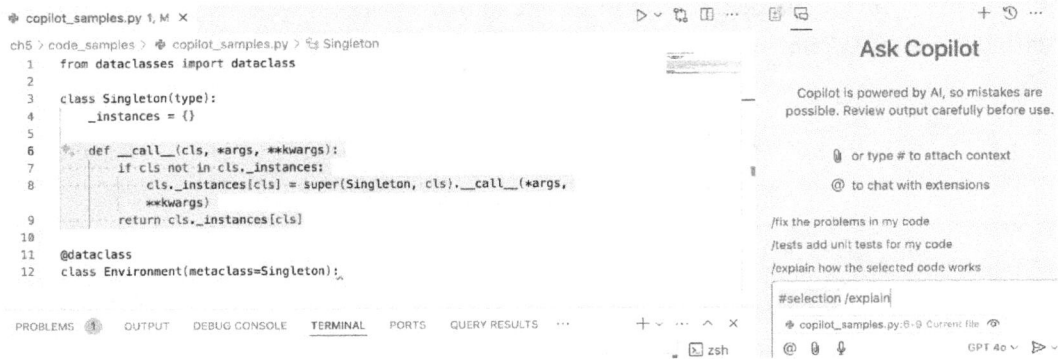

Figure 5.4: Using #selection /explain in VS Code/Copilot Chat

🔍 **Quick tip:** Need to see a high-resolution version of this image? Open this book in the next-gen Packt Reader or view it in the PDF/ePub copy.

📖 **The next-gen Packt Reader** is included for free with the purchase of this book. Scan the QR code OR go to packtpub.com/unlock, then use the search bar to find this book by name. Double-check the edition shown to make sure you get the right one.

This gives the chat context about the specific code snippet you want explained. For reference, here is the explanation we received for the selected code:

```
This code defines a Singleton metaclass in Python. A Singleton is a design
pattern that ensures a class has only one instance and provides a global
point of access to it.
Here's a breakdown of the code:
1. Class Definition: class Singleton(type):
This defines a metaclass named Singleton. In Python, a metaclass is a
class of a class that defines how a class behaves. A class that uses this
```

```
metaclass will follow the Singleton pattern.
2. Class Attribute: _instances = {}
This dictionary will store the single instances of the classes that use
this metaclass.
3. __call__ Method: def __call__(cls, *args, **kwargs):
This method is overridden to control the instantiation of the class.
cls refers to the class being instantiated.
*args and **kwargs are used to pass any arguments to the class
constructor.
4. Instance Check: if cls not in cls._instances:
This checks if an instance of the class already exists in the _instances
dictionary.
5. Instance Creation: cls._instances[cls] = super(Singleton, cls).__call__
(*args, **kwargs)
If the class is not in _instances, it creates a new instance using super()
and stores it in the _instances dictionary.
6. Return Instance: return cls._instances[cls]
This returns the instance of the class, ensuring that only one instance
exists.
In summary, this metaclass ensures that any class using it will only have
one instance, implementing the Singleton pattern.
```

Copilot identified the purpose of the Singleton metaclass and provided a clear explanation of its key components.

> **Note**
>
> As of January 2025, adding additional surrounding context to Copilot Chat is not yet supported in PyCharm.

Further narrowing the single task

While Copilot is already tailored to the three interaction modes, each aligned with a specific task, there are cases where the task scope can be further refined.

For example, extracting hardcoded strings with arguments or global variables requires providing more specific guidance instead of relying solely on the straightforward /fix command. Without additional context, the /fix command might generate broader suggestions.

For reference, here is an example of a /fix suggestion that unnecessarily proposes adding a __post_init__ method to the Environment class (see *Figure 5.5*).

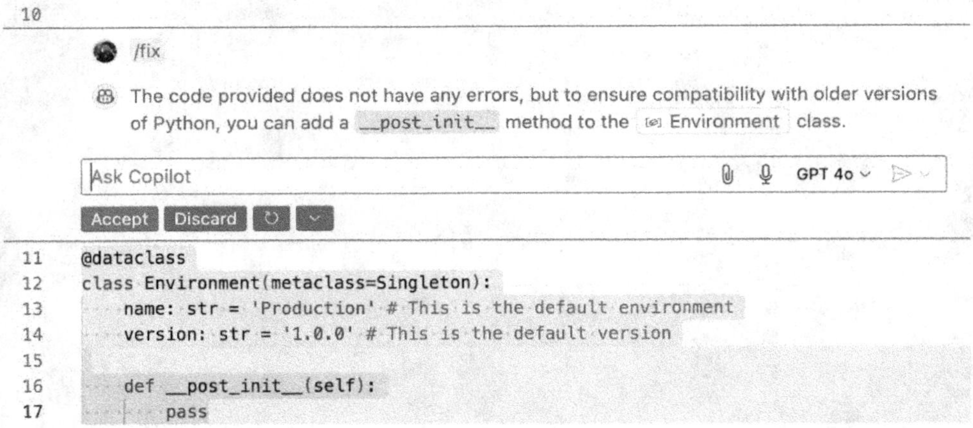

```
10
    ● /fix
    ⊞ The code provided does not have any errors, but to ensure compatibility with older versions
       of Python, you can add a __post_init__ method to the [◎] Environment  class.

    Ask Copilot                                          ⋃   ⎓   GPT 4o ⌄   ▷ ⌄
    Accept   Discard   ↻   ⌄
11  @dataclass
12  class Environment(metaclass=Singleton):
13      name: str = 'Production' # This is the default environment
14      version: str = '1.0.0' # This is the default version
15
16      def __post_init__(self):
17          pass
```

Figure 5.5: Copilot offers irrelevant fix

Always aim to include single-task instructions, even when using / commands. For instance, if the goal is to extract hardcoded values, you can specify that the desired fix, extract the hard-coded default values to global constants, alongside the /fix command. Narrowing down the single task in this way helps Copilot better understand your intent and produces more accurate recommendations:

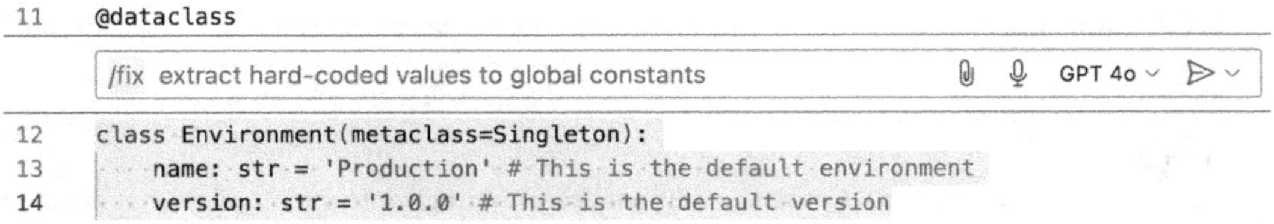

```
11  @dataclass

    /fix  extract hard-coded values to global constants       ⋃   ⎓   GPT 4o ⌄   ▷ ⌄
12  class Environment(metaclass=Singleton):
13      name: str = 'Production' # This is the default environment
14      version: str = '1.0.0' # This is the default version
```

Figure 5.6: Single task narrowed to extracting hardcoded values

In this example, Copilot effectively understands the task and successfully extracts the hardcoded values, proposing to extract DEFAULT_ENV_NAME and DEFAULT_ENV_VERSION:

/fix extract hard-coded values to global constants

To fix the code and extract hard-coded values to global constants, you can define the constants at the top of the file and use them in the [≡] Environment class.

```
Ask Copilot                                              🔗   🎤   GPT 4o ⌄   ▷ ⌄
Accept   Discard   ↻   ⌄
```

```
11   DEFAULT_ENV_NAME = 'Production' # This is the default environment
12   DEFAULT_ENV_VERSION = '1.0.0' # This is the default version
13
14   @dataclass
15   class Environment(metaclass=Singleton):
16       name: str = DEFAULT_ENV_NAME
17       version: str = DEFAULT_ENV_VERSION
```

Figure 5.7: Successful extraction of hardcoded values

In the green highlighted text in *Figure 5.7*, we can see that Copilot suggested extracting the hard-coded default values into global constants named DEFAULT_ENV_NAME and DEFAULT_ENV_VERSION.

This demonstrates how applying the single task principle and narrowing it further, even when using backslash commands such as \fix, helps us achieve more effective results when working with Copilot.

Specific instructions with type hints, docstrings, descriptive names, and unit tests

Copilot already preprocesses your files and surrounding context to include specific instructions, ensuring tailored code completions, analyses, and chat responses.

To follow the specificity practice more precisely in our prompts, we can incorporate type hints, docstrings, descriptive names, and unit tests into our code. These practices not only improve the quality and readability of the code but also help Copilot generate better implementations.

For instance, if our code involves handling environment versioning as integers, adding clear type hints and a meaningful name enables Copilot to better suggest appropriate default values:

```
@dataclass
class Environment(metaclass=Singleton):
    name: str = 'Production' # This is the default environment
    version: int = 1
            ⁇ int
```

Figure 5.8: Using type hints to specify desired completions

In *Lab 5.2*, we will explore how adding a failing unit test can assist Copilot in identifying and addressing issues in our code.

Short prompts without comment fluff

When working with Copilot, the goal is to supercharge our work without cluttering the code base we work on. To follow the short principle, we should avoid adding comment fluff, which we define as comments we would not include if not using Copilot and would likely remove after code generation, as they add no value to the implementation.

A better approach is to use meaningful names, type hints, docstrings, and unit tests when generating code, along with a lead-in cue to hint to Copilot that it should start its implementation.

For example, to instruct Copilot for code completion, it is better to provide a meaningful class signature that aligns with the intended implementation:

```
class TestSingleton(TestCase):
```

That is better than adding unnecessary comments such as the following:

```
# Implement a test case to verify the singleton behavior of the
Environment class
```

Similarly, prefer a docstring instead of comments:

```
def recursive_fibonacci(n):
    """
    Calculate the n-th Fibonacci number using a recursive approach.

    Args:
        n (int): The position in the Fibonacci sequence (0-indexed).

    Returns:
        int: The n-th Fibonacci number.

    Raises:
        ValueError: If n is a negative integer.

    Examples:
        >>> recursive_fibonacci(0)
        0
```

```
      >>> recursive_fibonacci(1)
      1
      >>> recursive_fibonacci(5)
      5
   """
```

That is better than using comments such as the following:

```
# implement the recursive_fibonacci function here
# The function should calculate the n-th fibonacci number using a
recursive approach
# The function should raise a ValueError if n is a negative integer
# the argument is n and the return type is an integer
# Examples:
# recursive_fibonacci(0) => 0
# recursive_fibonacci(1) => 1
# recursive_fibonacci(5) => 5
```

The former approach is not only more predictable for Copilot but also helps avoid clutter in the code base if the comment is kept after the class generation, or confusion about the code's origin if the comment is removed.

Also, prefer variable names with type hints instead of inline comments:

```
product: float =
```

Use the preceding code instead of the following:

```
# initialize a product variable to 1
```

Here, too, the former approach is more predictable to Copilot and avoids clutter in the code base.

Next, we will explore how to implement the five S's best practices with Copilot and apply them in the upcoming lab to fix a faulty implementation of a Singleton metaclass.

Lab 5.2 – Fixing faulty implementation with GitHub Copilot

In this lab, we will address a faulty Singleton implementation by adding a unit test to verify its Singleton behavior, then use Copilot to analyze the error and suggest a fix. This lab is inspired by a bug fix the author encountered earlier in her career, where an Environment class, intended to function as a Singleton, failed to preserve attribute changes across instances.

The initial faulty implementation of the `Singleton` metaclass was as follows:

```python
class Singleton(type):
    _instances = {}

    def __call__(cls, *args, **kwargs):
        if cls not in cls._instances:
            cls._instances[cls.__name__] = super(Singleton, cls).__call__
(*args, **kwargs)
        return cls._instances[cls.__name__]
```

This implementation is close to the correct implementation of a Singleton `__call__` function:

```python
class Singleton(type):
    _instances = {}

    def __call__(cls, *args, **kwargs):
        if cls not in cls._instances:
            cls._instances[cls] = super(Singleton, cls).__call__(*args,
**kwargs)
        return cls._instances[cls]
```

However, the faulty implementation searches for an instantiated class instance using the `cls` hash key but stores it under the `cls.__name__` key. This inconsistency causes a bug that prevents the Singleton from maintaining its intended behavior.

In this lab, we will address this logical error by first using Copilot to implement a unit test that evaluates the behavior of the metaclass and then asking Copilot to fix the bug.

Lab 5.2 guided walk-through

Open *Lab 5.2* in the book repository at `ch5/labs/lab52.py` and ensure that you have a stable internet connection and that GitHub Copilot is ready.

The starter code includes the faulty `Singleton` implementation along with an `import` statement for the `TestCase` class and the `main` runner from Python's `unittest` package:

```python
from dataclasses import dataclass
from unittest import TestCase, main

class Singleton(type):
    _instances = {}
```

```
    def __call__(cls, *args, **kwargs):
        if cls not in cls._instances:
            cls._instances[cls.__name__] = super(Singleton, cls).__call__
(*args, **kwargs)
        return cls._instances[cls.__name__]


@dataclass
class Environment(metaclass=Singleton):
    name: str = 'Production'
    version: int = 1


if __name__ == "__main__":
    main()
```

In the next steps, we will create a unit test to debug the faulty behavior of the Singleton metaclass, analyze why it fails, and correct the implementation accordingly.

To test a metaclass's behavior, we might want to include a class implementation that utilizes the Singleton and compare different instances of it, as follows:

```
def test_something(self):
    @dataclass
    Class A(metaclass=Singleton):
        a: int = 0
self.assertEqual(A(2), A())
```

To ensure Copilot follows this guideline, we will provide a lead-in cue to start the test case implementation by beginning with the class name. Type the following lead-in:

```
class TestSingleton
```

As you type, Copilot should recognize that you are attempting to test the Singleton metaclass. It may suggest a complete test case, but to tailor it more specifically to our requirements, accept only the first line, which should be as follows:

```
class TestSingleton(TestCase):
```

Continue by adding a descriptive name for the test case:

```
def test_singleton_should_return_same_instance(self):
```

Using descriptive names for unit tests is good practice, as it clearly conveys the purpose of the test and serves as a documentation tool.

At this point, Copilot may suggest an implementation involving the Environment class. However, the preferred approach is to test a designated class that uses the Singleton metaclass, as our goal is to validate the metaclass itself rather than the Environment class. Begin the implementation with the following:

```
@dataclass
class A(
```

At this point, Copilot should detect that we are testing an implementation of the metaclass. By combining the test name and the lead-in cue, it may suggest a unit test such as the following:

```
@dataclass
class A(metaclass=Singleton):
    a: int = 0


self.assertEqual(A(2), A())
```

This unit test verifies that an instance of A initialized with a non-default value of 2 should be equal to a new instantiation of the class without additional parameters, ensuring the Singleton behavior is maintained.

We will delve deeper into writing unit tests with GenAI applications in *Chapter 16*. For now, accept the suggested test case if it resembles the preceding one or tests similar functionality.

If you have completed all the steps correctly, your test class should look like this:

```
class TestSingleton(TestCase):
    def test_singleton_should_return_same_instance(self):
        @dataclass
        class A(metaclass=Singleton):
            a: int = 0


        self.assertEqual(A(2), A())
```

Please note that this test will fail because the `Singleton` implementation has not yet been corrected.

Next, execute the lab using the following shell command:

```
python -m unittest ch5/labs/lab52.py
```

This should result in a failing unit test:

```
⊗ .venv→  supercharge git:(main) ✗ python -m unittest ch5/labs/lab52_singleton.py
  F
  ========================================================================
  FAIL: test_singleton_behavior_should_return_same_instance (ch5.labs.lab52_singleton.TestSinglet
  test_singleton_behavior_should_return_same_instance)
  ------------------------------------------------------------------------
  Traceback (most recent call last):
    File "/Users/hila/PycharmProjects/private/supercharge/ch5/labs/lab52_singleton.py", line 26,
  test_singleton_behavior_should_return_same_instance
      self.assertEqual(A(2), A())
  AssertionError: TestS[13 chars]_singleton_behavior_should_return_same_instance.<locals>.A(a=2)
  TestS[13 chars]_singleton_behavior_should_return_same_instance.<locals>.A(a=0)


  ------------------------------------------------------------------------
  Ran 1 test in 0.001s

  FAILED (failures=1)
```

Figure 5.9: Failing unit test for Singleton behavior

Failure is expected because the __call__ method of the Singleton is not properly implemented. When a new instance of A is created, its attribute, a, is set to the default value of 0 instead of retaining the value from the previous instantiation of a=2.

If you are using VS Code, you can get an explanation of the terminal error by typing the following in the **Chat** window:

```
@terminal /explain the failing unit test
```

This prompt specifies that the context is the terminal, instructing Copilot to explain the test failure as shown in the terminal trace. Here is an example explanation generated by Copilot Chat using the *GPT-4o* model:

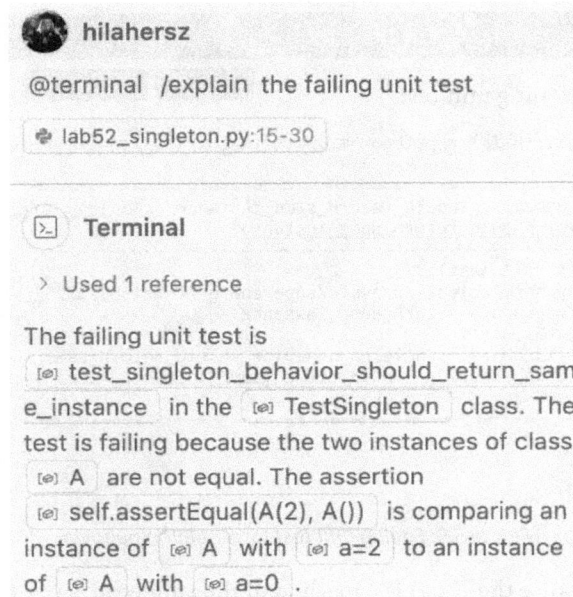

Figure 5.10: VS Code explanation for the failing unit test

Note that the objects in the explanation are clickable for added convenience. Clicking on objects such as A will direct you to their location in the code:

```
 9
 0      class TestSingleton(TestCase):
 1          def test_singleton_behavior_should_return_same_instance(self):
 2              @dataclass
 3              class A(metaclass=Singleton):
 4                  a: int = 0
 5
 6              self.assertEqual(A(2), A())
```

Figure 5.11: Clicking on A would highlight the objects in the file

The explanation correctly identifies that the incorrect implementation of the Singleton metaclass results in two different instances of the A class, causing the test to fail.

If you are using PyCharm, copy the failing traceback and paste it into the chat as follows, following the five S's:

```
CONTEXT: You will be provided with a failing Python unit test traceback
enclosed with {{{ TRACEBACK }}}.
TASK: Explain why the unit test is failing.
TRACEBACK: {{{
python -m unittest ch5/labs/lab52_singleton.py
F
========================================================================
FAIL: test_singleton_behavior_should_return_same_instance (ch5.labs.
lab52_singleton.TestSingleton.test_singleton_behavior_should_return_same_
instance)
------------------------------------------------------------------------
Traceback (most recent call last):
    File "supercharge/ch5/labs/lab52.py", line 26, in test_singleton_
behavior_should_return_same_instance
        self.assertEqual(A(2), A())
AssertionError: TestS[13 chars]_singleton_behavior_should_return_same_
instance.<locals>.A(a=2) != TestS[13 chars]_singleton_behavior_should_
return_same_instance.<locals>.A(a=0)
------------------------------------------------------------------------
Ran 1 test in 0.001s
FAILED (failures=1)
}}}
EXPLANATION:
```

This structured prompt, which includes surrounding context, a specific task to explain the failing unit test, the traceback with an enclosed alias, and a lead-in explanation cue, will help us understand why our test is failing.

For reference, here is a sample output from Copilot Chat in PyCharm that correctly identifies the cause of the failing test, specifically, the error in the singleton __call__ method implementation:

```
GitHub Copilot Chat                                      :  —        ⌂

Debugging Singleton Pattern in Python              🕐  +  ⋯      @

chars]_singleton_behavior_should_return_same_instance.<locals>.A(a
=2) != TestS[13
chars]_singleton_behavior_should_return_same_instance.<locals>.A(a
=0)</locals></locals>

<hr></hr> Ran 1 test in 0.001s

FAILED (failures=1)

}}}

EXPLANATION:
```

```
😎 GitHub Copilot                                        🖹  👍  👎

>   4 steps completed successfully

The unit test is failing because the assertEqual statement is
comparing two instances of the A class, but they are not equal.
The first instance is created with A(2), which sets the attribute
a to 2, while the second instance is created with A(), which uses
the default value of a (0).

In a singleton pattern, the same instance should be returned
every time the class is instantiated. However, the test is
failing because the __call__ method in the Singleton metaclass
does not correctly handle the arguments passed during
instantiation. It should ensure that the same instance is
returned regardless of the arguments.
```

Figure 5.12: Copilot Chat explanation for the failing unit test

Although this chat does not contain clickable elements, it accurately identifies the problem in the __call__ method that is not implemented correctly.

Now that we have identified the issue with the Singleton metaclass, we can adjust the __call__ method to properly maintain the single class instance design pattern.

To fix the issue, navigate to the __call__ method, highlight it, and prompt Copilot to fix the cls instantiation, as follows:

```
/fix cls instantiation
```

This prompt will suggest the correct fix for the cls._instances registry. For your reference, here is a sample output we received when using the Copilot extension in VS Code with the *GPT-4o* model:

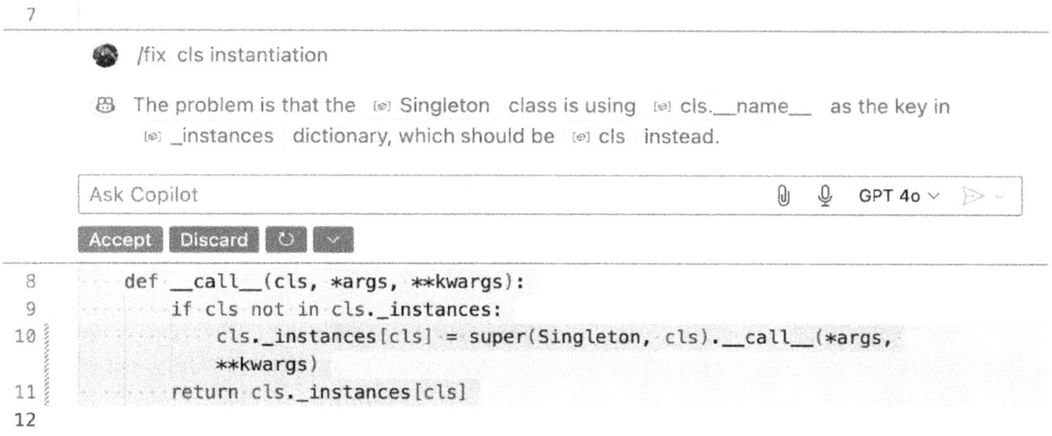

```
7

  /fix cls instantiation

  The problem is that the Singleton class is using cls.__name__ as the key in
  _instances dictionary, which should be cls instead.

  Ask Copilot                                    GPT 4o

  Accept   Discard

8     def __call__(cls, *args, **kwargs):
9         if cls not in cls._instances:
10            cls._instances[cls] = super(Singleton, cls).__call__(*args,
              **kwargs)
11        return cls._instances[cls]
12
```

Figure 5.13: Suggested fix for the cls instantiation

Copilot provided the correct implementation of the Singleton metaclass using cls._instances[cls] instead of cls._instances[cls.__name__].

Accept this solution. At this point, your code should appear as follows:

```
from dataclasses import dataclass
from unittest import TestCase, main

class Singleton(type):
    _instances = {}

    def __call__(cls, *args, **kwargs):
        if cls not in cls._instances:
            cls._instances[cls] = super(Singleton, cls).__call__(*args,
**kwargs)
        return cls._instances[cls]
```

Rerun the lab using the following shell command:

```
python -m unittest ch5/labs/lab52.py
```

The unit test should pass, confirming that the singleton is correctly implemented:

```
● .venv→  supercharge git:(main) python -m unittest ch5/labs/lab52.py
  .
  _____
  Ran 1 test in 0.001s

  OK
```

Figure 5.14: Test ran with no errors

The unit test verifies that a new instantiation of the A class retrieves the previously created instance with the argument of a=2, and the main() runner completes without errors.

Lab 5.2 analysis

In this lab, we debugged the Singleton implementation by creating a unit test that failed. Based on the failure explanation, we used Copilot to fix the error. To accomplish this, we applied the five S's best practices across five different prompts. Let us examine how each prompt emphasizes different practices of the five S's, helping us achieve more desirable results.

Prompt 1 – following the structured prompt principle with a lead-in cue

To create a test for the Singleton metaclass, we began with a code lead-in cue for Copilot:

```
class TestSingleton
```

We also followed the *short* best practice, by avoiding unnecessary comments. This was enough for Copilot to suggest the name class TestSingleton(TestCase) for the test class.

Prompt 2– providing specific and short prompt principles

To generate a unit test that utilizes the singleton as a metaclass, we used a descriptive test name, test_singleton_should_return_same_instance, along with a lead-in @dataclass decorator and class implementation:

```
@dataclass
class A(metaclass=Singleton):
```

This was sufficient for Copilot to understand that the test should validate the correct instantiation of the Singleton:

```
class TestSingleton(TestCase):
    def test_singleton_should_return_same_instance(self):
        @dataclass
        class A(metaclass=Singleton):
            a: int = 0


        self.assertEqual(A(2), A())
```

This test case compares two instances of the A class: one created with the default parameter and another with a specified parameter. If the Singleton is implemented correctly, the two instances should be equal.

Prompt 3 – adding surrounding context and focusing on a single task with VS Code

After running the failing unit test, we enhanced the prompt with the additional surrounding context and a single task by using the following:

```
@terminal /explain the failing unit test
```

This provided detailed information about the incorrect implementation of the __call__ method.

Prompt 4 – applying the five S's with PyCharm chat

When using PyCharm chat, we applied the same prompt techniques that work with ChatGPT. We used a *structured* prompt with the *surrounding* context, focusing on a *single* task, and created a *specific* and *short* prompt that led to an explanation of the traceback for the failing unit test.

Prompt 5 – narrowing down the single task to fix a method implementation

Once Copilot identified that the issue was with the __call__ method's cls instantiation, we provided the following /fix command with a narrowed-down single task:

```
/fix cls instantiation
```

This allowed Copilot to focus on the correct fix required from this method.

In summary, the five S's for crafting precise prompts are essential when interacting with any of GitHub Copilot's three interaction modes. They help refine the structure by incorporating lead-in cues, adding surrounding context to both chats and input statements, and narrowing the focus to the specific task. This approach makes instructions more precise while avoiding unnecessary comments and keeping prompts short and minimal.

In the upcoming chapters, we will explore advanced prompt engineering techniques to further enhance our ability to achieve even better results from the GenAI applications.

Summary

In this chapter, we explored how to apply the five S's best practices for crafting precise prompts using both OpenAI API and GitHub Copilot. With OpenAI API, we learned how to extract valuable information from Python objects, including attributes such as source code, docstrings, filenames, object types, and more. When working with Copilot, we examined which aspects of the five S's are already implemented and identified how we can use those more precisely to improve outputs from the GenAI application.

Through two interactive labs, we utilized the Singleton design pattern, commonly employed by Python developers to enforce a single class instance with a designated metaclass. Using OpenAI API, we generated documentation for the __call__ method of the Singleton. With GitHub Copilot, we constructed a unit test that failed due to an undesirable behavior caused by faulty implementation, analyzed the test failure, and assisted Copilot in fixing the implementation.

With this, we conclude *Part 1* of this book, in which we explored the best practices for crafting precise prompts in ChatGPT, OpenAI API, and GitHub Copilot.

By now, we have learned how to use OpenAI API, ChatGPT, and GitHub Copilot for a variety of use cases. We examined the costs associated with each tool and observed the OpenAI rate limits. We also explored Copilot's architecture, built on the foundation of OpenAI API, and gained insights into using ChatGPT's canvas editor effectively.

We discussed the three pillars of achieving quality outcomes from a GenAI application: model mastery, evaluation metrics, and precise prompts. We emphasized the role of precise prompts by implementing the five S's: structured prompts, surrounding context, single-task focus, specific instructions, and short prompts without unnecessary fluff.

Next, we move on to *Part 2*, where we will delve deeper into understanding the underlying LLMs, analyzing their risks and limitations, and learning how to take ownership of GenAI-generated code, including critically reviewing code created from colleagues' prompts.

Quiz time

Before you proceed to the next chapter, make sure that you can confidently answer the following questions:

Question 1: How can we incorporate information from Python objects when working with OpenAI API?

Answer: When working with OpenAI API, we often include data about Python objects such as functions, methods, classes, and variables. To extract details such as source code, docstrings, filenames, and object types, we can use special attributes (dunder) methods, or the built-in `inspect` package.

Question 2: Which of the five S's for precise prompts are implemented in OpenAI API system prompts?

Answer: OpenAI API system prompts incorporate surrounding context and single-task specifications, separated by a space. These prompts are reusable across different user prompts that are typically handled by a function such as `get_user_prompt`.

Question 3: How can we extend the structured prompt practice with GitHub Copilot?

Answer: GitHub Copilot handles much of the structuring automatically. Adding a lead-in cue, such as a function name (`def func_name`), variable type hint (`product: float =`), or a class name (`class ClassName`), serves as an effective cue for Copilot to begin the desired implementation.

Question 4: Are code comments such as `# implement the following function` effective when working with Copilot?

Answer: Such comments are considered fluff and do not enhance the code's readability or Copilot's output. Always prefer using lead-in cues instead of trivial comments.

Further reading

To learn more about the topics that were covered in this chapter, look at the following resources:

- Singleton design pattern, by Geeks for Geeks: `https://www.geeksforgeeks.org/singleton-method-python-design-patterns/`

- Metaclasses, by Real Python: `https://realpython.com/python-metaclasses/`

- Python dataclass documentation: `https://docs.python.org/3/library/dataclasses.html`

- The 3S's best practices for GitHub Copilot for VS Code: `https://techcommunity.microsoft.com/blog/azuredevcommunityblog/single-short-specific---prompting-github-copilot-for-visual-studio/4117226`

Part 2

Basics to Advanced LLM Prompting for GenAI Coding

In *Part 2* of this book, we explore how LLMs can be applied to consistently generate quality code. It begins with a high-level guide on how LLMs work and then applies them to different tasks. By the end of this part, you will understand which tools (ChatGPT, OpenAI API, and GitHub Copilot) can be best applied for a given task.

This part expands into prompt engineering, including advanced topics such as few-shot learning, Chain-of-Thought reasoning, iterative prompting, and chaining to better understand and refactor code. It concludes with an exploration of fine-tuning methods.

This part contains the following chapters:

- *Chapter 6, Behind the Scenes: How ChatGPT, GitHub Copilot, and Other LLMs Work*
- *Chapter 7, Reading and Understanding Code Bases with GenAI*
- *Chapter 8, An Introduction to Prompt Engineering*
- *Chapter 9, Advanced Prompt Engineering for Coding-Related Tasks*
- *Chapter 10, Refactoring Code with GenAI*
- *Chapter 11, Fine-Tuning Models with OpenAI*

6

Behind the Scenes: How ChatGPT, GitHub Copilot, and Other LLMs Work

While most of the chapters in this book provide hands-on guides to using GenAI models for coding, it is also useful to understand how they work under the hood. ChatGPT, OpenAI API, and GitHub Copilot are based around **large language models (LLMs)** that have been responsible for the sudden rise of GenAI not only in the technology space but across industries. By understanding how LLMs work, you will understand when they can be most effective, know their limitations, and appreciate their role in prompting. This will maximize your overall success with GenAI.

This chapter will introduce the following concepts:

- Statistical approach to finding similar letters
- Small and large language models for words
- Improving LLM output performance
- What are the limitations of LLMs?
- ChatGPT
- GitHub Copilot

Technical requirements

To get the most out of this chapter, ensure you have the following:

- GitHub Copilot account
- IDE – either VS Code or PyCharm
- OpenAI account with access to OpenAI API
- Access to the book's repository, available at `https://github.com/PacktPublishing/Supercharged-Coding-with-Gen-AI`
- Virtual environment set up in VS Code or PyCharm
- OpenAI API token

For assistance setting up a GitHub Copilot account, refer to *Chapter 3*. For instructions on setting up OpenAI API access and token generation, see *Chapter 2*. If you need help creating an OpenAI account or setting up a virtual environment in your IDE, refer to the *Appendix* for detailed guidance.

Statistical approach to LLMs

Many users of ChatGPT and other LLMs often have an incorrect impression of how LLMs work. They ask questions such as *What fraction of the internet do they understand?*. To introduce the underlying concepts, this section focuses on a simpler problem using just statistics. This will allow us to provide a foundation for discussing how models work before we shift into AI and deep learning. The question we will address is whether we can use probabilities to predict the next letter given a set of preceding letters. If we can, then we should be able to create true English from data without any understanding of linguistic orthography, phonology, morphology, or even general language.

For this sample problem, we will use a medium-sized dataset called the *Reuters-21578* dataset. It is available at the **UCI Machine Learning Repository** (`https://archive.ics.uci.edu/`) and consists of 21,578 different news wire articles, which are just text stories across different topics. While the main use of this dataset is to train and assess text classification algorithms, we are using this as a large corpus of text that has over 15 million letters. The rest of this section describes the process of using this corpus to predict the next letter using a statistical approach. A curious reader can experiment further with the provided code available in the GitHub repository for *Chapter 6*.

Our first analysis step is to look at the frequencies of individual letters. Although the dataset has not only letters but also numbers, punctuation, and other symbols, we will focus on just the letters and the spaces between words. We will also ignore the case and convert everything to lowercase. The frequencies of the individual letters are shown in *Figure 6.1*. The frequency of words typically follows **Zipf's law**, but not for letters. However, we do see the expected tapering of frequencies when sorted by letter, although the distribution is not as smooth due to the limited size of the dataset.

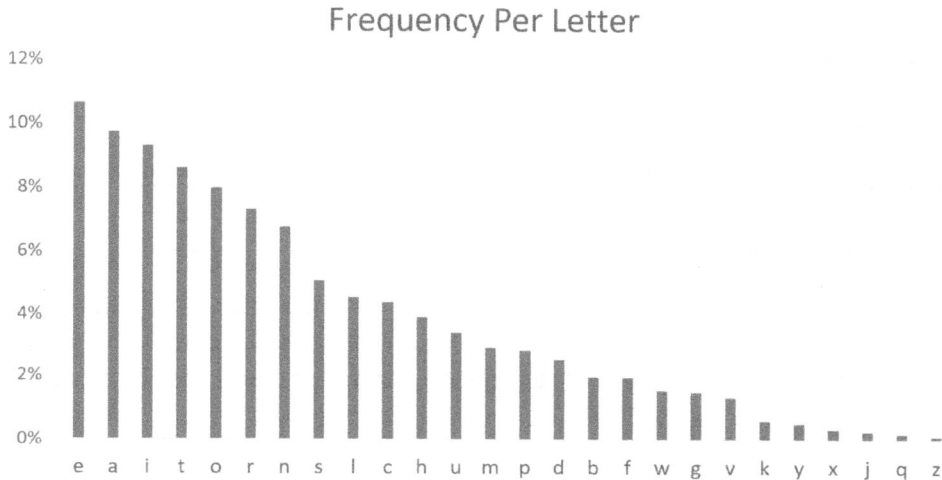

Figure 6.1: Letter frequencies for the Reuters-21578 dataset

With the frequencies or probabilities of the individual letters from *Figure 6.1*, we can produce words by sampling from this distribution. We can sample proportional to the frequency of the letters in the dataset and try to craft English words. We can do this by generating a random number with a uniform distribution between 0 and 100%. If it's < 12%, it would be an e. If it's in the 12 to (12+9)% range, then it would be t. If it's in the 19 to (19+8.5)% range, it would be a, and so on. The results of this approach are shown in *Figure 6.2*. Each row represents a different example to show some variation. As you can see, we have not replicated anything that looks vaguely like English:

1 eelnin ungia wwuetthgsaaeuuoiolifs ttelaroi ic so u dnli ohsaadoiolid
2 t ape ui preirl y ldueeseihenw eioxtincplastmtcteughct ivlrwataartrbi
3 ectee hcmasauisdeb eaeacwinsarsdu enti nuee dba io haqid kh aeeoa lr
4 aelplilvprag el nl einrileadneirearoafr ndstey m iser e hnpatfut hllbi
5 appdsmn rstthylan mvlccirefrrchneahbrgbmefw schnygtof mormde neehc

Figure 6.2: Creating "words" from using just the individual word frequencies

Using the individual frequencies of words doesn't use any context, and so it produces words that do not resemble English. Context in this case refers to the order of the letters that come before it. For instance, in the first line, no English words start with *wwu* or *tte* or *dn*. Similarly, the letter *q* is usually followed by *u* in English.

To augment this with the context of preceding letters, we can use conditional probabilities. In statistical terms, *p(x|y)* is read as the probability of *x* given *y*, and it means the probability of *x* occurring given that *y* occurs. Mathematically, the formal definition is as follows:

$$p(x|y) = \frac{p(x,y)}{p(x)}$$

If we think of playing cards, the probability of the queen of diamonds is 1/52, but the probability of the queen of diamonds given it is a queen is 1/4. The probability of a queen of diamonds given it is a diamond is 1/13.

In our context, we are going to use these conditional probabilities to compute the probability of the next letter. So, given the current letter is a *q*, the next letter is usually a *u*. In fact, we can build a table of all the possibilities written as percentages for each combination of letters. *Figure 6.3* shows the first letter as the column, and the conditional probability of the next letter as a row. For instance, *p(u|q)* is 90.3%.

	a	b	c	d	e	f	g	h	i	j	k	l	m	n	o	p	q	r	s	t	u	v	w	x	y	z
a	0.1	15.0	9.2	8.1	6.4	6.0	11.3	20.5	3.4	37.3	5.1	10.4	20.1	6.5	1.1	16.7	0.7	10.2	15.0	6.3	4.8	7.6	16.9	5.6	4.2	19.7
b	1.9	0.6	0.1	0.2	0.9	0.0	0.0	0.0	0.8	0.0	0.3	0.2	3.0	0.1	0.8	0.1	0.0	0.3	0.2	0.0	2.7	0.0	0.1	0.0	1.7	0.8
c	3.5	0.3	1.6	0.1	5.5	0.1	0.1	0.0	6.9	0.1	0.0	0.5	0.4	7.3	2.1	6.5	0.0	2.1	1.8	0.3	5.1	0.0	0.0	19.3	1.0	0.2
d	4.1	0.1	0.1	2.2	11.3	0.1	0.2	0.1	8.5	0.0	0.2	7.2	0.1	16.2	2.4	0.2	0.0	2.5	0.3	0.4	2.8	0.0	0.1	0.0	1.0	0.4
e	0.1	24.0	13.5	34.2	3.7	12.8	26.2	53.7	3.3	14.1	52.2	13.7	24.5	11.3	0.3	15.4	0.0	28.6	16.1	16.8	4.7	56.1	20.2	10.6	44.4	34.4
f	0.9	0.0	0.1	0.0	1.4	10.7	0.0	0.0	1.2	0.0	0.4	0.6	0.2	0.7	11.8	0.0	0.0	0.2	0.2	0.1	0.6	0.0	0.0	0.0	0.3	0.2
g	2.7	0.0	0.1	1.1	1.0	0.1	1.2	0.0	2.3	0.0	0.2	0.1	0.0	14.0	0.6	0.1	0.0	1.6	0.0	0.3	2.7	0.9	0.0	0.0	0.1	0.1
h	0.1	0.1	11.1	0.1	0.3	0.0	10.7	0.0	0.0	0.0	0.9	0.0	0.0	0.1	0.2	1.3	0.0	0.1	7.3	28.8	0.1	0.0	12.5	0.2	0.1	1.1
i	9.0	10.5	6.4	18.5	1.3	21.4	6.6	10.3	0.0	2.0	12.2	13.2	10.9	5.3	1.3	3.1	1.1	9.8	9.3	13.0	3.3	16.9	25.2	7.1	7.1	24.4
j	0.2	0.5	0.0	0.4	0.0	0.0	0.0	0.0	0.0	0.0	0.0	0.0	0.0	0.1	0.2	0.0	0.0	0.0	0.0	0.0	0.1	0.0	0.0	0.0	0.0	0.0
k	1.1	0.0	3.3	0.0	0.5	0.0	0.1	0.0	0.3	0.0	0.3	0.5	0.0	2.5	0.8	0.0	0.0	2.2	0.6	0.0	0.1	0.0	0.1	0.0	0.1	0.1
l	10.8	8.1	3.3	10.4	3.9	2.6	1.6	0.2	7.2	0.2	2.0	14.6	9.2	0.5	4.0	7.6	0.0	1.4	1.0	0.8	9.3	0.1	0.4	0.2	1.2	0.9
m	1.9	0.3	0.1	0.8	3.1	0.1	0.6	0.2	2.1	0.0	0.5	0.4	4.9	0.8	8.7	1.0	0.0	2.6	1.0	0.6	3.0	0.0	0.2	0.2	6.2	0.2
n	21.2	0.1	0.0	0.3	11.1	0.0	5.0	0.5	26.9	0.1	1.7	5.9	0.1	1.8	21.7	0.0	0.0	2.6	0.1	0.1	12.0	0.0	4.2	0.2	2.9	0.1
o	0.1	10.6	24.7	6.2	0.3	24.5	9.5	6.9	8.5	22.0	3.3	8.3	10.5	5.5	1.3	13.7	0.0	11.5	5.9	13.8	0.5	3.6	15.0	1.4	7.3	6.9
p	2.3	0.4	0.1	0.2	1.7	0.0	0.1	0.0	0.9	0.1	0.2	0.4	10.3	0.1	3.2	4.3	0.0	1.6	3.0	0.1	4.3	0.0	0.0	39.8	1.1	0.7
q	0.1	0.0	0.7	0.1	0.4	0.0	0.0	0.0	0.1	0.0	0.0	0.0	0.0	0.1	0.0	0.0	0.0	0.0	0.0	0.0	0.0	0.0	0.0	0.0	0.0	0.1
r	13.5	6.1	3.6	2.0	20.2	11.7	15.5	3.2	2.9	0.5	1.1	5.6	0.1	0.1	15.9	22.6	0.0	1.9	0.1	5.7	15.4	0.2	1.2	0.0	0.7	0.1
s	8.1	2.2	0.6	3.9	13.0	0.7	3.8	0.9	8.4	0.0	15.5	3.6	2.3	6.2	4.0	1.0	0.0	8.8	7.3	7.1	10.0	13.6	2.1	0.1	18.2	0.4
t	12.0	2.5	15.6	0.2	4.5	3.6	1.2	2.0	12.6	0.0	0.2	4.3	0.5	15.7	4.2	2.6	7.6	5.7	22.8	1.3	17.5	0.0	1.3	14.0	1.1	0.2
u	1.1	10.3	4.6	8.8	2.4	5.1	4.8	0.7	0.2	23.5	1.2	2.8	2.2	1.7	8.7	3.6	90.3	1.7	6.4	2.0	0.0	0.1	0.0	0.3	0.8	4.9
v	1.6	0.1	0.0	0.7	2.0	0.0	0.0	0.0	2.6	0.0	0.0	0.5	0.0	1.2	2.9	0.0	0.0	1.0	0.0	0.0	0.1	0.0	0.0	0.0	0.0	0.1
w	0.4	0.0	0.0	0.3	1.1	0.0	0.0	0.1	0.1	0.1	0.4	0.1	0.0	0.1	3.4	0.1	0.0	0.3	0.5	1.0	0.1	0.1	0.0	0.2	0.3	1.0
x	0.4	0.0	0.0	0.0	2.8	0.0	0.0	0.0	0.3	0.0	0.0	0.0	0.0	0.0	0.1	0.0	0.0	0.0	0.0	0.0	0.1	0.0	0.0	0.4	0.0	0.0
y	2.5	8.2	1.2	1.3	1.0	0.3	1.5	0.2	0.0	0.0	2.0	7.0	0.6	2.2	0.4	0.1	0.0	3.3	0.8	1.4	0.8	0.5	0.1	0.5	0.0	1.2
z	0.3	0.0	0.0	0.0	0.1	0.0	0.0	0.0	0.4	0.0	0.1	0.0	0.0	0.1	0.0	0.0	0.0	0.0	0.0	0.1	0.1	0.0	0.0	0.0	0.1	1.9

Figure 6.3: Percentage of conditional probabilities for next letters (rows) given letters (columns)

The sampling is more complicated in the conditional probability case, so let's use an example. To create text, we might assume that our last letter is a q. To choose the next letter, we randomly sample from the possibilities across all rows of the q column. We then generate a random value from 0 to 100% representing a random probability drawn from a uniform distribution for the next letter. We then consider which bucket the random number fell in. The letter a is 0.7%, b through h are all 0.0%. The letter l has a 1.1% chance. The letter t has a 7.6% chance, and the letter u has the largest probability of 90.3%. While it appears that these numbers do not sum to 100%, this is due to round-off errors only. If we select based on these probabilities, the most likely letter is u. We repeat the process with the u column, where the most likely letters are t, r, n, and s, and the least likely letters are q and u. You are likely wondering which words have these strange letters, but remember that there may be acronyms, email addresses, and foreign names included in the articles.

Now that we can generate words for conditional probabilities, does this approach work? *Figure 6.4* shows the results. The word lengths are much closer, and there are a couple of real words, such as it, as, and mag, but otherwise, they do not look like English words:

1 wmarerye icose verhe herer duvoucrpa tilllarast itout f cts coles t tere
2 quron ryeurod g tst venk es wedus d it pll inopo antopcol ediomoforen f
3 lzin terop zquntreve re h tha hentwhase ues tabr iningte as ithormarape
4 rhelds sa tonat ainserathaby sard d aran ido rerealdon itino iconderilos
5 bagalintenin bs cutr tha mag temes cr teat owa th ondes brsumesais t g t

Figure 6.4: Conditional probabilities for p(next_letter | current letter)

We can extend the model so that instead of just looking at a letter given its preceding single letter, we can consider a wider context. Specifically, we can consider the next letter given the preceding j letters using the probability *p(next_letter | preceding j letters)*. This makes the table much larger since the number of columns would increase from 26 to combinations of 2 letters, 3 letters, or more. For the next letter, based on all combinations of the 2 previous letters, the table would be 26 by $26^2 = 676$. For the next letter based on the previous 3 letters, the table would be 26 by $26^3 = 17,576$. However, with a longer context, we would expect better results. We will not show these larger tables of percentages or probabilities, but show the results instead.

The result for the preceding two letters is shown here:

1 laa fith any sh wilhipect thenbleraqi alevid can of the sid in majoin sai

2 sciall appoilliv the takems red trichater jappetted siserseparcess feradd

3 ccpcts allansdaidebt cilliculeve remagre yestom the prify she and saiday

4 onhasharce by williedit salichansaid compansucers sankin connotin farkell

5 goo cout ovelucce any annes and a prommit sers consainse theartment ths w

Figure 6.5: Conditional probabilities for p(next_letter | preceding 2 letters)

For the preceding three letters, the result is as follows:

1 axistraders vice resgel ince trial pital pare to company and on mate donal

2 uma in the feeds under heasonal behinance out ints comesterly also for dea

3 mies are it wcashelp included to thanted quota committe of converal insti

4 jave affere in gover see west rainly of apriculates als of the tradio estm

5 tiall bancember shings offection this in chanies anding for tration aprice

Figure 6.6: Conditional probabilities for p(next_letter | preceding 3 letters)

For the preceding four letters, this is the result:

1 frn in and corp told keeping an from years to market of about there listerd

2 ow fluctane cited under fight pct on the large share into mazda ways to the

3 orb states all year oper shr longer board if of worldwident effort said und

4 logan outstandar years for that they said the fund dives for the right pres

5 ority and its proving exposures said internative to tights income for throu

Figure 6.7: Conditional probabilities for p(next_letter | preceding 4 letters)

For the preceding five letters, the result is as follows:

1 o at such a president quarter eased prices in london said subsidiary said it

2 res average of a dry eder chemical difficulture deterior quickly export cred

3 ten land ship offer committee changed mexico portugal item for example price

4 men violated at federal of the projects to a strict of francs offer industry

5 f customers approval by their old starting earn that order the governments m

Figure 6.8: Conditional probabilities for p(next_letter | preceding 5 letters)

Finally, the result for the preceding six letters is the following:

1 aize subsidized by nippon is expects offer of the agreement earlier today to
2 ld start of corporate property owned from the exports of the chairman rich in
3 alty shortly the year from a floor and judicious market will come of the two
4 she city more discharge as its views last year as he said it would add some o
5 ed on industrial country in narrowed to buy up to the italian declined there

Figure 6.9: Conditional probabilities for p(next_letter | preceding 6 letters)

As we can see, the results improve substantially as we increase the context window. In fact, most of the output has real English words once we use the four preceding letters. With six preceding letters, the sentence flow starts to make some sense, which may be surprising since we are only looking at single letters.

It is important to understand what the model is learning. Although the statistics appear to be producing English words and even some meaningful sentences in *Figure 6.9*, it does not understand the concept of an English word or sentence structure. Furthermore, the model is not storing knowledge or facts of the English language or words. It is only storing the probabilities of the next letter from the preceding context. Our model focuses only on letters at this point, and the next section describes the extension to word-level models. If we had training data that was a thousand or a million times larger, it would be merely doing a better job of estimating the same frequencies.

Extending the model to words

Our English model, which builds language from letters, is quite limited. To produce meaningful language, we would need a much longer context of preceding words to understand the relationships between words spaced throughout a sentence. Furthermore, we don't think of language in terms of letters—we think in terms of words. With our 26 letters in English and a space, each of the preceding j positions can only have 27 possibilities, which means our model is relatively small.

Note

If we consider all combinations of the preceding 3 letters, there are 27 x 27 x 27, or about 20,000 possibilities of letters. With 15 million letters in the dataset and 20,000 combinations, we have a 750:1 ratio of training to combinations, which provides excellent training. The average person knows 42,000 words, so if we use all combinations of the preceding 3 words, it would be 42,000 x 42,000 x 42,000 ~ 7.4E13, or 74 trillion 3-word combinations possible, which is about 10x more than any PC hard disk can handle today. However, if we have 15 million letters and the average word plus a space character is 6 letters, then there would be 2.5 million words. The ratio of training to combinations drops to a 2.5 million:74 trillion ratio, or 1 in 30 million.

Based on the preceding information, we would need billions of times more data for similar accuracy using the statistical model.

As a model becomes more complex, it requires more training data. We can think of a model as a general function where we try to approximate a y value from different x values. This approximation process determines the best function parameters from a set of training data (x, y) pairs representing the input, x, and the output, y. In the case of a linear model, the model must learn the best slope and y-intercept to represent the data. The training data is collected and designed to be representative of future data so that when the model fits well, it can be useful to predict future y values.

Of course, most models are not simple linear models or functions. There may be multivariate inputs with billions of parameters and large output dimensionality. Learning from such large datasets requires significantly larger training data. Consider fitting a linear or a higher-order linear model to a set of data points, as shown in *Figure 6.10*:

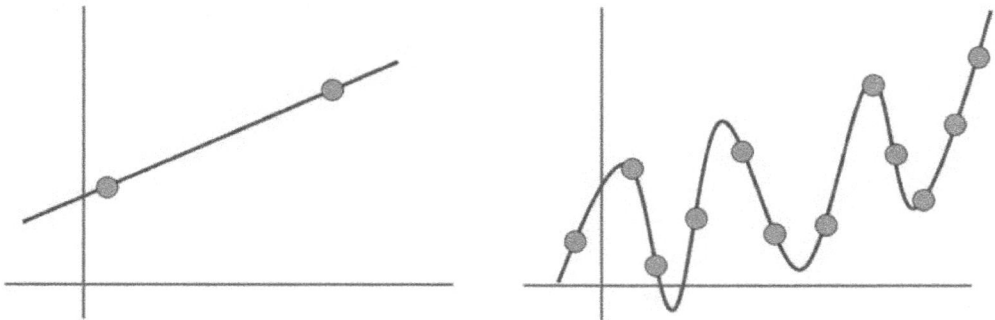

Figure 6.10: The number of training data points increases as the model becomes more complex

We can fit a line with just two points, perhaps, but the seventh-order model on the right needs far more data points to accurately fit. AI models often require data for trillions of parameters, which introduces a problem where the model may suffer from insufficient training data available. The accuracy of the model depends on the number of parameters in the model and the size of its training dataset.

To summarize, the example with letters showed that a statistical model could approximate English language words with a moderate training dataset since the number of combinations is reasonably small. However, we need to store the probabilities of each letter given all preceding letter contexts, which can be quite large. For even the context of just three preceding words, the frequencies are prohibitive to store. In addition to the storage challenge, we would need vast quantities of data to fill a word frequency table to achieve modest prediction accuracy, which is not readily available. The next section uses AI rather than statistics to overcome these challenges for words.

Small and large language models for words

The statistical model clearly worked well for a medium-sized dataset with a small model based on letters. Since grammar and meaning function at the word level, we need to be able to accurately predict the next word rather than the next letter. Since the number of possible next words is far larger than the number of next letters, the model will need to be many orders of magnitude larger. If we think about code or even text, there are no datasets that are billions of times larger. AI methods, and specifically LLMs, provide solutions that enable predictions more efficiently than just probabilities. We describe two methods in this section: word2vec and the Transformer deep learning model.

Word2vec

The **word2vec model** is arguably a small language model that uses a simple neural network. Inspired by biology, neural networks are a particular type of machine learning algorithm that learn from data. Although there are a variety of neural network models, this type learns a mathematical function. Each output neuron is a nonlinear function of the weighted sum of the input values. In the training step, the weights are adjusted so that the input values will predict the output values.

As an example, a neural network could learn to predict whether today is a good day to play tennis based on the inputs of temperature, wind, precipitation, and humidity. The training data would use past decisions to play tennis (output=1) or not play (output=0), and the corresponding weather conditions. With only this data, a neural network could learn to classify future good days for tennis based on the weather. The learned weights for wind and precipitation might be large negative values since high wind speeds and precipitation make tennis unplayable.

Developed by Google in 2013, the word2vec algorithm (`https://en.wikipedia.org/wiki/Word2vec`) trained a model to predict the target word from the context of two words before and after that word. They also developed the opposite problem of predicting the surrounding context from a single word. Essentially, this is equivalent to the next word prediction using the presence of adjacent words rather than only preceding words. Backed with an efficient training algorithm, the results proved reasonably predictive. Of greater importance, *the word2vec weights formed an embedding of the word or numeric vector representation that quantified the semantic and syntax function of words*. In other words, the word2vec model learns to associate every trained word with a numeric vector of numbers. These vectors can be compared, which is useful for comparing the similarity of word meanings.

Deep learning

Deep learning is a subset of neural networks that involves learning functions of functions, essentially. That is, the outputs of one layer form the inputs to a second layer, creating a deep stack of functions. The **Universal Approximation Theorem** proved that neural networks could learn to approximate any mathematical function, given a two-layer network under certain conditions. Research has found that creating deep neural networks with tens, hundreds, or thousands of layers is an efficient way of achieving accurate results. In each layer, the model adjusts its weights based on the training data to learn functions with the results passed as input to subsequent layers.

In 2017, a new deep learning architecture called the Transformer was published in a famous paper called *Attention is All You Need* from Google, the link to which can be found in the *Further reading* section. Rather than relying on the context of adjacent words, the Transformer architecture efficiently learns the relationship between all words in a sentence. The training process learns the relationship between words using a masking process, through which it hides each word separately and learns to predict it from all the other words in each sentence.

A deep learning network describes an architecture in machine learning with a specific number of inputs, outputs, layers, nodes per layer, inter-node connections, and weights throughout. Like the previously described linear model, the architecture describes the solution and is trained to solve a specific problem. LLMs are the result of training a deep learning network on large volumes of text. They learn to correctly predict the next word much better than statistical and word2vec models. Similar to the statistical next-letter prediction models, they can iteratively predict the next word to generate sentences, paragraphs, and full texts. Researchers have found that by training on ever larger volumes of text (or code), the accuracy continues to improve, so many LLMs have been developed that use increasingly larger network sizes and more training data.

LLMs by themselves offer significant capabilities in next-word prediction, but they are continuing to expand into new areas of intelligence. Many of the breakthroughs are now coming from various techniques that improve the performance of their respective LLMs. The next section describes some steps that users can take with an LLM to improve the outputs of LLMs.

Improving LLM output performance

If the LLM does not answer questions well, there are four general courses of action: improving prompt engineering, adding more data through the context window, providing examples (few-shot learning), fine-tuning, and **retrieval-augmented generation (RAG)**. These will be discussed in this section.

Prompt engineering

The discipline of prompt engineering has recently emerged as a human interface to the LLM. Users or programs can send commands to, ask questions of, and apply research reasoning through the LLM. The discipline involves applying specific wording to maximize the chance of correct outputs without producing erroneous or biased outputs, including hallucinations. The process of writing prompts is often an iterative process where it may require multiple rounds to achieve the desired output. Most of the prompts discussed in this book focus on a single task with specific and clear wording, which is considered good practice. The *five S's* framework outlined in this book provides a useful general-purpose structured approach to writing the prompts. We'll cover more on prompt engineering techniques in later chapters.

Adding context

As discussed in this chapter, LLMs are not databases that store data, nor are they an oracle of all knowledge (yet). They can perform a limited number of tasks and answer a finite number of questions without further enhancements. To enable question-answering, interactive chats, or other tasks such as code generation, the user can send the LLM both the question as well as additional information within a **context window**.

> Note
>
> The context window is somewhat analogous to a human's short-term memory in that it has a limited size and may forget older information. However, the context window is generally large enough to include documents, earlier inputs, and returned outputs. A document can be provided as context, and the prompt engineer can ask questions of the document.

Depending on the size of the context window, all or part of earlier outputs from the system and past inputs are automatically included in the next prompts associated with that user, so an entire dialog or thought process is included in every interaction with the LLM. A short context window might only allow a few papers to be uploaded and summarized together, while a longer context window could enable a book to be uploaded with multiple interactive sessions kept as context. This approach has several advantages over an LLM system, which will be discussed next as ways of improving results.

Providing examples

The context window allows for documents and other data to be included along with the prompt or question, but it also allows for examples. A prompt may ask the LLM to return a particular nugget of information in a specific format. In many cases, this will be successful, and this is called **zero-shot learning**. That is, there are no examples of how the LLM should form a response—it just uses its baseline approach. However, the prompts can include one example of an input and an output as part of the prompt. This is called **one-shot learning**. If multiple examples are provided, this is called **few-shot learning**. While many examples can be used depending on the context window length, there is a law of diminishing returns. However, it is an effective approach to instruct the LLM to tailor its outputs to meet a specific need. We will discuss few-shot learning in depth in *Chapter 8*.

Fine-tuning

Training an LLM from scratch may cost $100 million to learn the trillions of weights that are trained on prose, poetry, drama, literature, and science. Due to the prohibitive cost, it will not be trained often. In fact, it is typically two years out of date, which means it does not have any recent events or information. It also likely doesn't have personal or corporate documents included in its training. One solution discussed is to provide these in a context window. As discussed in *Chapter 2*, for pay-for-service LLMs such as OpenAI, every transaction has two costs: a cost to send information to the LLM and a cost for the output produced, both based on the length of the information. As the amount of input information and the number of calls with the same information increase, it may become a costly solution.

Fine-tuning offers an alternative to repeatedly sending a large context to the LLM. It essentially adds a limited supplemental dataset to the LLM training in the form of documents or examples. The training *fine-tunes* the weights of the neural network by making minor adjustments that are sufficient to produce improved outputs. Fine-tuning provides a cost-efficient way of improving outputs without repeatedly sending large contexts of data to the LLM. We will dive deeper into fine-tuning in *Chapter 11*.

Retrieval-augmented generation

RAG solves two major problems with the LLMs. First, OpenAI and ChatGPT are not databases of information, so they cannot retrieve information like a web search. Second, their training data is typically two years old and does not include personal or corporate documents. The RAG architecture integrates the LLM with external information from a web search, database, or set of documents. RAG uses the LLM to interpret the input from a user and then retrieves blocks of text from various sources that it finds to be closely related to the input. The LLM then processes the combination of the input and retrieved data to form an answer or response using the standard LLM processing. Essentially, RAG fills the context window with candidate answers relevant to the question based on a search and then instructs the LLM to perform its usual summary or question-answering on that context window. This enables a full system with an LLM to perform web searches on current information or focus on specific documents when generating output.

Each of the approaches described in this section is widely used to improve LLM results. While research continues to advance LLM capabilities, it is important to understand their limitations, which are discussed in the next section.

What are the limitations of LLMs?

With both the statistical approach for the letters and the LLM approach for words, there is no formal knowledge that many expect, given its ability to answer many questions. There is no extensive knowledge base of topics, common sense, or anything except the word patterns it has learned. What is surprising to researchers is the fact that the learned patterns and their relationships somehow enable LLMs to perform new tasks for which they have never been trained. For instance, LLMs have even shown some capability in some foreign languages that are not part of their training set, through a process called **zero-shot cross-linguistic transfer**. Even if the output has been trained, one may get slightly different results each time from a prompt due to the randomness in the system. Much of the research in the prompt engineering area focuses on how to receive consistent and correct outputs from LLMs by crafting the prompts with specific phrases, commands, and context.

The deep learning approach will almost always produce syntactically correct and plausible-looking output, but some of the output may be prone to **hallucinations**. There have been some famous cases where the output was completely incorrect, technically wrong, and sometimes just made up. A professor was accused of assault on a school trip that never happened. Many students have been caught using ChatGPT since none of their references existed. Even a US government health report was caught citing facts of a made-up reference. These incidents can be found in the *Further reading* section. Hallucinations often occur when there is insufficient training to support a particular output. The statistical methods do not have such an issue since they only sample from the previously seen patterns.

It is currently nearly impossible to know in which areas exactly the LLM has expertise, and in which areas they have limited training. A few years ago, the training of LLMs was generally released as part of its research publication. In the past couple of years, much of the LLM training has become more secretive, so we do not know exactly which sources were used and cannot exactly predict their domains of capability. However, OpenAI has been trained extensively on both texts and code in multiple languages. OpenAI's philosophy is to provide safe and beneficial general AI across many domains. ChatGPT is a specialization using an OpenAI LLM and is discussed in the next section.

ChatGPT

Launched by OpenAI in November 2022, ChatGPT was developed on the **GPT-3.5** model. It became a focal point of the AI growth since it worked through a conversational interface, unlike the programming interface of other LLMs. The dialog-driven interface requires it to track the history of the conversation, even across sessions. ChatGPT is a specialization of the LLM with improved conversational capability.

One of the key technology improvements was the use of **reinforcement learning from human feedback (RLHF)**, which improved the dialog capability through training and feedback to give better responses. As discussed earlier, fine-tuning can improve the LLM's performance for specific tasks. RLHF goes one step further and incorporates feedback from users to adjust the weights. As a result, it delivers results that incorporate human preferences and even reasoning capabilities in terms of responses and answers to questions.

ChatGPT continues to be a leader in the growth of AI, in part due to its easy web interface that makes it widely accessible with minimal training. It has led to greater research in **natural language processing (NLP)** and multiple use cases. Although it can write code, its capabilities are limited as compared to GitHub Copilot, which extends the GPT model for generative coding, as described in the next section.

GitHub Copilot

GitHub Copilot was officially announced as a collaboration between GitHub, Microsoft, and OpenAI, specifically for writing code, in 2021, and opened for technical review. At the time, it started with the GPT-3 instance from OpenAI, and the three companies collaboratively trained it to focus on code development, resulting in the OpenAI Codex. After GPT-4 was released, GitHub Copilot adopted it and released GitHub Copilot X. Its optimization focuses on code completion, fixing bugs, code comments, and tests based on billions of lines of code training beyond the GPT models. The combination of the underlying GPT model with the code-training focus enables the two-way natural language and computer language code writing and explanation.

GitHub Copilot uses a combination of technologies to provide its coding experience. When writing code from a single file, it sends at least part of the current file through the internet to the Copilot server. It will also use the prompt and other open files that are open within their respective VS Code or PyCharm IDE for context. It uses this context to search for similar code using the RAG approach, and then sequentially generates code one token at a time. The amount of code sent to the Copilot server is based on the context length and certainly costs.

If part of your open code and possibly data is being sent to Copilot, it is natural to be concerned about security. The information is encrypted when sent to and from Copilot. The exchange context resides in memory but is deleted without being stored or used for training. The **GitHub Copilot Trust Center** page, available at `https://copilot.github.trust.page/`, provides more information about their data security, privacy, and related issues. It includes suggestions, feedback, prompts, and user engagement data. None of the code exchanged while using GitHub Copilot is used for training their system.

Summary

Statistical and AI approaches can learn patterns from sequential data such as text or code, which can efficiently predict the next symbol. Due to the range of possible words, deep learning methods scale well to efficiently predict the next words much better than statistical techniques and have become the standard. Even so, they require vast training sets of text and code and an expensive computational process to be effective.

While LLMs are highly effective, they are not perfect and are limited by their training set of data and perhaps the time it was trained. The output can be limited for various domains and time periods, which can result in hallucinations. While research continues in these areas, some solutions to improve results include effective prompt engineering, providing contextual information such as documents or examples, fine-tuning, and the RAG approach.

OpenAI and ChatGPT are trained on general data and code, and are quite effective at generating code. GitHub Copilot is built upon OpenAI and, with significant additional training on code, is more efficient at generating code, tests, comments, and more.

Quiz time

Before you proceed to the next chapter, make sure that you can confidently answer the following questions:

Question 1: How is the deep learning approach for words similar to and different from the statistical approach described for letters in this chapter?

Answer: Both the deep learning approaches and statistical approaches generate new text or code using a combination of their trained model and randomness. Even though they are both trained on data, they rely on randomness to select from the probable next words, which means their outputs can be different each time. In both cases, if they are trained with insufficient data, they may not produce satisfactory results. Neither has a conceptual understanding of the inputs or outputs, so both are relying on patterns of inputs to predict patterns of outputs.

The deep learning approach is orders of magnitude more efficient in predicting the range of possible next words or code using complex, less interpretable models. While both could easily predict the next letters with a large training set, the conditional probabilities would not be able to scale to predict next words as the deep learning approach can.

Question 2: How is GitHub Copilot different from OpenAI in terms of code development?

Answer: OpenAI was optimized for general knowledge, and GitHub Copilot was optimized for code generation. GitHub Copilot took the human language capabilities of GPT-4 from OpenAI and further trained it on billions of lines of code, comments, and documentation. In this way, it serves as a pair programmer with the ability to generate code from text, explain code as text, write tests from code, and write comments from code.

Further reading

To learn more about the topics that were covered in this chapter, take a look at the following resources:

- *Zipf's law*: https://en.wikipedia.org/wiki/Zipf's_law
- Mikolov, Tomas; Chen, Kai; Corrado, Greg; Dean, Jeffrey (16 January 2013). *Efficient Estimation of Word Representations in Vector Space*: https://en.wikipedia.org/wiki/Word2vec
- Vaswani, Ashish; Shazeer, Noam; Parmar, Niki; Uszkoreit, Jakob; Jones, Llion; Gomez, Aidan N; Kaiser, Łukasz; Polosukhin, Illia (December 2017). *Attention is All You Need*. In I. Guyon, U. Von Luxburg, S. Bengio, H. Wallach, R. Fergus, S. Vishwanathan, and R. Garnett (ed.). 31st Conference on **Neural Information Processing Systems** (**NIPS**). Advances in Neural Information Processing Systems. Vol. 30. Curran Associates, Inc.: https://arxiv.org/abs/1706.03762
- Pranav Dixit. *US law professor claims ChatGPT falsely accused him of sexual assault, says 'cited article was never written'*. Business Today: https://www.businesstoday.in/technology/news/story/openai-chatgpt-falsely-accuses-us-law-professor-of-sexual-harassment-376630-2023-04-08
- Loreben Tuquero. *RFK Jr.'s health report shows how AI slips fake studies into research*: https://www.poynter.org/fact-checking/2025/rfk-jr-fake-citations-medical-journals/
- *GitHub Copilot Trust Center page*: https://copilot.github.trust.page/

Subscribe for a free eBook

New frameworks, evolving architectures, research drops, production breakdowns—AI_Distilled filters the noise into a weekly briefing for engineers and researchers working hands-on with LLMs and GenAI systems. Subscribe now and receive a free eBook, along with weekly insights that help you stay focused and informed.

Subscribe at `https://packt.link/TRO5B` or scan the QR code below.

7

Reading and Understanding Code Bases with GenAI

Writing code is rarely an isolated task. We will typically have to incorporate our Python snippets into a larger code base that includes project files, often structured under a /src folder, along with dependencies listed in a requirements.txt file and other non-project files, such as a **Dockerfile** that defines container specifications.

In this chapter, we will work with a code base that computes the **Manhattan distance** between two matrices represented as pandas DataFrames. With the help of ChatGPT, GitHub Copilot, and OpenAI API, we will explore how various GenAI tools can support us in efficiently understanding both non-project files and the main business logic. We will also examine how generating calls with sample parameters can improve our understanding of more complex code.

Here are the key topics covered in this chapter:

- Reading and understanding the code base structure
- Using LLMs to explain code
- Interpreting non-project files
- Creating calls with example parameters

Technical requirements

To get the most out of this chapter, ensure you have the following:

- GitHub Copilot account
- IDE – either VS Code or PyCharm
- OpenAI account with access to OpenAI API
- Access to the book's repository, available at `https://github.com/PacktPublishing/ Supercharged-Coding-with-Gen-AI`
- Virtual environment set up in VS Code or PyCharm
- OpenAI API token

For assistance setting up a GitHub Copilot account, refer to *Chapter 3*. For instructions on setting up OpenAI API access and token generation, see *Chapter 2*. If you need help creating an OpenAI account or setting up a virtual environment in your IDE, refer to the *Appendix* for detailed guidance.

Reading and understanding the code base structure

So far in the book, we have mostly explored code snippets that are limited to a single Python file. In this chapter, we will shift our focus and see how GenAI tools can support us in reading and understanding a broader code base.

Getting to know a code base usually involves reading through a variety of files. For instance, when a developer encounters a new project, they might do the following:

Explore entry points such as `main.py` or `app.py`

Identify the main project files, often found in a `/src` directory

Look for container and dependency management files such as `Dockerfile` and `requirements.txt`

Experiment with specific parts of the code

In this book's repository, we provide a small code base example located under `ch7/`. Here is a directory tree view of its contents:

```
ch7/
├── app.py
├── src/
│   └── manhattan.py
```

```
├── Dockerfile
├── README.md
├── requirements.txt
```

In this tree view, the core business logic that we will explore next is located in src/manhattan.py. In addition, we have the following:

app.py, which serves as the entry point and handles basic **Hypertext Transfer Protocol (HTTP)** POST requests, routing them to the business logic. As introduced in *Chapter 2*, HTTP POST is a standard method for sending data to a server.

Dockerfile, a text file that outlines the steps and dependencies needed to build a container image for running the application. We will return to this later in the chapter.

requirements.txt, which lists the application's dependencies, such as *pandas* and *Flask*, as introduced in *Chapter 2*.

README.md, a markdown file commonly used to provide documentation about a code base. In our case, it includes examples of how to use the application.

Next, we will introduce the Manhattan distance, which serves as the core business logic of our application.

Introducing the Manhattan distance

In this chapter, our code focuses on calculating the **Manhattan distance** between two points. This distance is defined as the sum of the absolute differences along each dimension. In two-dimensional space, we can relate this to classic computer games such as *Pacman*, where movement is restricted to vertical or horizontal directions, with no diagonal steps allowed. For example, consider Pacman and a ghost positioned in locations (1,1) and (3,2), respectively, in *Figure 7.1*.

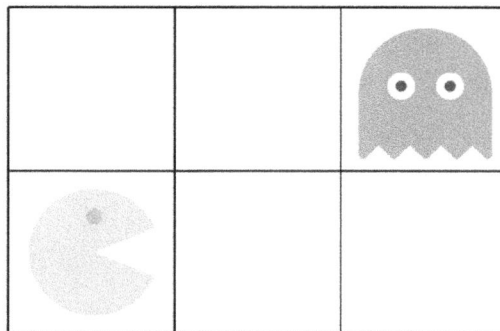

Figure 7.1: Pacman and ghost positions

In this figure, the characters can move either horizontally or vertically. The Manhattan distance between them is two units along the x axis and one unit along the y axis, which totals 3:

$$\text{Manhattan Distance} = |3 - 1| + |2 - 1| = 3$$

A simple Python implementation for calculating this distance might look like this:

```
def get_manhattan_distance(
        x1: Tuple[int, int],
        x2: Tuple[int, int],
) -> int:
    x_dist: int = abs(x1[0] - x2[0])
    y_dist: int = abs(x1[1] - x2[1])

    dist: int = x_dist + y_dist
    return dist
```

In this implementation, we use two-dimensional vectors represented as `Tuple[int, int]` to represent a position on a board. However, the Manhattan distance can be generalized to higher dimensions computed between matrices of floats, as we will see next.

Manhattan distance for matrices

The Manhattan distance, also referred to as the **L1 norm**, extends naturally to higher-dimensional data. It is widely used in image analysis when comparing two images and in machine learning research when evaluating prediction errors.

To compute the Manhattan distance between matrices, we can use pandas `DataFrame` objects. *pandas* is a standard library for data manipulation and should be listed in the book's `requirements. txt` file and already installed in your virtual environment.

Here is an example of a DataFrame with two rows, A and B, and three columns labeled a, b, and c:

```
import pandas as pd

df1: pd.DataFrame = pd.DataFrame(
    data={
        "A": [1, 2, 3],
        "B": [4, 5, 6],
    },
    index=["a", "b", "c"],
)
```

We can implement the Manhattan distance using the *pandas* methods .abs() for absolute values and .sum() for summing along axes:

```
def get_manhattan_distance(
        df1: pd.DataFrame,
        df2: pd.DataFrame,
) -> np.float64:
    element_wise_dist: pd.DataFrame = (df1 - df2).abs()
    dist: float = element_wise_dist.sum().sum().astype(float)
    return dist
```

The distance calculation uses .sum() twice: first to sum across rows, and then again to sum the resulting column totals. We convert the result to a float to standardize the output, since summing over integer values may return a *NumPy* int64 data type.

Let's take these two DataFrames:

```
A = [[1 3]
 [2 4]]
B = [[5 7]
 [6 8]]
```

Calling get_manhattan_distance on these will return the following:

```
|5-1| + |6-2| + |7-3| + |8-4| = 16
```

Now that we have a clear understanding of the core business logic and supporting code around the distance computation, we can explore how GitHub Copilot, ChatGPT, and OpenAI API can help us navigate and familiarize ourselves with the code base.

Using LLMs to explain code

In *Chapter 3*, we noted that GitHub Copilot does not include the entire code base in the prompt. This is due to context window limitations, potential cost, and the fact that much of the content may not be relevant to the specific task.

However, this does not prevent GenAI from helping us understand the code bases we are working with. Rather than relying blindly on **Large Language Models (LLMs)** to identify key components, we will explore how to request explanations for both simple elements and more complex scenarios.

Using the /explain command with GitHub Copilot

GitHub Copilot includes several slash commands, among them the /explain command, which is available in both the inline chat and the chat window. Unlike code completion tasks, the output of this prompt is explanatory text covering arguments, data transformations, and return values.

The command can be used alone or with extra instructions. For example, in PyCharm, we can ask Copilot to explain the get_manhattan_distance function by placing the cursor anywhere within the function signature, opening the inline chat window, typing /explain, and hitting *Enter*, as shown in *Figure 7.2*:

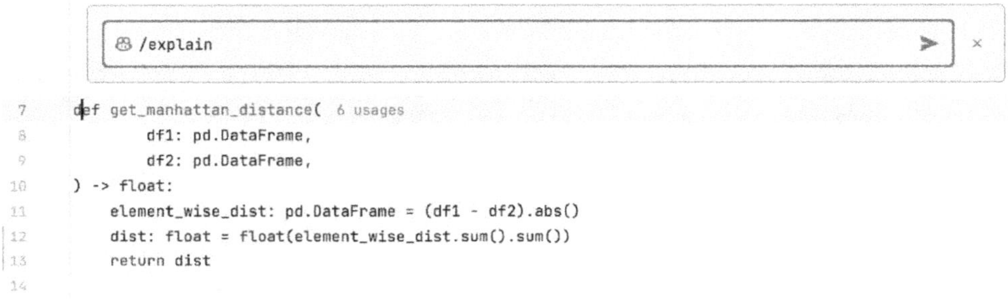

```
7    def get_manhattan_distance( 6 usages
8            df1: pd.DataFrame,
9            df2: pd.DataFrame,
10   ) -> float:
11       element_wise_dist: pd.DataFrame = (df1 - df2).abs()
12       dist: float = float(element_wise_dist.sum().sum())
13       return dist
14
```

Figure 7.2: Using GitHub Copilot /explain for methods

Another available option is to select the contents of the function, open a chat window, and type /explain. Note that in VS Code, you will need to choose @workspace /explain by either typing it directly or selecting the /explain @workspace option in the drop-down menu after typing / explain, as shown in *Figure 7.3*:

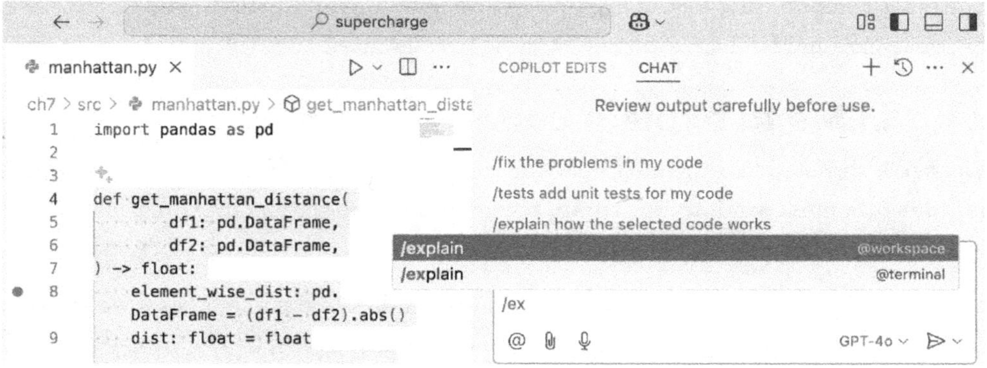

Figure 7.3: Choosing @workspace /explain in VS Code chat

For either IDE, Copilot is likely to yield a general explanation about the purpose of the function, the data transformation, and the returned value, as shown in *Figure 7.4*.

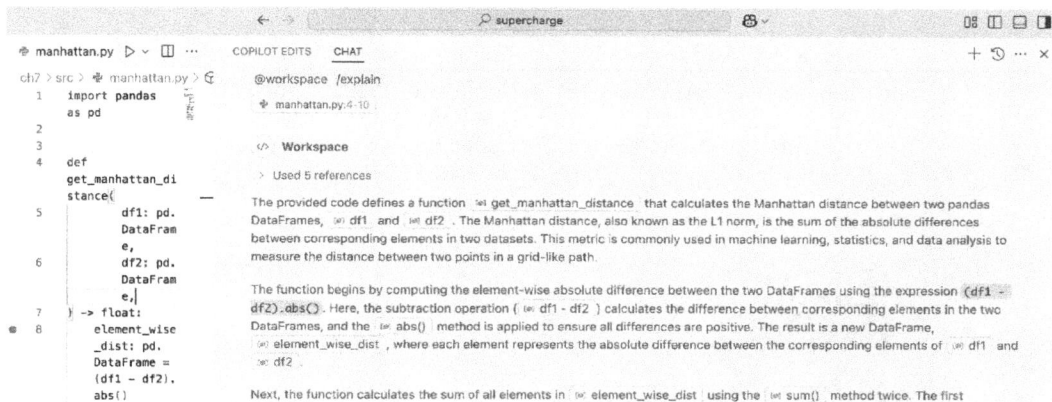

Figure 7.4: Sample /explain output in VS Code

If we wanted a broader analysis of the arguments and their type, for example, we could use this prompt:

```
/explain argument types
```

This should yield an extended explanation about the arguments, as shown in *Figure 7.5*.

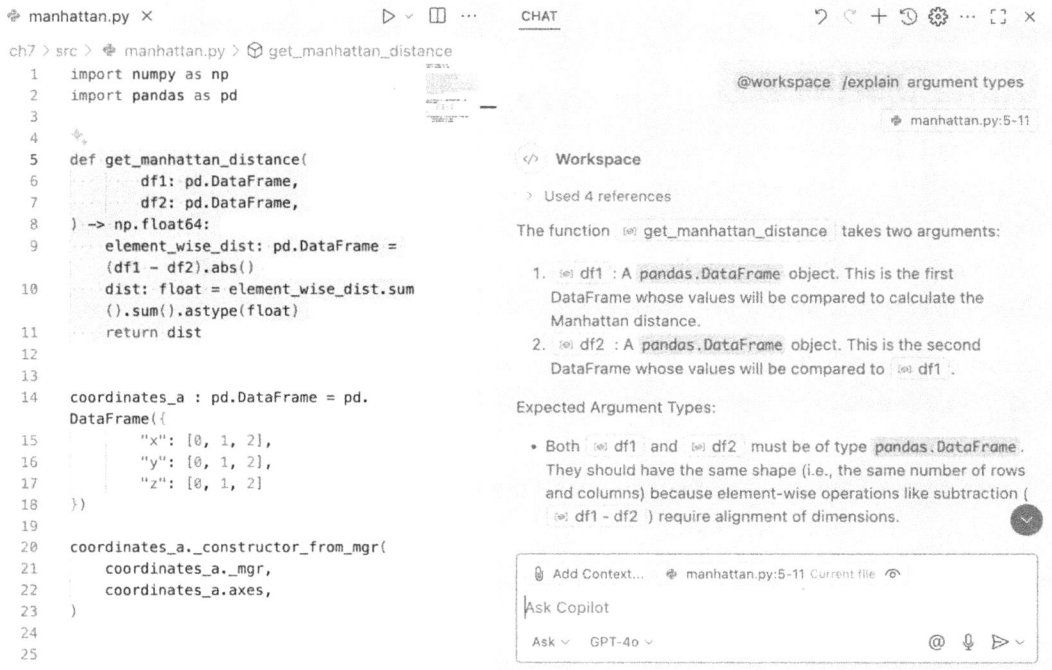

Figure 7.5: Extended /explain argument types with GitHub Copilot

🔍 **Quick tip:** Need to see a high-resolution version of this image? Open this book in the next-gen Packt Reader or view it in the PDF/ePub copy.

🔒 **The next-gen Packt Reader** is included for free with the purchase of this book. Scan the QR code OR go to packtpub.com/unlock, then use the search bar to find this book by name. Double-check the edition shown to make sure you get the right one.

Here, we see a detailed explanation of the arguments df1 and df2, including a note that df2 is expected to have the same shape as df1 for the function to work properly. This expectation is not mentioned in the plain /explain prompt, but when we ask about a specific aspect of the code, we get a more in-depth explanation.

Next, we will see how we can replicate this outcome through direct prompting with ChatGPT and OpenAI API.

Using ChatGPT to explain code

While Copilot includes a built-in slash command for code explanations, we can apply the **five S's framework** introduced in *Chapter 4* to achieve similar results with ChatGPT, even when using older or more cost-effective models such as *GPT-4o*. Unlike GitHub Copilot, which follows predefined instructions about what to explain based on the Python object, ChatGPT allows us to tailor the explanation to our specific needs.

For instance, the following prompt focuses on describing the function's purpose, its arguments and types, the data flow, expected output, and possible edge cases:

```
CONTEXT: you are provided with:
1. A Python function enclosed with {{{ FUNCTION }}}
2. Explanation points enclosed with {{ HEADERS }}}.
TASK: Explain the function using the explanation points.
FUNCTION: {{{ ...omitted for brevity ... }}}
HEADERS: {{{
1. Function's purpose
```

```
2. Arguments and their types
3. Step-by-step data flow
4. Output and its types
5. Potential edge cases
}}}
```

EXPLANATION:

When using *GPT-4o* with this structure, we received an explanation that covered all bullet points with the headers, as partially shown in *Figure 7.6*:

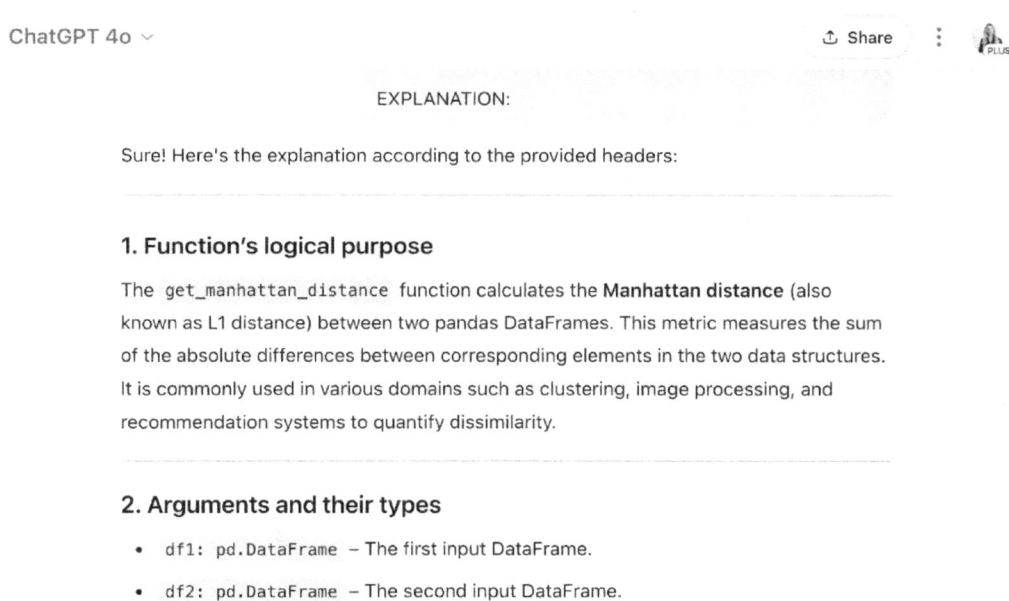

ChatGPT 4o ∨   ⬆ Share   ⋮   👤
                                                                                       PLUS

EXPLANATION:

Sure! Here's the explanation according to the provided headers:

---

1. Function's logical purpose

The `get_manhattan_distance` function calculates the **Manhattan distance** (also known as L1 distance) between two pandas DataFrames. This metric measures the sum of the absolute differences between corresponding elements in the two data structures. It is commonly used in various domains such as clustering, image processing, and recommendation systems to quantify dissimilarity.

---

2. Arguments and their types

* `df1`: `pd.DataFrame` – The first input DataFrame.
* `df2`: `pd.DataFrame` – The second input DataFrame.

Figure 7.6: ChatGPT returned extended explanation

For reference, here is the output generated by ChatGPT under the edge cases header, which adds value by uncovering situations where the function might fail or produce unexpected behavior:

```
5. Edge cases
Shape mismatch: If df1 and df2 do not have the same shape, the subtraction
operation will raise a ValueError.
Non-numeric columns: If the DataFrames contain non-numeric data, the
subtraction operation will raise a TypeError or produce NaNs that affect
the result.
Missing values (NaNs): If either DataFrame contains NaNs, the output
```

```
distance may be NaN unless explicitly handled beforehand.
Empty DataFrames: If both inputs are empty DataFrames, the result will be
0.0.
```

Although writing a prompt for ChatGPT might take slightly more effort compared to using the /explain command, it can be worthwhile when we need more targeted explanations, such as uncovering edge cases.

Next, we will demonstrate how to achieve this using OpenAI API, which may be more appropriate for scenarios where the repository becomes larger and we want to generate explanations for many functions programmatically.

Using OpenAI API to explain code

Using the same prompt structure from ChatGPT, we can make a programmatic call to OpenAI, following the best practices introduced in *Chapter 5*.

We will define the same system prompt components that mirror our ChatGPT prompt:

```python
SURROUND = """... omitted for brevity ..."""
SINGLE_TASK = "... omitted for brevity..."
HEADERS = """...omitted for brevity"""
```

We will add a get_user_prompt function that merges the HEADERS prompt piece with the source code of the function:

```python
def get_user_prompt(func: callable) -> str:
    return f"""
    FUNCTION: {{{{{{ {inspect.getsource(func)} }}}}}}
    HEADERS: {{{{{{ {POINTS} }}}}}}
    EXPLANATION:
    """
```

Then, we can call OpenAI API using the *gpt-4o-mini* model:

```python
if __name__ == "__main__":
    client: OpenAI = OpenAI()

    system_prompt = f"{SURROUND} {SINGLE_TASK}"
    user_prompt = get_user_prompt(get_manhattan_distance)

    completion: ChatCompletion = client.chat.completions.create(
```

```
        model="gpt-4o-mini",
        messages=[
            {"role": "system", "content": system_prompt},
            {"role": "user", "content": user_prompt},
        ],
    )
    print("Explanation:", completion.choices[0].message.content)
```

Just as with ChatGPT, we will receive a detailed explanation of the function, covering all points specified. For reference, here is a sample output from running this script:

```
Function's purpose: < ... omitted for brevity ... >
Arguments and their types: The function takes in two arguments:
* df1: a pandas DataFrame, which represents the first set of data.
* df2: a pandas DataFrame, which represents the second set of data. Both
dataframes are expected to have the same shape and structure for the
calculation to be valid.
Step-by-step data flow: < ... omitted for brevity ... >
Potential edge cases:
* If df1 and df2 have different shapes, the function may raise a value
error due to the inability to perform element-wise operations on
differently-sized frames.
* If either of the DataFrames is empty, the function will return a
distance of 0.0 as there are no elements to compute differences from.
* Handling of NaN (Not a Number) values might need to be considered,
as this could affect the calculations when present in either of the
DataFrames.
```

The output here also provides an overview of the edge cases. In later chapters of the book, we will explore how to make use of this when designing a test suite for functions.

Next, we will explore how to extend the use of the /explain command beyond .py files using various GenAI tools.

Explaining non-project files

The /explain command is not limited to .py files or core business logic. For instance, in our Manhattan distance code base, we can use Copilot to interpret an entire non-project file or a specific section of it.

Explaining an entire file

There are times when we may want a summary of a complete non-project file. For example, consider the `requirements.txt` file in our project:

```
pandas==2.2.3
flask==3.1.0
```

To get a general explanation, we can highlight the entire content with the cursor, then open the inline chat or chat window and enter `/explain`. *Figure 7.7* shows an example of this using the chat window in VS Code:

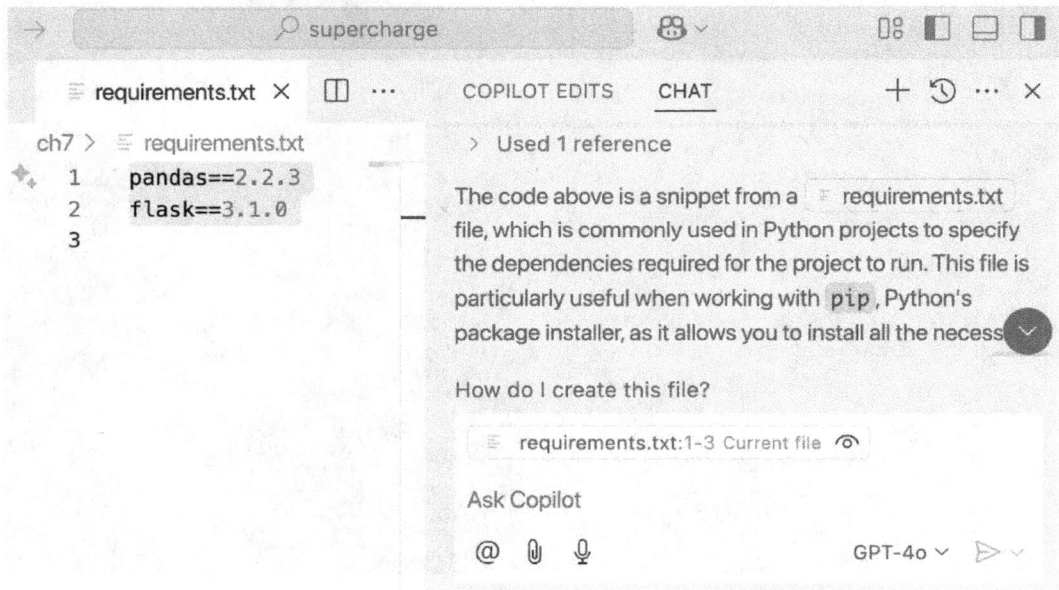

Figure 7.7: Chat window explanation of a full file highlighted content

In this case, Copilot accurately recognized that `requirements.txt` lists the dependencies needed for the code base to run properly. For common non-project files, we can generally expect reliable explanations since LLMs have encountered many similar examples during training.

Next, we will look at how to ask for a more detailed explanation of a specific line within a non-project file by providing the right context.

Explaining with context

While it is useful to understand a file as a whole, there are often specific lines that may be unclear and require a deeper explanation.

Take the Dockerfile from our Manhattan distance project as an example. **Docker** is a widely used tool among software developers for packaging applications in a consistent and reproducible way. A key element in this process is the Dockerfile, a plain text file typically placed at the project root that outlines the environment setup. This includes specifying a base image (such as a Python environment), listing dependencies (like the *pandas* library), and providing commands to build and run the container (such as opening a port to receive HTTP POST requests).

Below is the Dockerfile we used for our Manhattan distance application:

```
FROM python:3.10-slim

WORKDIR /app

COPY requirements.txt .
RUN pip install -r requirements.txt

COPY . .

EXPOSE 5000

CMD ["python", "app.py"]
```

Copilot can provide an explanation for the entire file, but there are times when we want to focus on a specific line. For instance, we may want to understand the meaning of EXPOSE 5000. Although it might seem like this command publishes port 5000 for incoming requests, it serves as documentation only. The application will still need to explicitly expose this port when launching the container, using a shell command such as docker run -p 5000:5000. When we highlight just this line and request an explanation, Copilot incorporates context from nearby lines, the filename and extension, and other signals to generate a relevant and accurate response, as shown in *Figure 7.8*:

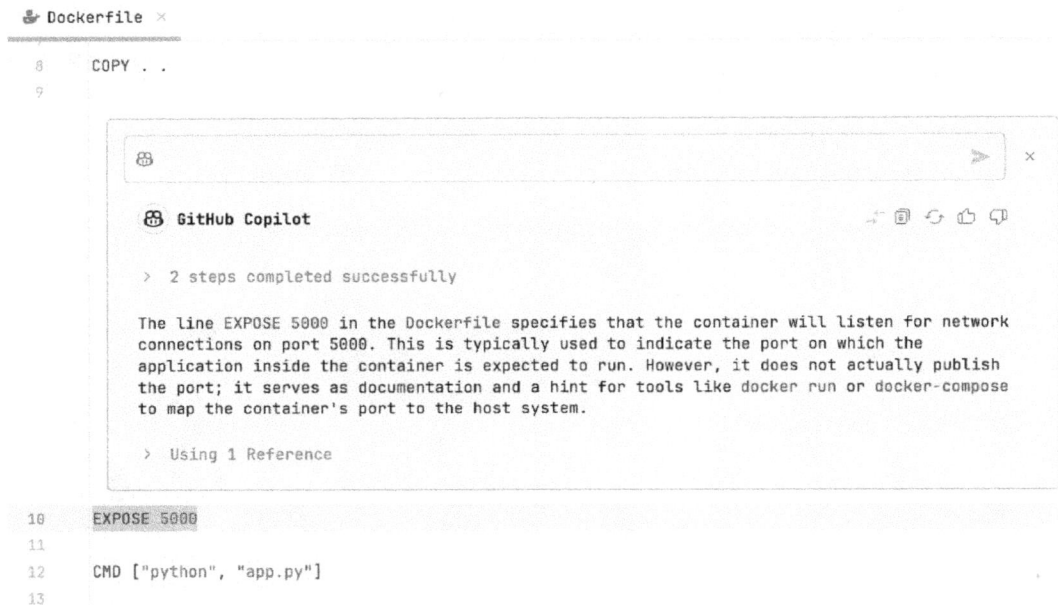

```
🐳 Dockerfile ×

8     COPY . .
9
```

```
  🐙                                                                    ➤      ×

  🐙 GitHub Copilot                                             ⌁ 🗐 🔁 👍 👎

  >  2 steps completed successfully

  The line EXPOSE 5000 in the Dockerfile specifies that the container will listen for network
  connections on port 5000. This is typically used to indicate the port on which the
  application inside the container is expected to run. However, it does not actually publish
  the port; it serves as documentation and a hint for tools like docker run or docker-compose
  to map the container's port to the host system.

  >  Using 1 Reference
```

```
10    EXPOSE 5000
11
12    CMD ["python", "app.py"]
13
```

Figure 7.8: Copilot explanation about exposed port from the Dockerfile

Copilot correctly identified that the port specification indicates the port on which the application is listening. For common files such as Dockerfile, the plain /explain command usually provides a sufficient one-line explanation.

Next, we will explore how to get similar explanations in non-project files working with ChatGPT.

Explaining non-project files with ChatGPT

When seeking an explanation for a specific line within a non-project file or the entire file itself, the best practice is to provide the full content of the file along with the line in question and the standard filename and extension. In the case of a Dockerfile, there is no extension (such as .txt or .py), so simply specifying Dockerfile is sufficient.

For instance, if we want to understand the role of an exposed port in a Dockerfile, we should include both the entire file contents and the specific line to get a more accurate explanation, as demonstrated in the following prompt:

```
CONTEXT: you are provided with:
1. A Dockerfile enclosed with {{{ DOCKERFILE }}}
2. A line from the file enclosed with {{{ LINE }}}.
TASK: Explain the purpose of the line.
DOCKERFILE: {{{ ...omitted for brevity... }}}
LINE: {{{EXPOSE 5000}}}
EXPLANATION:
```

This prompt effectively identifies the function of the line in the Dockerfile, as shown in *Figure 7.9*:

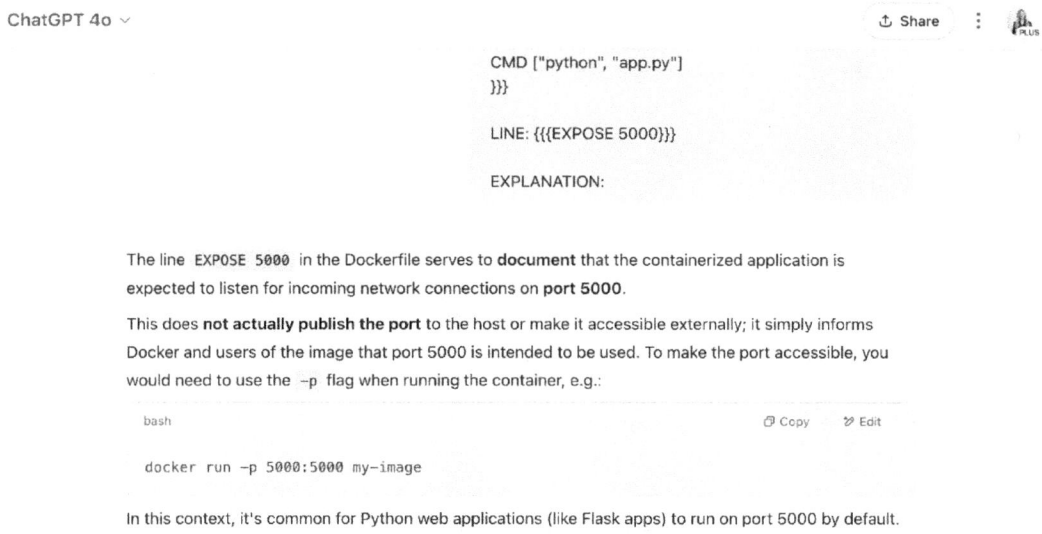

ChatGPT 4o ∨   ⬆ Share   ⋮   🧍

CMD ["python", "app.py"]
}}}

LINE: {{{EXPOSE 5000}}}

EXPLANATION:

The line `EXPOSE 5000` in the Dockerfile serves to **document** that the containerized application is expected to listen for incoming network connections on **port 5000**.

This does **not actually publish the port** to the host or make it accessible externally; it simply informs Docker and users of the image that port 5000 is intended to be used. To make the port accessible, you would need to use the `-p` flag when running the container, e.g.:

```bash
docker run -p 5000:5000 my-image
```

In this context, it's common for Python web applications (like Flask apps) to run on port 5000 by default.

Figure 7.9: Expose 5000 line explanation in ChatGPT

In general, when using ChatGPT to explain a line of code or a line from a non-project file, it is helpful to include a broader context than just the target line. For example, when explaining a method within a class, include the entire class definition. If a function uses a custom argument type, include the definition of that type as well. This leads to more precise and useful explanations. Later in the chapter, we will introduce debugging strategies for complex scenarios where a simple textual explanation does not provide sufficient insight into the purpose of a code block.

Next, we will explore how to use a similar approach when working with OpenAI API.

Explaining non-project files with OpenAI API

Similar to ChatGPT, we can use OpenAI API to explain specific lines from non-project files. Let us revisit the `Dockerfile` example and apply a comparable system prompt:

```
SURROUND = """you are provided with:
1. A Dockerfile enclosed with {{{ DOCKERFILE }}}
2. A line from the file enclosed with {{{ LINE }}}."""
SINGLE_TASK = "Your task is to explain the purpose of the line."
```

Unlike earlier examples where we passed a function's source code to OpenAI API, this time we want to send the entire `Dockerfile` content. We can do this by using Python's built-in open function inside the get_user_prompt function:

```
def get_user_prompt(path: str, line: str) -> str:
    with open(path, 'r') as file:
        dockerfile_content = file.read()

    return f"""
DOCKERFILE: {{{{{{ {dockerfile_content} }}}}}}
LINE: {{{{{{ {line} }}}}}}
EXPLANATION:
"""
```

We can then call OpenAI API using the following code:

```
if __name__ == "__main__":
    client: OpenAI = OpenAI()

    system_prompt = f"{SURROUND} {SINGLE_TASK}"
    user_prompt = get_user_prompt(
'../../ch7/Dockerfile', 'EXPOSE 5000')

    completion: ChatCompletion = client.chat.completions.create(
        model="gpt-4o-mini",
        messages=[
            {"role": "system", "content": system_prompt},
            {"role": "user", "content": user_prompt},
```

```
        ],
    )
    print("Explanation:", completion.choices[0].message.content)
```

For reference, running this script produced the expected result, identifying the line's purpose as specifying the port to be exposed. Here is an example output:

```
Explanation: The line `EXPOSE 5000` in the Dockerfile serves to inform
Docker that the application running inside the container will be listening
for incoming network connections on port 5000.
When a container is created from this Docker image, port 5000 will be
exposed for external communications, making it possible for users or other
applications to connect to the service provided by the application running
in the container. However, it is important to note that this command does
not actually publish the port; to make the port accessible from outside
the Docker environment, the user must explicitly map it to a port on the
host machine when running the container, typically using the `-p` option
with the `docker run` command.
In summary, `EXPOSE 5000` is a documentation feature that indicates the
intended service port and enhances the understandability of the Docker
container's purpose.
```

To conclude, both ChatGPT and OpenAI API can deliver accurate results even when using smaller models such as *GPT-4o*, if we supply the necessary context, including the filename and extension if it exists, its contents, and the specific line we want explained.

GitHub Copilot is best suited for quick, informal explanations. For more control over the prompt and instructions, ChatGPT is a better fit. When a programmatic solution is required, OpenAI API becomes the preferred choice.

Next, we will explore how to harness the power of GenAI to handle more advanced cases where a simple explanation is not enough, and interaction with the object is required for deeper understanding.

Creating calls with example parameters

As our Python objects or non-project files become more complex, a straightforward explanation might not be enough to help us understand the code in front of us. This is especially true when the Python object is part of a class, lacks type hints in its signature, contains no docstring, and strays from best practices.

Take, for instance, the private method _constructor_from_mgr in the widely used pandas
DataFrame class. This method constructs a DataFrame from a set of data blocks and their associated axes. For your reference, here is the source code, which lacks argument type hints, a
docstring, or any reference to tests:

```python
def _constructor_from_mgr(self, mgr, axes) -> DataFrame:
    df = DataFrame._from_mgr(mgr, axes=axes)

    if type(self) is DataFrame:
        # This would also work `if self._constructor is DataFrame`, but
        #  this check is slightly faster, benefiting the most-common case.
        return df

    elif type(self).__name__ == "GeoDataFrame":
        # Shim until geopandas can override their _constructor_from_mgr
        #  bc they have different behavior for Managers than for
DataFrames
        return self._constructor(mgr)

    # We assume that the subclass __init__ knows how to handle a
    #  pd.DataFrame object.
    return self._constructor(df)
```

One issue here is the naming of the first argument. Although it is called manager, a name typically
associated with the _mgr property of a DataFrame, it refers to a block of data, which is essentially
the cell content without axis labels. This misleading name, combined with the absence of type
hints, a docstring, or proper testing, makes the code block hard to understand for both humans
and GenAI applications.

For reference, here is the explanation output from Copilot when prompting /explain from a
PyCharm inline chat:

```
The _constructor_from_mgr method is a helper function in the DataFrame
class. It is used to create a new DataFrame instance from a given
BlockManager (or ArrayManager) and its associated axes.
Key Points:
1. Parameters:
```

```
mgr: The BlockManager or ArrayManager that holds the actual data for the
DataFrame.
axes: The axes (index and columns) for the new DataFrame.
2. Return Value:
It returns a new DataFrame object constructed from the provided manager
and axes.
Example Snippet:
def _constructor_from_mgr(self, mgr, axes) -> DataFrame:
    df = DataFrame._from_mgr(mgr, axes=axes)


Here, _from_mgr is a class method that initializes a DataFrame from the
given manager and axes. This method ensures that the new DataFrame is
properly aligned with the provided data structure.
```

This output includes all the elements we are looking for, such as arguments, the return value, and some level of data transformation. However, deciphering the explanation can be just as challenging as deciphering the code itself. We propose a better approach by debugging the code using the generated content.

Debugging with GitHub Copilot

Copilot is built for code generation, which makes it useful for interacting with our Python code. If we take the get_manhattan_distance function as an example, prompting Copilot with a partial call to the function can result in a completion that includes example arguments.

We can do this by writing the function call directly:

```
get_manhattan_distance(
```

Or, we can do it by assigning the result to a variable with a matching type hint for the function's return value:

```
d: float = get_manhattan_distance(
```

In both cases, Copilot is expected to generate two `DataFrame` arguments for the function. An example of this kind of completion in PyCharm is shown in *Figure 7.10*:

```
4
5      def get_manhattan_distance(  7 usages   ⊥ Hila Paz Herszfang
6              df1: pd.DataFrame,
7              df2: pd.DataFrame,
8      ) -> np.float64:
9          element_wise_dist: pd.DataFrame = (df1 - df2).abs()
10         dist: float = element_wise_dist.sum().sum().astype(float)
11         return dist
12
13
14     distance = get_manhattan_distance(
15         df1=pd.DataFrame([[1, 2], [3, 4]]),
           df2=pd.DataFrame([[5, 6], [7, 8]]),
16     )
17
```

Figure 7.10: Sample call completed by GitHub Copilot

Keep in mind that if your IDE automatically inserts a closing bracket,), after you type the opening one, (, you may need to press *Enter* to activate Copilot's suggestion.

This generated completion can serve as an entry point for interacting with the function through the debugger. In PyCharm, we can initiate debug mode by right-clicking the filename and selecting **Debug**, as illustrated in *Figure 7.11*:

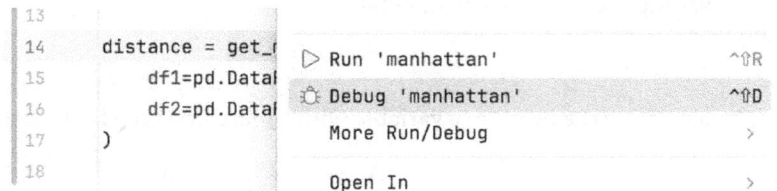

```
13
14     distance = get_       ▷ Run 'manhattan'           ^⇧R
15         df1=pd.Datal
16         df2=pd.Datal      ⚙ Debug 'manhattan'         ^⇧D
17     )
                             More Run/Debug                 >
18
                             Open In                        >
```

Figure 7.11: Debug mode in PyCharm

In VS Code, debugging is done by clicking the **play** icon in the top-right corner and selecting **Python Debugger: Debug Python File**, as shown in *Figure 7.12*:

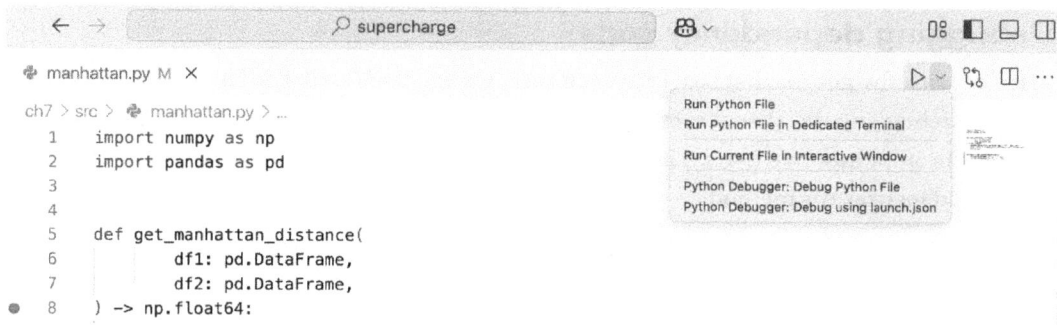

Figure 7.12: Running the Debugger in VS Code

Running the file in debug mode allows us to step through the code line by line, offering a clearer under-standing of its internal workings. For example, when using PyCharm's debugger, we can inspect the variables within the function and follow the data transformation as it happens, as seen in *Figure 7.13*:

Figure 7.13: Debug mode in PyCharm showing internal function arguments

This gives us visibility into the intermediate values within `get_manhattan_distance`.

The authors frequently rely on debugging to interact with the code they read and write. This hands-on approach supports faster development of intended functionality and offers deeper insights into complex code logic. This far exceeds reading source code, using GenAI explanations, or consulting docstrings.

Next, we will explore how generating sample calls can help us better understand complex code blocks, such as the `_constructor_from_mgr` method in the pandas `DataFrame` class.

Debugging dependency code

Just like with the `get_manhattan_distance` case, we can use Copilot to help generate sample code for debugging the `_constructor_from_mgr` method. Since this is a class method, we will split our prompt into two parts. The first prompt generates a sample instance of the class, and the second invokes the method.

We will begin by asking Copilot to complete a `DataFrame` instance. A sample prompt may look like this:

```
coordinates_a : pd.DataFrame =
```

This prompt offers sufficient context for Copilot to suggest an assignment. As shown in *Figure 7.14*, Copilot begins by proposing an initial completion for a `pd.DataFrame`.

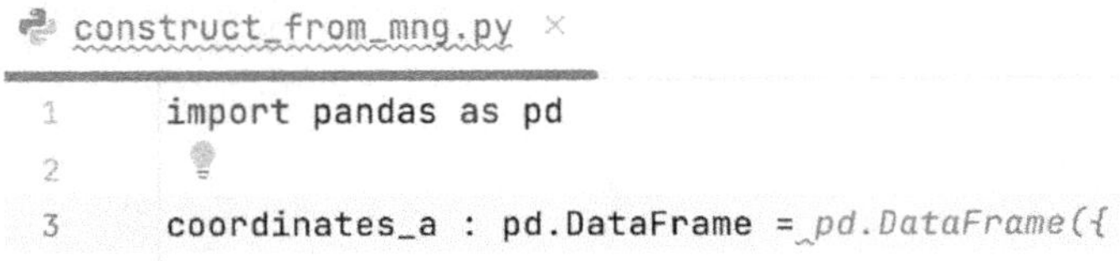

```
construct_from_mng.py  ×

1     import pandas as pd
2
3     coordinates_a : pd.DataFrame = pd.DataFrame({
```

Figure 7.14: Initial completion in PyCharm

When we accept the suggestion, Copilot typically proposes sample data that fits the DataFrame's name, as illustrated in *Figure 7.15*:

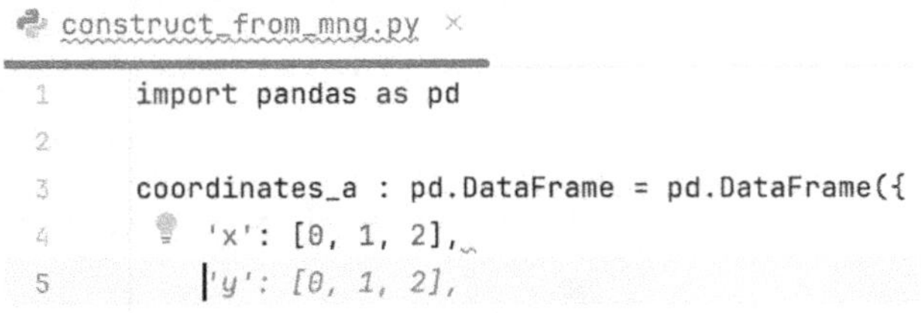

```
construct_from_mng.py  ×

1     import pandas as pd
2
3     coordinates_a : pd.DataFrame = pd.DataFrame({
4         'x': [0, 1, 2],
5         'y': [0, 1, 2],
```

Figure 7.15: Chained completion in PyCharm

At this point, we can either trigger additional columns by accepting chained suggestions or type `}` to flag to Copilot that we do not want any additional columns. We then move on to the method call with the following prompt:

```
coordinates_a._constructor_from_mgr(
```

Note that your IDE may automatically complete the closing bracket, `)`. In that case, press *Enter* between the brackets to let Copilot generate a completion suggestion.

For example, in *Figure 7.16*, Copilot proposes using the coordinates_a._mgr and coordinates_a. axes properties as the calling parameters.

```
 3    coordinates_a : pd.DataFrame = pd.DataFrame({
 4          "x": [0, 1, 2],
 5          "y": [0, 1, 2],
 6          "z": [0, 1, 2]
 7    })
 8
 9    coordinates_a._constructor_from_mgr(
10        coordinates_a._mgr,
          coordinates_a.axes,
      )
11
```

Figure 7.16: Parameter completion

With the two proposed parameters, we can debug the method as shown in *Figure 7.17* and gain a better understanding of its behavior.

```
construct_from_mng.py        frame.py ×
511      class DataFrame(NDFrame, OpsMixin):
660
661          def _constructor_from_mgr(self, mgr, axes) -> DataFrame:    axes: [RangeIndex(start=0, stop=3, step=1), Index(['x', 'y', 'z'],
●                df = DataFrame._from_mgr(mgr, axes=axes)
663      |
664          if type(self) is DataFrame:
665              # This would also work `if self._constructor is DataFrame`, but
666              #  this check is slightly faster, benefiting the most-common case.
667              return df
668
669          elif type(self).__name__ == "GeoDataFrame":
670              # Shim until geopandas can override their _constructor_from_mgr
671              #  bc they have different behavior for Managers than for DataFrames
672              return self._constructor(mgr)
```

Figure 7.17: Debugging _constructor_from_mgr using Copilot's suggestion

To conclude, Copilot can supercharge the process of debugging sections of the code base, allowing us to better understand both simple and complex implementations. We rely heavily on debugging as a daily practice to deepen their understanding of the code they interact with.

Next, we will explore how ChatGPT and OpenAI API offer distinct characteristics that we can utilize.

Customizing call parameters with ChatGPT and OpenAI

GitHub Copilot is generally better suited for quickly generating debugging calls to trigger Python objects, as it can access relevant context, such as the class code, when we are working with a method. For cases where we want specific characteristics of the sample parameters, prompting ChatGPT and OpenAI may be more suitable.

For example, to generate suitable arguments for debugging the get_manhattan_distance function, we might want five rows and three columns, and can use the following prompt:

```
CONTEXT: you are provided with:
1. A Python function enclosed with {{{ FUNCTION }}}
2. Arguments requirements enclosed with {{ REQUIREMENTS }}}.
TASK: Call the function with the data requirements
FUNCTION: {{{ ... omitted for brevity ... }}}
REQUIREMENTS: {{{
1. 5 rows
2. 3 columns
3. floats and integers in cells
}}}
CALL:
```

For reference, the output is shown in *Figure 7.18*:

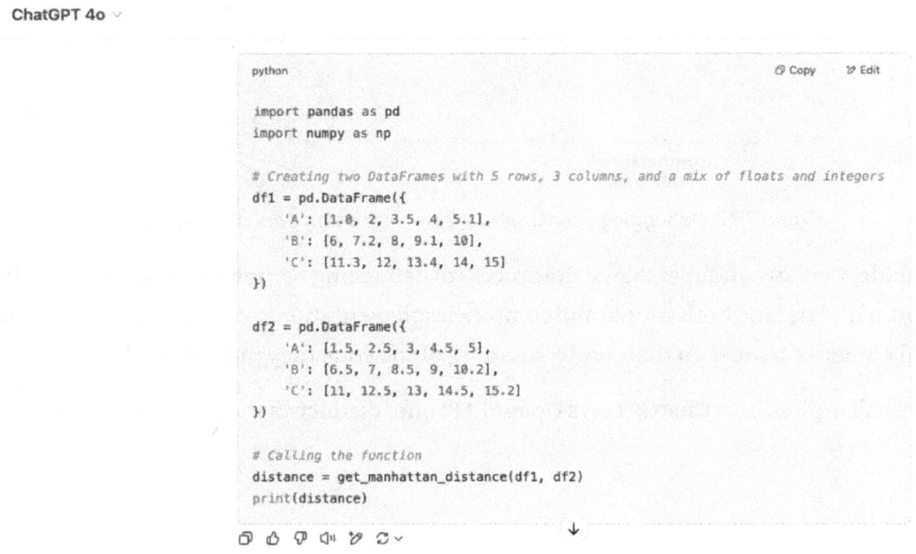

```python
import pandas as pd
import numpy as np

# Creating two DataFrames with 5 rows, 3 columns, and a mix of floats and integers
df1 = pd.DataFrame({
    'A': [1.0, 2, 3.5, 4, 5.1],
    'B': [6, 7.2, 8, 9.1, 10],
    'C': [11.3, 12, 13.4, 14, 15]
})

df2 = pd.DataFrame({
    'A': [1.5, 2.5, 3, 4.5, 5],
    'B': [6.5, 7, 8.5, 9, 10.2],
    'C': [11, 12.5, 13, 14.5, 15.2]
})

# Calling the function
distance = get_manhattan_distance(df1, df2)
print(distance)
```

Figure 7.18: Call parameters for get_manhattan_distance

In this example, both DataFrames, df1 and df2, have the same shape of five rows and three columns, which makes them appropriate arguments for the function call.

The OpenAI API call is similar, and you can find the full script at `ch7/prompts/openai_debug.py` for later reference.

To conclude, we turn to ChatGPT and OpenAI API when our data requirements are beyond trivial for a quick completion that Copilot might otherwise handle well. Later in the book, we will explore how to build on these data generation methods to create a robust test suite.

Debugging dependency code

When using ChatGPT or OpenAI API to generate test code for a dependency package, it is important to provide enough context for the model to produce a desirable call. The amount of context required depends on how widely the library is used. For standard packages such as *pandas*, including just the relevant method may be enough. For custom or private repository classes, it is usually best to include the entire class definition.

For example, the DataFrame class in pandas is about 12,000 lines long, which is too much to include in a prompt. However, because pandas is highly popular, we can provide only the_constructor_from_mgr method and still receive a relevant response.

Below is a sample prompt used with ChatGPT to generate a call to the _constructor_from_mgr method:

```
CONTEXT: Given Pandas DataFrame 2.2.3 class, you are provided with:
1. Pandas DataFrame method to be called enclosed with {{{ FUNCTION }}}
2. Arguments requirements enclosed with {{ REQUIREMENTS }}}.
TASK: Generate a method call with sample parameters that meet the data
requirements.
FUNCTION: {{{ ... omitted for brevity ... }}}
REQUIREMENTS: {{{
1. 5 rows
2. 3 columns
3. floats and integers in cells
}}}
CALL:
```

Figure 7.19 shows an example output from *GPT-4o* in response to this prompt.

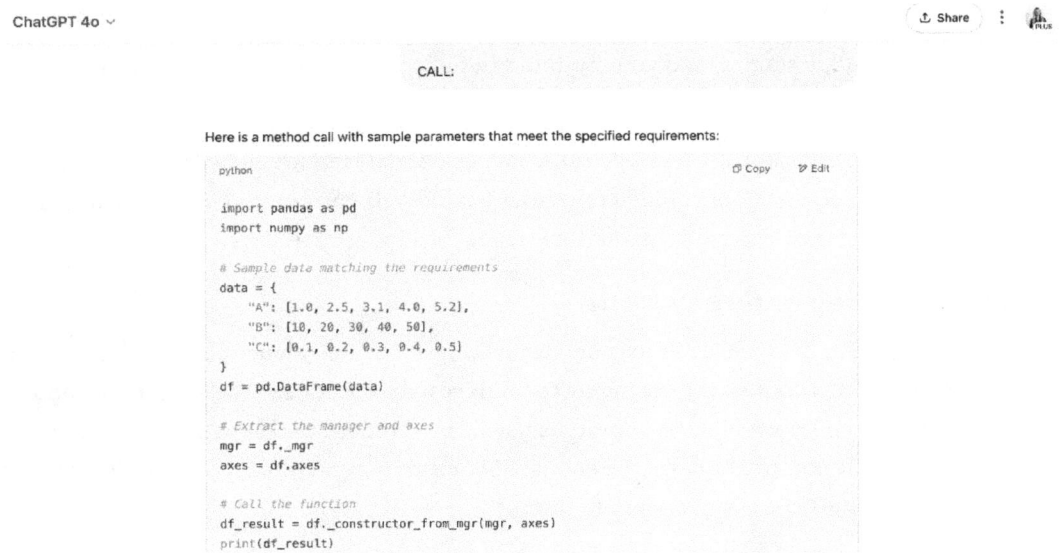

ChatGPT 4o ⌄   ⬆ Share   ⋮   🎈

CALL:

Here is a method call with sample parameters that meet the specified requirements:

```python
import pandas as pd
import numpy as np

# Sample data matching the requirements
data = {
    "A": [1.0, 2.5, 3.1, 4.0, 5.2],
    "B": [10, 20, 30, 40, 50],
    "C": [0.1, 0.2, 0.3, 0.4, 0.5]
}
df = pd.DataFrame(data)

# Extract the manager and axes
mgr = df._mgr
axes = df.axes

# Call the function
df_result = df._constructor_from_mgr(mgr, axes)
print(df_result)
```

Figure 7.19: Sample test call to _constructor_from_mgr

Here, ChatGPT successfully generated a method call using df._mgr and df.axes, producing a DataFrame with the required dimensions.

Since OpenAI API follows a similar pattern, we have provided the full script in ch7/prompts/ openai_debug_pandas.py for reference.

In later chapters, we will build on this approach to supercharge the generation of robust test suites.

Putting it all together

Now that we have reviewed different approaches to shorter objects, explored tailored explanations for Python objects and non-project files, considered programmatic concerns, and looked at scenarios where a textual explanation is not sufficient, we can summarize everything in a pros and cons table for each of the tools:

GenAI app	Pros	Cons
GitHub Copilot	Provides quick responses with relevant context. It supports the use of /explain as is and allows us to add additional requirements.	Does not support tailored explanations, such as when we need to include edge cases for get_manhattan_distance.
ChatGPT	Enables tailored explanations and gives us flexibility to add or remove context.	Requires more effort to craft prompts.
OpenAI API	Suitable for programmatic solutions and automation.	Significantly more effort compared to GitHub Copilot and ChatGPT.

In our own work, we typically begin with Copilot when we need an explanation. As our requirements expand, we move to Copilot's chat window, ChatGPT, or OpenAI API. When dealing with more complex objects, we always recommend incorporating debugging into the reading process to better understand the code.

Summary

In this chapter, we expanded our focus beyond .py files and explored how GenAI can help us understand entire code bases. Using GitHub Copilot, we applied the /explain command in its plain form as well as with more tailored instructions to grasp the role of the get_manhattan_distance function. We also applied this command to understand non-project files such as requirements. txt and Dockerfile.

Next, we used ChatGPT to craft prompts that offered useful explanations about edge cases and argument types. We then moved on to OpenAI API to generate a script that programmatically provided multiple explanations with one call.

We concluded by generating sample values that are useful for interacting with our code through the debugger. This approach is especially helpful when dealing with more complex implementations.

In the next chapter, we will dive into prompt engineering techniques to improve the quality of our generated code. Through **few-shot learning**, also known as **in-context learning**, we will guide Copilot, ChatGPT, and OpenAI API to follow a specific style guide aligned with our production standards. We will also explore additional techniques to shape prompts for better outcomes.

Quiz time

Before you proceed to the next chapter, make sure that you can confidently answer the following questions:

Question 1: How can we address explanations of complex Python objects?

Answer: In cases where the object is relatively simple, we can utilize the GitHub Copilot `/explain` slash command to help us better grasp the arguments, data transformation, and return values. For more complex objects, we can use debugging by generating calls to the object with GitHub Copilot, ChatGPT, and OpenAI API.

Question 2: When asking ChatGPT to explain a single line in a Dockerfile, what context should be added?

Answer: It is recommended to include the full contents of the Dockerfile along with the filename and extension, and the specific line in question. This gives ChatGPT the context needed for a more accurate explanation.

Further reading

To learn more about the topics that were covered in this chapter, look at the following resources:

- Dockerfile, Wikipedia: `https://realpython.com/primer-on-python-decorators/`
- PyCharm debugging: `https://www.jetbrains.com/help/pycharm/part-1-debugging-python-code.html#step`
- VS Code debugging: `https://code.visualstudio.com/docs/python/debugging`

Unlock this book's exclusive benefits now

Scan this QR code or go to `packtpub.com/unlock`, then search for this book by name.

Note: Keep your purchase invoice ready before you start.

8

An Introduction to Prompt Engineering

In this chapter, we will introduce the practice of **prompt engineering**, a field of study that started in 2020, which offers advanced techniques for refining prompts to achieve more reliable, predictable, and desirable outcomes in **large language model (LLM)**-based applications.

We will focus on an effective prompt engineering technique for code generation with GenAI: few-shot learning, also known as in-context learning. This approach, when used in the context of code-related tasks, guides the model toward producing outputs that align with a specific coding style or objective.

We will focus on how the few-shot learning technique can enhance the model's output for more accurate and style-consistent code generation. While there are many different uses of few-shot learning in code-related tasks, the focus on style is a useful example for maintaining consistency in a repository. This includes enforcing type hints, adding docstrings, or following a specific logging convention. By aligning the generated code with the required style guide, we can reduce the need for manual customization and accept the GenAI output as-is.

In this chapter, we will cover the following topics:

- Utilizing prompt engineering for coding
- Enhancing prompts with few-shot examples
- Leveraging few-shot learning with ChatGPT

- Working with few-shot learning for OpenAI API
- Crafting a style guide for GitHub Copilot
- Introducing more prompt engineering techniques

Technical requirements

To get the most out of this chapter, ensure you have the following:

- GitHub Copilot account
- IDE – either VS Code or PyCharm
- OpenAI account with access to OpenAI API
- Access to the book's repository, which includes the prompt samples and style guides featured in this chapter, available at `https://github.com/PacktPublishing/Supercharged-Coding-with-Gen-AI`
- Virtual environment set up in VS Code or PyCharm
- OpenAI API token

For assistance setting up a GitHub Copilot account, refer to *Chapter 3*. For instructions on setting up OpenAI API access and token generation, see *Chapter 2*. If you need help creating an OpenAI account or setting up a virtual environment in your IDE, refer to the *Appendix* for detailed guidance.

Utilizing prompt engineering for coding

In *Chapter 4*, we explored the three pillars of achieving quality output: **model mastery**, **evaluation metrics**, and **precise prompts**. We also discussed how following the five S's best practices for prompts (structured, surrounded, single-tasked, specific, and short) can significantly enhance the quality of model output. Using OpenAI's example of an effective prompt, we demonstrated how aligning with these principles, such as focusing exclusively on error fixes and providing a clear list of issues to address, could improve results.

As tasks grow more complex, advanced techniques are essential to guide models toward achieving desired outcomes. LLMs may need additional instructions to adhere to a specific style guide, pass a unit test suite, or fix reproducibility issues.

Since the advent of LLMs in 2020, prompt engineering has developed into a practice that refines and structures prompts to achieve better results and address more complex scenarios. There are now many strategies that guide the model toward more desirable outcomes, including the following:

- Structuring prompts in a way that aligns with LLM capabilities
- Providing additional context to clarify the problem
- Including specific guidelines for the desired output
- Guiding the model through a reasoning process
- Defining constraints and boundaries for the expected output
- Providing external feedback to iteratively refine results

In coding-related tasks, prompt engineering is valuable for a variety of applications including creating style guides for code refactoring, breaking down complex challenges into manageable steps, and generating production-standard code. We will explore in depth a range of prompt engineering techniques designed to supercharge various stages of the **software development life cycle (SDLC)** throughout this book.

Next, we will take an in-depth look at the few-shot learning technique, which incorporates specific guidelines for desired outputs, and examine its impact on shaping the coding style of the model's suggestions. Later in the chapter, we will preview other prompt engineering techniques that will be explored in detail in later chapters.

Enhancing prompts with few-shot examples

Few-shot learning, also known as **in-context learning**, is a prompt engineering technique where we include a few examples of desirable outputs directly within the prompt. This method can be extended to incorporate examples of incorrect output or edge cases, enabling the model to differentiate between what constitutes a good result and what does not. By analyzing these patterns, the model can infer how to structure an optimal response for the given task.

To delve deeper into the research behind this approach, refer to *Language Models are Few-Shot Learners* by Brown et al. (https://arxiv.org/abs/2005.14165v4).

Few-shot learning research demonstrates how, with a few examples (or **shots**) of input-output pairs, a model can infer patterns from the relationships between these examples and complete tasks in a style consistent with the provided samples. For instance, the following prompt, taken from the study, illustrates the predictability and consistency of an LLM when solving arithmetic problems. Utilizing few-shot prompting increases the predictability of the output, as the model is likely to generate responses that align with the style of the provided few-shot examples as shown here:

```
Instruction: Solve the following arithmetic problems.
Examples:
Problem: What is 5 + 3?
Answer: 8
Problem: What is 12 - 4?
Answer: 8
Problem: What is 7 × 6?
Answer: 42
Problem: What is 15 ÷ 3?
Answer:
```

The model's output was as follows:

```
5
```

Compared to prompts that only specify the task (Solve the following arithmetic problem), this example-based approach reduces ambiguity. The model aligns its output more closely to the expected structure, providing only the number as the answer, without additional explanation or formatting inconsistencies.

Few-shot prompting is a useful technique for a variety of coding-related tasks, such as code re-factoring, code analysis, and code generation. By including specific examples in the prompt, we can guide the model to produce outputs that align with our desired patterns.

Few-shot learning for code refactoring

In a code refactoring scenario, we may want to transform print statements into structured logger messages, a common practice for maintaining production-level software. Replacing the variety of print statements across many files is both error-prone and tedious. However, we can use an LLM with a prompt with clear instructions and a few examples. For example, we can enrich a request to refactor the following print message:

```
print('Error! File not found: passwords.txt')
```

We can refactor it to a log message, with a few examples:

```
Old: print('Process started for config.txt')
Refactored: logger.info('Processing started', extra={'stage': 'start',
file: 'config.txt'})

Old: print('Warning! Could not load user data from user_info.csv')
Refactored: logger.warning('User data failed to load', extra={'module':
'user_loader', 'status': 'failure', file: 'user_info.csv'})

Old: print('Error! File not found: passwords.txt')
Refactored:
```

> 💡 **Quick tip**: Enhance your coding experience with the **AI Code Explainer** and **Quick Copy** features. Open this book in the next-gen Packt Reader. Click the **Copy** button
>
> **(1)** to quickly copy code into your coding environment, or click the **Explain** button
>
> **(2)** to get the AI assistant to explain a block of code to you.

```
                                                    Copy      Explain
function calculate(a, b) {                           1          2
  return {sum: a + b};
};
```

📖 **The next-gen Packt Reader** is included for free with the purchase of this book. Scan the QR code OR visit packtpub.com/unlock, then use the search bar to find this book by name. Double-check the edition shown to make sure you get the right one.

The examples in this prompt highlight the distinctions between different logging levels with examples of transforming `print` messages into `info` and `warning` logging messages. The examples also demonstrate static log messages with additional information provided through the `extra` parameter.

Next, we will see how enhancing our prompt with few-shot examples improves the output we get from ChatGPT.

Leveraging few-shot prompting with ChatGPT

When using ChatGPT, if applying the **five S's framework** from *Chapter 4* does not produce the desired results, we can enhance our prompts with a few-shot approach. In this case, we will still follow the five S's framework but incorporate **indexed variables** that represent a series of inputs and outputs for the task.

Few-shot structure

A typical approach to implement few-shot prompting in ChatGPT is by extending the five S's framework to include indexed variables such as {{{ Input_i }}} and {{{ Output_i }}}. This implies that the context references these variables, for example:

```
CONTEXT: You are provided with:
1. Python snippet enclosed with {{{ OLD }}}
2. Examples enclosed with {{{ OLD_i }}} followed by a desirable output
enclosed with {{{ REFACTORED_i }}}
```

We then supply the `OLD_i` and `REFACTORED_i` examples, followed by {{{ OLD }}}, as such:

```
OLD_1: {{{ }}}
REFACTORED_1: {{{ }}}
OLD_2: {{{ }}}
REFACTORED_2: {{{ }}}
...
OLD: {{{ }}}
```

Overall, a ChatGPT prompt that uses few-shot examples can be structured in this way:

```
CONTEXT: You are provided with:
1. ...
2. Examples enclosed with {{{ Input_i }}} followed by a desirable output
```

```
enclosed with {{{ Output_i }}}
TASK: ...
Input_1: {{{ ... }}}
Output_1: {{{ ... }}}
Input_2: {{{ ... }}}
Output_2: {{{ ... }}}
...
Input: {{{ }}}
CUE:
```

The labels for inputs and outputs should reflect their relationship and remain consistent across examples. For example, when solving arithmetic problems, question and answer are appropriate labels. When transforming print statements to log messages or performing other refactoring tasks, old and refactored make more sense.

Improvement in output with code refactoring

Let us examine a case where we want to refactor print statements into structured logging. This involves using appropriate logging levels, enforcing static messages, and including extra parameters.

To observe the default behavior without applying a few-shot approach, we can navigate to https://chatgpt.com/, start a new conversation with the *GPT-o3-mini-high* model, and prompt it to refactor a print statement into a log message using the following:

```
CONTEXT: You are provided with a Python snippet enclosed with {{{ OLD }}}.
TASK: Refactor the snippet to a log message.

OLD: {{{ print('Error! File not found: passwords.txt') }}}

REFACTORED:
```

The *GPT-o3-mini-high* model excels at coding tasks and is likely to generate a log message with an error level. However, without explicit instructions on structuring the log message, it may not use a logger instance nor distinguish the static log message from additional details such as the filename, as shown in *Figure 8.1*:

ChatGPT o3-mini-high ⌄   ⬆ Share

> TASK: Refactor the snippet to a log message.
>
> OLD: {{{ print('Error! File not found: passwords.txt') }}}
>
> REFACTORED:

Reasoned about log message refactoring for 5 seconds >

```python
import logging

logging.error("File not found: passwords.txt")
```
⎘ Copy

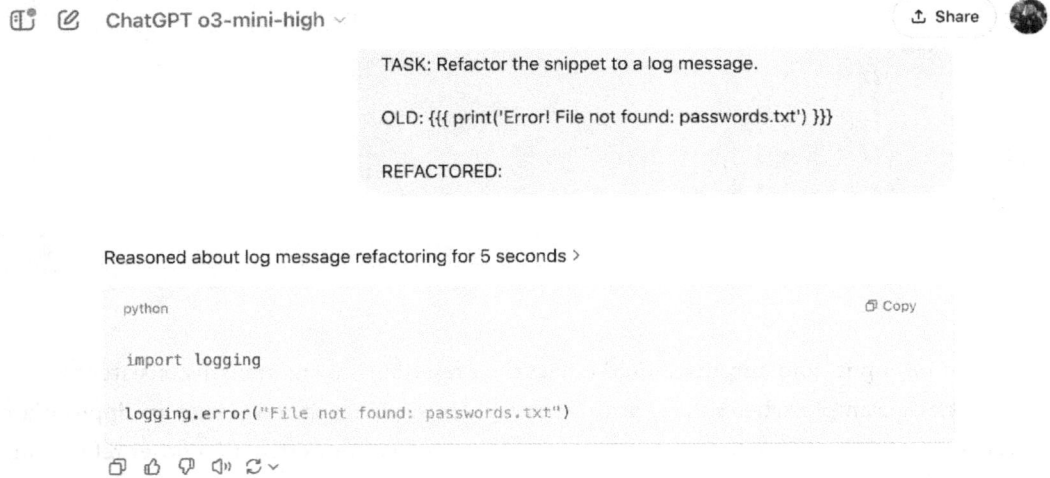

Figure 8.1: Working with Canvas in ChatGPT

We can improve the model's output by providing few-shot examples demonstrating how to extract key details from a `print` statement and use a logger instance. For example, we can refactor a `print` message to include a filename and verbosity setting:

```
print('Process started for config.txt with verbose=True')
```

We can refactor it into a structured log message:

```
logger.info('Processing started', extra={'verbose': True, file: 'config.
txt'})
```

This example highlights the extraction of essential details to improve logging clarity. Similarly, we can add another example with `print` statements containing user and file path information:

```
print('Warning! Could not load user U-232 data from user_info.csv')
```

We can refactor it into the following structured log message:

```
logger.warning('User data failed to load', extra={'user': 'U-232', 'file':
'user_info.csv'})
```

A complete prompt with these few-shot examples might be structured as follows:

```
CONTEXT: You are provided with:
1. Python snippet enclosed with {{{ OLD }}}
2. Examples enclosed with {{{ OLD_i }}} followed by a desirable output
enclosed with {{{ REFACTORED_i }}}
```

```
TASK: Refactor the snippet to a log message.
OLD_1: {{{ print('Process started for config.txt with verbose=True') }}}
REFACTORED_1: {{{ logger.info('Processing started', extra={'verbose':
True, file: 'config.txt'}) }}}
OLD_2: {{{ print('Warning! Could not load user U-232 data from user_info.
csv') }}}
REFACTORED_2: {{{ logger.warning('User data failed to load',
extra={'user': 'U-232', 'file': 'user_info.csv'}) }}}
OLD: {{{ print('Error! File not found: passwords.txt') }}}
REFACTORED:
```

Providing these two examples as guidance for the model will capture the desired output, as illustrated in *Figure 8.2*:

Figure 8.2: Improved logging suggestion

This time, the model successfully extracted the parameters from the static log message and used the logger instance instead of a direct logging message, following the patterns demonstrated in the few-shot examples. We will revisit logging practices in greater detail in *Chapter 15*, so stay tuned.

Next, we will explore how adopting a Python-formatted **style guide** with Copilot can go beyond traditional linting and code formatting tools. This few-shot approach is proactive, adaptable, and context-aware, enabling Copilot to predict our intended implementation easily.

Crafting a style guide for GitHub Copilot

GitHub Copilot functions as a personalized AI assistant, predicting our next coding moves. Because LLMs excel at imitating style, Copilot quickly adapts to any style preferences it observes during a session.

For example, suppose we have a file named ch8/code_samples/math_calculations.py with two functions (get_area and get_arithmetic_mean), both implemented without type hints and with single-line function signatures:

```
import numpy as np


def get_area(radius):
    return np.pi * radius ** 2


def get_arithmetic_mean(x1, x2):
    return (x1 + x2) / 2
```

If we then start typing a new function signature for get_euclidean_distance, Copilot is likely to generate an implementation in the same style, with no type hints and one-line signatures, as shown in *Figure 8.3*:

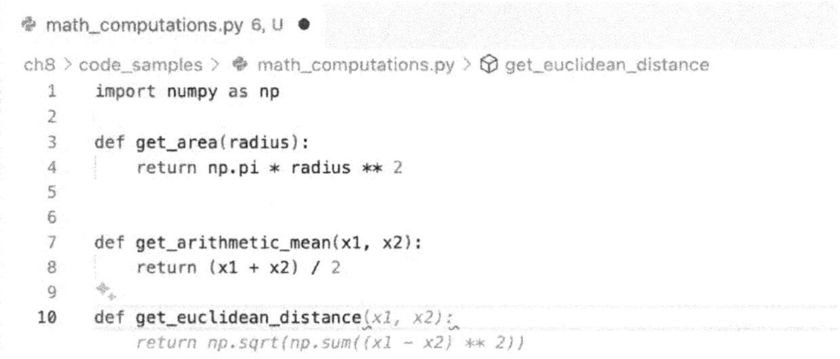

```
math_computations.py 6, U ●

ch8 > code_samples > math_computations.py > get_euclidean_distance
1    import numpy as np
2
3    def get_area(radius):
4        return np.pi * radius ** 2
5
6
7    def get_arithmetic_mean(x1, x2):
8        return (x1 + x2) / 2
9
10   def get_euclidean_distance(x1, x2):
         return np.sqrt(np.sum((x1 - x2) ** 2))
```

Figure 8.3: Copilot preserving our coding style

Alternatively, if our code implements type hints, hanging indents, and docstrings, Copilot will generate suggestions that reflect this updated style. For example, here is an alternate implementation of get_area and get_arithmetic_mean:

```
import numpy as np
def get_area(
        radius: float,
```

```
    ) -> float:
    """

    Compute the area of a circle given its radius.
    """

    area: float = np.pi * radius ** 2
    return area
def get_arithmetic_mean(
        x1: float,
        x2: float,
        ) -> float:
    """

    Compute the arithmetic mean of two numbers.
    """

    arithmetic_mean: float = (x1 + x2) / 2
    return arithmetic_mean
```

Based on this coding preference, *Figure 8.4* shows the suggested implementation of get_euclidean_distance reflecting the new coding style:

```
math_computations.py 1, U  ●

ch8 > code_samples > math_computations.py > get_eucleadian_distance
 3    def get_area(
 6        """
 7        Compute the area of a circle given its radius.
 8        """
 9        area: float = np.pi * radius ** 2
10        return area
11
12
13    def get_arithmetic_mean(
14            x1: float,
15            x2: float,
16            ) -> float:
17        """
18        Compute the arithmetic mean of two numbers.
19        """
20        arithmetic_mean: float = (x1 + x2) / 2
21        return arithmetic_mean
22
23
24    def get_eucleadian_distance(
            x1: float,
            y1: float,
            x2: float,
            y2: float,
            ) -> float:
        """
        Compute the Euclidean distance between two points.
        """
        eucleadian_distance: float = np.sqrt((x2 - x1) ** 2 + (y2 - y1) ** 2)
        return eucleadian_distance
25
```

Figure 8.4: Copilot's adapted coding style

As developers, we would like a more robust method for informing Copilot of our preferred style guidelines without having to repeat them every session. We can achieve this by using a few-shot learning approach: creating a dedicated style guide file, as we will see next.

Style guide file

A simple way to include our preferred style guide in Copilot is to maintain a single file outside the main project folder that we can copy and paste in place when we start a new Copilot session. Copying and pasting this file's content makes our coding style part of the active session, although we hope that future versions of Copilot will introduce a more convenient method. For example, a sample file located at ch8/code_samples/style_guide.py, shown in *Figure 8.5*, includes two functions: get_area and get_arithmetic_mean.

```python
style_guide.py M ✕

ch8 > code_samples > style_guide.py > ...
 1   import numpy as np
 2
 3   def get_area(
 4           radius: float,
 5           ) -> float:
 6       area: float = np.pi * radius ** 2
 7       return area
 8
 9
10   def get_arithmetic_mean(
11           x1: float,
12           x2: float,
13           ) -> float:
14       arithmetic_mean: float = (x1 + x2) / 2
15       return arithmetic_mean
16
```

Figure 8.5: Style guide

This file does not include a docstring, as adding one is considered a separate task from implementing the function. We will explore this topic in more detail in later chapters.

Next, if we open a new file at ch8/code_samples/distances.py and begin typing the signature of get_euclidean_distance, Copilot is likely to generate an implementation that aligns with that formatting, as shown in *Figure 8.6*:

```
⬧ style_guide.py M        ⬧ distances.py 1, U  ●

ch8 > code_samples >  ⬧ distances.py >  ⬡ get_eucleadian_distance
   1    def get_eucleadian_distance(
                    x1: float,
                    x2: float,
                    y1: float,
                    y2: float,
                    ) -> float:
               distance: float = ((x2 - x1) ** 2 + (y2 - y1) ** 2) ** 0.5
               return distance
```

Figure 8.6: Preserved coding style

Our coding preferences remain consistent in the new file, showing that Copilot has effectively captured our desired style. In later chapters, we will explore how adding more Python elements, such as decorators, to the style guide can further refine and expand our preferred coding approach.

Style guide as a next-generation code formatter

If you are used to code formatters or linters, you will notice that implementing a style guide may remind you of a code formatting initiative, but is more advanced. First, because the style guide approach is proactive rather than reactive, we get suggestions already formatted the way we want. Second, it offers more flexibility: we can adopt the *show, don't tell* method by simply demonstrating our preferred style to Copilot. Finally, we can go beyond traditional formatters by including preferences such as type hints, which are not always clear using older methods.

Next, we will explore how to apply few-shot learning with OpenAI, using this technique to re-factor code at scale.

Working with few-shot learning for OpenAI API

For large-scale tasks, such as generating code implementations from function signatures, we can use OpenAI API programmatically and apply few-shot learning to illustrate the desired outcome effectively. To do this, we provide indexed examples of input and output and reference these examples in the system prompt.

The system prompt should reference the indexed input and output examples as follows:

```
SURROUND = """You are provided with:
1. A [...] enclosed with {{{ INPUT }}}.
2. Example [...] enclosed with {{{ INPUT_i }}} followed by the
corresponding [...] enclosed with {{{ OUTPUT_i }}}."""
SINGLE_TASK = "Your task is to [...]."
system_prompt = f"{SURROUND} {SINGLE_TASK}"
```

Next, we update the `get_user_prompt` function to include the provided examples, ensuring that the labels align with those in the system prompt:

```
def get_user_prompt(some_input: str, few_shots: list) -> str:
    prompt = ""
    for i, (input_, output_) in enumerate(few_shots):
        prompt += f"""
INPUT_{i + 1}:  {{{{{{ {input_} }}}}}}
OUTPUT_{i + 1}:       {{{{{{ {output_} }}}}}}"""

    prompt += f"""
INPUT:         {{{{{{ {some_input} }}}}}}
OUTPUT:
"""
    return prompt
```

Similarly, we replace `INPUT_i` and `OUTPUT_i` with task-specific labels, such as `FUNCTION_i` and `CODE_i` for code completion tasks.

Implementing code with OpenAI API

In *Chapter 2*, we built a code completion program that generates a Python implementation based on a function signature. For example, when implementing `print_fibonacci_sequence`, we provided a prompt that requested only the function's implementation, without additional explanations or output samples.

A more effective approach is to include a few examples that demonstrate the desired output format. For instance, we can provide implementations for `get_area` and `get_arithmetic_mean`, both based solely on their function signatures:

```
INPUT_1 = """def get_area(radius: float) -> float:"""
```

```
OUTPUT_1 = """def get_area(radius: float) -> float:
    area: float = np.pi * radius ** 2
    return area"""


INPUT_2 = """def get_arithmetic_mean(x1: float, x2: float) -> float:"""


OUTPUT_2 = """def get_arithmetic_mean(x1: float, x2: float) -> float:
    arithmetic_mean: float = (x1 + x2) / 2
    return arithmetic_mean"""


FEW_SHOTS = [
    (INPUT_1, OUTPUT_1),
    (INPUT_2, OUTPUT_2),
]
```

With these examples, we can construct a system prompt and user prompt that encourage the model to generate only the function implementation without additional explanations. The system prompt would be structured as follows:

```
SURROUND = """You are provided with:
1. A Python function signature enclosed with {{{ FUNCTION }}}.
2. Example signatures enclosed with {{{ FUNCTION_i }}} followed by the
corresponding implementation enclosed with {{{ CODE_i }}}.
"""
SINGLE_TASK = "Your task is to implement the function."
```

Next, we define a function to generate the user prompt, ensuring consistency with the system prompt's structure:

```
def get_user_prompt(signature: str, few_shots: list) -> str:
    prompt = ""
    for i, (input_, output_) in enumerate(few_shots):
        prompt += f"""
    FUNCTION_{i + 1}:  {{{{{{ {input_} }}}}}}
    CODE_{i + 1}:      {{{{{{ {output_} }}}}}}"""

    prompt += f"""
    FUNCTION:         {{{{{{ {signature} }}}}}}
```

```
    CODE:
    """

    return prompt
```

For the implementation of `print_fibonacci_sequence`, we define the system and user prompts as follows:

```
system_prompt = f"{SURROUND} {SINGLE_TASK}"
user_prompt = get_user_prompt("def print_fibonacci_sequence(n: int) ->
None:", FEW_SHOTS)
```

Finally, we call the API with the following snippet:

```
client: OpenAI = OpenAI()

completion: openai.ChatCompletion = (
    client.chat.completions.create(
        model="gpt-4o-mini",
        messages=[
            {"role": "system", "content": system_prompt},
            {"role": "user", "content": user_prompt},
        ],
    ))
print(completion.choices[0].message.content)
```

By structuring the prompt this way, the model is more likely to follow the expected output format. Running the preceding example, which is available in `ch8/code_samples/openai_fibonacci.py`, we got the following function implementation:

```
def print_fibonacci_sequence(n: int) -> None:
    a, b = 0, 1
    for _ in range(n):
        print(a, end=' ')
        a, b = b, a + b
    print() # To add a newline after printing the sequence
```

This implementation aligns with our provided examples and does not include surrounding explanations.

Fine-tuning as a better approach to OpenAI API

When scaling projects, **fine-tuning** offers a more effective way to specialize a model for a specific task, such as generating code in a preferred style. This process involves training a pre-trained model such as *GPT-4o-mini* on a set of high-quality examples, allowing it to adjust its internal settings to better align with our preferences. We will explore this topic in greater detail in *Chapter 11*.

Having explored few-shot learning with ChatGPT, GitHub Copilot, and OpenAI API, we will now introduce additional prompt engineering techniques, which we will examine in greater detail in the upcoming and later chapters of the book.

Introducing more prompt engineering techniques

Variations of few-shot prompting can include edge cases, progressively complex examples, or contrastive examples that highlight both correct and incorrect outcomes. These variations on few-shot prompting enhance a model's ability to generalize across diverse task requirements. The examples in this chapter on type hinting and style formatting are just the tip of the iceberg of how prompt engineering can be used.

In other scenarios of the SDLC, we will see how using different prompt engineering techniques can become handy.

Bug fix at scale with prompt engineering

Refer to the OpenAI example of effective prompts for fixing buggy code, enhanced with the refinements discussed in *Chapter 4*:

```
CONTEXT: You will be provided with Python code in the Python editor with
description enclosed with {{{ DESCRIPTION }}}
that may contain errors enclosed with {{{ ERRORS }}}.
TASK: Fix the errors in the code.

DESCRIPTION: {{{ Execute 10 multiplication quizzes for the user and
validate the answer }}}
```

```
ERRORS: {{{
1. Compilation
2. Reproducibility of random number generation
3. Logical scoping of variable assignments
4. Error handling for input casting
}}}
```

While this prompt successfully identified all errors in the code, we cannot guarantee that GenAI applications will consistently capture all errors in different code snippets.

To improve results, we can explore techniques such as iterative prompting, where the output is verified for compilation and refined through model reiteration if needed. Template-based prompting can enforce a specific format for error descriptions, ensuring consistency and clarity in the output. Additionally, chain-of-thought prompting helps guide the model through a logical reasoning process, improving its ability to understand and fix code issues. Let's explore these in the next subsections.

Iterative prompting

Iterative prompting involves engaging the model repeatedly within a feedback loop that refines its output based on evaluations of previous responses. This feedback can be manual, such as asking ChatGPT to revise its response to address unidentified errors, or automated, such as compiling code generated by OpenAI API or running it against a suite of unit tests. The resulting feedback, whether a traceback error message or failed test results, can be reintroduced to the model, continuing the cycle until specific criteria are satisfied.

For instance, if the goal is to address compilation issues, an iterative mechanism could involve attempting to compile the output and feeding the traceback error messages back to the model for refinement if the code fails to compile:

```
for i in range(10):
    try:
        exec(user_code)
        print(f"successfully compiled:\n {user_code}")
        break
    except SyntaxError as se:
        user_code = get_refined_output(user_code, traceback.format_exc())
```

Here, we will repeatedly prompt the model with traceback messages from the suggested code until it successfully compiles. Alternatively, we could evaluate the code by running it against a test suite or using other evaluation mechanisms, which we will explore in later chapters of the book.

Template-based prompting

Template-based prompting involves providing specific guidelines for structuring the desired output. For instance, when fixing code, we may want to understand the type of error being addressed, such as whether it is a compilation error, a logical issue, or something else. In such cases, the output could follow this structure:

```
This code requires fix because of { ERROR TYPE}. The fixed code is { CODE
}.
```

To guide the model toward generating this output, we include hints about the template within the context and provide a structure like this:

```
CONTEXT: You will be provided with Python code enclosed with {{{ CODE }}}
that does not compile, and an error traceback enclosed with {{{ TRACEBACK
}}}, along with a template of the output enclosed with {{{ TEMPLATE }}}.
TASK: Fix the errors in the code using the provided template.
TEMPLATE: This code requires a fix because of { ERROR TYPE }. The fixed
code is { CODE }.
```

Here, we guide the model by providing a specific template that includes placeholders for the error type and the fixed code. This approach differs from few-shot prompting in how the output is constructed; rather than offering input-output examples, we define the structure of the output with variables for the model to populate. These two techniques can be used independently or in combination to achieve the desired results.

Chain-of-thought prompting

Chain-of-thought (CoT) prompting involves guiding the model through a step-by-step reasoning process toward a final answer. In coding, we apply CoT by referencing functions that are yet to be implemented, serving as a reasoning framework for the GenAI tool, which later fills in the implementation details. For instance, when validating that a code has no bugs, the process may involve the following steps:

1. Validating syntax
2. Checking compilation
3. Ensuring reproducibility across runs

Using CoT, we can explicitly reference functions that handle each of these steps while leaving the actual implementation for GenAI to complete. In code, this might look like this:

```python
def validate_no_bugs_in_source_code(sc: str) -> None:
    validate_syntax(sc)
    validate_compilation(sc)
    validate_reroducibility_across_runs(sc)
```

Here, `validate_no_bugs_in_source_code` outlines the logical steps needed to verify that the source code is bug-free but does not contain implementation details. GenAI tools are particularly effective at generating low-level implementations, and when typing the first referenced function, `validate_syntax`, Copilot can generate a suitable implementation, as illustrated in *Figure 8.7*:

```python
 chain_of_thought.py 3, R  ●

ch8 > code_samples >  chain_of_thought.py > ...
 1  import ast
 2
 3
 4  def validate_no_bugs_in_source_code(sc: str) -> None:
 5      validate_syntax(sc)
 6      validate_compilation(sc)
 7      validate_reroducibility_across_runs(sc)
 8
 9
10  def validate_syntax(sc: str) -> None:
11      try:
            ast.parse(sc)
        except SyntaxError:
            raise ValueError("Syntax error in source code")
12
```

Figure 8.7: GitHub Copilot suggested implementation of validate_syntax

CoT is one of the most effective prompt engineering techniques for coding tasks, and we will explore its applications further in the upcoming chapters.

Exploring additional methods

This book covers a selection of prompt engineering techniques among the many available. For a broader exploration of prompting strategies, *Unlocking the Secrets of Prompt Engineering: Master the art of creative language generation to accelerate your journey from novice to pro* by Packt delves into numerous other techniques applicable to diverse use cases.

Summary

In this chapter, we introduced few-shot learning as a prompt engineering technique to guide LLMs toward more predictable and desired outcomes. We demonstrated its application in scenarios such as implementing a specific logging structure and following a particular coding style.

We explored how to implement few-shot prompting across different GenAI applications. In ChatGPT and OpenAI API, we utilized specific keyword combinations such as `question` and `answer` or `old` and `refactored` to structure the few-shot examples. With GitHub Copilot, we leveraged a style guide file to influence code completion output.

We also introduced additional prompt engineering techniques that are valuable for scaling bug fixes. Iterative prompting enables models to refine their output by utilizing feedback from compilation checks until the code compiles successfully. Template-based prompting leads the model toward producing outputs with a specific structure. Furthermore, CoT prompting breaks down solutions into clear, step-by-step reasoning processes.

In the next chapters, we will delve deeper into the mechanics of CoT, and chaining, and see how to apply them with ChatGPT, OpenAI API, and GitHub Copilot.

Quiz time

Before you proceed to the next chapter, make sure that you can confidently answer the following questions:

Question 1: When should we use prompt engineering?

Answer: Prompt engineering should follow best practices to achieve desirable outcomes from LLMs. However, when standard guidelines are insufficient, advanced prompting techniques may be necessary. In this chapter, we saw how few-shot learning helped align outputs with a specific style guide, making results more predictable and desirable.

Question 2: Can we use plain English to describe the desired outcome instead of providing few-shot examples in code?

Answer: While it is theoretically possible to use plain English to describe coding styles and desired outputs, this approach is less effective. Like mathematical equations or music notes, code acts as a concise and precise notation system. LLMs, trained extensively on code, interpret it more accurately than plain-text descriptions.

Further reading

To learn more about the topics that were covered in this chapter, take a look at the following resources:

- *PEP-8 Style Guide for Python Code*: `https://peps.python.org/pep-0008/`
- Brown, T. B., Mann, B., Ryder, N., Subbiah, M., Kaplan, J., Dhariwal, P., ..., and Amodei, D. (2020). *Language Models are Few-Shot Learners*. OpenAI. Retrieved from `https://arxiv.org/abs/2005.14165v4`
- Sahoo, P., Singh, A. K., Saha, S., Jain, V., Mondal, S., and Chadha, A. (2024). *A systematic survey of prompt engineering in large language models: Techniques and applications*. Indian Institute of Technology Patna, Stanford University, and Amazon AI. Retrieved from `https://arxiv.org/abs/2402.07927v1`

Subscribe for a free eBook

New frameworks, evolving architectures, research drops, production breakdowns—AI_Distilled filters the noise into a weekly briefing for engineers and researchers working hands-on with LLMs and GenAI systems. Subscribe now and receive a free eBook, along with weekly insights that help you stay focused and informed.

Subscribe at `https://packt.link/TRO5B` or scan the QR code below.

9

Advanced Prompt Engineering for Coding-Related Tasks

Some coding tasks extend beyond simple, single-task initiatives. For these more complex scenarios, advanced prompt engineering techniques such as **chain of thought (CoT)** and **chaining** can be highly effective when working with **large language models (LLMs)**. This chapter will explore how to use these techniques when working with OpenAI API, ChatGPT, and GitHub Copilot on challenges that often require more than just the initial prompt to achieve the desired output.

We will walk through an example of implementing a geometric mean calculator for portfolio returns that handles negative net returns. By applying CoT prompting, we will guide the model with explicit reasoning steps and achieve desirable results, even with a lighter model such as **GPT-4o mini**. Then, using chaining, we will improve the initial implementation by enhancing its type hints and refining the docstring.

This chapter covers the following topics:

- Extending the prompt implementation scope
- Leveraging CoT reasoning for code completion
- Using prompt chaining with LLMs

Technical requirements

To get the most out of this chapter, ensure you have the following:

- GitHub Copilot account
- IDE – either VS Code or PyCharm
- OpenAI account with access to OpenAI API
- Access to the book's repository, available at `https://github.com/PacktPublishing/Supercharged-Coding-with-Gen-AI`
- Virtual environment set up in VS Code or PyCharm
- OpenAI API token

For assistance with setting up a GitHub Copilot account, refer to *Chapter 3*. For instructions on setting up OpenAI API access and token generation, see *Chapter 2*. If you need help creating an OpenAI account or setting up a virtual environment in your IDE, refer to the *Appendix* for detailed guidance.

Extending the prompt implementation scope

Until now, we have mainly worked with short functions spanning only a few lines of code, applying our best practices for prompt precision to generate effective code using GitHub Copilot, OpenAI, and ChatGPT.

However, in many real-world scenarios, our tasks will not fit within such a narrow scope. We may need to handle input casting, switch cases, or adapt implementations beyond a raw mathematical formula. This chapter explores how we can extend the scope of coding tasks by applying advanced prompt engineering techniques.

Extending the geometric mean scope

Let us revisit the geometric mean implementation from *Chapter 3*. The geometric mean is a method of averaging numbers that have a multiplicative nature, such as financial portfolio growth rates, population growth rates, or drug concentrations that change exponentially over time. The geometric mean is defined as the nth root of the product of the inputs, as follows:

$$\text{Geometric Mean} = \left(\prod_{i=1}^{n} x_i \right)^{\frac{1}{n}}$$

For a more detailed explanation of the concept, refer to *Chapter 3*.

However, when some of the inputs are negative, such as net portfolio returns, the standard formula becomes insufficient. For example, consider IBM's stock returns from 2000 to 2002, where two years had negative returns:

```python
IBM_YEARLY_RETURNS: Dict[str, float] = {
    "2000": -0.2084,
    "2001": 0.4300,
    "2002": -0.3547
}
```

If we were to use the geometric mean formula as is, we would get an average yearly return of 32%:

$$G = (-0.2084 \cdot 0.4300 \cdot -0.3547)^{\frac{1}{3}} = (0.031)^{\frac{1}{3}} = 0.32$$

This result, however, is incorrect. A $1,000 investment in IBM stock in 2000 would shrink to approximately $730 by the end of 2002, reflecting a total decline of about 27%. Thus, we would expect an average annual return closer to -10%.

One way to handle negative returns is by using gross returns instead. This involves converting net returns to gross values, computing their product, and extracting the nth root:

```python
from typing import Dict
import numpy as np


def get_average_return(
    net_returns: Dict[str, float],
) -> float:
    # Step 1: Calculate the yearly gross returns
    gross_returns: np.ndarray = np.array(list(net_returns.values())) + 1

    # Step 2: Calculate the geometric mean of the gross returns
    power: float = 1 / len(gross_returns)
    gross_average: float = np.prod(gross_returns) ** power

    # Step 3: Calculate the net average return
    net_average: float = gross_average - 1

    return net_average
```

Applying this function to IBM's returns produces an average return of -10%:

```
net_returns: [-0.2084, 0.43, -0.3547]
gross_returns: [0.7916, 1.43, 0.6453]
gross_average: 0.9006
net_average: -0.099
```

This implementation is more extensive than the functions we have generated so far, so it may require more advanced techniques to get desirable results with minimal iterations.

Next, we will compare baseline responses from GitHub Copilot, ChatGPT, and OpenAI API, examining their limitations and potential pitfalls.

Evaluating baseline outputs

In *Chapter 6*, we discussed how GitHub Copilot, ChatGPT, and OpenAI API each have strengths in different coding-related tasks. Copilot excels at code completion but can fall short when generating larger blocks of starter code. ChatGPT is better suited for producing more extensive initial code, though it often includes longer functions with excessive comments and computations. OpenAI API requires more effort to craft effective prompts but offers greater flexibility through programmatic automation and control over prompt history. For a refresher on these differences, you can revisit *Chapter 6*.

These differences become apparent when implementing the geometric mean for portfolio returns over multiple years. Each tool requires different strategies to refine and enhance the quality of the generated output.

GitHub Copilot baseline

To apply best practices for prompt precision with Copilot, we can start by providing the function signature for get_geometric_mean as follows:

```
def get_geometric_mean(
    net_returns: Dict[str, float],
) -> float:
    ...
```

This gives Copilot a clear starting point with the function name, an argument specifying the use case of net returns, and an expected return type. However, this prompt alone may not be sufficient to guide Copilot in handling negative inputs, as demonstrated in *Figure 9.1*.

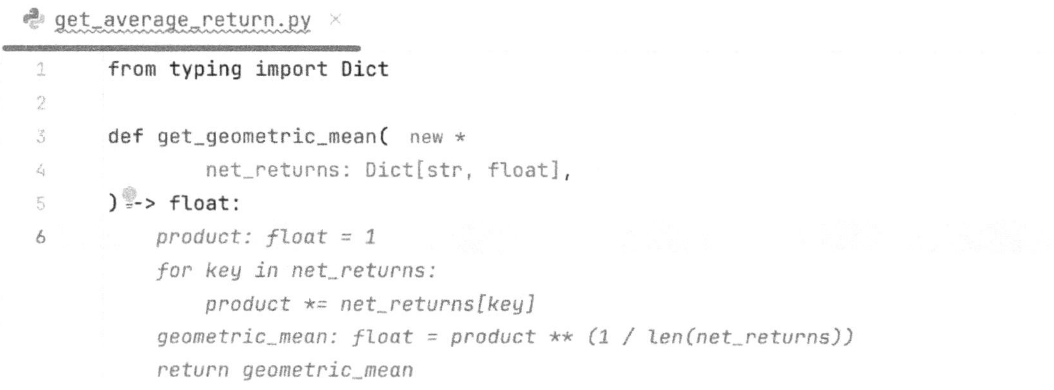

```python
get_average_return.py

1    from typing import Dict
2
3    def get_geometric_mean( new *
4            net_returns: Dict[str, float],
5    ) -> float:
6        product: float = 1
        for key in net_returns:
            product *= net_returns[key]
        geometric_mean: float = product ** (1 / len(net_returns))
        return geometric_mean
```

Figure 9.1: Copilot's completion does not support negative net returns

This implementation would yield incorrect results for negative inputs and should not be used. Later in the chapter, we will see how CoT can help us get the correct implementation we are after.

ChatGPT baseline

ChatGPT, on the other hand, presents a different challenge. While newer models, such as o3, excel at deeper reasoning (as discussed later in this chapter) and may produce more accurate implementations, more effort is required to prompt ChatGPT effectively than with Copilot. Additionally, achieving a coding format that aligns with our preferences is more challenging.

To replicate the GitHub Copilot implementation, we used the following prompt:

```
CONTEXT: You are provided with a Python function signature enclosed with
{{{ FUNCTION }}}.
TASK: implement the function.
FUNCTION: {{{ defget_geometric_mean(\n\t\tnet_returns: Dict[str,
float],\n) -> float: }}}
CODE:
```

Using the o3-mini-high model, we generated a functionally correct implementation. However, the resulting code was cluttered with excessive inline comments and docstrings, making it time-consuming to clean up. *Figure 9.2* illustrates this output in ChatGPT.

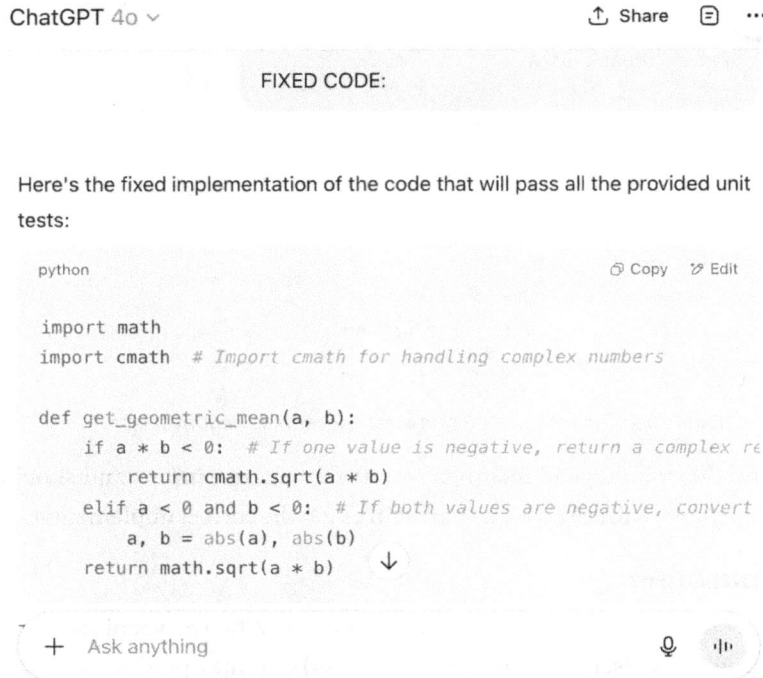

ChatGPT 4o ⌄   ↥ Share ▤ ⋯

FIXED CODE:

Here's the fixed implementation of the code that will pass all the provided unit tests:

```python
import math
import cmath  # Import cmath for handling complex numbers

def get_geometric_mean(a, b):
    if a * b < 0:  # If one value is negative, return a complex re
        return cmath.sqrt(a * b)
    elif a < 0 and b < 0:  # If both values are negative, convert
        a, b = abs(a), abs(b)
    return math.sqrt(a * b)     ↓
```

+   Ask anything   🎤 ⑊

Figure 9.2: ChatGPT implementation

🔍 **Quick tip**: Need to see a high-resolution version of this image? Open this book in the next-gen Packt Reader or view it in the PDF/ePub copy.

🔒 **The next-gen Packt Reader** is included for free with the purchase of this book. Scan the QR code OR go to packtpub.com/unlock, then use the search bar to find this book by name. Double-check the edition shown to make sure you get the right one.

For reference, the proposed code by ChatGPT is as follows:

```python
import math
from typing import Dict


def get_geometric_mean(net_returns: Dict[str, float]) -> float:
    """ [... omitted for brevity ...] """
    if not net_returns:
        return 0.0
    # Calculate the product of (1 + return) for each net return
    product = math.prod(1 + r for r in net_returns.values())
    n = len(net_returns)
    # Compute the nth root of the product and subtract 1 to get the
geometric mean
    geometric_mean = product ** (1 / n) - 1
    return geometric_mean
```

This code is functionally correct but includes several undesired elements:

- Unnecessary docstring
- Input validation
- Excessive comments
- Inline computations

Later in the chapter, we will explore how CoT and chaining requests to the initial implementation can help us achieve the desired output.

OpenAI API baseline

We used the o3-mini-2025-01-31 model via OpenAI API and found that its output closely mirrored what ChatGPT produced. To evaluate this, we ran the script located at `ch9/baseline/baseline_openai.py`, using the following system and user prompts:

```python
SURROUND = "You are provided with a Python function signature enclosed
with {{{ FUNCTION }}}."
SINGLE_TASK = "Your task is to implement the function."

SRC_CODE = """def get_geometric_mean(\n\tnet_returns: Dict[str, float],\n)
-> float:"""
```

```python
def get_user_prompt(src: str) -> str:
    return f"""
FUNCTION: {{{{{{ {src} }}}}}}

CODE:
"""
```

We then called the model using the following code:

```python
if __name__ == '__main__':
    client: OpenAI = OpenAI()
    system_prompt = f"{SURROUND} {SINGLE_TASK}"
    user_prompt = get_user_prompt(SRC_CODE)
    completion: ChatCompletion = client.chat.completions.create(
        model="o3-mini-2025-01-31",
        messages=[
            {"role": "system", "content": system_prompt},
            {"role": "user", "content": user_prompt},
        ],
    )
    output = completion.choices[0].message.content
    print(output)
```

The output generated by OpenAI API was very similar to the one produced by ChatGPT, as seen in the following sample result:

```python
def get_geometric_mean(net_returns: Dict[str, float]) -> float:
    # Return 0.0 if there are no returns (could alternatively raise an
exception)
    if not net_returns:
        return 0.0
    import math

    # Calculate the product of (1 + return) for each period
    product = 1.0
    n = len(net_returns)
    for r in net_returns.values():
        product *= (1 + r)
```

```
# Compute the geometric mean: nth root of product then subtract 1
geom_mean = math.pow(product, 1 / n) - 1
return geom_mean
```

In this implementation, the functionality is correct, but the formatting is less than ideal due to excessive inline comments, unnecessary input validation, and even an import statement placed inside the function. Later in the chapter, we will see how to refine this implementation using CoT and chaining to achieve desirable results even when working with lower-cost models such as GPT-4o mini.

In summary, as our implementation scope expands beyond simple and short functions, applying more advanced techniques becomes essential to achieving the desired results.

Next, we will see how we can utilize advanced prompt engineering techniques and get the implementation we want faster, and see which application (either Copilot, OpenAI API, or ChatGPT) is most suitable for each technique.

Leveraging CoT reasoning with LLM

In *Chapter 8*, we explored how guided reasoning with CoT can help LLMs produce better code by following a step-by-step reasoning process. This step-by-step thinking encourages models to tackle problems in a structured way, leading to more accurate and desirable outputs.

As a simple exercise, consider the following sequence:

17, 34, 14, 28, 8, 16

This sequence follows two rules – first, multiply the previous number by 2 to get the next one; then subtract 20 to get the following number:

$34 = 17 \times 2$

$14 = 34 - 20$

$28 = 14 \times 2$

$8 = 28 - 20$

$16 = 8 \times 2$

The next number should be -4, which is 16 - 20. However, prompting Copilot to predict the next number in the sequence is not straightforward, as shown in *Figure 9.3*.

```python
 get_average_return.py ×
1    from typing import Dict
2
3    def get_geometric_mean( new *
4            net_returns: Dict[str, float],
5    ) -> float:
6        product: float = 1
         for key in net_returns:
             product *= net_returns[key]
         geometric_mean: float = product ** (1 / len(net_returns))
         return geometric_mean
```

Figure 9.3: Copilot fails to predict the correct next number

In this case, Copilot failed to predict the next number accurately, suggesting 4 instead of -4. This demonstrates that the model did not fully grasp the sequence's logic. To improve the outcome, we can guide the model by prompting it to reason through the relationship between the current number and the previous one before making a final prediction, as shown in *Figure 9.4*.

```python
 cot_copilot.py ×
1    # What is the next number in the sequence?
2
3    # Number 1: 17
4    # Number 2: 34. Relationship to Number 1: 2
5    # Number 3: 14. Relationship to Number 2: -20
6    # Number 4: 28. Relationship to Number 3: 2
7    # Number 5: 8. Relationship to Number 4: -20
8    # Number 6: 16. Relationship to Number 5: 2
9    # Number 7: 6. Relationship to Number 6: -20
```

Figure 9.4: Reasoning steps provided for the next number

Figure 9.4 shows that, by adding comments in rows 4-8, Copilot predicted the next number in the sequence correctly and also explained its reasoning for the final number, 6. Similarly, as we will explore later in this chapter, incorporating reasoning steps into our coding tasks can help the model produce more desirable outcomes.

CoT in the GPT-o series

CoT has proven so effective across a range of domains requiring complex reasoning that it was built into the GPT-o series. This means the model will automatically identify the necessary steps to complete a task before arriving at the final answer.

For the sequence completion example we explored earlier in the chapter, we could use the GPT-o1 model without additional guidance, as shown in *Figure 9.5*.

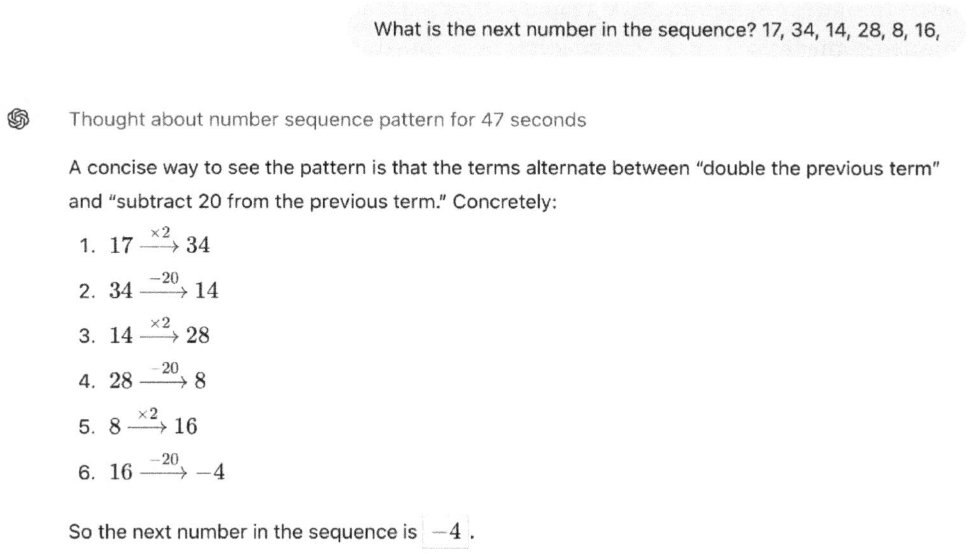

What is the next number in the sequence? 17, 34, 14, 28, 8, 16,

⬡ Thought about number sequence pattern for 47 seconds

A concise way to see the pattern is that the terms alternate between "double the previous term" and "subtract 20 from the previous term." Concretely:

1. $17 \xrightarrow{\times 2} 34$

2. $34 \xrightarrow{-20} 14$

3. $14 \xrightarrow{\times 2} 28$

4. $28 \xrightarrow{-20} 8$

5. $8 \xrightarrow{\times 2} 16$

6. $16 \xrightarrow{-20} -4$

So the next number in the sequence is -4 .

Figure 9.5: Built-in CoT in o1

From the ChatGPT output, we can see that the model recognized this as a sequence pattern task, with an internal process for handling reasoning in such cases. The model took 47 seconds to process the task, which included problem analysis, problem recognition, and estimating the next number, as shown in *Figure 9.6*.

ChatGPT o1 ∨

What is the next number in the sequence? 17, 34, 14, 28, 8, 16,

⚙ Analyzing the sequence

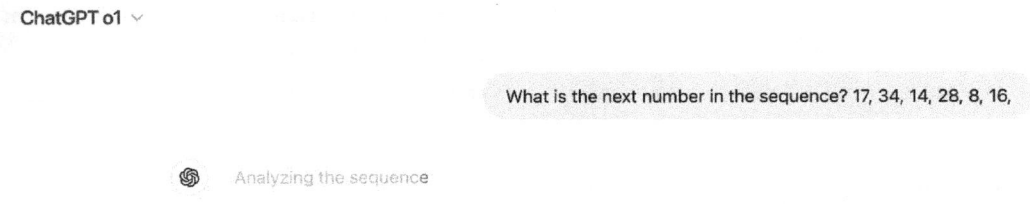

Figure 9.6: Thought process in ChatGPT

Here, we can see that ChatGPT is analyzing the sequence, which is one of the reasoning steps in CoT to get to the final answer.

o-series adoption

Models from the o series are now available through ChatGPT and OpenAI API. However, they come at a higher cost than their predecessors, as illustrated in *Figure 9.7*:

Our latest models

Reasoning models for complex, multi-step problems

OpenAI o1	OpenAI o3-mini
Frontier reasoning model that supports tools, Structured Outputs, and vision | 200k context length	Small cost-efficient reasoning model that's optimized for coding, math, and science, and supports tools and Structured Outputs | 200k context length
Price	**Price**
Input: $15.00 / 1M tokens	Input: $1.10 / 1M tokens
Cached input: $7.50 / 1M tokens	Cached input: $0.55 / 1M tokens
Output: $60.00 / 1M tokens	Output: $4.40 / 1M tokens

Figure 9.7: Costs of o-series models for OpenAI API calls

The o1 model, for example, is priced at $15 per million input tokens and $60 per million output tokens, making it six times more expensive than GPT-4o and 1,000 times more expensive than GPT-4o mini, as shown in *Figure 9.8*.

GPT models for everyday tasks

GPT-4.5	GPT-4o	GPT-4o mini
Largest GPT model designed for creative tasks and agentic planning, currently available in a research preview | 128k context length	High-intelligence model for complex tasks | 128k context length	Affordable small model for fast, everyday tasks | 128k context length
Price	**Price**	**Price**
Input: $75.00 / 1M tokens	Input: $2.50 / 1M tokens	Input: $0.150 / 1M tokens
Cached input: $37.50 / 1M tokens	Cached input: $1.25 / 1M tokens	Cached input: $0.075 / 1M tokens
Output: $150.00 / 1M tokens	Output: $10.00 / 1M tokens	Output: $0.600 / 1M tokens

Figure 9.8: GPT-4o pricing for OpenAI API calls

Due to this significant cost difference, o-series models are used less frequently in applications. When selecting the right model for yourself or your company, it is important to weigh the trade-off between cost and output quality. If more affordable models, such as GPT-4o, deliver satisfactory results and meet expectations, it may be prudent to continue using them. However, the o1 and o3 models have been shown to give significantly better outcomes, so it might be worth using them first or as a fallback, even at a higher cost.

Using CoT for GitHub Copilot

The CoT approach is one of our most frequently used strategies when working with GitHub Copilot. When applied effectively, it can simplify the development of entire code segments, leading to cleaner and more readable implementations.

This method involves structuring the reasoning process by referencing functions that have yet to be implemented. For example, when calculating the geometric mean for net returns, we can break it down into three logical steps:

1. Convert input to gross returns.
2. Compute the geometric mean of the gross returns.
3. Convert back to the net returns.

Expressing these steps in code involves defining each operation as a function, as shown in the following code:

```
def get_average_return(
    net_returns: Dict[str, float],
) -> float:
    gross_returns: np.ndarray = get_gross_returns(net_returns)
    gross_average: float = get_geometric_mean(gross_returns)
    net_average: float = get_net_average(gross_average)
    return net_average
```

This function does not include any implementation details and only outlines the functions or steps to be completed. Since the functions are not yet implemented, typing their names in an IDE may look like an error, as shown in *Figure 9.9*:

```
 5
 6       def get_average_return(  ≜ Hila Paz Herszfang *
 7             net_returns: Dict[str, float],
 8       ) -> float:
 9           gross_returns: np.ndarray = get_gross_returns(net_returns)
10           gross_average: float = get_geometric_mean(gross_returns)
11           net_average: float = get_net_average(gross_average)
12           return net_average
13       💡
```

Figure 9.9: Error underline in the CoT definition

This underlying error indicator is expected and resolved as Copilot generates the implementation for the function at hand.

This reasoning approach facilitates the generation of accurate and predictable code when working with the AI pair programmer. As each function is implemented (such as get_gross_returns, get_geometric_mean, etc.), Copilot learns enough context to write the correct provided parameters, how the return value is used, and the expected type hints.

Additionally, we can predict how Copilot will complete the code and in what order. The implementation will follow the sequence of function calls in get_average_return. Indeed, as we press *Enter* twice and start typing def, Copilot will suggest an implementation for get_gross_returns, as shown in *Figure 9.10*:

```
1        from typing import Dict
2
3        import numpy as np
4
5
6        def get_average_return(    ≛ Hila Paz Herszfang ⋆
7                net_returns: Dict[str, float],
8        ) -> float:
9            gross_returns: np.ndarray = get_gross_returns(net_returns)
10           gross_average: float = get_geometric_mean(gross_returns)
11           net_average: float = get_net_average(gross_average)
12           return net_average
13
14           ⚘
15       def get_gross_returns(  new ⋆
                net_returns: Dict[str, float],
         ) -> np.ndarray:
             gross_returns: np.ndarray = np.array(list(net_returns.values())) + 1
             return gross_returns
```

Figure 9.10: Copilot predicts the implementation of the first called function

Once we accept the implementation and hit *Enter* twice again, Copilot will suggest the next function in the call sequence, get_geometric_mean, as shown in *Figure 9.11*:

```
6        def get_average_return(    ≛ Hila Paz Herszfang ⋆
7                net_returns: Dict[str, float],
8        ) -> float:
9            gross_returns: np.ndarray = get_gross_returns(net_returns)
10           gross_average: float = get_geometric_mean(gross_returns)
11           net_average: float = get_net_average(gross_average)
12           return net_average
13
14
15       def get_gross_returns(  1 usage  ≛ Hila Paz Herszfang ⋆
16               net_returns: Dict[str, float],
17       ) -> np.ndarray:
18           gross_returns: np.ndarray = np.array(list(net_returns.values())) + 1
19           return gross_returns
20
21           ⚘
22       def get_geometric_mean(
```

Figure 9.11: Copilot predicting the next function definition

Here, we did not need to type anything. Just a two-line break, resembling the space between get_average_return and get_gross_returns, was enough to trigger a fully predictable implementation in this file. This demonstrates the optimal use of Copilot, truly leveraging the power of an AI pair programmer. For your reference, here is the full implementation suggested by Copilot:

```python
def get_gross_returns(
    net_returns: Dict[str, float],
) -> np.ndarray:
    gross_returns: np.ndarray = np.array(
        list(net_returns.values())
    ) + 1
    return gross_returns


def get_geometric_mean(
    gross_returns: np.ndarray,
) -> float:
    gross_average: float = np.prod(gross_returns) ** (
        1 / len(gross_returns)
    )
    return gross_average


def get_net_average(
    gross_average: float,
) -> float:
    net_average: float = gross_average - 1
    return net_average
```

This implementation successfully captures the intended logic, and its structuring across different levels of abstraction is superior to what even the most advanced o3 models produce via ChatGPT and OpenAI API. This serves as a strong example of how effective prompting techniques can outperform more powerful and costly models.

Educating your colleagues

Next time you notice a colleague trying to use inline comments in GitHub Copilot such as # step 1: Compute the gross returns, suggest they try using CoT instead. This approach will not only be more efficient and a better way to use Copilot, but it will also help the team maintain higher-quality code.

Next, we will explore how to replicate the desired outputs with ChatGPT and OpenAI API, even when using more affordable models such as GPT-4o mini.

CoT for the geometric mean with ChatGPT

The same CoT approach can be applied to coding tasks, such as implementing a get_average_ return function that supports negative returns. Rather than supplying the function signature, we will provide a full implementation of get_average_return as we did with Copilot and prompt the model to complete the lower-level details. A prompt for this might look like the following:

```
CONTEXT: You are provided with a Python function enclosed with {{{
FUNCTION }}} that calls functions that should be completed.
TASK: Implement the missing functions.
FUNCTION: {{{def get_average_return(\n\t\tnet_returns: Dict[str,
float],\n) -> float: \n\tgross_returns: np.ndarray = get_gross_
returns(net_returns) \n\tgross_average: float = get_geometric_mean(gross_
returns) \n\tnet_average: float = get_net_average(gross_average) \n\
treturn net_average }}}
CODE:
```

This prompt outlines the necessary reasoning steps to generate the correct code. For reference, here is the output produced by ChatGPT using the GPT-4o mini model with the given prompt:

```python
def get_gross_returns(net_returns: Dict[str, float]) -> np.ndarray:
    """ ... omitted for brevity ... """
    return np.array([1 + net_return for net_return in net_returns.
values()])


def get_geometric_mean(values: np.ndarray) -> float:
    """ ... omitted for brevity ... """
    return np.prod(values) ** (1 / len(values))


def get_net_average(gross_average: float) -> float:
    """ ... omitted for brevity ... """
    return gross_average - 1


def get_average_return(net_returns: Dict[str, float]) -> float:
    gross_returns: np.ndarray = get_gross_returns(net_returns)
    gross_average: float = get_geometric_mean(gross_returns)
```

```
net_average: float = get_net_average(gross_average)
return net_average
```

This output is more satisfactory than the baseline, even though it was generated with GPT-4o model instead of the more advanced O-series. It no longer includes inline comments or input validation, which significantly reduces the amount of manual editing required. Later in the chapter, we will see how chaining can help produce even more polished results that are ready to use as is.

Next, we will apply this approach using OpenAI API.

CoT with OpenAI API

We can leverage CoT prompting and provide a full implementation of `get_average_return` as we did with Copilot and ChatGPT. The system and user prompts may look as follows:

```
SURROUND = "You are provided with a Python function enclosed with {{{
FUNCTION }}} that calls functions that should be completed."
SINGLE_TASK = "Your task is to implement the missing functions."

def get_user_prompt(func: callable) -> str:
    return f"""
    FUNCTION: {{{{{{ {inspect.getsource(func)} }}}}}}

    CODE:
    """
```

We will integrate these prompt pieces into an OpenAI API call, including the system prompt, user prompt, and a GPT-4o mini model, as shown here:

```
if __name__ == '__main__':
    client: OpenAI = OpenAI()
    system_prompt = f"{SURROUND} {SINGLE_TASK}"
    user_prompt = get_user_prompt(get_average_return)

    completion: ChatCompletion = client.chat.completions.create(
        model="gpt-4o-mini",
        messages=[
            {"role": "system", "content": system_prompt},
            {"role": "user", "content": user_prompt},
        ],
```

```
    )

    output = completion.choices[0].message.content
    print(output)
```

Note that the code sample can be found in this book's repository at ch9/cot/cot_openai.py. For reference, here is sample output from the call:

```
import numpy as np
from typing import Dict

def get_gross_returns(net_returns: Dict[str, float]) -> np.ndarray:
    """Convert net returns to gross returns."""
    return np.array([1 + r for r in net_returns.values()])

def get_geometric_mean(gross_returns: np.ndarray) -> float:
    """Calculate the geometric mean of a numpy array of gross returns."""
    return np.prod(gross_returns) ** (1 / len(gross_returns))

def get_net_average(gross_average: float) -> float:
    """Convert gross average back to net average."""
    return gross_average - 1
def get_average_return(net_returns: Dict[str, float]) -> float:
    ... omitted for brevity ...
```

Here, we obtained a better implementation than the baseline, maintaining the desired level of abstraction and avoiding input validation and inline comments.

While leveraging CoT is highly effective when using GitHub Copilot, it is not always sufficient to produce ready-to-use code with ChatGPT or OpenAI API. To address this, we can incorporate chaining through follow-up prompts, as we will demonstrate next.

Using prompt chaining for LLMs

Prompt chaining is another highly effective prompt engineering technique that helps us achieve better results from LLMs. It involves breaking down tasks into smaller, sequential steps that are more efficiently completed individually.

For instance, when implementing get_average_return, we may want to enhance ChatGPT's or OpenAI's initial output by adding type hints and avoiding inline calculations in the return statement. With GitHub Copilot, we might want to construct a barebones implementation first and add a Google Style docstring later.

Although we could include all these elements in the initial prompt, it is often more natural and effective to start with an implementation that is functionally correct. From there, we can refine the code step by step through a series of follow-up prompts.

Chaining with ChatGPT

Applying chaining with ChatGPT is very intuitive given that the UI is already designed for a conversational style. The chat history helps us reference previous prompt pieces without needing to retype them.

For instance, say that we wanted to improve the implementation of get_average_return with a Google Style docstring rather than an arbitrary one, and type hints to variables in all functions. Including all these elements in one prompt would defy the single-task best practice and result in suboptimal outputs. Instead, we recommend the following approach:

- For chained prompts with the same context, focus only on the new task
- For chained prompts with a different context, such as adding test cases, use a full prompt following the five S's best practices

For the task of coding get_average_return, adding type hints for variables, revising the docstring to be in a Google Style format, and adding a test suite can be done with the following strategy:

- **Prompt 1:** Write the full code prompt using the five S's for the get_average_return implementation with a CoT.
- **Prompt 2:** Add type hints to all variables.
- **Prompt 3:** Change the docstring to Google Style.
- **Prompt 4:** Write unit tests. In this step, we will specify the test cases we want to cover, creating a new context. As a result, we need to provide a complete prompt that follows the five S's best practices.

For example, prompt 2, which focuses on the single task of removing comments, is simply as follows:

```
Add type hints to all variables.
```

This will produce an updated implementation without the inline comments, as shown in *Figure 9.12*.

```python
import numpy as np
from typing import Dict

def get_gross_returns(net_returns: Dict[str, float]) -> np.ndarray:
    """
    Convert net returns (e.g., 0.05 for 5%) to gross returns (e.g., 1.05).
    """
    gross_returns: np.ndarray = np.array([1 + r for r in net_returns.values()])
    return gross_returns

def get_geometric_mean(gross_returns: np.ndarray) -> float:
    """
    Compute the geometric mean of an array of gross returns.
    """
    product: float = np.prod(gross_returns)
```

Figure 9.12: Added type hints to variables

The initial implementation has been updated to include type hints for variables across the different functions. For instance, in the first function, get_gross_returns, the gross_returns variable is now correctly annotated with the np.ndarray type and returned in the following line.

In prompt 3, the focus shifts to improving the docstring. We continue with a single-task prompt:

```
include Google Style docstring.
```

This prompt is expected to yield a better implementation, as demonstrated in *Figure 9.13*.

ChatGPT 4o ⌄   ⬆ Share

> include Google Style docstring.

Sure! Here's the version with full **Google Style docstrings** and all **variable type hints**:

```python
import numpy as np
from typing import Dict

def get_gross_returns(net_returns: Dict[str, float]) -> np.ndarray:
    """Converts net returns to gross returns.

    Args:
        net_returns (Dict[str, float]): A dictionary of net returns,
            where the key is typically a time period and the value is the net return

    Returns:
        np.ndarray: An array of gross returns (e.g., 1.05 for a 5% net return).
    """
    gross_returns: np.ndarray = np.array([1 + r for r in net_returns.values()])
```

Figure 9.13: Refined docstring

The result confirms that we successfully obtained the desired docstring for the get_gross_return function in Google Style format. For reference, here are the docstrings generated by ChatGPT for the get_geometric_mean, get_net_average, and get_average_return functions:

```python
def get_geometric_mean(gross_returns: np.ndarray) -> float:
    """Calculates the geometric mean of gross returns.
Args:
    gross_returns (np.ndarray): An array of gross returns.

Returns:
    float: The geometric mean of the gross returns.
"""

... omitted for brevity ...

def get_net_average(gross_average: float) -> float: """Converts gross
average return to net average return.
Args:
    gross_average (float): The geometric mean of gross returns.
```

```
Returns:
    float: The corresponding net average return.
"""

... omitted for brevity ...

def get_average_return(net_returns: Dict[str, float]) -> float:
"""Calculates the geometric mean of net returns from a dictionary of net
returns.
Args:
    net_returns (Dict[str, float]): A dictionary of net returns per
period.

Returns:
    float: The geometric mean of the net returns.
"""

... omitted for brevity ...
```

In later chapters of the book, we will explore a more robust approach to generating docstrings, along with additional chained tasks such as input validation, monitoring, and unit testing.

One limitation of the ChatGPT interface is the lack of control over how prompts are constructed and sent to the underlying model, especially as the conversation grows longer. In the next section, we will see how to gain more control over the chat history by using OpenAI API.

Selective history with OpenAI API

When working with OpenAI API for chained tasks, we can take a selective approach and explicitly choose which parts of the conversation history to include in each prompt.

Let us consider the first three prompts from the previous ChatGPT session:

- **Prompt 1**: Leverage CoT for the get_average_return implementation
- **Prompt 2**: Add type hints
- **Prompt 3**: Refine the docstring

A straightforward way to replicate this workflow with OpenAI API is to continuously append the chained prompt and the corresponding output to our messages list, as shown here:

```
messages = [{"role": "system", "content": system_prompt}]

prompt_1 = get_user_prompt(get_average_return)
```

```python
prompt_2 = "Add type hints to all variables."
prompt_3 = "include Google Style docstring."

for prompt in [prompt_1, prompt_2, prompt_3]:
    messages.append({"role": "user", "content": prompt})

completion: ChatCompletion = client.chat.completions.create(
    model="gpt-4o-mini",
    messages=messages,
)

output: str = completion.choices[0].message.content
messages.append({"role": "assistant", "content": output})
```

In this naive setup, each user prompt and corresponding model response is appended to the conversation history. By the time we reach prompt_3, we expect the output to closely resemble what ChatGPT would generate. For reference, here is a sample response from the API that successfully produced a correct implementation, complete with Google Style docstrings and properly typed variables:

```python
def get_gross_returns(net_returns: Dict[str, float]) -> np.ndarray:
    """Convert net returns to gross returns.

    Args:
        net_returns (Dict[str, float]): A dictionary where keys are identifiers
        (such as tickers) and values are net return values (as decimal).

    Returns:
        np.ndarray: An array of gross returns corresponding to the net returns.
    """
    gross_returns: np.ndarray = np.array([1 + return_value for return_value in net_returns.values()])
    return gross_returns
```

For reference, the full script can be found in ch9/chaining/naive_chaining_openai.py.

The naive approach works reasonably well when there are fewer than 5 follow-up prompts. However, as the chain grows, so does the length of the accumulated prompt, leading to increased token usage. For instance, running the preceding script peaked at 1,253 tokens by prompt_3, as illustrated in *Figure 9.14*.

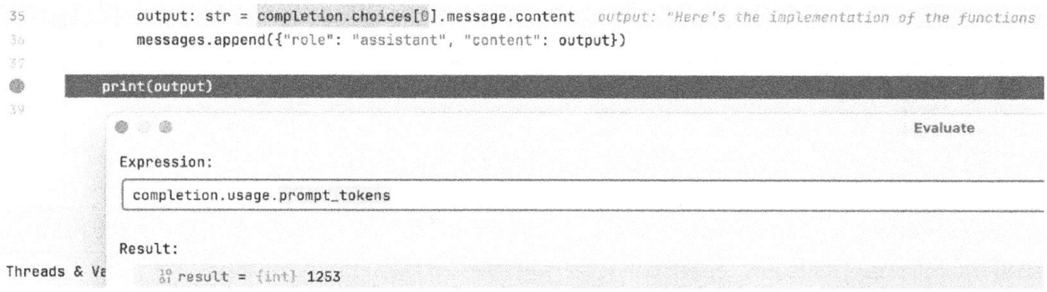

Figure 9.14: prompt_3 with 1,253 tokens

As more prompts are added, the total token count increases, which results in higher usage costs and the risk of distracting the LLM from the specific task at hand.

A more efficient alternative for longer chains is a selective history strategy, where only the relevant parts of the interaction are passed along. Instead of including the entire interaction history in each follow-up request, we can simply pass the code generated in response to the first prompt, along with a new system prompt tailored to the next transformation task.

To isolate just the code from the assistant's response, we can use the following utility function:

```python
def get_refactor_user_prompt(assistant_output: str) -> str:
    code: str = re.sub(
        r"(.*?)```python(.*?)```(.*)",
        r"\2",
        assistant_output,
        flags=re.DOTALL
    ).strip()

    user_prompt: str = f"""
OLD: {{{{{{ {code} }}}}}}
REFACTORED:
"""

    return user_prompt
```

This extracts the relevant code and formats it into a new user prompt for the next step in the chain.

In contrast to the static system prompt used in the naive approach, we now update the system prompt with each task:

```
prompt_1: str = f"{SURROUND} {SINGLE_TASK}"
prompt_2: str = "You are provided with a Python code enclosed in {{{
FUNCTION }}}. Your task is to add type hints to all variables."
prompt_3: str = "You are provided with a Python code enclosed in {{{
FUNCTION }}}. Your task is to include Google Style docstring."
```

We can then use a `prompts` dictionary to associate each prompt with the appropriate input-generation function, linking `prompt_1` to `get_user_prompt` for the initial implementation, and the subsequent prompts to `get_refactor_user_prompt` for the refactoring steps:

```
prompts: Dict[str, callable] = {
    prompt_1: get_user_prompt,
    prompt_2: get_refactor_user_prompt,
    prompt_3: get_refactor_user_prompt}
```

This allows us to generate the user prompt dynamically for each task using the correct function:

```
for prompt, func in prompts.items():
    completion: ChatCompletion = client.chat.completions.create(
        model="gpt-4o-mini",
        messages=[
            {"role": "system", "content": prompt},
            {"role": "user", "content": func(next_input)},
        ],
    )
    next_input: str = completion.choices[0].message.content
```

Notice how each API call now contains only a system prompt and a single user message. This keeps the interaction focused, passing along only what is necessary rather than the full chain of previous prompts and outputs.

For reference, here is a sample output from `prompt_3` using the selective history strategy:

```
def get_gross_returns(net_returns: Dict[str, float]) -> np.ndarray:
    """

    Convert net returns to gross returns.
```

```
Gross Return is calculated as:
Gross Return = 1 + Net Return.

Args:
    net_returns (Dict[str, float]): A dictionary where keys are
identifiers (e.g., asset names) and values are the corresponding net
returns.

Returns:
    np.ndarray: An array of gross returns derived from the provided
net returns.
    """
    gross_returns: np.ndarray = np.array([1 + net_return for net_return in
net_returns.values()])
    return gross_returns
```

This output mirrors the quality of the naive approach, including type hints and a Google Style docstring. The key difference is efficiency: using selective history, we reduced the token count to just 296, which is less than 25% of the naive approach, as shown in *Figure 9.15*:

```
Expression:
  completion.usage.prompt_tokens

Result:
  result = {int} 296
```

Figure 9.15: Selective history reduces input tokens by over 75%

As chained tasks become more complex, the selective history strategy helps keep prompts short and focused. In later chapters, we will explore additional use cases for chaining across various stages of the **Software Development Life Cycle (SDLC)**.

In summary, OpenAI API allows both automated execution of chaining and control over prompt history. By including only relevant information, we can reduce costs and help the model concentrate on the specific task at hand.

In the final subsection of this chapter, we will look at how chaining can be applied with GitHub Copilot, where we aim for the initial implementations to already follow the desired formatting.

Chaining with Copilot

When working with Copilot for code completion tasks, we can also leverage chaining by breaking down the task into smaller steps. For tasks that go beyond the barebones implementation, such as adding docstrings, input validations, logs, and tests, it is best to align with a chained approach. For the chained tasks, we can use the chat interaction mode with Copilot. In later chapters of the book, we will see how to leverage code completion for chained tasks as well.

For example, a chaining flow to extend get_average_return with a docstring and input validation might look as follows:

1. **Initial task**: Implement get_average_return with CoT.
2. **Chained task 2**: Add docstrings to all functions.
3. **Chained task 3**: Add input validation.

After generating the initial implementation of get_average_return, as shown earlier in the chapter, we can proceed to the second chained task, which focuses on adding docstrings to all functions in the file.

In VS Code, we can use Copilot Edits for this task by opening the chat window and selecting **Edit**. We will ensure that the working set includes the current file, ch9/chaining/get_average_return. py, and enter the following prompt:

```
Add Google Style docstring to all functions.
```

This prompt will result in suggestions for adding type hints to the variables, as shown in *Figure 9.16*.

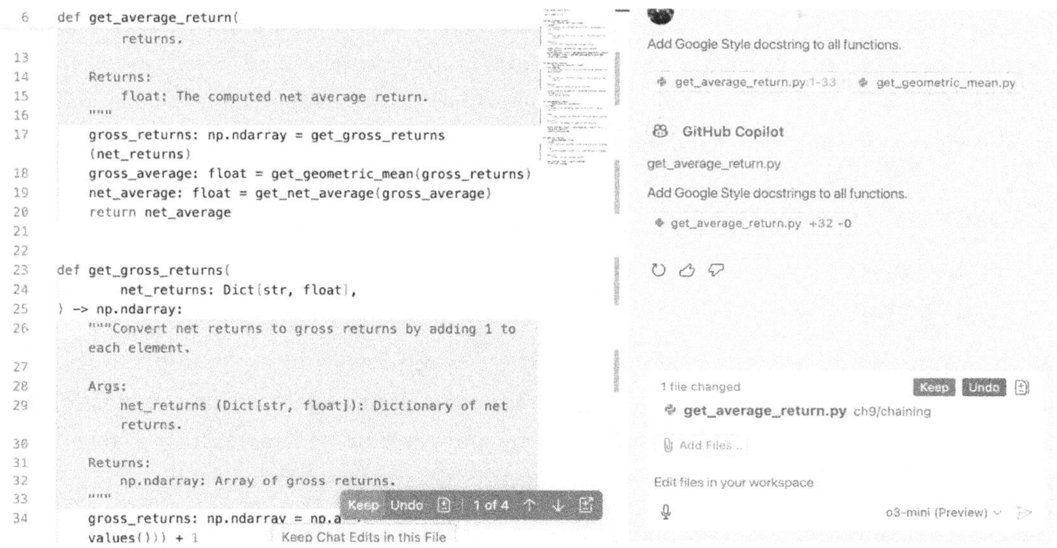

```
 6    def get_average_return(
           returns.
13
14       Returns:
15           float: The computed net average return.
16       """
17       gross_returns: np.ndarray = get_gross_returns
         (net_returns)
18       gross_average: float = get_geometric_mean(gross_returns)
19       net_average: float = get_net_average(gross_average)
20       return net_average
21
22
23    def get_gross_returns(
24           net_returns: Dict[str, float],
25    ) -> np.ndarray:
26       """Convert net returns to gross returns by adding 1 to
         each element.
27
28       Args:
29           net_returns (Dict[str, float]): Dictionary of net
             returns.
30
31       Returns:
32           np.ndarray: Array of gross returns.
33       """
34       gross_returns: np.ndarray = np.a
         values())) + 1
```

Add Google Style docstring to all functions.

⊕ get_average_return.py:1-33   ⊕ get_geometric_mean.py

🐙 GitHub Copilot

get_average_return.py

Add Google Style docstrings to all functions.

⊕ get_average_return.py +32 -0

1 file changed   Keep Undo

⊕ **get_average_return.py** ch9/chaining

Add Files...

Edit files in your workspace

o3-mini (Preview)

Keep Undo   1 of 4 ↑ ↓

Keep Chat Edits in this File

Figure 9.16: Suggested edits to add a docstring

Here, we can see that Copilot correctly added a docstring to all functions with our preferred Google Style; for example, in line 26, a correct description of get_gross_return was added to the function.

In PyCharm, open GitHub Copilot Chat by clicking the Copilot icon in the bottom menu and selecting **Open GitHub Copilot Chat** or using the *Ctrl + Shift + C* keyboard shortcut. Enter the following prompt:

```
Add Google Style docstring to all functions.
```

Copilot will suggest the necessary edits, adding a docstring to all functions, as seen in *Figure 9.17*:

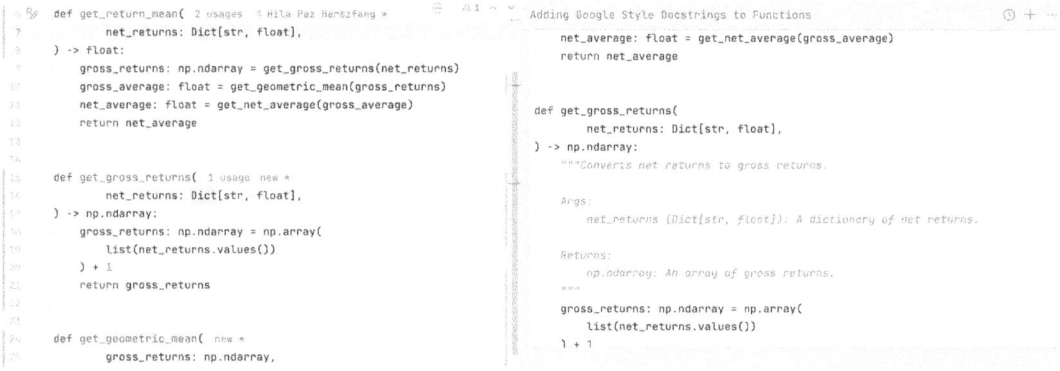

```
def get_return_mean( 2 usages  Hila Paz Herszfang *
        net_returns: Dict[str, float],
) -> float:
    gross_returns: np.ndarray = get_gross_returns(net_returns)
    gross_average: float = get_geometric_mean(gross_returns)
    net_average: float = get_net_average(gross_average)
    return net_average


def get_gross_returns( 1 usage  new *
        net_returns: Dict[str, float],
) -> np.ndarray:
    gross_returns: np.ndarray = np.array(
        list(net_returns.values())
    ) + 1
    return gross_returns


def get_geometric_mean( new *
        gross_returns: np.ndarray,
```

Adding Google Style Docstrings to Functions

```
        net_average: float = get_net_average(gross_average)
        return net_average


def get_gross_returns(
        net_returns: Dict[str, float],
) -> np.ndarray:
    """Converts net returns to gross returns.

    Args:
        net_returns (Dict[str, float]): A dictionary of net returns.

    Returns:
        np.ndarray: An array of gross returns.
    """
    gross_returns: np.ndarray = np.array(
        list(net_returns.values())
    ) + 1
```

Figure 9.17: Suggested edits to add a docstring using PyCharm

In both VS Code and PyCharm, Copilot suggests the appropriate docstring for each function. Later in this book, we will apply chaining along with other prompt engineering techniques to address SDLC tasks. For example, in *Chapter 14*, we will explore how to combine CoT and chaining to profile the runtime and space complexity of our code.

Summary

In this chapter, we explored how to achieve desirable outcomes from LLMs by effectively applying CoT and chaining for coding tasks with an extended scope.

With CoT prompting, we saw how introducing reasoning steps into our prompts enables the model to handle more nuanced challenges, such as implementing a geometric mean function that supports negative net returns. We used function names as intermediate reasoning steps, while relying on Copilot, ChatGPT, and OpenAI API to fill in the implementation details.

Through chaining, we began with an initial implementation that is functionally correct and iteratively improved by adding type hints and refining docstrings. When using OpenAI API, we introduced a selective history approach to make chaining more efficient, which still holds as the chain of tasks gets longer.

In the next chapter, we will delve deeper into refactoring code with GenAI applications. Later in the book, we will introduce advanced prompt engineering techniques at various stages of the SDLC.

Quiz time

Before you proceed to the next chapter, make sure that you can confidently answer the following questions:

Question 1: Is prompt engineering always necessary when working with GenAI?

Answer: Not always. For tasks with a smaller scope, such as implementing a short function, the five S's framework is often enough to guide the model toward a good result. Prompt engineering becomes more important when the task grows in complexity, requiring us to either break it into smaller parts or guide the model with reasoning steps to help it succeed.

Question 2: How is CoT applied with GitHub Copilot?

Answer: To apply CoT with Copilot, we specify our reasoning steps in abstracted functions. This approach helps Copilot understand the reasoning behind the desired implementation, allowing it to generate the next lines of code with minimal input, often just by hitting *Enter*.

Question 3: Is chat history irrelevant when using prompt chaining?

Answer: No. In chaining, we make use of the previously provided context and supporting data, such as code specifications and reasoning steps, and refer to them again, just as we would reference variables in our code. When additional context is needed, such as test cases to include in our test suite, we rebuild the full prompt.

Further reading

To learn more about the topics that were covered in this chapter, refer to the following resources:

- Geometric mean in financial applications, Wikipedia: `https://en.wikipedia.org/wiki/Geometric_mean#Financial`

- OpenAI learning to reason (CoT): `https://openai.com/index/learning-to-reason-with-llms/`

10

Refactoring Code with GenAI

Software developers write in programming languages to instruct a computer to perform specific tasks. The source code in the programming language is translated by a compiler or interpreter into executable computer instructions. One might conclude that programming is only artificial communication with a computer, but it is much more than that.

The true, implicit goal of a computer program is to communicate with other developers. Once code is written, it is frequently read many times, hours, weeks, or even years later, by the same or other developers. The developers will read the code to understand it, debug it, and integrate it with other systems. The goal must be to communicate with the precision required by software, while maintaining clarity for future developers.

Thus, code is written once but read many times. Before GenAI code generation became common, Python practitioners invested significant effort into code quality and style. Today, we can use prompting techniques with GenAI to enhance code quality and style more efficiently.

In *Chapter 7*, we introduced techniques for quickly reading and debugging GenAI-generated code. In this chapter, we will focus on using GenAI for **refactoring**, which means rewriting existing code to improve readability, structure, or performance while preserving its original functionality.

We will examine a poorly implemented function that computes the distance between two matrices. By applying the five S's framework for prompt precision as introduced in *Chapter 4*, we will convert a nested loop into a vectorized operation. With **chain-of-thought (CoT)** prompting, we will restructure the function and delegate implementation details to GitHub Copilot, ChatGPT, and OpenAI API.

Topics covered in this chapter include the following:

- Introducing code refactoring
- Refactoring for better structure with GenAI
- Refactoring for performance with GenAI

Technical requirements

To get the most out of this chapter, ensure you have the following:

- GitHub Copilot account
- IDE – either VS Code or PyCharm
- OpenAI account with access to OpenAI API
- Access to the book's repository, available at `https://github.com/PacktPublishing/Supercharged-Coding-with-Gen-AI`
- Virtual environment set up in VS Code or PyCharm
- OpenAI API token

For assistance setting up a GitHub Copilot account, refer to *Chapter 3*. For instructions on setting up OpenAI API access and token generation, see *Chapter 2*. If you need help creating an OpenAI account or setting up a virtual environment in your IDE, refer to *Appendix* for detailed guidance.

Introducing code refactoring

Code is intended as communication to future software developers. Code that effectively and clearly communicates the purpose and mechanisms is described as **clean code**.

As described by Robert C. Martin (better known as *Uncle Bob*), clean code can be achieved through refactoring. Code refactoring is not merely modifying code, but a disciplined approach to continuously improving code. One aspect is removing the indiscriminate **code smell** that qualitatively characterizes poorly written code (see *Further reading*). A second aspect is improving the code's actual design, which should improve its readability and maintainability. This is critical since firms spend an estimated 75% of their software development costs on the evolution and maintenance of software (Sommerville).

Software developers frequently dedicate time to refactoring, which involves rewriting sections of existing code while keeping the original functionality and purpose intact. The goal is to improve readability, structure, or performance. This is particularly evident in **Agile** software development, where continuous refactoring is linked to the sustainable evolution of code. The **Extreme Programming** (**XP**) agile methodology explicitly embraces refactoring along with ideals of collective ownership and the use of **Test-Driven Development** (**TDD**), as will be discussed in *Chapter 13*.

IDEs such as PyCharm and VS Code offer built-in tools for tasks such as extracting variables, functions, and methods, renaming code elements, and formatting code. Still, they fall short when it comes to more complex scenarios such as extracting a function from non-consecutive lines of code.

Next, we will use an example of a function that computes two types of distances and identify hidden issues caused by poor implementation. Later in the chapter, we will refactor it using GenAI tools.

Manhattan and Euclidean distance

In *Chapter 7*, we introduced the **Manhattan distance** between two matrices, also known as the **L1 norm**, defined as the sum of absolute differences between corresponding elements. The code example provided used a *Flask* application that receives matrix data through HTTP requests. If you need a refresher on this topic, refer to *Chapter 7*.

Another way to measure the distance between matrices is the **Euclidean distance**, which is simply the straight-line distance. In two dimensions, the distance between points *(x1, y1)* and *(x2,y2)* is calculated as follows:

$$\text{Distance} = \sqrt{(x_1 - x_2)^2 + (y_1 - y_2)^2}$$

When applied to a pair of two-dimensional matrices X and Y of the same shape (with the same number of rows and columns), the distance is calculated as follows:

$$\text{Distance} = \sqrt{\sum_{i=1}^{n}\sum_{j=1}^{m}(X_{ij} - Y_{ij})^2}$$

This measure is also referred to as the **L2 norm** or **Frobenius** norm. It is widely used in tasks such as image similarity and machine learning, where it often represents the *squared error* of a prediction.

Implementing the distance function

If we want to implement a function that computes both L1 and L2 norms based on a request, one way to approach this is to build upon our *Chapter 7* implementation of the Manhattan distance (L1) and extend it to include the Euclidean distance (L2) as well. A sample implementation, although poorly written, is as follows:

```python
@app.route("/distances", methods=["POST"])
def calculate_distance():
    data = request.get_json()
    dist_type = data.get("distance")
    if dist_type == "L1":
        print("Info: computing L1 distance...")
        a = data.get("df1")
        b = data.get("df2")
        dist = np.sum(np.abs(a - b))
        return jsonify({"distance": dist})
    elif dist_type == "L2":
        print("Info: computing L2 distance...")
        a = data.get("df1")
        b = data.get("df2")
        dist_2 = 0
        for i in range(len(a)):
            for j in range(len(a[i])):
                dist_2 += (a[i][j] - b[i][j]) ** 2
        dist = np.sqrt(dist_2)
        return jsonify({"distance": dist})
```

💡 **Quick tip:** Enhance your coding experience with the **AI Code Explainer** and **Quick Copy** features. Open this book in the next-gen Packt Reader. Click the **Copy** button (1) to quickly copy code into your coding environment, or click the **Explain** button (2) to get the AI assistant to explain a block of code to you.

```
                                              Copy      Explain
function calculate(a, b) {
  return {sum: a + b};                          1           2
};
```

📖 **The next-gen Packt Reader** is included for free with the purchase of this book. Scan the QR code OR visit packtpub.com/unlock, then use the search bar to find this book by name. Double-check the edition shown to make sure you get the right one.

Maintaining this code may be challenging. For example, reading the parameters a and b is duplicated, so if we want to add validations such as checking that both matrices have the same shape, we need to do it twice. Such duplication of code is considered poor programming practice. If we plan to add unit tests, every test needs to mock the request. Adding another distance function would make the function even longer and harder to read.

Next, we will categorize the several types of refactoring and see how they apply to this example.

Types of refactoring

When we refactor code, our goal is to maintain its functionality while improving its quality. There is always a risk that the modifications will break the code or inadvertently change the functionality. To avoid this, unit tests should be in place before making any significant changes to ensure that the code still runs correctly. In addition, refactoring should be performed as a set of incremental changes that do not alter the behavior of the code.

The term **refactoring** alone is not specific enough to define a single task, according to the **five S's framework** introduced in *Chapter 4*. The changes we aim to make can vary from simple tasks such as renaming a variable to more extensive efforts such as redesigning an entire module.

To achieve clean code, there are several common refactoring approaches. First, larger and more complex functions should be divided into several that perform a single task. Second, duplicate code should be removed or abstracted by the **Do not Repeat Yourself (DRY)** principle. Variables and functions should be named for clarity. This principle also applies to arbitrary numeric constants and strings, so there should not be hardcoded values (also referred to as **magic numbers**), but instead have these values assigned to a meaningful constant name.

We typically divide refactoring tasks into three categories:

- **Readability**: This includes tasks such as renaming objects, removing redundant imports or excessive comments, introducing constants instead of hardcoded numbers, or adding type hints. For example, within the implementation of `calculate_distance`, we might change the name of the variable `a` to `df1` to indicate that it represents a matrix in the request. We might also want to add type hints to the request parameters.

- **Structure change**: This involves organizing code in a better way, such as extracting long code blocks into functions or classes. For example, within the implementation of `calculate_distance`, we might replace `print` statements with `logger` calls, improving how our code handles output. We might also extract the `L1` and `L2` calculations into separate functions.

- **Performance**: This means adjusting the implementation to better handle space or runtime constraints. For example, within the implementation of `calculate_distance`, instead of using a nested `for` loop to calculate `L2`, we might apply vectorization using the *NumPy* library to improve efficiency.

There are already good capabilities for refactoring code, particularly for readability, using the built-in tools of our IDEs, as we will see next.

Improving readability before GenAI

Modern IDEs such as VS Code and PyCharm offer built-in refactoring tools that help improve code readability. For example, in PyCharm, we can right-click a parameter we would like to rename and select **Refactor | Rename** to update the variable and all its references within the relevant scope (in this case, the calculate_distance function). This option is illustrated in *Figure 10.1.*

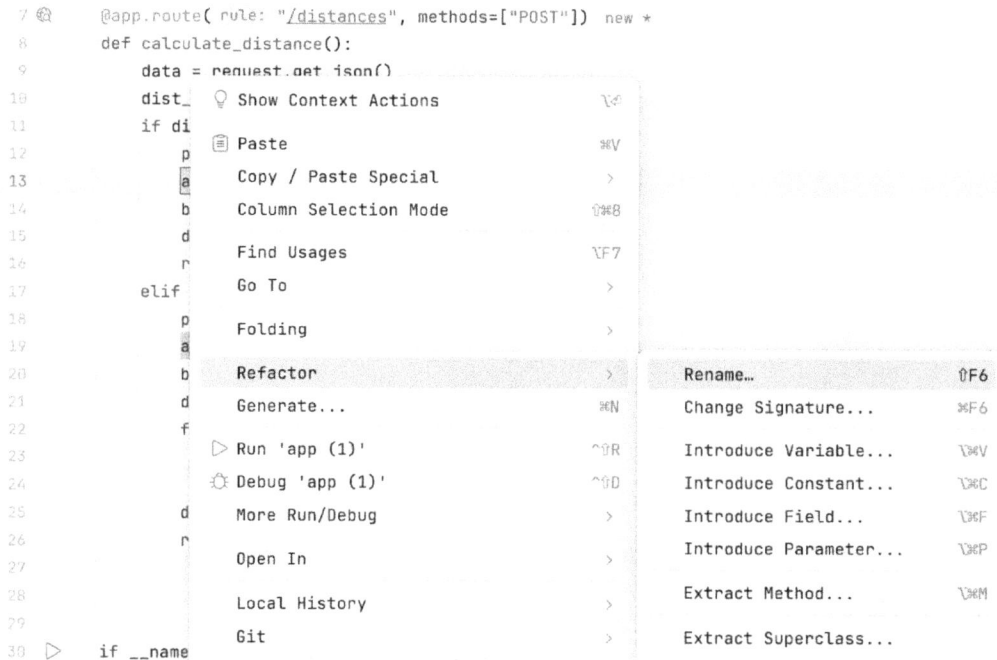

Figure 10.1: PyCharm built-in refactoring tools for refactoring/renaming

This figure also highlights other refactoring options such as changing a callable signature, extracting constants or methods, and more. The authors frequently use these features when refining existing code.

Similarly, VS Code allows us to right-click the parameter we want to change and select **Rename Symbol** to update the variable and all its references within the relevant scope, as shown in *Figure 10.2*.

```
 7   @app.route("/distances", methods=["POST"])
 8   def calculate_distance():
 9       data = request.get_json()
10       dist_    Go to Definition              F12    e")
11       if di   Go to Declaration
12          p    Go to Type Definition                 distance...")
13          a    Go to Implementations         ⌘ F12
14          b    Go to References              ⇧ F12
15          d    Peek                     >            b))
16          r    Find All References       ⌥⇧F12     ": dist})
17       elif    Find All Implementations
18          p    Show Call Hierarchy       ⌥⇧H       distance...")
19          a    Show Type Hierarchy
20          b    Copilot                   >
21          d    Rename Symbol                 F2
22          f    Change All Occurrences        ⌘F2
23               Format Document           ⌥⇧F       i])):
                 Format Document With...
```

Figure 10.2: VS Code Rename Symbol

The **Rename Symbol** option appears fourth from the bottom in the figure and performs a similar renaming operation as in PyCharm.

Next, we will explore the limitations of these built-in tools. Later in the chapter, we will use GenAI to address those challenges.

Limitations of code refactoring with IDE tools

PyCharm and VS Code offer powerful refactoring features, but these are still limited.

For example, we may want to extract argument parsing logic for a, b, and dist_type into a separate function, such as the following:

```
def parse_request_parameters(r: request) -> Tuple[np.ndarray, np.ndarray,
str]:
    a = np.array(r["df1"])
    b = np.array(r["df2"])
    dist_type = r["distance"]
    return a, b, dist_type
```

This kind of structural refactoring helps reduce code duplication. However, current IDE tools are unable to extract these three parameters into a single function because they are not written in consecutive lines in the original implementation, as shown in *Figure 10.3*.

```
8
      /distances
9     @app.route( rule: "/distances", methods=["POST"])  new *
10    def calculate_distance():
11        data = requ  ⊘ Cannot perform the Extract Method refactoring using the selected elements
12        dist_type =
13        if dist_type == "L1":
14            print("Info: computing L1 distance...")
15            a = data.get("df1")
16            b = data.get("df2")
17            dist = np.sum(np.abs(a - b))
18            return jsonify({"distance": dist})
```

Figure 10.3: Limitation of extracting a code block to a function

Quick tip: Need to see a high-resolution version of this image? Open this book in the next-gen Packt Reader or view it in the PDF/ePub copy.

The next-gen Packt Reader is included for free with the purchase of this book. Scan the QR code OR go to packtpub.com/unlock, then use the search bar to find this book by name. Double-check the edition shown to make sure you get the right one.

In this figure, we cannot extract dist_type, a, and b into a separate function since the lines are not written in a continuous block. As functions become more complex, this approach might no longer be practical.

Next, we will examine how to handle structural refactoring challenges that are beyond the capabilities of IDE tools alone.

Refactoring with chain-of-thought

In *Chapter 9*, we introduced **chain-of-thought** (**CoT**) as a key prompt engineering technique for working with GenAI to generate code. This method involves writing a high-level function as the prompt, while leaving the implementation details for the GenAI application to complete.

When refactoring code, we want to include the old implementation as an additional context for the model. This can help it better understand the intended functionality. For instance, in the case of the `calculate_distance` function, the previous implementation can clarify which parameters need to be extracted from the JSON request: a, b, and `dist_type`.

Refactoring for a better structure

When reviewing the implementation of the `calculate_distance` function, we can break it down into three main steps:

1. Extracting the request parameters
2. Deciding whether to compute L1 (Manhattan) or L2 (Euclidean) distance
3. Calculating the distance

A CoT prompt that reflects these steps could look like this:

```
@app.route("/distances", methods=["POST"])
def calculate_distance():
    a, b, dist_type = parse_request_parameters(request)
    dist_func = {"L1": get_manhattan_dist, "L2": get_euclidean_dist}.
get(dist_type)
    dist = dist_func(a, b)
    return jsonify({"distance": dist})
```

In this high-level implementation, we can observe the three main steps:

1. Call a function called `parse_request_parameters` that should return the values for a, b, and `dist_type`.
2. Map `dist_function` based on the value of `dist_type` from the request.
3. Compute the distance using a and b.

Note that we have considerable flexibility in how we map dist_type to a function. This could involve more than an inline dictionary, such as using a function or an external dictionary. A less Pythonic but also acceptable approach would be to use a switch-case structure or an if-else block.

With this function in place, we can now explore how to implement a complete prompt for GitHub Copilot, ChatGPT, and OpenAI API.

CoT for refactoring with GitHub Copilot

When using GitHub Copilot, the best practice is to start our prompt with the same function signature as the function we want to refactor. This tells Copilot that we are planning to re-implement the function. Note that Copilot may already suggest an implementation based on the signature alone. However, such an implementation is only as good as asking ChatGPT to refactor a function, since the prompt is not specific enough. For reference, one early completion that Copilot produced from the signature alone is shown in *Figure 10.4*.

```
 7   @app.route("/distances", methods=["POST"])
 8   def calculate_distance():
 9       data = request.get_json()
         dist_type = data.get("distance")
         if dist_type == "L1":
             print("Info: computing L1 distance...")
             a = np.array(data.get("df1"))
             b = np.array(data.get("df2"))
             dist = np.sum(np.abs(a - b))
             return jsonify({"distance": dist})
         elif dist_type == "L2":
             print("Info: computing L2 distance...")
             a = np.array(data.get("df1"))
             b = np.array(data.get("df2"))
             dist_2 = 0
             for i in range(len(a)):
                 for j in range(len(a[i])):
                     dist_2 += (a[i][j] - b[i][j]) ** 2
             dist = np.sqrt(dist_2)
             return jsonify({"distance": dist})
10
11
12   @app.route("/distances", methods=["POST"])
13   def calculate_distance():
```

Figure 10.4: Copilot produced a weak refactoring suggestion

In this example, the refactoring involved converting the a and b parameters to NumPy arrays. While this vectorization can be beneficial in some cases, it may be unnecessary in others. To guide Copilot toward a more suitable output, we use the CoT approach by providing the full CoT high-level implementation as shown earlier in the chapter. Like in *Chapter 9*, Copilot is expected to generate the implementations of the missing functions called by the high-level implementation, as illustrated in *Figure 10.5*.

```
7   @app.route("/distances", methods=["POST"])
8   def calculate_distance():
9       a, b, dist_type = parse_request_parameters(request)
10      dist_func = {"L1": get_manhattan_dist, "L2": get_euclidean_dist}.get
        (dist_type)
11      dist = dist_func(a, b)
12      return jsonify({"distance": dist})
13
14
15  def parse_request_parameters(request):
```

Figure 10.5: CoT approach triggers an implementation of missing functions

In this case, Copilot correctly proposed starting with the parse_request_parameters function. Once accepted, it suggested a correct implementation for parsing a, b, and dist_function, as shown in *Figure 10.6*.

```
7   @app.route("/distances", methods=["POST"])
8   def calculate_distance():
9       a, b, dist_type = parse_request_parameters(request)
10      dist_func = {"L1": get_manhattan_dist, "L2": get_euclidean_dist}.get
        (dist_type)
11      dist = dist_func(a, b)
12      return jsonify({"distance": dist})
13
14
15  def parse_request_parameters(request):
        data = request.get_json()
        a = np.array(data.get("df1"))
        b = np.array(data.get("df2"))
        dist_type = data.get("distance")
        return a, b, dist_type
16
```

Figure 10.6: Copilot implementation for parse_request_parameters

Here, Copilot effectively used the context from the previous version of the function. It suggested reading the value of a from the df1 key in the request JSON, b from df2, and dist_type from distance. This highlights how providing relevant context can lead to desirable results.

For reference, here are the three implementations Copilot generated:

```python
def parse_request_parameters(request):
    data = request.get_json()
    a = np.array(data.get("df1"))
    b = np.array(data.get("df2"))
    dist_type = data.get("distance")
    return a, b, dist_type


def get_manhattan_dist(a, b):
    print("Info: computing L1 distance...")
    return np.sum(np.abs(a - b))


def get_euclidean_dist(a, b):
    print("Info: computing L2 distance...")
    dist_2 = 0
    for i in range(len(a)):
        for j in range(len(a[i])):
            dist_2 += (a[i][j] - b[i][j]) ** 2
    return np.sqrt(dist_2)
```

These functions mirror the original logic from calculate_distance while offering improved abstraction and avoiding code duplication. In a later section of the chapter, we will explore how to refactor for performance, including replacing nested loops with vectorized operations.

Next, we will explore how to apply the CoT approach for refactoring with ChatGPT and OpenAI API. This requires a bit more effort to set up effectively.

Leveraging CoT for refactoring with ChatGPT and OpenAI API

Just like GitHub Copilot, we can also make use of ChatGPT and OpenAI API to refactor our code to have a better structure. To achieve this, we need to provide these tools with both the original implementation for context and the new structure we want to complete.

A structural refactoring prompt for ChatGPT can follow this general template:

```
CONTEXT: You are provided with
1. Python function enclosed with {{{ fUNCTION }}} with calls to missing
implementations.
2. Old implementation enclosed with {{{ OLD }}} for reference.
TASK: implement the missing functions.
FUNCTION: {{{ ... omitted for brevity ... }}}
OLD: {{{ ... omitted for brevity ...}}}
CODE:
```

Note that in contrast to CoT for new code, refactoring prompts requires giving ChatGPT both the new structure of the function and the reference implementation enclosed in {{{ OLD }}}. This format is like how we prompt Copilot and produces desirable results that preserve functionality, even when using more cost-effective models such as *GPT-4o*. *Figure 10.7* shows the output we received from *GPT-4o* for this prompt.

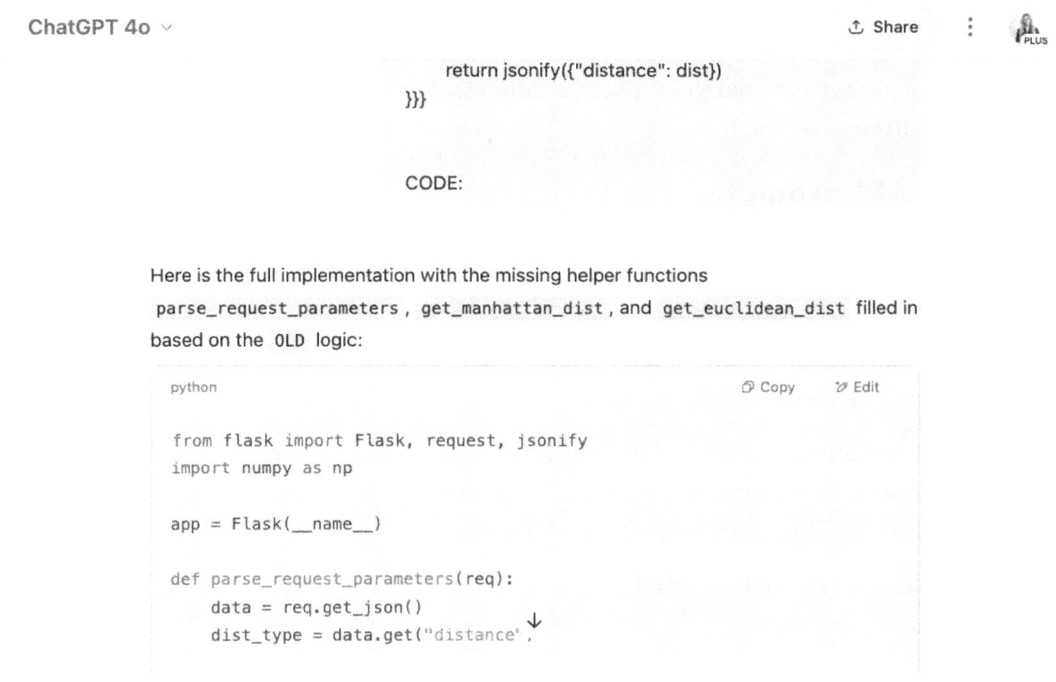

Figure 10.7: ChatGPT suggested refactoring

Here is the implementation for the missing functions proposed by ChatGPT:

```
def parse_request_parameters(req):
    data = req.get_json()
    dist_type = data.get("distance")
    a = np.array(data.get("df1"))
    b = np.array(data.get("df2"))
    return a, b, dist_type


def get_manhattan_dist(a, b):
    print("Info: computing L1 distance...")
    return float(np.sum(np.abs(a - b)))


def get_euclidean_dist(a, b):
    print("Info: computing L2 distance...")
    return float(np.sqrt(np.sum((a - b) ** 2)))
```

This output resembles the structure Copilot suggested, focusing on extracting the distance calculations into smaller functions and removing redundancy. One notable difference is that ChatGPT was more consistent and used NumPy vectorization for both distance functions, and not just the Manhattan distance method.

OpenAI API prompt

When we refactor code for improved structure, GitHub Copilot and ChatGPT often prove to be more suitable than OpenAI API. This is because using the API typically requires more manual effort to craft the prompt programmatically. OpenAI API becomes more practical only when we need to scale changes across multiple similar functions, and we find that refactoring the structure with CoT might not be one of these cases.

In summary, GenAI supports the restructuring of existing code by combining prior implementations with new instructions. We recommend trying this technique with code you encounter in your day-to-day work or even in third-party libraries.

Next, we will briefly introduce refactoring for performance using GenAI, a topic we will cover more extensively in *Chapter 14*.

Performance refactoring with GenAI

Performance refactoring refers to changes made to the code that preserve its functionality while improving runtime or memory efficiency. One common approach is to use **vectorized computations**. These can reduce the runtime by benefiting from cache, lower overhead, and parallel computation.

For instance, in the GitHub Copilot implementation of calculate_distance example, this would mean replacing a nested for loop with a vectorized computation of the Euclidean distance. We will explore further runtime and space complexity in *Chapter 14*, including when and why to scale system capacity and the trade-offs involved. Until then, let us demonstrate how a simple optimization through vectorization might be applied.

Performance refactoring with GitHub Copilot

As with the CoT approach, we will leverage the context of existing code along with our desired structure. This time, we will specify the library we would like to implement a code block instead of the original implementation.

For example, consider the function Copilot extracted for us to compute the Euclidean distance:

```python
def get_euclidean_dist(a, b):
    print("Info: computing L2 distance...")
    dist_2 = 0
    for i in range(len(a)):
        for j in range(len(a[i])):
            dist_2 += (a[i][j] - b[i][j]) ** 2
    return np.sqrt(dist_2)
```

This function computes the squared distance dist_2 and then returns its square root.

To vectorize the squared distance computation, we can use NumPy, a widely used Python library that supports optimized operations on arrays and matrices. In our prompt, our goal is to preserve the original logic:

1. Compute the squared distance
2. Compute the distance

To guide Copilot toward the desired refactoring, we can add a cue using a NumPy function call. The first prompt would be placed near the squared distance step:

```python
Dist_2 = np.
```

This is shown in *Figure 10.8*:

```
28          def get_euclidean_dist(a, b):  1 usage  new *
29      💡      print("Info: computing L2 distance...")
30              dist_2 = np.sum((a - b) ** 2)
31
32
33              dist_2 = 0
34              for i in range(len(a)):
35                  for j in range(len(a[i])):
36                      dist_2 += (a[i][j] - b[i][j]) ** 2
37              return np.sqrt(dist_2)
```

Figure 10.8: Prompt with an np. library call as a cue

Then, for the square root step, we would add another cue:

```python
dist = np.
```

This is sufficient context for Copilot to complete the correct implementation using NumPy, as shown in *Figure 10.9*:

```
28    def get_euclidean_dist(a, b):  1 usage  new *
29        print("Info: computing L2 distance...")
30     💡 dist_2 = np.sum((a - b) ** 2)
31        dist = np.|sqrt(dist_2)
32
33
34        dist_2 = 0
35        for i in range(len(a)):
36            for j in range(len(a[i])):
37                dist_2 += (a[i][j] - b[i][j]) ** 2
38        return np.sqrt(dist_2)
```

Figure 10.9: Copilot recognized the correct function from the cue

These inline completions can be highly effective. However, before applying performance optimizations, it is important to determine whether scaling or optimizing code is necessary. We will explore these considerations further in *Chapter 14*.

Next, we will look at how to achieve the same outcome using ChatGPT and OpenAI.

Performance refactoring with ChatGPT and OpenAI

When using ChatGPT and OpenAI API for performance refactoring tasks such as vectorizing computations, common transformations such as adopting the NumPy package can be achieved by following the **five S's best practices**, as introduced in *Chapter 4*. Like in *Chapter 7*, where we include the full file content in the prompt along with the specific line we want to explain, here, we also provide the complete function implementation together with the files that need refactoring.

Here is a sample prompt template that can be used in ChatGPT:

```
CONTEXT: You are provided with:
1. A Python function implementation enclosed with {{{ FUNCTION }}}
2. Lines to be refactored enclosed with {{{ OLD }}}
3. A library to be used in the new code enclosed with {{{ LIBRARY }}}
TASK: Return a new implementation for the old lines using the specified
library.
FUNCTION: {{{ ... }}}
OLD: {{{      ... }}}
```

```
LIBRARY: {{{ ... }}}

REFACTORED CODE:
```

Note that in this template, we are not requiring the model to follow the same sequence of steps as in Copilot, such as first computing dist_2 and then applying the square root. This allows ChatGPT to suggest more common implementations that may take a different route. By specifying LIBRARY, we are explicitly guiding the GenAI tools toward an expected solution.

> **Important note**
>
> In *Chapter 14*, we will learn how to replace the library constraint with constraints on runtime and space capacity. If we do not specify either constraints or a library, the model will suggest the most popular implementation, which may not align with our goals. As a result, the response often lacks specific instructions and does not follow the five S's framework.

For reference, let us consider a vectorization prompt for the get_euclidean_distance function that is available in this book's repository at ch10/prompts/performance_refactoring_chatgpt. txt. The response we got from ChatGPT with the *GPT-4o* economic model is shown in *Figure 10.10*.

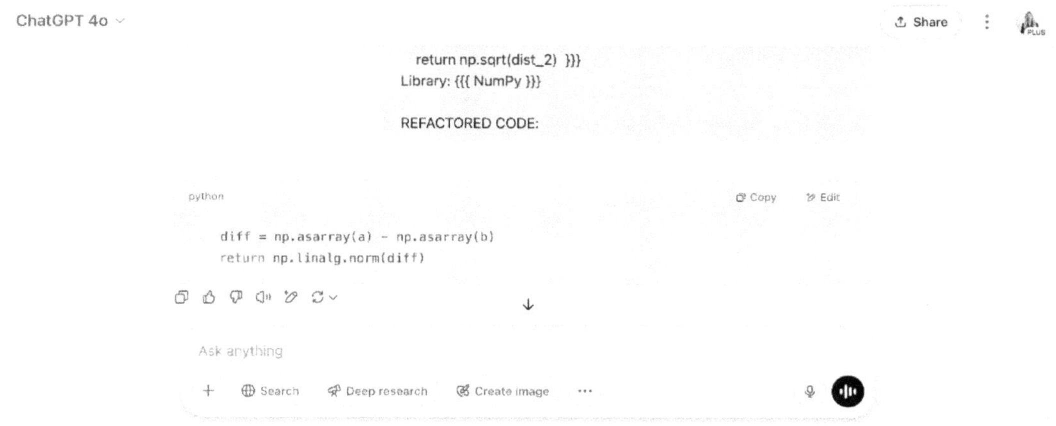

Figure 10.10: ChatGPT proposed vectorized implementation

The implementation shown in the figure is a common implementation for calculating Euclidean distance. It vectorizes the element-wise distance and then uses the linear algebra module in NumPy to compute the norm. This version is typically easier to read and more flexible than what Copilot suggested.

> **Note**
>
> This prompt structure can be reused when comparing implementations across multiple libraries offering similar functionality. For instance, when evaluating alternatives between SciPy and NumPy, this format allows us to generate and compare implementations quickly.

Next, we will look at how to achieve equivalent results using OpenAI API.

Vectorizing with OpenAI API

Creating a prompt for OpenAI API usually takes more effort than using ChatGPT to get comparable results. This approach is most suitable when we want to produce multiple new implementations at scale, such as converting many for loops to vectorized NumPy expressions.

To create a system prompt, we can adapt our ChatGPT prompt structure into two components:

```
SURROUND = """You are provided with:
1. A Python function implementation enclosed with {{{ FUNCTION }}}
2. Lines to be refactored enclosed with {{{ OLD }}}
3. A library to be used in the new code enclosed with {{{ LIBRARY }}}."""
SINGLE_TASK = "Your task is to return a new implementation for the old
lines using the specified library."

LINES = """dist_2 = 0
for i in range(len(a)):
    for j in range(len(a[i])):
        dist_2 += (a[i][j] - b[i][j]) ** 2
"""
```

We can define a get_user_prompt function as such:

```
def get_user_prompt(func: callable, library: str, lines: str) -> str:
    return f"""
    FUNCTION: {{{{{{ {inspect.getsource(func)} }}}}}}
```

```
    LINES: {{{{{{ {lines} }}}}}}

    LIBRARY: {{{{{{ {library} }}}}}}

    REFACTORD:
    """
```

We can then use both prompts when calling the service:

```
if __name__ == "__main__":
    client: OpenAI = OpenAI()

    system_prompt = f"{SURROUND} {SINGLE_TASK}"
    user_prompt = get_user_prompt(get_euclidean_distance, "NumPy", LINES)

    completion: ChatCompletion = client.chat.completions.create(
        model="gpt-4o-mini",
        messages=[
            {"role": "system", "content": system_prompt},
            {"role": "user", "content": user_prompt},
        ],
    )
    print("Explanation:", completion.choices[0].message.content)
```

For reference, the full script is available in `ch10/prompts/performance_refactoring_openai.py`. The output we obtained was equivalent to the result from ChatGPT.

To conclude, GitHub Copilot is the quickest way to get performance refactoring suggestions. ChatGPT is more suitable when we want widely adopted implementations or to quickly assess different libraries' implementations with a reusable prompt. OpenAI API is helpful in less common cases when we want to generate bulk transformations across many files or a large code base.

More advanced performance refactoring

In *Part 3* of the book, *Chapter 14* will address runtime and space complexity optimization. We will demonstrate how combining code completion tools with prompt engineering techniques such as **chaining** can help us find the right balance between space and time complexity.

We will use GitHub Copilot, ChatGPT, and OpenAI to assess the program's current performance, estimate its runtime and space complexity in terms of **Big-O notation**, and introduce optimized solutions to extend input capacity with minimal trade-off. Stay tuned for a detailed exploration of these topics.

Summary

In this chapter, we explored how GitHub Copilot, ChatGPT, and OpenAI API can assist in rewriting code while preserving its original functionality. These tools can enhance readability, improve structure, and boost performance.

Clean code is a shared goal among software developers, especially as projects grow and become complex. Most IDEs already offer strong built-in tools for refactoring, which we frequently use. However, when those tools reach their limits, GenAI can step in. It can support structural refactoring by using CoT techniques with the original implementation, or it can optimize performance through the five S's framework.

Although refactoring is useful, writing clean and structured code from the start is usually simpler. In the next chapter, we will introduce **fine-tuning** with OpenAI API as an alternative to **few-shot learning**. Fine-tuning enables us to adapt a pretrained model to a specific domain, such as generating clean and well-organized code. Unlike prompt engineering, fine-tuning separates the specialization process from the prompt itself, which can be beneficial for larger-scale projects.

Quiz time

Before you proceed to the next chapter, make sure that you can confidently answer the following questions:

Question 1: Why do we need GenAI for refactoring tasks if IDEs already provide built-in tools?

Answer: While built-in tools are powerful, they have limitations. For example, they can only extract code blocks to external functions when the lines are written consecutively in a single block. GenAI allows us to restructure Python objects more flexibly, using the CoT technique with the original implementation as a reference.

Question 2: How does the CoT approach differ when refactoring existing code compared to generating new code?

Answer: When generating new code, we typically describe the high-level function we want GenAI to complete. For refactoring, we also include the original implementation in the prompt. This helps GenAI understand the intended functionality, such as parsing specific JSON request keys or assigning them to specific variable names.

Further reading

To learn more about the topics that were covered in this chapter, look at the following resources:

Clean Code: A Handbook of Agile Software Craftsmanship by Robert C. Martin (aka Uncle Bob): `https://www.amazon.com/Clean-Code-Handbook-Software-Craftsmanship/dp/0132350882`

Code smell: `https://en.wikipedia.org/wiki/Code_smell`

Refactoring: Improving the Design of Existing Code, Second Edition: `https://www.amazon.com/Refactoring-Improving-Existing-Addison-Wesley-Signature/dp/0134757599`

Design Patterns: Elements of Reusable Object-Oriented Software: `https://www.amazon.com/Design-Patterns-Elements-Reusable-Object-Oriented/dp/0201633612`

Mariane Anaya. *Clean Code in Python: Develop maintainable and efficient code, Second Edition*, 2021: `https://www.packtpub.com/en-us/product/clean-code-in-python-9781800560215`

Kent Beck and Cynthia Andres, *Extreme Programming Explained: Embrace Change*, 2004: `https://www.amazon.com/Extreme-Programming-Explained-Embrace-Change/dp/0321278658`

Ian Sommerville. *Software Engineering*, 2015: `https://www.amazon.com/Software-Engineering-10th-Ian-Sommerville/dp/0133943038`

Subscribe for a free eBook

New frameworks, evolving architectures, research drops, production breakdowns—AI_Distilled filters the noise into a weekly briefing for engineers and researchers working hands-on with LLMs and GenAI systems. Subscribe now and receive a free eBook, along with weekly insights that help you stay focused and informed.

Subscribe at `https://packt.link/TR05B` or scan the QR code below.

11

Fine-Tuning Models with OpenAI

Concluding *Part 2*, this chapter explores how to train **large language models (LLMs)** to specialize in completing a specific task. This is achieved by **fine-tuning** the model's parameters, known as **weights**, through the OpenAI platform. This is quite like the prompt engineering strategy **few-shot learning**, sometimes referred to as **in-context learning**, which we introduced earlier in the book as a technique for helping the model to specialize in a particular domain. Fine-tuning, however, is best suited for larger-scale projects where we want to separate the specialization aspect from the actual prompt.

We will delve into a use case where this specialization of the model is required to produce code while avoiding comments clutter. We will examine how outputs from the *GPT-4o mini* model may be programmatically correct but fail to follow our style guidelines and requirements for concise explanations and code comments. We will construct a fine-tuning **JSONL** file with high-quality examples that illustrate desired outcomes, initiate a fine-tuning job through the OpenAI website, and compare the improved results with the output of the base model.

This chapter covers the following topics:

- Fine-tuning LLMs toward a specialization
- Experimenting with the OpenAI Playground
- Crafting a JSONL file for fine-tuning
- Fine-tuning a model with the OpenAI GUI
- Comparing our results

Technical requirements

To get the most out of this chapter, ensure you have the following:

- An OpenAI account with access to OpenAI API
- Access to the book's repository, available at `https://github.com/PacktPublishing/Supercharged-Coding-with-Gen-AI`

For instructions on setting up OpenAI API access, see *Chapter 2*. If you need help with creating an OpenAI account, refer to the *Appendix* for detailed guidance.

Fine-tuning LLMs toward a specialization

When working on complex coding tasks with LLMs, we may need to employ **prompt engineering** techniques. In *Chapter 8*, we saw how including a few examples in the prompt implicitly instructs the model to follow the expected coding style when writing code. This *show, don't tell* approach effectively guides the model by enriching our existing prompt, as illustrated in *Figure 11.1*:

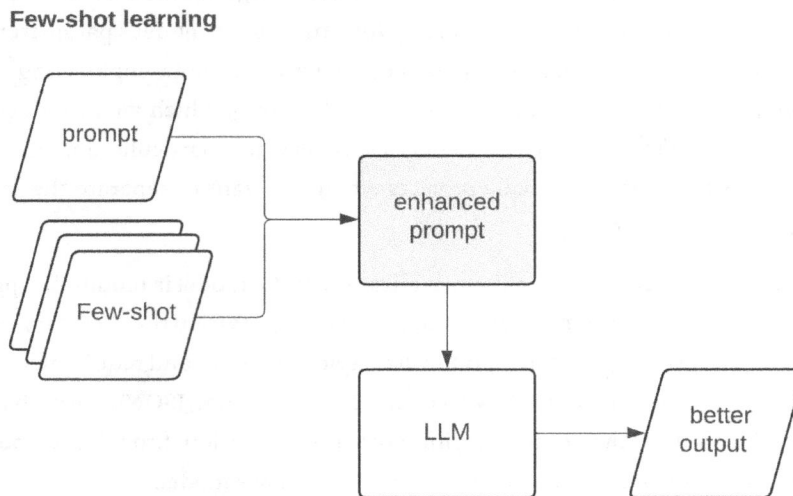

Figure 11.1: Few-shot learning prompt enrichment

By using this approach, the model adapts to produce outputs that align with the examples provided, effectively *specializing* in the given task.

LLMs specialization

A **specialization** for LLMs focuses on a specific task or a set of closely related tasks. Here are some examples of specializations you might want your model to develop:

- Generating completion code that follows a specific coding style
- Creating a unit test suite that covers key scenarios such as happy paths, bad inputs, edge cases, and error handling
- Assessing the quality of a function's docstring
- Refactoring for loops into comprehensions

We typically identify a specialization as either a single system prompt or a set of closely related system prompts, each incorporating the surrounding context and a single-task focus. These tasks are generally non-trivial for an LLM, such as code completion to reverse a string, requiring additional effort in prompt crafting, such as prompt engineering or fine-tuning.

For certain tasks, few-shot learning can be particularly effective. For example, if refactoring for loops into comprehensions never involves more than two levels of nesting, providing a few examples in the prompt may be sufficient to achieve reliable results.

However, for deeper specializations, such as breaking longer functions into helper functions to improve code quality, we may need to incorporate a larger set of training examples with the desired output, rather than just a few. We might include examples of naming conventions and indentation. Some examples may show the extraction of code blocks into helper functions, and others may show how to eliminate unnecessary explanations that come along with the code. Including all these examples directly in the prompt increases the prompt's length and, therefore, the cost associated with the input token length. It also makes it harder to maintain.

Fine-tuning an LLM

Fine-tuning a model is a process that aims to achieve better outputs by using a pre-trained model such as GPT-4o mini and training it toward a specialization using a small set of **training examples** that depict the intended output. The fine-tuning process adjusts the model's parameters (or **weights**, as discussed in *Chapter 6*) to achieve the desired outcomes shown in the provided examples. This specialization process is shown in *Figure 11.2*:

Fine-tuning

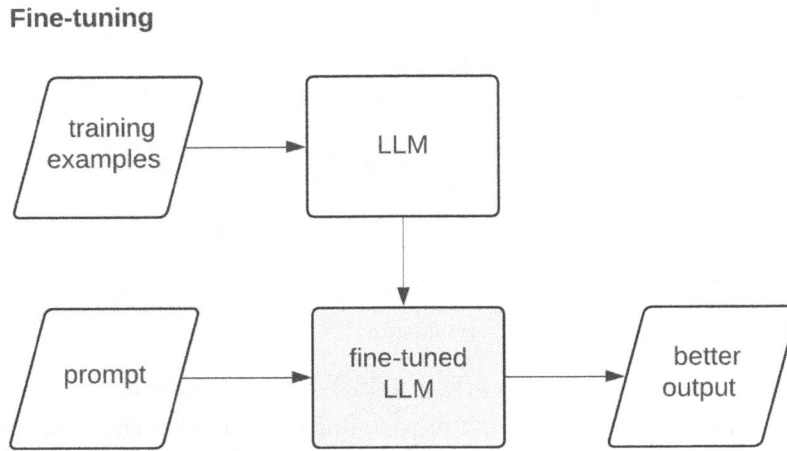

Figure 11.2: Leveraging fine-tuning for a better output

The specialization process uses the crafted training examples to fine-tune the LLM, resulting in a new LLM that is ready to be prompted without requiring further examples in the prompts.

Favoring fine-tuning over prompt engineering

Based on studies, and confirmed with our experience, fine-tuning requires more training examples than few-shot learning because the examples are retraining the model's parameters, rather than simply being part of the prompt. In this chapter, we use 15 examples, which is slightly above the OpenAI API's minimum of 10 for initiating a fine-tuning job. For more complex cases, tens or even hundreds of examples may be necessary, which can be time-consuming to find.

Fortunately, for most of our daily coding tasks, we will find that few-shot learning is sufficient where only a few examples are needed. However, for larger-scale projects, or when few-shot learning does not meet our needs, fine-tuning may be a better alternative. Generally, it is good practice to begin with the few-shot technique and turn to fine-tuning only when the results are not satisfactory.

Task specializing in cleaner code

In *Chapter 7*, we noted that LLMs often include explanations and example usage along with the code. The LLMs also add code comments when function implementations become longer to compensate for less readable code. When working with higher-quality code, we may prefer the model to return only the code without extra explanations. Additionally, rather than relying on comments in lengthy functions, we might want the model to break the logic into smaller, more manageable functions.

This is a perfect use case for fine-tuning since the effort invested in creating a training file of examples is justified as it can be applied to an entire repository using short prompts alone. Later in the book, we will explore how fine-tuning supports advanced refactoring initiatives, such as extracting logging, monitoring, and error-handling responsibilities into separate functions.

Next, we will explore how to experiment with the OpenAI API Playground and observe that the *GPT-4o mini* model requires improvements in its output implementation. Later in the chapter, we will address these improvements through the fine-tuning process.

Experimenting with the OpenAI API Playground

In this section, we will use OpenAI's **graphical user interface** (GUI) Playground to quickly view our results for a given **preset**, which represents a combination of a model and the selected call parameters. This interface is an excellent tool for rapid experimentation and for comparing models before implementing them programmatically in our software.

To access the Playground, ensure that your OpenAI account has credits applied to unlock *tier 1*, as explained in *Chapter 2*. Then, go to https://platform.openai.com/playground/chat. You can also reach it by navigating to the home page, https://platform.openai.com, selecting **Play-ground** from the top-right menu, and then choosing the **Chat** option from the left menu. The opening screen of the Playground is shown in *Figure 11.3*:

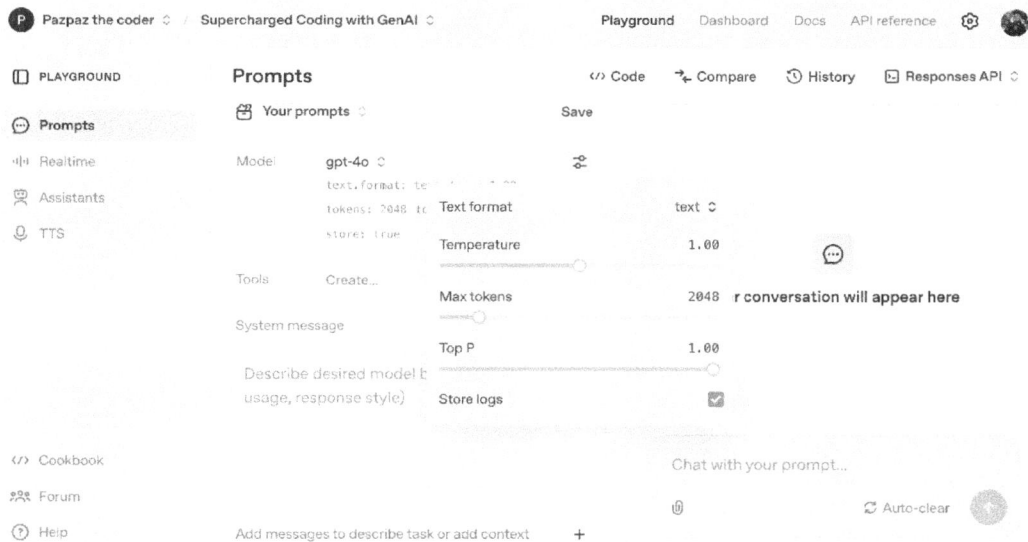

Figure 11.3: Opening screen of the Playground interface for OpenAI

On this page, we can craft prompts for OpenAI, as introduced in *Chapter 2*, and try different presets. This includes the system and user prompts, along with parameters such as temperature and maximum tokens. Additional parameters include the following:

- **Top P** is an alternative to the temperature, setting a minimal probability threshold that the model's output must meet. In some cases, higher values can prevent hallucinations.
- The **Store logs** checkbox saves the prompt so it can be restored later.

We can also modify the response format and add functions. These topics will be discussed in detail in later chapters of this book.

Note that the experimentation in the Playground is free for tier 1 or higher accounts, but not all models are available. For instance, as of April 2025, *GPT-o1* and *GPT-o1-preview* models are not available in the reasoning models for experimentation. *Figure 11.4* shows the available models.

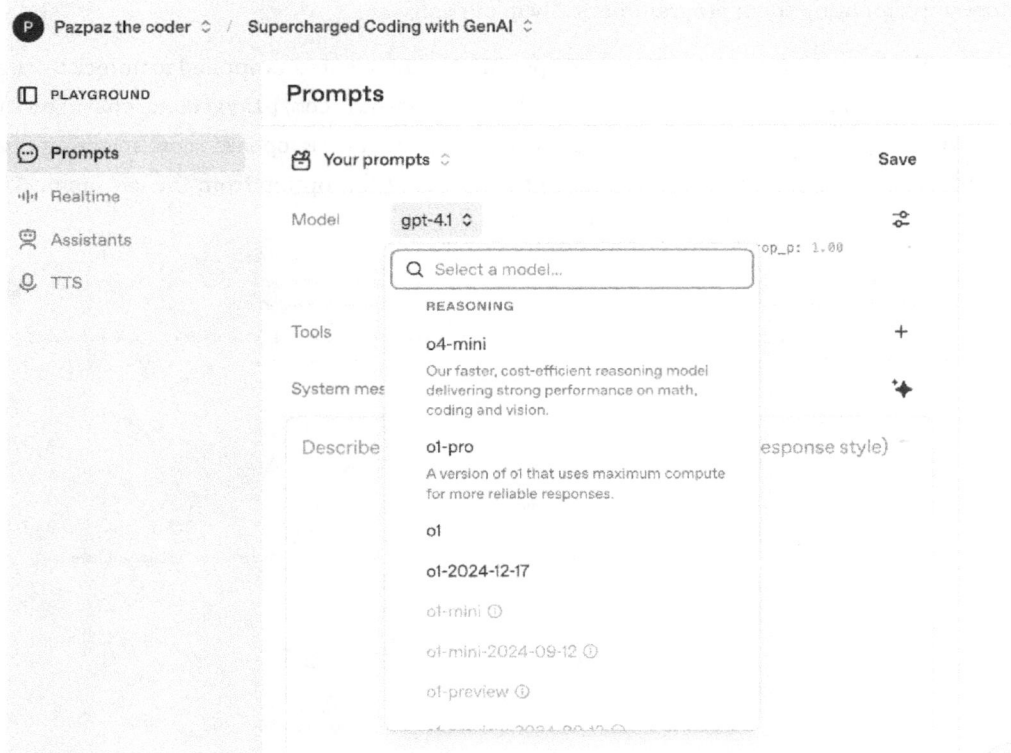

Figure 11.4: Available reasoning models in the OpenAI API Playground

For the examples in this chapter, we will use the *GPT-4o mini 2024-07-18* model, which is cheaper to use with the API compared to the *GPT-o* series models.

Computing quadratic roots with GPT-4o mini

As a benchmark for the model output, we will evaluate how GPT-4o mini handles implementing functions that extend beyond a few lines of code, such as computing the quadratic roots of the equation $ax^2 + bx + c = 0$. To find the roots of this equation, we compute the two values that satisfy the quadratic formula:

$$x_{1,2} = \frac{-b \pm \sqrt{b^2 - 4ac}}{2a}$$

In our case, we want to return the roots only when they are real, which occurs when the discriminant $b^2 - 4ac$ is larger than or equal to 0.

To obtain a function implementation that returns the real roots only, we define the function signature:

```
def get_quadratic_roots_only_if_real (a:int, b:int, c:int) -> Tuple[float,
float]
```

We will use this function signature in our prompt to the model. As usual, we will structure our prompt according to the five S's framework, as introduced in *Chapter 4*, where the system prompt provides the surrounding context and specifies the single task to be completed, and the user prompt includes supplementary details, such as the function signature and a lead-in cue.

For the system prompt, we will add the following instruction:

```
You will be provided with a Python function signature enclosed with {{{
FUNCTION }}}. Your task is to implement it.
```

This instruction provides the model with sufficient context for the code completion task using a Python function signature.

For the user prompt, we will ask it to implement the get_quadratic_roots_only_if_real function and include the CODE lead-in cue:

```
FUNCTION: {{{def get_quadratic_roots_only_if_real (a:int, b:int, c:int) ->
Tuple[float, float] }}}
CODE:
```

The function's name, `get_quadratic_roots_only_if_real`, signals the model to return the quadratic roots only if they are real.

Implementing the quadratic roots calculator

A typical approach to computing quadratic roots and returning them if they are real involves the following steps:

1.   Compute the discriminant $b^2 - 4ac$.

2.   Verify that the discriminant is positive so that the roots are real.

3.   Return the two roots if real.

Since this function requires more than just a few lines of code, the LLM is likely to introduce comments within the code and include surrounding explanations with the implementation.

For reference, *Figure 11.5* shows the explanation provided by the model before the actual code implementation.

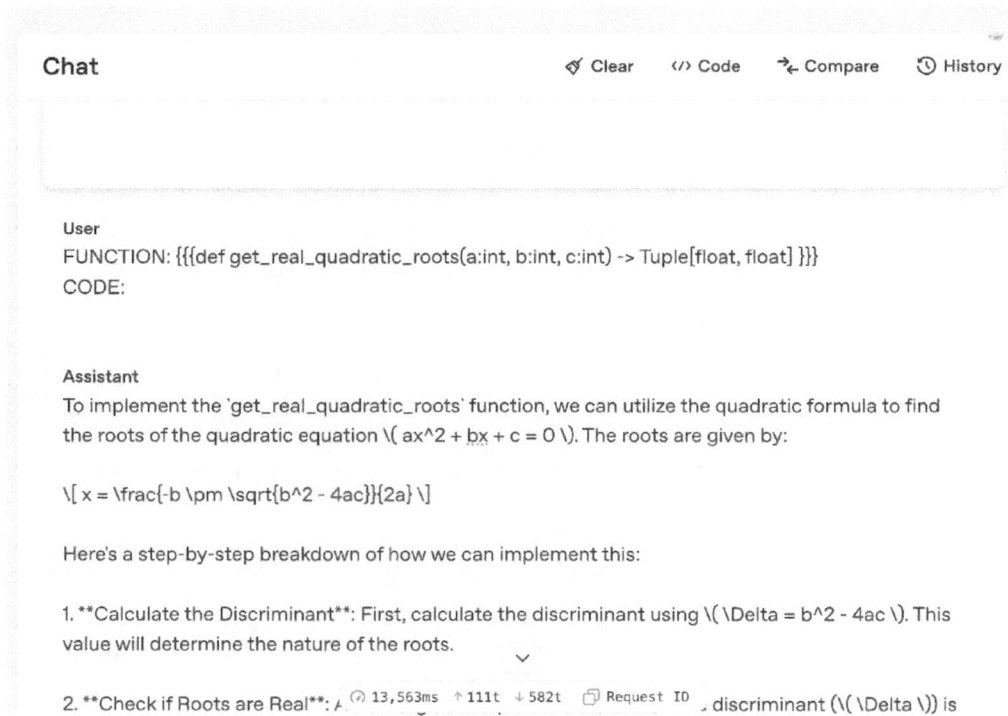

Figure 11.5: Base model output with supplementary explanations

The following is the code output generated by the model:

```python
import math
from typing import Tuple
def get_quadratic_roots_only_if_real(a: int, b: int, c: int) ->
Tuple[float, float]:
    # Calculate the discriminant
    discriminant = b * b - 4 * a * c
    # If discriminant is negative, there are no real roots
    if discriminant < 0:
        raise ValueError("The equation does not have real roots.")
    # Calculate the two solutions using the quadratic formula
    sqrt_disc = math.sqrt(discriminant)
    x1 = (-b + sqrt_disc) / (2 * a)
    x2 = (-b - sqrt_disc) / (2 * a)
    return (x1, x2)
```

This implementation covers all three required steps: computing the discriminant, checking for real roots, and returning the two solutions when appropriate. However, the solution includes redundant explanations and a function that is cluttered with comments. Later in the chapter, we will see how fine-tuning can help us achieve improved results by fine-tuning the LLM to return only code for code completion tasks.

Next, we will see how to prepare the training data to fine-tune the GPT-4o mini model. We will later compare this model with those of the default GPT-4o mini model.

Crafting a JSONL file for fine-tuning

One of the initial challenges in fine-tuning a model is gathering enough training examples. When fine-tuning a model through OpenAI, a minimum of 10 training examples is required. However, for most tasks that are beyond trivial, tens or even hundreds of examples might be necessary, depending on the task. According to OpenAI's official documentation, satisfactory results are typically achieved with 50 training examples.

In our case, where we want to fine-tune a model to produce outputs consisting solely of code without comments, 15 examples are sufficient, as we will see later in the chapter. When crafting our training set, we will utilize two techniques: desirable examples that are like few-shot learning and **contrastive learning**. Contrastive learning builds on the idea of in-context learning by first presenting an incorrect or incomplete output, followed by an additional user-assistant prompt pair that provides the desired output. For more details, see the *Further reading* section in this chapter.

Fine-tuning file structure

We will upload a JSONL file as the training data for our fine-tuning process, where each line in the file is a valid JSON object representing one training example. A minimal prompt should include a system prompt and a training example with a user prompt and an assistant prompt. Each assistant prompt is attributed with a weight of 0 for undesirable output and 1 for desirable output. In the following desirable example, the assistant prompt has a weight of 1, and line breaks have been added for clarity:

```
{"messages": [
  {"role": "system", "content": "You will be provided with a Python
function signature enclosed with {{{ FUNCTION }}}. Your task is to
implement it."},
  {"role": "user", "content": "FUNCTION: {{{def get_euclidean_distance(x1,
y1, x2, y2):}}}\n CODE: "},
  {"role": "assistant", "content": "def get_euclidean_distance(x1, y1, x2,
y2): \n return ((x1-x2)**2 + (y1-y2)**2)**0.5", "weight": 1}
]}
```

This format may look familiar, as it resembles the `messages` parameter used in OpenAI API calls. However, in this case, we assign a weight to the assistant message. The preceding example is a training instance included in the `fine_tuning.jsonl` file for this chapter, located at `ch11/fine_tuning.jsonl`, demonstrating the expected implementation of the `get_euclidean_distance` function.

A minimal training line template should be as follows, containing at least one user prompt and one assistant prompt. Here, too, line spaces are added for clarity:

```
{"messages": [
{"role": "user", "content": "Your Content Here"},
{"role": "assistant", "content": "Your desired output here", "weight":
1}]}
```

We could also incorporate a system prompt if it helps refine the specialization, as we will explore later in the chapter.

With contrastive learning examples, we will include additional user prompt and assistant prompt pairs. The first pair represents an undesirable output and is assigned a weight of 0, as such:

```
{"messages": [
{"role": "system", "content": "...omitted for brevity..."},
{"role": "user", "content": "FUNCTION: {{{def sum_of_squares(n: int) ->
int:}}}\n CODE: "},
{"role": "assistant", "content": "Sure! here is the code:\n\n```python\
ndef sum_of_squares(n: int) -> int:\n return sum(i * i for i in range(1, n
+ 1))\n```", "weight": 0},
{"role": "user", "content": "Include only code."},
{"role": "assistant", "content": "def sum_of_squares(n: int) -> int:\n
return sum(i * i for i in range(1, n + 1))", "weight": 1}]}
```

In this example, we provide two sets of user and assistant messages. The initial assistant response is undesirable because it includes explanatory text alongside the code, so it is assigned a weight of 0. The second user prompt corrects this by explicitly instructing the assistant to provide only the code, and this response is given a weight of 1.

Strategy

A practical approach to constructing a fine-tuning training file is to start with the simplest cases of desired outputs and gradually introduce more complex examples to cover the specialization we want the model to develop. While the few-shot examples we saw in *Chapter 8* included one or two cases, for fine-tuning, we will use 15 examples, allocating 7-8 examples to each of the following objectives:

- **Code-only**: Positive and contrastive
- **No comments**: Positive and contrastive

These examples will be sufficient to generate code without surrounding explanations and without comments within the function. The complete JSONL file is available in this book's repository at ch11/fine_tuning.jsonl. Next, we will present a single example from each of the preceding objectives.

Code-only — five training examples

In these cases, we will include simple implementations of functions spanning 1-2 lines. Each example consists of a single user and assistant prompt pair, ensuring that the output consists solely of code. Take the following example:

```
{"messages": [
{"role": "system", "content": "You will be provided with a Python function
signature enclosed with {{{ FUNCTION }}}. Your task is to implement it."},
{"role": "user", "content": "FUNCTION: {{{def get_arithmetic_mean(a,
b)}}}\n CODE: "},
{"role": "assistant", "content": "def get_arithmetic_mean(a, b): \n return
(a+b)/2", "weight": 1}]}
```

In this example, we provide a desirable implementation of get_arithmetic_mean without any surrounding explanations. Note that the actual JSONL line contains no extra line breaks. This is an example of the training pattern with just a single positive example indicated by the weight 1. Additionally, we will include three more examples for the get_euclidean_distance, reverse_string, is_even, and is_odd functions.

Contrastive code-only — three training examples

In addition to providing high-quality examples, we can also include contrastive examples. These scenarios involve an initial assistant response that is undesirable, such as including explanations or comments in the code, followed by a chained request to refine the output into a more desirable version. The chained user prompt should follow the best practices introduced in *Chapter 9*, such as the following:

- Include code only
- Remove code comments
- Extract lower-level details to functions

As introduced in *Chapter 9*, when crafting chained prompts, we avoid unnecessary phrasing such as *"Your answer is wrong!"* since it does not follow the *short* best practice and adds no value. Instead, we should determine whether the assistant's output is significantly incorrect or if only minor adjustments are needed.

In the first case, if the output is far off, the user prompt should be refined to produce a more desirable result, and this example should not be included in our training data. In the second case, if the model's output only requires minor refinements, we should focus on providing clear guidance on the necessary adjustments, such as instructing the model to return only code or extract low-level details into helper functions. This type of direction is more precise and informative.

For example, the following is a contrastive code-only training example for an implementation of `is_palindrome`, where the first assistant prompt includes an explanation along with the code. This output is marked with a weight of 0 to indicate undesirability. It is followed by a chained user prompt instructing the assistant to return only the code, leading to a refined implementation with a weight of 1:

```
{"messages": [
{"role": "system", "content": "...omitted..."},
{"role": "user", "content": "FUNCTION: {{{def is_palindrome(s: str) ->
bool:}}}\nCODE: "},
{"role": "assistant", "content": "A palindrome is a word, phrase, or [...]
otherwise `False`.\n\n```python\ndef is_palindrome(s: str) -> bool:\n s =
s.lower()\n return s == s[::-1]\n```", "weight": 0},
{"role": "user", "content": "Include code only."},
{"role": "assistant", "content": "def is_palindrome(s: str) -> bool:\n s =
s.lower()\n return s == s[::-1]", "weight": 1}]}
```

The final assistant message consists solely of the implementation code and is assigned a weight of 1 to indicate a desirable output. The fine-tuning file also includes similar contrastive examples for `sum_of_squares` and `flatten_list_of_lists`.

Code with no comments — five examples

In these examples, we focus on functions that go beyond simple 1-2 line implementations, breaking down more complex tasks into lower-level abstraction functions. This approach enhances readability in the main function and eliminates the need for inline comments. For instance, consider the implementation of `get_reversed_longer_string`, which takes two strings as input and returns the reverse of the longer string. It can be structured as follows:

```
def get_reversed_longer_string(s1:str, s2: str) -> str:
longer_s = get_longer_string(s1, s2)
reversed_longer_s = reverse_string(longer_s)
return reversed_longer_s
```

```
def get_longer_string(s1, s2):
return s1 if len(s1) > len(s2) else s2


def reverse_string(s):
return s[::-1]
```

While more concise implementations exist, they may be less readable. The preceding structure keeps get_reversed_longer_string clear and shifts the implementation details to dedicated lower-level functions.

To include this approach in our training examples, we will add the following:

```
{"messages": [{"role": "system", "content": "...omitted for brevity..."},
{"role": "user", "content": "FUNCTION: {{{def get_reversed_longer_
string(s1, s2):}}}\n CODE: "},
{"role": "assistant", "content": "def get_reversed_longer_string(s1,
s2):\n longer_s = get_longer_string(s1, s2)\n reversed_longer_s = reverse_
string(longer_s)\n return reversed_longer_s\n\ndef get_longer_string(s1,
s2):\n return s1 if len(s1) > len(s2) else s2\n\ndef reverse_string(s):\n
return s[::-1]", "weight": 1}]}
```

This aligns with our preferred coding style of extracting lower-level functionality into separate functions. Similarly, we will include example implementations for the following:

- get_max_multiplication_from_lists
- get_maximal_second_element_squared
- get_sum_of_absolute_differences
- get_highest_even

These five implementations will demonstrate the separation of abstraction levels in functions, serving as a guideline for the fine-tuning process.

Contrastive no comments – two examples

To complete our dataset, we will include examples of initial implementations with excessive comments, followed by a refined version where low-level details are extracted into separate functions. For instance, consider a function that, given a list of lists, computes the average of the second elements of each sublist:

```
get_average_of_second_elements(numbers: List[List[int]])
```

This function involves more complex logic than our previous examples, which may lead to an implementation with excessive comments. To steer the model toward a solution that separates levels of abstraction, we first provide an implementation with inline comments, followed by a chained prompt that refines the output. An initial incorrect assistant response might look like this:

```
def get_average_of_second_elements(numbers: List[List[int]]) -> float:
    if not numbers: # Check if the input list is empty
        return 0
    second_elements = [sublist[1] for sublist in numbers] # Extract second
elements
    return sum(second_elements) / len(second_elements) # Compute the
average
```

While this implementation is correct, the inline comments add unnecessary fluff. When including this negative example in our dataset, we assign it a weight of 0.

Next, we chain a user prompt requesting a refinement:

```
Extract low level details to functions
```

This results in a cleaner implementation:

```
import statistics
def get_average_of_second_elements(numbers: List[List[int]]) -> float:
    second_elements = get_second_elements(numbers)
    return statistics.mean(second_elements)
def get_second_elements(numbers: List[List[int]]) -> List[int]:
    return [sublist[1] for sublist in numbers]
```

By abstracting the extraction logic into a separate function, get_average_of_second_elements remains more readable. The corresponding example looks like this:

```
{"messages": [{"role": "system", "content": "...omitted for brevity..."},
{"role": "user", "content": "FUNCTION: {{{def get_average_of_second_
elements(numbers: List[List[int]]):}}}\n CODE: "}, {"role": "assistant",
"content": "def get_average_of_second_elements(numbers: List[List[int]])
-> float:\n if not numbers: # Check if the input list is empty\n return
0\n \n second_elements = [sublist[1] for sublist in numbers] # Extract
second elements\n return sum(second_elements) / len(second_elements) #
Compute the average", "weight": 0},
{"role": "user", "content": "Extract low level details to functions"},
{"role": "assistant", "content": "import statistics\n\n\ndef get_average_
```

```
of_second_elements(numbers: List[List[int]]) -> float:\n second_elements
= get_second_elements(numbers)\n return statistics.mean(second_elements)\
n\n\ndef get_second_elements(numbers: List[List[int]]) -> List[int]:\n
return [sublist[1] for sublist in numbers]", "weight": 1}]}
```

Additionally, we will include a similar contrastive example for get_smallest_squared, bringing our total to 15 training examples.

With the finalized JSONL dataset, we can now proceed with fine-tuning using OpenAI's GUI.

Fine-tuning a model with the OpenAI GUI

Fine-tuning an LLM with OpenAI can be done either programmatically via an API call or through OpenAI's GUI. In this chapter, we will focus on using the GUI to initiate fine-tuning jobs.

Costs of fine-tuning a model

Fine-tuning an LLM comes with two types of costs:

- **Job cost:** As of April 2025, fine-tuning a model costs $3 per 1M tokens. For reference, the JSONL file provided earlier, which contains approximately 12K tokens (2K tokens in the file × 6 iterations), would cost around $0.04 to fine-tune. There are no associated storage costs for the model or training files.

- **Application:** The pricing of using a fine-tuned model depends on the base model used. For instance, the cost for GPT-4o mini-based models is $0.30 per 1M input tokens and $1.20 per 1M output tokens, and much cheaper than the GPT-4o models, as illustrated in *Figure 11.6*:

Fine-tuning our models

Customize our models to get even higher performance for your specific use cases.

GPT-4o	GPT-4o mini
Fine-tuning price	**Fine-tuning price**
Input: $3.750 / 1M tokens	Input: $0.30 / 1M tokens
Cached input: $1.875 / 1M tokens	Cached input: $0.15 / 1M tokens
Output: $15.000 / 1M tokens	Output: $1.20 / 1M tokens
Training: $25.000 / 1M tokens	Training: $3.00 / 1M tokens

Figure 11.6: Fine-tuning costs for GPT-4o models

As of April 2025, using a fine-tuned GPT-4o mini model costs exactly twice as much as using the model without fine-tuning. However, while the per-token cost is higher, a fine-tuned model can be more efficient, as its specialization allows for more concise inputs and outputs, potentially reducing overall costs.

To check the latest pricing for current and legacy models, visit OpenAI's pricing page: `https://openai.com/api/pricing/`.

With these costs in mind, we can now proceed with initiating the fine-tuning process.

Initiating a fine-tuning job

We can fine-tune a model using our JSONL file directly through OpenAI's API GUI. While fine-tuning can also be done programmatically, we will focus on the GUI method since it is by far the most common way.

To initiate the job, go to OpenAI's platform home page at `https://platform.openai.com/`, click on **Dashboard** in the upper-right menu, and then select **Fine-tuning** from the left-hand menu, as shown in *Figure 11.7*:

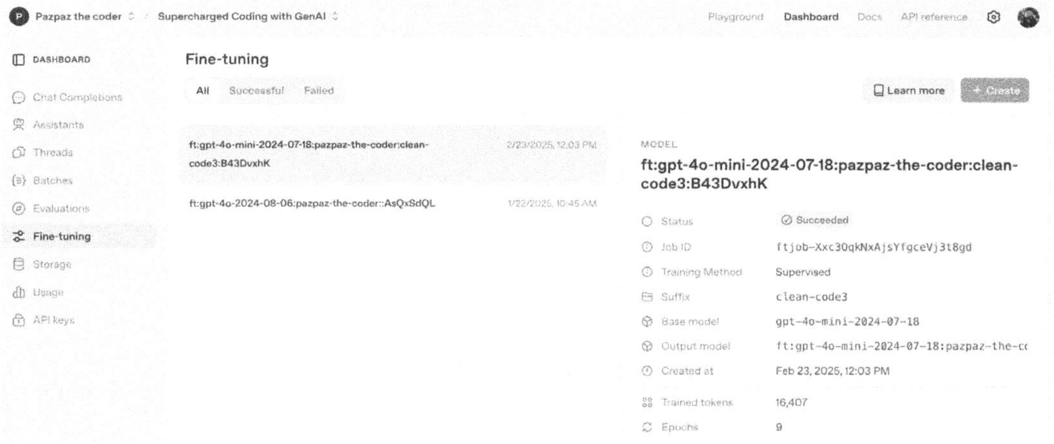

Figure 11.7: Fine-tuning page in the OpenAI API platform

To start a new fine-tuning job, click the **Create** button in the upper-right corner of the screen. This will open the setup popup, as shown in *Figure 11.8*:

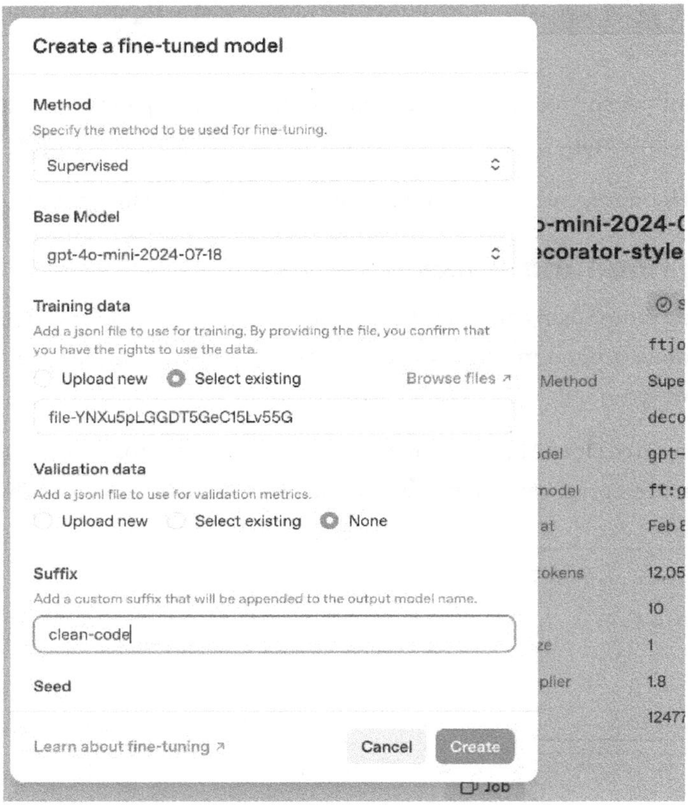

Figure 11.8: Fine-tuning job popup

We used the following settings for fine-tuning:

- **Method: Supervised** mode. Based on our experience, this is the most effective approach for coding style specialization.

- **Base Model: gpt-4o-mini 2024-07-18** (or the latest available mini model). This model provides sufficient results for our use case and is cost-effective.

- **Training data**: The JSONL file introduced earlier in the chapter.

- **Suffix** (optional): This is appended to the model's name for identification and does not need to be unique across fine-tuning jobs. We added the `clean-code` suffix for future reference.

Now, we can start the fine-tuning job by clicking **Create**.

With 15 training examples, the process should take about five minutes to complete. Once finished, a success message will appear, as shown in *Figure 11.9*:

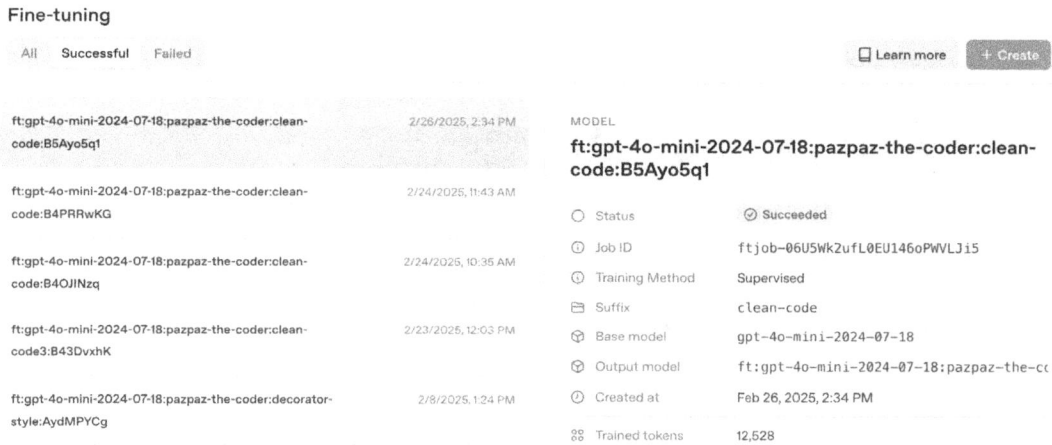

Figure 11.9: Successful completion of fine-tuning job

The fine-tuning job processed 12,500 tokens, running six iterations (or **epochs**) of our file, which contains approximately 2,000 tokens. The fine-tuned model can be used in any OpenAI API call or accessed through the Playground, as we will explore later in this chapter.

To monitor the cost of the fine-tuning job, navigate to the OpenAI usage page at `https://platform.openai.com/usage`, scroll down to **Spend categories**, and review the fine-tuning expenses, as shown in *Figure 11.10*:

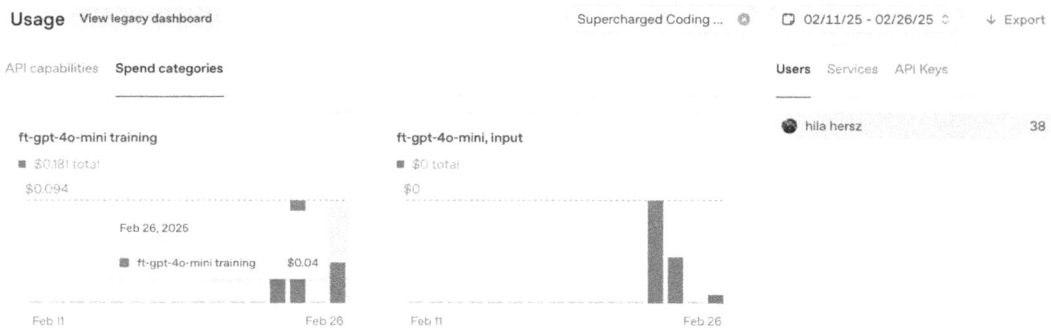

Figure 11.10: Incurred fine-tuning costs

Here, we can see that fine-tuning the model with 15 training examples and 12K tokens resulted in a total cost of $0.04.

Using the fine-tuned model

The fine-tuned model can be accessed either through the OpenAI Playground or programmatically. In *Figure 11.9*, OpenAI gave a formal name for our fine-tuned model under **Output model**, in the following format:

```
ft:{base model}:{account name}:{fine-tuning suffix}:{id}
```

For example, our model's name is shown here, but your model will be named differently:

```
ft:gpt-4o-mini-2024-07-18:pazpaz-the-coder:clean-code:B5Ayo5q1
```

To use the fine-tuned model in code, replace the standard model reference:

```
completion: openai.ChatCompletion = (
    client.chat.completions.create(
        model="gpt-4o-mini",
        messages=[{...}]))
```

The updated call using the fine-tuned model will look as follows:

```
completion: openai.ChatCompletion = (
    client.chat.completions.create(
        model="ft:gpt-4o-mini-2024-07-18:pazpaz-the-coder:clean-
code:B5Ayo5q1",
        messages=[{...} ))
```

The fine-tuned model is also available in the OpenAI Playground, as shown in *Figure 11.11*:

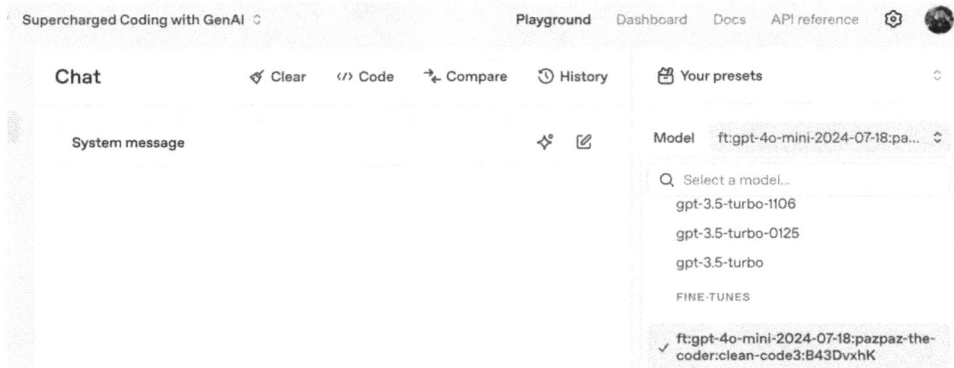

Figure 11.11: Playground models, including our fine-tuned model

Within the Playground interface, we can compare its results with the base model, which we will explore next.

Comparing our results

Now that we have fine-tuned our custom model, we can evaluate how its outputs compare to those of the base model. To do this, navigate to the OpenAI Playground, `https://platform.openai.com/playground/chat`, select **gpt-4o-mini-2024-07-18** as the base model, and click on **Compare**, as shown in *Figure 11.12*:

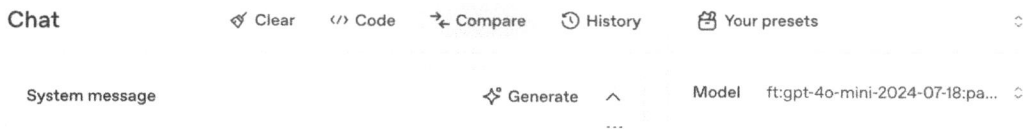

Figure 11.12: Playground comparison selecting the base model to compare

Next, add the fine-tuned model, as shown in *Figure 11.13*:

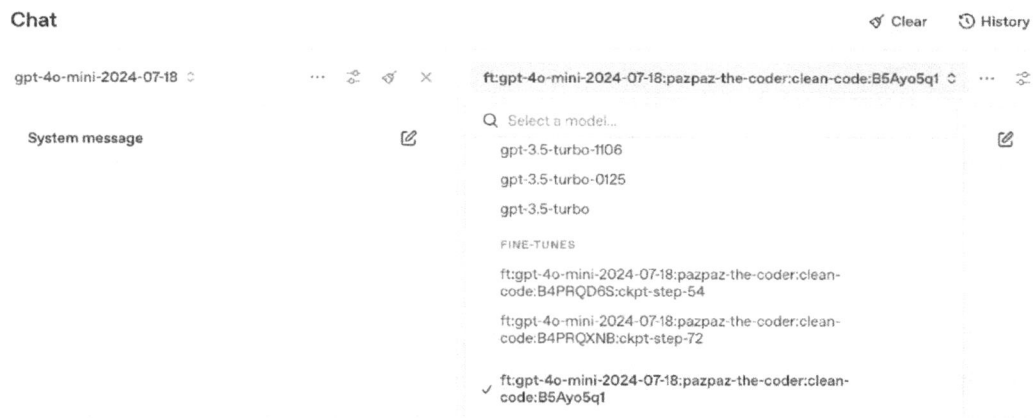

Figure 11.13: Adding a model for comparison

We will use the same system message from earlier in the chapter that will be applied to both models:

```
You will be provided with a Python function signature enclosed with {{{
FUNCTION }}}. Your task is to implement it.
```

Next, we will enter the same user message as earlier in the chapter:

```
FUNCTION: {{{def get_quadratic_roots_only_if_real(a:int, b:int, c:int) ->
Tuple[float, float] }}}
CODE:
```

Our comparison can be run by clicking **Run**, generating responses from both models. The base model's output includes explanations and inline comments, while the fine-tuned model provides a more structured implementation, as shown in *Figure 11.14*:

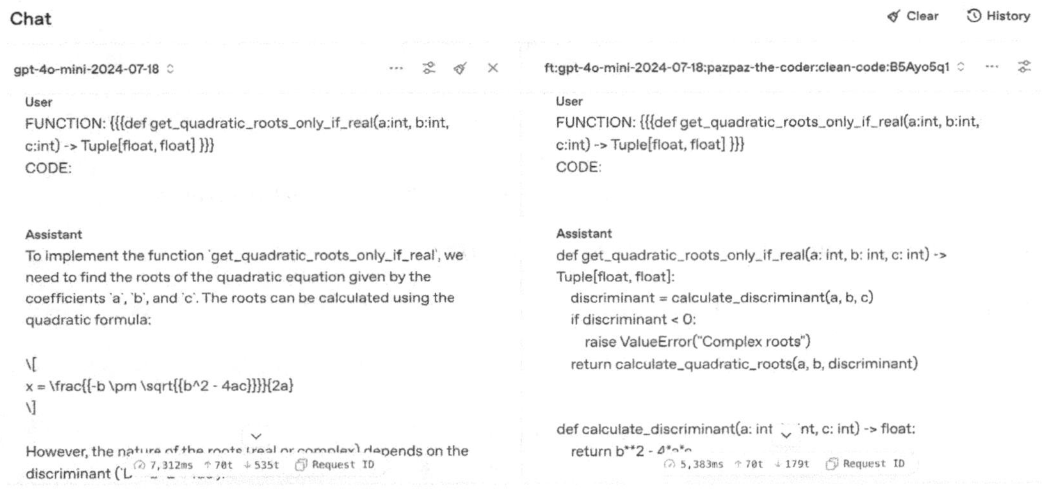

Figure 11.14: Comparing the base model (left) and the fine-tuned model (right)

The fine-tuned model returns a cleaner implementation that abstracts computations into separate functions, keeping the main function concise and readable. For your reference, here is the full implementation proposed:

```
def get_quadratic_roots_only_if_real(a: int, b: int, c: int) ->
Tuple[float, float]:
    discriminant = calculate_discriminant(a, b, c)
    if discriminant < 0:
        raise ValueError("Complex roots")
    return calculate_quadratic_roots(a, b, discriminant)
def calculate_discriminant(a: int, b: int, c: int) -> float:
    return b**2 - 4*a*c
def calculate_quadratic_roots(a: int, b: int, discriminant: float) ->
Tuple[float, float]:
```

```
    root1 = (-b + discriminant**0.5) / (2*a)
    root2 = (-b - discriminant**0.5) / (2*a)
    return root1, root2
```

This output aligns with our fine-tuning objective of separating computations into helper functions while keeping the primary function, get_quadratic_roots_only_if_real, clear. Additionally, the base model generates 535 tokens, compared to 179 tokens from the fine-tuned model. Despite the higher per-token cost of the fine-tuned model, it is ultimately more cost-efficient.

To conclude, we successfully fine-tuned the model to specialize in returning clean, code-only outputs. This targeted specialization was achieved with 15 JSONL examples, using a combination of positive and contrastive learning to guide the model's behavior.

Fine-tuning enables us to adapt a pre-trained LLM for specific tasks, making it especially valuable for automated and large-scale coding projects. In later chapters, we will explore ways to further improve fine-tuning, such as refining the training data to separate validation logic from core functionality.

Fine-tuning in action

Currently, we use just two fine-tuned models for coding tasks. The first is for code implementation as we constructed in this chapter, providing an alternative perspective on new implementations. The other is for docstring maintenance, ensuring that a function's code remains consistent with its docstring. For more narrowly scoped tasks, few-shot learning is usually sufficient and preferable since it requires less effort. In general, fine-tuning is only considered when simpler prompt engineering techniques are ineffective or when the project operates at a repository-wide scale, making the investment worthwhile.

We encourage you to experiment frequently with prompt engineering and fine-tuning. In the next section of the book, we will introduce additional **software development life cycle (SDLC)** use cases that you can start applying to your code base right away.

Summary

In *Part 2* of the book, we explored LLMs in greater depth. We explained how they work, what they excel at, and how to leverage prompt engineering techniques to achieve more effective results. We also covered strategies for evaluating their outputs to ensure reliability.

This chapter took the concept of few-shot learning a step further by demonstrating how to fine-tune an LLM to specialize on a given task. Through positive and contrastive training examples, we guided the model to generate function implementations based solely on their signatures, returning clean code without inline comments. This approach can be applied more broadly to tasks such as generating unit test suites, maintaining docstring quality, or refactoring for loops across an entire repository.

With this deeper understanding of LLMs, prompt engineering, and output evaluation, we now have the essential tools to become supercharged coders. We can determine the best tool for a given task, whether ChatGPT, OpenAI API, or Copilot, and craft prompts that maximize effectiveness using best practices and advanced techniques. Moreover, we now have the skills to assess the quality of the model's output with confidence.

In the third part of the book, we will apply this knowledge to advanced SDLC tasks. We will explore how GenAI can assist in areas such as documentation, testing, scaling applications for runtime and memory efficiency, logging, monitoring, and error handling. Some tasks will rely on the five S's framework for coding-related tasks, while others will require more advanced prompt engineering strategies or fine-tuning to achieve optimal results.

Quiz time

Before you proceed to the next chapter, make sure that you can confidently answer the following questions:

Question 1: When is fine-tuning a good approach?

Answer: Fine-tuning is beneficial for large-scale projects where a repetitive task needs to be performed consistently, such as generating function implementations from signatures while following specific coding standards. Instead of relying on few-shot learning or complex prompt engineering techniques within each request, fine-tuning allows the specialization process to be separate from the prompt, making it easier to maintain and, in some cases, more cost-effective.

Question 2: What are the costs involved in fine-tuning?

Answer: Fine-tuning involves two types of costs:

- **Training cost:** A one-time cost incurred when running the fine-tuning job.
- **Usage cost:** Fine-tuned models typically have higher per-token costs for input and output compared to their base models. For example, with GPT-4o mini, using fine-tuned models costs twice as much as those from the base model.

However, the true cost of fine-tuning lies in the time and effort required to carefully construct training examples that ensure the model aligns with the desired specialization.

Question 3: Why does fine-tuning require more training samples than few-shot learning?

Answer: The specialization process in fine-tuning is fundamentally different from few-shot learning. In few-shot learning, examples are simply provided within the prompt, guiding the model without altering its internal parameters.

Fine-tuning, on the other hand, adjusts the model's weights to align with the desired behavior. Given that the base model was pre-trained on vast amounts of data, requiring tens or even hundreds of fine-tuning examples is relatively modest in comparison to the scale of its original training.

Further reading

To learn more about the topics that were covered in this chapter, take a look at the following resources:

- Brown, T. B., Mann, B., Ryder, N., Subbiah, M., Kaplan, J., Dhariwal, P., ... & Amodei, D. (2020). *Language Models are Few-Shot Learners*. OpenAI. Retrieved from `https://arxiv.org/abs/2005.14165v4`

- Deepchecks on contrastive learning: `https://www.deepchecks.com/glossary/contrastive-learning/`

- OpenAI API fine-tuning: `https://www.datacamp.com/tutorial/fine-tuning-large-language-models`

- OpenAI API request parameters: `https://platform.openai.com/docs/api-reference/responses/create`

- Data camp fine-tuning tutorial for LLMs: `https://www.datacamp.com/tutorial/fine-tuning-large-language-models`

Unlock this book's exclusive benefits now

Scan this QR code or go to packtpub.com/unlock, then search for this book by name.

Note: Keep your purchase invoice ready before you start.

Part 3

From Code to Production with GenAI

In *Part 3* of this book, we branch from simple coding to the full **software development life cycle (SDLC)**. We first focus on writing docstrings, followed by testing, since these are almost universally required for production-ready code. The next advanced topic is scaling applications for systems in terms of runtime and memory. The part will also cover logging, monitoring, and error handling.

The techniques for completing these SDLC steps build on both the five S's framework and advanced prompt engineering techniques discussed in *Part 2*.

The final chapter examines the current trends, including vibe coding, and suggests what might be next for the field of GenAI.

This part contains the following chapters:

- *Chapter 12, Documenting Code with GenAI*
- *Chapter 13, Writing and Maintaining Unit Tests*
- *Chapter 14, GenAI for Runtime and Memory Management*
- *Chapter 15, Going Live with GenAI: Logging, Monitoring, and Errors*
- *Chapter 16, Architecture, Design, and the Future*

12

Documenting Code with GenAI

In *Part 3* of the book, we will introduce advanced practices from the **software development life-cycle (SDLC)** when working with ChatGPT, OpenAI API, and GitHub Copilot. Using the five S's framework introduced in *Chapter 4*, and prompt engineering techniques introduced in *Chapter 8* and *Chapter 9*, we will see how to productionize our Python applications.

In this chapter, we will introduce docstrings for Python objects, which already has a built-in slash command (i.e., /doc) with GitHub Copilot. We can use this slash command with the vanilla format or extend it with specific docstring requirements. Docstrings are already a feature of most IDEs as a template structure where arguments will be formatted with a fixed style, but the standard template does not include any descriptive information about the function or its parameters beyond their name. GitHub Copilot will usually produce a full docstring for high-quality code.

The topics covered in this chapter include the following:

- Introducing software documentation
- Using GenAI to write docstrings
- Finding outdated docstrings with GitHub Copilot, ChatGPT, and OpenAI API
- Practical insights

Technical requirements

To get the most out of this chapter, ensure you have the following:

- GitHub Copilot account
- IDE – either VS Code or PyCharm
- OpenAI account with access to OpenAI API
- Access to the book's repository, available at `https://github.com/PacktPublishing/Supercharged-Coding-with-Gen-AI`
- Virtual environment set up in VS Code or PyCharm
- OpenAI API token

For assistance setting up a GitHub Copilot account, refer to *Chapter 3*. For instructions on setting up OpenAI API access and token generation, see *Chapter 2*. If you need help creating an OpenAI account or setting up a virtual environment in your IDE, refer to the *Appendix* for detailed guidance.

Introducing software documentation

Software engineers not only write a lot of code, but they also need to read and understand code written by others. The code could be written the same day by other developers or be part of a legacy system maintained over multiple decades. While clean, well-written code is a critical aspect, code documentation is also a fundamental way of communicating with other developers.

Software documentation comes in multiple forms that serve different needs. Technical documentation includes the comments in source code, API descriptions, database schemas, and software architecture diagrams. User documentation is a guide on how an end user can use software. The software engineering process also adds specific documentation on requirements, specifications, testing plans, CI/CD pipelines, sprint planning, and much more. This chapter focuses on the documentation of the source code.

A general guideline is that the documentation should focus on the "why" rather than the "what." That is, the code is readable and one can figure out what it does, but the reason for its implementation is what should be documented. The rationale is that well-written code is self-explanatory about what it does, but the reason for the code (the why) can be better understood through documentation. The code documentation can therefore explain the code, improve its readability, and aid later software maintenance.

In Python, the convention for documentation within the code is the docstring. Docstrings typically occur at the beginning of Python modules, classes, and methods. The purpose is to explain their function and the reason for their inclusion. Python's docstrings are enclosed in triple quotes (single or double quotes) even if they are just one line. However, for the most common docstrings used to document methods, they should include arguments, return types, and any exceptions raised.

Docstrings serve a few different purposes. First, they provide documentation for a module, class, method, or function for developers. They can be compiled into formal documentation resources. In addition, these forms of documentation are accessible using Python's help() function. Using docstrings makes the code easier to maintain, which reduces the lifetime cost of code.

The second purpose of docstrings is based on **Miller's Law**, also known as the Magical Number Seven, Plus or Minus Two. Based on George Miller's 1956 paper (https://psychclassics.yorku. ca/Miller/), it states that humans can retain 5 to 9 pieces of information in their working memory. A software developer trying to understand even a medium-length Python file must understand the interaction of several methods. The docstring and naming conventions facilitate a quick understanding of the abstracted methods.

Although docstrings may appear to be standard, there are actually four common formats. The **PEP 257** convention is the official Python standard, consisting of a single line with no string formatting that emphasizes readability. The **Google style** is among the most common and still emphasizes readability. It uses multi-line formatting for the arguments passed in, method returns, and exceptions raised. The **NumPy/SciPy style** is widely used, but primarily for scientific software. It has similar content to the Google style but uses different formatting. The **reStructuredText (reST)** or **Sphinx style** includes more detailed information than the others. This style is used by the Sphinx documentation generator, which produces HTML, PDF, and LaTeX documentation manuals directly from the source code with full hyperlinking and other advanced features. This chapter will focus on both single-line **PEP 257** and **Google styles** due to their widespread use, but other styles are directly supported by requesting specific docstring styles. We have included a few sources in the *Further reading* section that describe comment styles for Python in more detail.

Working with the /explain GitHub Copilot command

As a working example in this chapter, we use Flask routines that support the distance calculation found in *Chapter 10*. The base code is shown in the GitHub repository and copied for reference here:

```python
from flask import Flask, request, jsonify
import numpy as np


app = Flask(__name__)


@app.route("/distances", methods=["POST"])
def calculate_distance():
    data = request.get_json()
    dist_type = data.get("distance")
    a = np.asarray(data.get("df1"))
    b = np.asarray(data.get("df2"))
    if a.shape != b.shape:
        return jsonify({"error": "Matrices must have the same shape"})
    if dist_type == "L1":
        dist = np.sum(np.abs(a - b))
        return jsonify({"distance": dist})
    elif dist_type == "L2":
        dist = np.sqrt(np.sum((a - b) ** 2))
        return jsonify({"distance": dist})
    else:
        return jsonify({"error": "Invalid distance type"})
```

In VS Code, by simply highlighting the method, right-clicking and selecting Copilot, and selecting **Generate Docs** as shown in *Figure 12.1*, a docstring can be automatically written. Note that we have ignored **Generate Docstring** shown under **Copilot**. That command is VS Code's template approach for docstrings, which creates placeholders for the docstring and parameters but does not use any AI to write the comment or description.

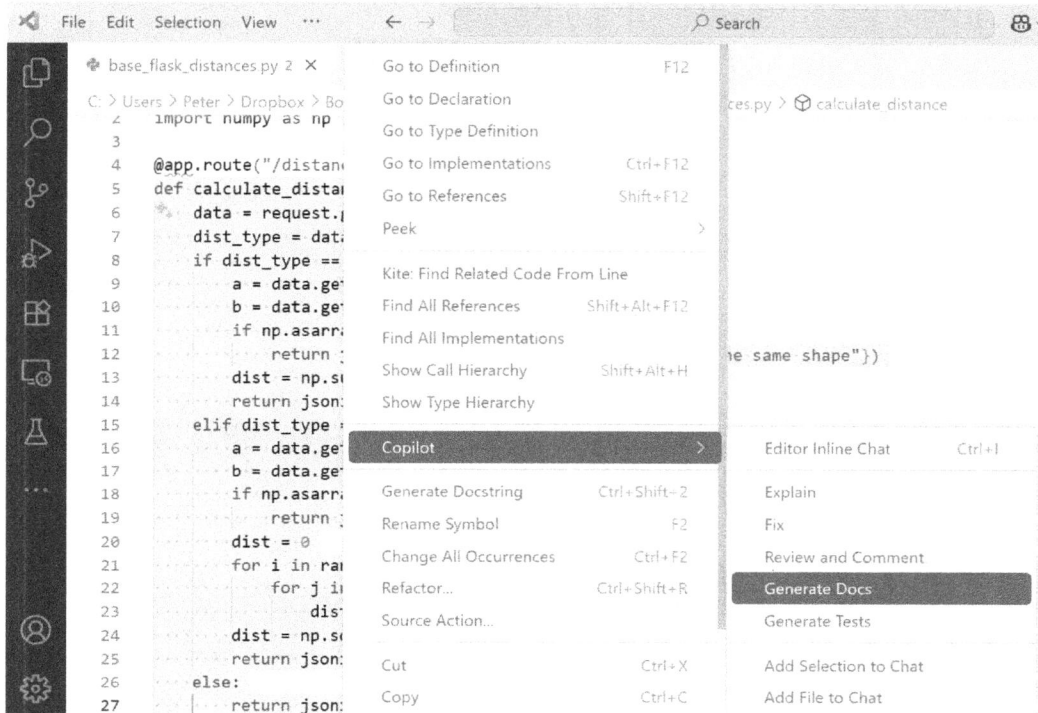

Figure 12.1: By highlighting the method and right-clicking, Copilot generates a docstring

The generated docstring is shown in *Figure 12.2.* Trying this several times, we obtained several variations on the docstring, some of which had exceedingly long lines or different formats, and some included different information. Regardless, the docstring format has a simple one-line description, but the remainder has a random format that does not follow any of the style guides. Specifically, the "expects..." section of the docstring is unclear.

```
4    @app.route("/distances", methods=["POST"])
5    def calculate_distance():
6        """
7        Calculate the distance between two matrices based on the specified distance type.
8
9        This function expects a JSON payload with the following structure:
10       {
11           "distance": "L1" or "L2",  # Type of distance metric to use
12           "df1": [[...], [...]],      # First matrix (list of lists)
13           "df2": [[...], [...]]       # Second matrix (list of lists)
14       }
15
16       Returns:
17           - A JSON response containing the calculated distance if the input is valid.
18           - A JSON error message if the matrices have different shapes or if the distance type is invalid.
19
20       Distance types:
21           - "L1": Manhattan distance (sum of absolute differences).
22           - "L2": Euclidean distance (square root of the sum of squared differences).
23
24       Error cases:
25           - If the matrices `df1` and `df2` do not have the same shape, an error message is returned.
26           - If the `distance` type is not "L1" or "L2", an error message is returned.
27       """
```

Figure 12.2: GitHub Copilot produces a vague docstring for a poorly constructed function

Another common case is for GitHub Copilot to produce multiple lines of text as the docstring, excluding the parameters, returns, and so on. *Figure 12.2* fails in this respect, with two lines of explanation followed by the expects (This endpoint expects...) and returns sections. While both multi-line and one-line docstrings exist, the preference is for one line rather than an elaborate description, particularly for low-level methods. If such a method requires multiple lines, it is often considered good practice to refactor the method into multiple simpler methods that each perform a single task.

Copilot's docstring creation is usually quite good, but can occasionally be incorrect. As in the previous example, you will encounter cases where it does not perform well. Some of these cases are due to the complexity of the underlying code. Rather than fixing the docstring, a preferred solution would be to refactor the code into a simpler form and recreate docstrings. In many cases, the /explain function is quite informative. In *Figure 12.3*, we apply /explain to the same code by using the GitHub Copilot Editor Inline Chat from within the same function:

CHAT

</> Workspace

⟩ Used 8 references

The provided code defines a Flask route function, [◉] calculate_distance , which computes the distance between two matrices based on the specified distance type. It uses JSON data from an HTTP request to determine the type of distance calculation (L1 or L2) and the input matrices (df1 and df2). The function handles errors, such as mismatched matrix shapes, and returns the computed distance or an error message as a JSON response.

The function begins by extracting the JSON payload from the request using [◉] request.get_json() and retrieves the distance type. If the distance type is L1 , the function calculates the Manhattan distance (sum of absolute differences) between the two matrices. It first ensures that the matrices have the same shape using [◉] np.asarray(a).shape != np.asarray(b).shape . If the shapes mismatch, it returns an error message. Otherwise, it computes the Manhattan distance using [◉] np.sum(np.abs(a - b)) and returns the result.

If the distance type is L2 , the function calculates the Euclidean distance (square root of the sum of squared differences). Similar to the L1 case, it checks for shape mismatches and returns an error if the shapes differ. The Euclidean distance is computed using nested loops to iterate over each element of the matrices, summing the squared differences, and then taking the square root of the total. The result is returned as a JSON response.

If the distance type is neither L1 nor L2 , the function returns an error message indicating an invalid distance type. This ensures that the function handles unexpected input gracefully.

The code relies on NumPy functions like [◉] np.asarray to ensure the input is treated as arrays and [◉] np.sum for efficient summation. It also uses Flask's [◉] jsonify to format the responses. However, the nested loops in the L2 calculation could be replaced with a more efficient NumPy operation, as NumPy is optimized for array-based computations. Additionally, the repeated shape-checking logic could be refactored into a helper function to improve code readability and reduce redundancy.

↺ 👍 👎

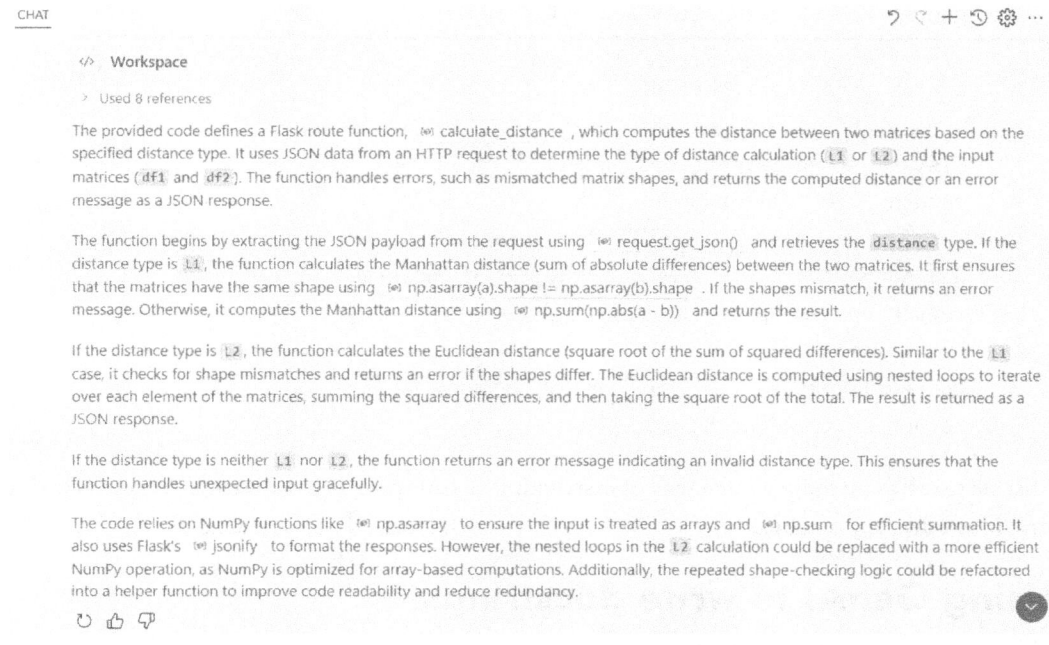

Figure 12.3: Using /explain for calculate_distance describes a complex method

A similar functionality occurs within the GitHub Copilot Chat with the /explain calculate_distance() command, which often returns explanations that are more verbose. Although both provide a clear explanation, their content is technically complex, which is why we recommend refactoring the code as shown:

```python
import numpy as np
from flask import Flask, request, jsonify


app = Flask(__name__)


@app.route("/distances", methods=["POST"])
def calculate_distance():
    a, b, dist_type = parse_request_parameters(request)
    dist_func = {"L1": get_manhattan_dist, "L2": get_euclidean_dist}.
get(dist_type)
    dist = dist_func(a, b)
    return jsonify({"distance": dist})
```

```
def parse_request_parameters(request):
    data = request.get_json()
    a = np.array(data.get("df1",))
    b = np.array(data.get("df2",))
    dist_type = data.get("distance")
    return a, b, dist_type

def get_manhattan_dist(a: np.ndarray, b: np.ndarray) -> float:
    return np.sum(np.abs(a - b))

def get_euclidean_dist(a: np.ndarray, b: np.ndarray) -> float:
    return np.sum((a - b) ** 2)
```

This section has introduced one way of instructing GenAI to write a docstring. The next section provides other approaches.

Using GenAI to write docstrings

This section describes different techniques for creating docstrings for a single method and for a full Python file. Docstrings improve code readability and are often required by organizations as part of their **continuous integration/continuous development (CI/CD)** pipelines. Using GenAI to create docstrings can increase the speed of the software development process.

Docstring for a single method

The simplest approach to generating a docstring in VS Code is simply typing three double quotes """" or the equivalent in single quotes on a blank line following the method signature, as shown in *Figure 12.4*, with results shown in the code block that follows, which can be accepted by pressing tab:

```
def get_euclidean_distance(a: np.ndarray, b: np.ndarray) -> float:
    '''
    return np.sum((a - b) ** 2)
```

Figure 12.4: Initiating the request for a docstring with three single or double quotes

```
def get_euclidean_dist(a: np.ndarray, b: np.ndarray) -> float:
    '''Calculates the squared Euclidean distance between two arrays.'''
    return np.sum((a - b) ** 2)
```

As we can see, it describes the method but is the simplest form of the **PEP 257** style with a single line string and no parameters or return values.

If we want to have a different docstring style, we can request it using the Copilot Editor Inline Chat (/doc `Google style`) or any other specified style. *Figure 12.5* shows the results for the Google style.

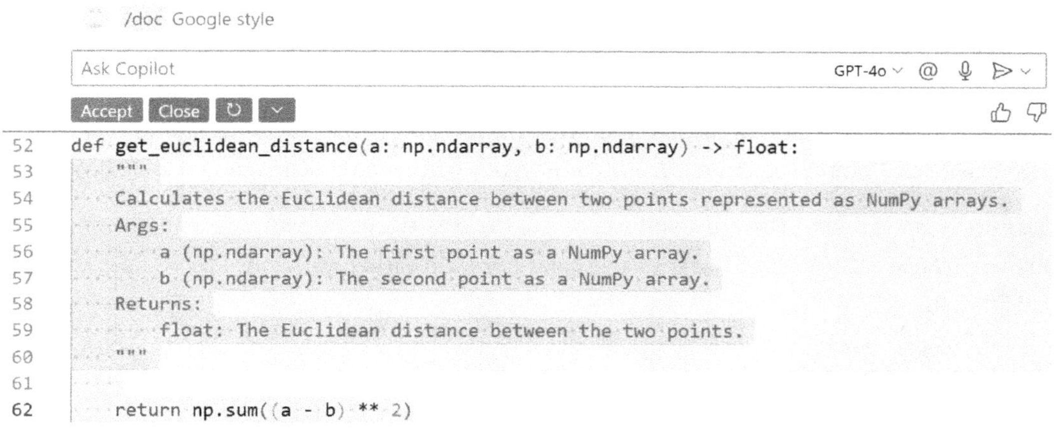

Figure 12.5: Docstring in Google style using the inline /doc Google style

This approach with the online Editor Inline Chat will not create docstrings for all the methods within a file. Other techniques for working at a file level are discussed next.

Similarly, with the GitHub Copilot chat, we can highlight a single method, such as get_euclidean_ dist, and request a Google-style docstring using the /doc `Google style` command. Shown on the left of *Figure 12.6*, the original (above) and new (below) docstrings are presented with the options to keep or undo the changes.

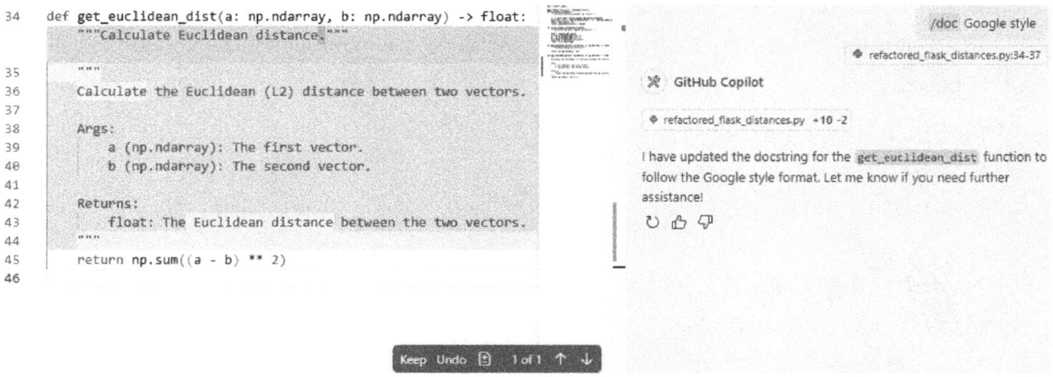

Figure 12.6: Using GitHub Copilot chat on a single method to change to Google style

Docstrings for an entire file

GitHub Copilot and ChatGPT can be used to produce docstrings for all methods within a single file at once using the chat mode, which can be quite useful. This may not work with the inline chat, depending on the version you are using of VS Code or PyCharm, so the code may be produced in the chat window and will have to be copied and pasted back into the code base. We find this approach useful at the end of the day, when you are trying to submit code before a deadline. In practice, though, we recommend writing docstrings with the code since the GenAI should be verified, which is best accomplished when writing the code. A later section, *Finding outdated docstrings with GitHub Copilot, ChatGPT, and OpenAI API,* will describe strategies for stale comments.

The first step is asking GitHub Copilot to write the docstrings for your current Python file, as shown in *Figure 12.7*. We will use the same code as we did earlier, using the Flask-based distance calculation.

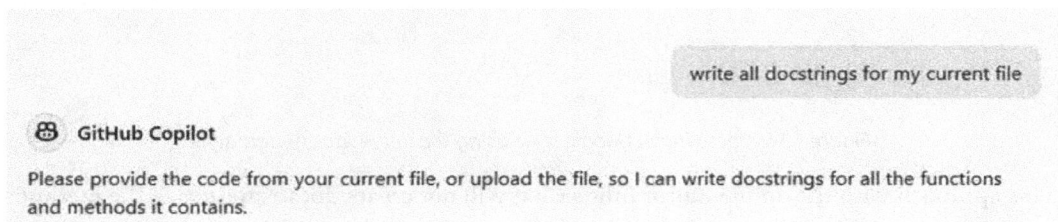

write all docstrings for my current file

GitHub Copilot

Please provide the code from your current file, or upload the file, so I can write docstrings for all the functions and methods it contains.

Figure 12.7: GitHub Copilot chat request to produce docstrings for the entire file

After uploading or pasting the file, the results are shown in the following code block. The results appear in the chat and must be copied from it to the code development window. We have not specified the type of docstring, and it may default to the Google style or the equivalent of /doc Google style. By modifying the prompt to /doc single line style, the code will produce the corresponding single-line docstrings. Both versions are included in the GitHub repository for this book.

```python
from flask import Flask, request, jsonify

app = Flask(__name__)

@app.route("/distances", methods=["POST"])
def calculate_distance():
```

```python
    """Calculate distance between two vectors."""

    a, b, dist_type = parse_request_parameters(request)
    dist_func = {"L1": get_manhattan_dist, "L2": get_euclidean_dist}.
get(dist_type)
    dist = dist_func(a, b)
    return jsonify({"distance": dist})

def parse_request_parameters(request):
    """Parse and validate request parameters."""

    data = request.get_json()
    a = np.array(data.get("df1",))
    b = np.array(data.get("df2",))
    dist_type = data.get("distance")
    return a, b, dist_type

def get_manhattan_dist(a: np.ndarray, b: np.ndarray) -> float:
    """Calculate Manhattan distance."""

    return np.sum(np.abs(a - b))

def get_euclidean_dist(a: np.ndarray, b: np.ndarray) -> float:
    """Calculate Euclidean distance."""

    return np.sum((a - b) ** 2)
```

```
                                                          Copy        Explain
function calculate(a, b) {
  return {sum: a + b};                                     1            2
};
```

With these methods, we can create documentation for a single method or an entire file. Refactoring code often leads to a problem where the code and the docstrings are out of sync. The next section discusses strategies to overcome this problem.

Finding outdated docstrings with GitHub Copilot, ChatGPT, and OpenAI API

A frequent debate among software engineers is whether documentation should be written when writing the code or later, when the code has stabilized. One line of thinking is that the docstring (and test cases) should be written at the same time. The primary argument is that the intention of the code is clearest when the developer is working through its logic and understands its purpose. The problem is that, as code is routinely refactored, the docstring comments and test cases must be adapted, making the original versions obsolete. The other line of thinking is that the documentation can and should be written later, once the code settles, to minimize the repeated rewriting of the comments.

New GenAI technology makes the debate irrelevant since it offers two solutions. The first solution is simply to regenerate and update all the comments at the method or file level. The previous section described this strategy. We can use GitHub Copilot or ChatGPT to write the docstrings for the entire file, which will update or redo all the docstrings.

The second strategy is more specific in that it can detect outdated or **stale** comments so that these can be manually or automatically adjusted. The advantage of this approach is that individual methods can be updated, leaving previously generated or verified comments unchanged. If we have individually written, verified, or otherwise invested effort in the docstrings, we do not want them to be overwritten.

For the comments, we have taken the previous example and created two versions of the Euclidean distance by copying one and modifying the code. The new code is shown here. As you can see, the first method returns the Euclidean distance and the second method returns the Euclidean distance squared, yet the docstrings have not been updated and are, in fact, identical due to our copy and paste approach.

```python
def get_euclidean_dist(a: np.ndarray, b: np.ndarray) -> float:
    """Return the squared Euclidean (L2) distance between two arrays."""
    return np.sqrt(np.sum((a - b) ** 2))



def get_euclidean_squared_dist(a: np.ndarray, b: np.ndarray) -> float:
    """Return the squared Euclidean (L2) distance between two arrays."""
    return np.sum((a - b) ** 2)
```

Using GitHub Copilot or ChatGPT, we can simply ask whether any of the docstrings are out of sync, as shown in *Figure 12.8*. The approach cleverly recognizes the squared root function call in get_euclidean_dist and suggests an update to the docstring:

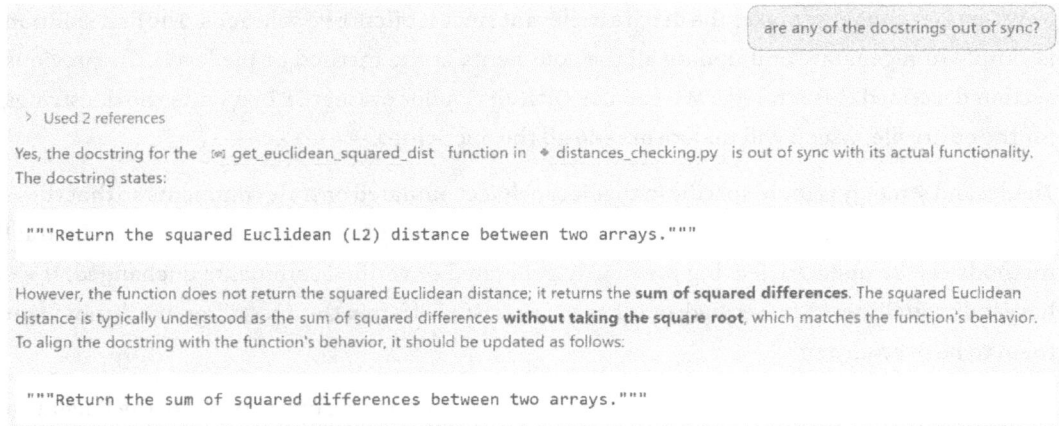

> Used 2 references

Yes, the docstring for the 🔲 get_euclidean_squared_dist function in ◆ distances_checking.py is out of sync with its actual functionality. The docstring states:

```
"""Return the squared Euclidean (L2) distance between two arrays."""
```

However, the function does not return the squared Euclidean distance; it returns the **sum of squared differences**. The squared Euclidean distance is typically understood as the sum of squared differences **without taking the square root**, which matches the function's behavior. To align the docstring with the function's behavior, it should be updated as follows:

```
"""Return the sum of squared differences between two arrays."""
```

Figure 12.8: Using GitHub Copilot to identify stale docstrings

A better approach is to use OpenAI API to compare the code and docstrings individually across a file. The sample code can be found in the repository for this chapter called openai_docstring_review.py, which runs on the distance_versions.py file. The resulting output is shown next for each of the methods.

The output explains the logic and provides an answer as to whether the docstring correctly corresponds to the code implementation. It correctly identifies that the get_euclidean_dist method does not match.

```
Function: calculate_distance
Docstring: Calculate distance between two arrays from a POST request.
Source: @app.route("/distances", methods=["POST"])
def calculate_distance():
<...code deleted for space...>
Matches: The docstring matches the implementation. Both the docstring and
the function's purpose convey that the function is designed to calculate
the distance between two arrays based on parameters received from a POST
request. Therefore, the conclusion is:
MATCHES: Yes


Function: get_euclidean_dist
Docstring: Return the squared Euclidean (L2) distance between two arrays.
```

```
Source: def get_euclidean_dist(a: np.ndarray, b: np.ndarray) -> float:
<…code deleted for space…>
Matches: The provided docstring states that the function returns
the "squared Euclidean (L2) distance between two arrays," but the
implementation actually returns the Euclidean distance (not squared) by
taking the square root of the sum of squared differences. Therefore, the
docstring does not accurately describe the implementation.

Thus, the conclusion is that the docstring does NOT match the
implementation.
Function: get_euclidean_squared_dist
Docstring: Return the squared Euclidean (L2) distance between two arrays.
Source: def get_euclidean_squared_dist(a: np.ndarray, b: np.ndarray) ->
float:
<…code deleted for space…>

Matches: The docstring and the function implementation match. The function
`get_euclidean_squared_dist` computes the squared Euclidean distance (also
known as the L2 distance) between two numpy arrays `a` and `b`, and the
docstring accurately describes this functionality.

Therefore, the answer is:
MATCHES

Function: get_manhattan_dist
Docstring: Return the Manhattan (L1) distance between two arrays.
Source: def get_manhattan_dist(a: np.ndarray, b: np.ndarray) -> float:
<…code deleted for space…>
Matches: MATCHES: Yes
```

The chapter has covered several techniques for creating docstrings. It has also introduced different strategies for finding problems with stale comments. In the next section, we provide recommendations based on how we approach writing docstrings with GenAI.

Practical insights

Given the choices of GitHub Copilot, ChatGPT, and OpenAI API, we find that Copilot is the most convenient for writing docstrings. The convenience of pair programming in the integrated environment simply makes it easier to request documentation, rather than copying and pasting code to other places. Copilot chat can usually accurately locate stale comments by itself. One issue we have encountered is that the context of sending code to Copilot is not visible. If you copy code and ask if the comments are current, it may miss some methods that were not included in the context. This can be solved by copying and pasting the code in place to renew the context.

We recommend that the docstrings be created after writing the code for each method, or at least after the code for a method has stabilized, if not after each refactoring. We further suggest checking that the docstring accurately reflects the implementation. At the beginning of the chapter, we discussed that documentation should reflect why a particular method was written rather than describing what the code does. The current technology is quite reasonable for the what but ignores the why, which is an opportunity for software engineers to elaborate.

Summary

Docstrings are a standard practice for maintaining high-quality code. They enable future readers of the software to understand the code, which is important for debugging, feature enhancements, and more. We recommend docstrings be included as soon as the code has been written. GitHub Copilot offers multiple ways of writing docstrings for a single method, including three single or double quotes, using the Copilot menus on a highlighted method. These approaches will produce single-line docstrings, the Google docstring style, or others when specified as a command.

A challenge in writing software is keeping docstrings up to date with the code. All methods can identify discrepancies between the code and docstrings, which is the preferred method for identifying issues that can be resolved. Alternatively, docstrings can be updated at a method or file level, replacing any existing docstrings.

Quiz time

Before you proceed to the next chapter, make sure that you can confidently answer the following questions:

Question 1: What are three ways of generating docstrings for code?

Answer: The three ways discussed in this chapter are as follows:

1. GitHub Copilot can recommend code by opening " " " or ' ' ' for a method on the line after the method signature

2. GitHub Copilot can be invoked by highlighting a method and using its menu to generate a docstring

3. ChatGPT or Copilot can be used to add docstrings to all methods

Question 2: What are two approaches for keeping docstrings consistent with the underlying code?

Answer: The first approach is simply overwriting any docstrings. This ensures that the GenAI produces a docstring for all methods based on the underlying code. If a docstring were inconsistent, then it would be overwritten. Unfortunately, this overwrites all previously created docstrings, which may be undesirable if you have invested time and effort into writing or checking any of them.

The second approach uses GitHub Copilot or ChatGPT to ask if there are discrepancies between the code and the docstrings. One can also use OpenAI API to match each code implementation against the docstring and return whether they match on a case-by-case basis as was shown with the openai_docstring_review.py, sample code. Any of the options in the second approach are preferred if docstrings are current and verified.

Question 3: Given that GenAI can produce quality docstrings, is it necessary to check the docstrings, or can they simply be regenerated?

Answer: While the quality is usually quite high, inaccurate docstrings can confound future developers. It is strongly recommended to use GenAI to save time, but to use human intelligence to verify that they are correct. At the present time, trust but verify is the best approach.

Further reading

- Miller's Law, also known as Magic Number 7 plus or minus 2: `https://en.wikipedia.org/wiki/The_Magical_Number_Seven,_Plus_or_Minus_Two`

- Types of docstring formats: `https://www.geeksforgeeks.org/python-docstrings/`

- Further formatting of docstrings: `https://www.linkedin.com/pulse/python-docstrings-formats-samuel-thomas/`

Subscribe for a free eBook

New frameworks, evolving architectures, research drops, production breakdowns—AI_Distilled filters the noise into a weekly briefing for engineers and researchers working hands-on with LLMs and GenAI systems. Subscribe now and receive a free eBook, along with weekly insights that help you stay focused and informed.

Subscribe at `https://packt.link/TRO5B` or scan the QR code below.

13

Writing and Maintaining Unit Tests

The task of software engineering can be interpreted as the ability to deliver quality products that contribute to the business value of customers. In this age of technology, customers have high standards and demand excellence.

The notion of quality has been interpreted in different ways over the years. However, here are two key aspects:

- That it must meet the user requirements
- It must be free of defects

These two requirements are captured by verification and validation processes, which assert that the software achieves the intended goal without any defects. There are many software engineering techniques that aim to achieve these goals, including code reviews, pair programming, and so on, but the most common is testing. Although there are many books that focus on the art and practice of software testing, this chapter focuses on unit testing, which is the most widely used approach. **Test-driven development (TDD)** is a popular agile approach for software development. Rather than writing the code first and ensuring it functions correctly with unit tests, TDD involves writing the unit test cases first and subsequently writing the minimum code that passes the tests. Proponents of the practice claim superior code quality and an inherently testable design. In this chapter, we will refer to the primary code under development as the **implementation code**, and the unit tests as the **test code**.

With GenAI coding, one can argue that testing is even more critical than conventional programming. The generative AI process involves crafting code based on comments and/or method signatures from other code, which lacks the precision that a developer would normally apply, given the trade-off for supercharged, faster coding. Unit testing serves as a check that the code functions correctly, as specified by tests. Combined with code inspection while creating the code, it offers a check of correctness.

This chapter is dedicated to working with both GitHub Copilot and ChatGPT to supercharge our creation of unit tests. In this chapter, we will cover the following topics:

- Unit tests with GenAI
- Data-driven tests
- Test-driven development
- Sample data creation with GenAI
- Practical insights

Technical requirements

To get the most out of this chapter, ensure you have the following:

- A GitHub account
- Access to your preferred IDE – either VS Code or PyCharm
- Access to the book's repository available at `https://github.com/PacktPublishing/Supercharged-Coding-with-Gen-AI`
- A virtual environment set up in your preferred IDE, VS Code, or PyCharm

For assistance setting up a GitHub Copilot account, refer to *Chapter 3*. For instructions on setting up OpenAI API access and token generation, see *Chapter 2*. If you need help creating an OpenAI account or setting up a virtual environment in your IDE, refer to the *Appendix* for detailed guidance.

Unit tests with GenAI

GenAI can save considerable time in writing unit tests. As the name suggests, each unit test is designed to test a single unit or aspect of the code. In fact, they are focused on the smallest fragments of code that can be separated and tested in isolation. Together, they provide confidence that the code functions correctly at the component level and provide an early signal of issues when the code is refactored. The same developer typically writes the code implementation and unit tests. The unit tests prove that the code functions correctly, as understood, and may also help define the requirements.

By their nature, unit tests require a deep understanding of the business and software requirements and how each method fulfills those requirements. One must consider the intended functionality as well as the variety of edge cases for each method separately and incorporate those into the test framework. This includes decisions on the test framework, method call, test nomenclature, assertion form, and the actual test. IDEs can certainly help with the test framework, but the actual test requires developer time, thought, and perhaps a strategy. These often become hurdles for junior or less motivated developers who perhaps see them as superfluous to the core software coding task. The current GenAI tools provide two-way functionality in writing unit tests for existing code as a common approach or writing code from existing unit tests, which is TDD.

The GenAI capability is not a substitute for testers or testing, but makes skilled testers much more efficient. The developer can write more tests in less time and focus on the more complex cases. The generic and simpler unit tests can be written by GenAI, usually with high accuracy. However, if the resulting tests are incomplete, one can request or prompt the GenAI to create additional tests to provide better coverage and confidence in the code.

As example code, we use the concept of creating n-grams for a given text string, which we introduced in *Chapter 6*. **N-grams** are simply adjacent groups of N letters starting at any and every point within a string without exceeding the left or right side of the string. For example, the 3-grams from the sequence "abcde" are ["abc", "bcd", "cde"]. Since we wanted to limit the range of possible characters, we only considered lowercase letters and spaces, but left tabs and line feeds. Uppercase letters were converted to lowercase, and both numbers and symbols were removed. Additionally, since English type uses single spaces, we replaced all adjacent spaces with a single space. This portion of the code is as follows:

```python
import re

def lowercase_remove_punct_numbers(text, supercharte=True):
    return re.sub(r'[^a-z\s]', '', text.lower())

def multiple_to_single_spaces(text):
    letters_single_spaces = re.sub(r'\s+', ' ', text)
    return letters_single_spaces

def create_ngrams(text, n) -> list:
    '''create a list of n-gram tuples from the input text.'''
    processed_text = lowercase_remove_punct_numbers(text)
    single_space_processed = multiple_to_single_spaces(processed_text)
```

```
    u = [single_space_processed[i:i+n] for i in range(len(single_space_
processed)-n+1)]
    return u


if __name__ == "__main__":
    text = "This is a sample text $ABC% for creating n-grams."
    n = 3
    print(create_ngrams(text, n))
```

The output of this function is a list of 3-grams that span the text input string:

```
['thi', 'his', 'is ', 's i', ' is', 'is ', 's a', ' a ', 'a s', ' sa',
'sam', 'amp', 'mpl', 'ple', 'le ', 'e t', ' te', 'tex', 'ext', 'xt ', 't
a', ' ab', 'abc', 'bc ', 'c f', ' fo', 'for', 'or ', 'r c', ' cr', 'cre',
'rea', 'eat', 'ati', 'tin', 'ing', 'ng ', 'g n', ' ng', 'ngr', 'gra',
'ram', 'ams']
```

If we start unit testing and have not set up the testing framework, we can use GitHub Copilot Chat with the prompt @workspace /setupTests, which will present an option to use either of the two main frameworks: pytest or unittest, as shown in *Figure 13.1*. The instructions are useful if you are installing unittest for the first time.

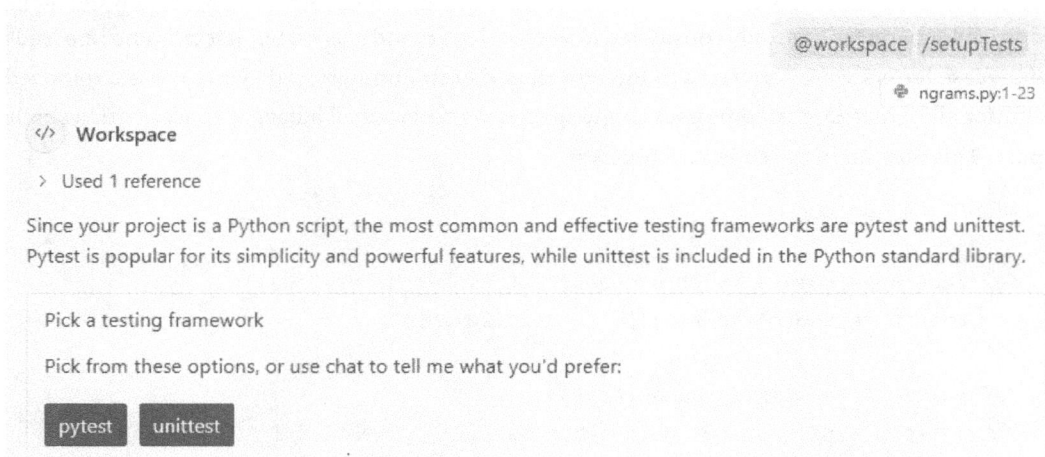

Figure 13.1: @workspace /setupTests provides a choice of the two main test frameworks

To generate unit tests, first select a single method from the implementation code, such as the lowercase_remove_punct_numbers code. Then, type the @workspace /tests generate unit tests command. Alternatively, explicitly type the name of the target method, such as @workspace

/tests generate unit tests for lowercase_remove_punct_numbers, into the GitHub Copilot Chat. It will first explain the tests that it will generate and then write the corresponding unit test file. The test explanation is shown in *Figure 13.2*:

> @workspace /tests generate unit tests for lowercase_remove_punct_numbers
>
> 🐍 ngrams.py:1-19
>
> </> Workspace
>
> > Used 1 reference
>
> Here is the unit test file for the [◎] lowercase_remove_punct_numbers function using the **unittest** framework:
>
> Plan:
>
> 1. Import the [◎] lowercase_remove_punct_numbers function using an absolute import.
> 2. Write test cases to cover:
>   ○ Text with punctuation, numbers, and uppercase letters.
>   ○ Text with only lowercase letters.
>   ○ Text with spaces and special characters.
>   ○ Empty string input.

Figure 13.2: The test plan from GitHub Copilot is provided along with the code for the method

The user will be prompted to save the resulting test file. The following code shows an example of what the output unit tests may look like, although it will vary in order and even the number of tests:

```python
import unittest
from src.ngrams import lowercase_remove_punct_numbers

# File: test_ngrams.py

class TestLowercaseRemovePunctNumbers(unittest.TestCase):
    def test_mixed_input(self):
        text = "Hello, World! 123"
        expected = "hello world"
        self.assertEqual(lowercase_remove_punct_numbers(text), expected)

    def test_lowercase_only(self):
        text = "this is a test"
        expected = "this is a test"
        self.assertEqual(lowercase_remove_punct_numbers(text), expected)
```

```python
    def test_punctuation_and_numbers(self):
        text = "!@#$%^&*()1234567890"
        expected = ""
        self.assertEqual(lowercase_remove_punct_numbers(text), expected)

    def test_empty_string(self):
        text = ""
        expected = ""
        self.assertEqual(lowercase_remove_punct_numbers(text), expected)

    def test_spaces_and_special_characters(self):
        text = "   Hello!!   World??   "
        expected = "   hello   world   "
        self.assertEqual(lowercase_remove_punct_numbers(text), expected)

if __name__ == "__main__":
    unittest.main()
```

The test code is quite reasonable in the sense that it mostly proves that the regular expressions and lowercase are correct. The tests can be run from the parent level using the `python -m unittest test_lowercase_remove_punct_numbers.py` command.

Creating tests is an iterative process, and some of the test functions created by GenAI may be unnecessary or incorrect. In other cases, additional tests may be warranted, and the GitHub Copilot Editor Inline Chat is useful for creating those tests from within the test file. As an example, we used /tests with a request to include 10-digit phone numbers to prove they would be correctly handled, which produced inline code in the test file. This process is shown in *Figure 13.3*:

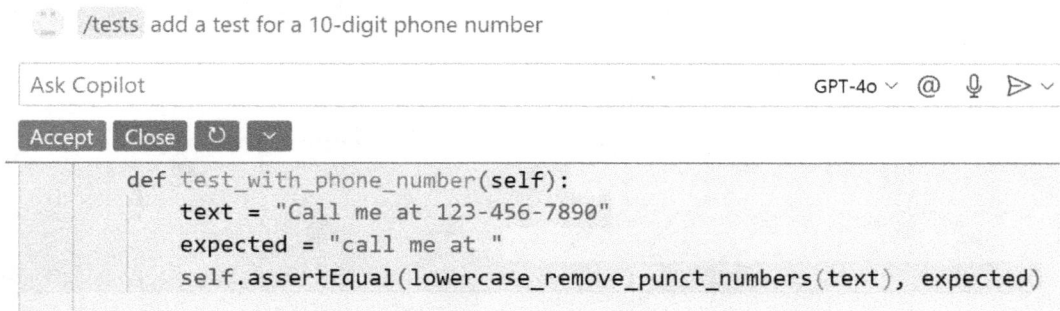

/tests add a test for a 10-digit phone number

Ask Copilot   GPT-4o ∨   @   🎤   ▷ ∨

Accept   Close   ↻   ∨

```python
    def test_with_phone_number(self):
        text = "Call me at 123-456-7890"
        expected = "call me at "
        self.assertEqual(lowercase_remove_punct_numbers(text), expected)
```

Figure 13.3: Using Editor Inline Chat within the test code to add a new test

In some cases, the Editor Inline Chat is more convenient since it will add directly to the code, whereas GitHub Copilot Chat may create a new test file. In either case, a request for a single test, such as a phone number or punctuation, may result in multiple additional tests. The developer can accept or reject these tests individually with the click of a button. Reviewing tests is important since the accuracy of the tests relates to the correctness of the code.

Rather than write tests for each method separately, the entire file can be converted into unit tests. Using GitHub Copilot chat and the @workspace /tests create unit tests for ngrams. py command, Copilot will often, but not always, produce a test plan for each of the methods in ngrams.py. Then, it will create an output test file that you must name to save. Using the unittest conventions, each method will have its own class of one or more unit tests within that file. The full set of tests is not shown here but can be found in the test_ngrams.py file in the book's GitHub repository.

There are guidelines for adding additional tests to the test file using a comment format. By typing a comment (starting with # in Python), GitHub Copilot reads the comment and suggests code. Although it should be equivalent, we have found this approach to sometimes be less accurate than using the Editor Inline Chat or GitHub Copilot Chat. As shown in *Figure 13.4*, the expected answer incorrectly includes numbers that should have been removed:

```
102     # test create_ngrams with 10-digit phone numbers including area codes
103         def test_phone_number(self):
104             self.assertEqual(
105                 create_ngrams("(123) 456-7890", 2),
106                 ["12", "23", "34", "45", "56", "67", "78", "89", "90"]
107             )
```

Figure 13.4: This test, generated from the #comment, incorrectly includes numbers

Revising the test with the #test create_ngrams with a 10-digit phone number and make sure the numbers are removed request resulted in fewer numbers included in the test. However, the variability of the unit tests with correct and incorrect responses means that checking them must be part of the verification process.

If we repeat a similar process of adding a zip code of the form 12345-6789 using the Editor Inline Chat feature, the results are more promising, as shown in *Figure 13.5*. Not only did it correctly produce the test, but it also added several additional tests. However, as a note of caution, the Inline Chat did not always produce accurate tests and sometimes incorrectly included numbers.

/tests add a new test for a zip code of the form of five digits - 4 digits

```
Ask Copilot                                                          GPT-4.1 ∨  @  🎤  ▷∨
```

Accept | Close | ↻ | ∨

```
108        def test_zip_code(self):
109            # Should remove all digits and punctuation, leaving only spaces (if any)
110            self.assertEqual(
111                create_ngrams("12345-6789", 2),
112                []
113            )
114
115        def test_longer_ngram(self):
116            self.assertEqual(
117                create_ngrams("abcdefg", 5),
118                ["abcde", "bcdef", "cdefg"]
119            )
120
121        def test_ngram_with_spaces(self):
122            self.assertEqual(
123                create_ngrams("a b c", 3),
124                ["a b", " b ", "b c"]
125            )
126
```

Figure 13.5: The tests from Editor Inline Chat produced a correct test and others as well

This section has described how GitHub Copilot can create unit tests from the implementation code, either for a single method or an entire file. The next section describes how ChatGPT can achieve similar results.

ChatGPT for testing

ChatGPT can also be used to write unit tests. An example prompt to write Python unit tests is as follows:

You are a Python testing assistant.

Given Python code enclosed within {{ }}}, generate unit tests using the unittest framework. For each function or method in the code:

1. Create a corresponding test method within a unittest.TestCase subclass.

2. Use meaningful test method names that reflect the function being tested.

3. Include appropriate assertions based on the function's logic and expected behavior.

4. Use mock objects or patching where necessary (e.g., for I/O, APIs, or external dependencies).

5. If a function has multiple logical branches or edge cases, include test cases for them.

6. Do not include the original code in the output—only the test code.

7.Import any modules or classes necessary for the tests to run.
8.Format your output as a complete, valid Python test file using the unittest module.

Input:
python
{{{
# Paste Python code here
}}}

Output:

Applying this template to the `ngrams.py` code produced seven different tests without further elaboration. The file is listed in `test_ngrams_chatgpt.py` in the GitHub repository for the book. One of the tests created was incorrect and subsequently failed, as shown in *Figure 13.6*. The test incorrectly suggests that a $ and s are equivalent, instead of replacing the dollar symbol with a space.

```
12        def test_lowercase_remove_punct_numbers_with_symbols(self):
13            self.assertEqual(
14                lowercase_remove_punct_numbers("Te$ting #punctu@ation &numbers 456"),
15                "testing punctuation numbers "
16            )
```

PROBLEMS ②   OUTPUT   DEBUG CONSOLE   TERMINAL   PORTS

```
....F..
=======================================================================
FAIL: test_lowercase_remove_punct_numbers_with_symbols (tests.test_ngrams_chatgpt.TestTextUtils.test_lowerc
ase_remove_punct_numbers_with_symbols)
-----------------------------------------------------------------------
Traceback (most recent call last):
  File "C:\Users\PeterH\Documents\Euro 2025\Book Writing\testing chapter\src\tests\test_ngrams_chatgpt.py",
 line 13, in test_lowercase_remove_punct_numbers_with_symbols
    self.assertEqual(
AssertionError: 'teting punctuation numbers ' != 'testing punctuation numbers '
- teting punctuation numbers
+ testing punctuation numbers
?    +
```

Figure 13.6: ChatGPT produced one incorrect test out of seven for ngrams.py

When prompted `Are there additional tests that should be included?`, ChatGPT produced an additional set of tests shown in *Figure 13.7*, each with code, and offered to convert them into a code library:

Summary of Suggested Additions

Function	Suggested New Tests
`lowercase_remove_punct_numbers`	Empty string, all punctuation, all alpha, mixed whitespace
`multiple_to_single_spaces`	Empty, only whitespace, already spaced
`create_ngrams`	Empty, small/large `n`, edge alignment cases

Figure 13.7: Additional ChatGPT tests that it suggested when prompted

As a supplement to the unit tests, additional tests can also be run directly within ChatGPT and included in the overall test suite. The `test_ngrams_chatgpt_extra.py` file in the GitHub repository shows the tests generated. In addition to running the tests in ChatGPT, this platform also explains why tests fail. *Figure 13.8* presents a valuable discussion of the test failure and the handling of tabs and newlines, which could be a failed test or an issue with the original code. Such insight into the code will help improve the overall quality. ChatGPT made suggestions to change the tests and rerun them:

❌ Failed Test 1: `test_lowercase_remove_punct_numbers_whitespace_mix`

Why it failed:

The function `lowercase_remove_punct_numbers` preserves tabs (`\t`) and newlines (`\n`) as whitespace, but your test expected them to be replaced with regular spaces.

Fix:

The `re.sub(r'[^a-z\s]', '', text.lower())` pattern retains all whitespace characters (`\s` includes tab, newline, space). So the actual return includes `\t` and `\n`.

✅ **Update the test to reflect actual behavior** or modify the function to normalize whitespace. Here's the adjusted test:

python Copy Edit

```python
def test_lowercase_remove_punct_numbers_whitespace_mix(self):
    self.assertEqual(lowercase_remove_punct_numbers("ABC\tDEF\nGHI"), "abc\tdef\nghi")
```

Figure 13.8: Explanation of a failed text from ChatGPT

ChatGPT is clearly effective at writing unit tests, even if it requires multiple requests. It is also possible to write other kinds of tests, such as data-driven tests, which is the topic of the next section.

Data-driven tests

The GitHub Copilot or ChatGPT prompt can enable data-driven or random testing that supplements the unit test coverage. Using the `Generate data driven tests for lowercase_remove_punct_numbers` prompt with Copilot gave the following code:

```python
import unittest
from src.ngrams import lowercase_remove_punct_numbers


class TestLowercaseRemovePunctNumbers(unittest.TestCase):
    def test_data_driven(self):
        test_cases = [
            # (input, expected_output)
            ("Hello, World! 123", "hello world "),
            ("ABCdef", "abcdef"),
            ("1234!@#$", ""),
            ("A1! b2@ C3#", "a b c"),
            ("", ""),
            ("     ", "     "),
            ("Python3.8_is#awesome!", "pythonisawesome"),
            ("No PUNCTUATION", "no punctuation"),
            ("MiXeD CaSe &*^%", "mixed case "),
            ("newline\nTab\tSpace ", "newline\ttab\tspace "),
        ]
        for input_text, expected in test_cases:
            with self.subTest(input=input_text):
                self.assertEqual(lowercase_remove_punct_numbers(input_
text), expected)


if __name__ == "__main__":
    unittest.main()
```

This file can be found as `test_data_driven_ngrams.py` in the book's GitHub repository. This example and the unit tests in the previous section show how GenAI can create tests from the implementation code. GitHub Copilot and ChatGPT use this code to identify meaningful test cases, including many edge cases. To improve the coverage, additional tests can be written manually, semi-manually with GenAI, or by simply requesting additional tests. These unit tests can be extended similarly to other types of testing, such as integration testing, performance testing, and A/B testing.

As discussed in these two sections, both unit tests and data-driven tests can be written using GenAI from the implementation code. While creating test code from the implementation code works, one should consider writing the tests first rather than the implementation. This approach is called test-driven development and is described in the next section.

Test-driven development

Test-driven development (TDD) is one component of the **Extreme Programming (XP)** agile software methodology proposed by Kent Beck in the 1990s. Two of his books can be found in the *Further reading* section. The main concept of TDD is that the unit tests are written first and subsequently fail since there is no code to support them. The software engineer then writes the code until the tests pass. It is widely accepted that this practice improves code design and enhances testability. Empirical studies such as that by Mäkinen & Jürgen Münch (`https://link.springer.com/chapter/10.1007/978-3-319-03602-1_10`) generally support the value of TDD. The approach also focuses the software engineer on passing tests rather than adding other features.

Whether to write tests first or last often becomes a religious debate with devout followers on either side. We will not attempt to resolve the issue here. If we believe that GenAI always writes perfect code that exactly and cleanly meets all the requirements, then it does not matter whether the tests or the code are used to write the other. A recent 2024 IEEE study by Jiri et al. (`https://ieeexplore.ieee.org/document/10685204`) showed that unit tests written by humans have fewer errors than unit tests by GenAI, but the technology is advancing rapidly and closing this gap. This leaves us with a conundrum that the code may be flawed, and the tests may not be perfect, yet we need both to be accurate. The more common convention of software engineers is to write the code using GenAI and then use GenAI to write the tests, which mirrors their development practice. With TDD, there is a potential to write the perfect tests, perhaps with GenAI, and then use GenAI to prove that the implementation passes the tests and their perceived requirements. In fact, we can go further and use GenAI to iterate and craft the code that meets these requirements.

As an example for this section, we will use the intersection of two rectangles problem, which simply identifies the overlapping area between two rectangles. To simplify the problem, we restrict the rectangle definition to use two points—the x and y coordinates of the lower-left and upper-right corners of the rectangle. In our notation, the rectangle is represented as (*xll, yll, xur, yur*) as shown in *Figure 13.9*:

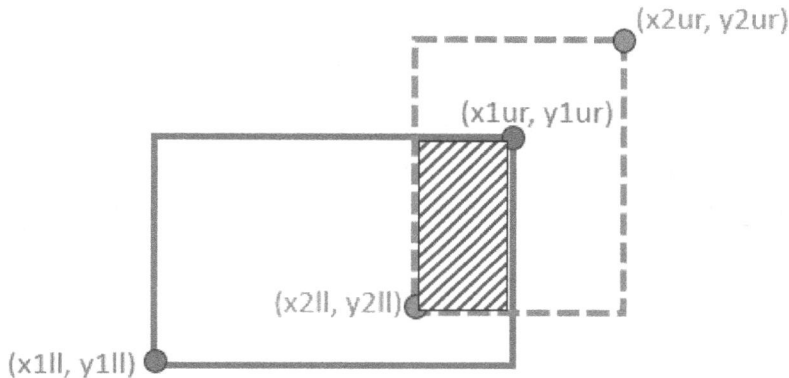

Figure 13.9: Intersecting rectangle problem

Rather than immediately start coding the result, we will instead consider the various test cases, which are broken down into the following:

1. Intersecting rectangles (*Figure 13.10*):

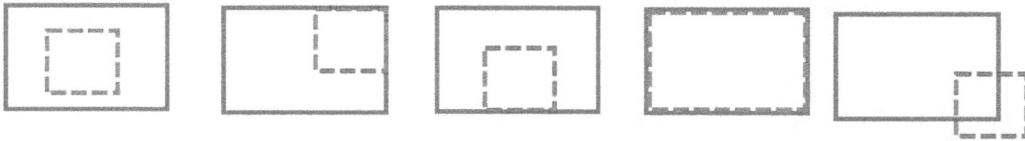

Figure 13.10: Example test cases for overlapping rectangles

2. Non-intersecting rectangles (*Figure 13.11*):

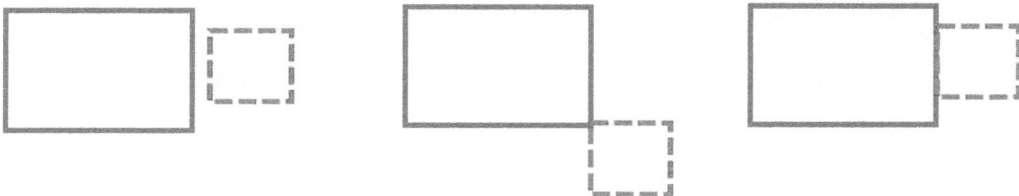

Figure 13.11: Example test cases for non-overlapping rectangles

3.   Invalid rectangles (*Figure 13.12*):

Figure 13.12: Example test cases for invalid rectangles that fail our definition

As part of the TDD process, we begin by coding the unit tests using GenAI. Using descriptive test names facilitates the accurate creation of the test code. A few tests are shown to illustrate the idea in the following code snippet (the full file with 21 unit tests is available in the book's GitHub repository as test_rectangle_intersection.py):

```python
import unittest
from rectangle_intersection import rect_intersection_area

class TestRectangleIntersectionArea(unittest.TestCase):
    def test_intersecting_rectangles(self):
        rect1 = (0, 0, 4, 4)
        rect2 = (2, 2, 6, 6)
        self.assertEqual(rect_intersection_area(rect1, rect2), 4)

    def test_intersecting_rectangles_swapped(self):
        rect1 = (2, 2, 6, 6)
        rect2 = (0, 0, 4, 4)
        self.assertEqual(rect_intersection_area(rect1, rect2), 4)

    def test_non_intersecting_rectangles(self):
        rect1 = (0, 0, 2, 2)
        rect2 = (3, 3, 5, 5)
        self.assertEqual(rect_intersection_area(rect1, rect2), 0)
```

For the tests to appropriately fail as the next step of the TDD process, we need a stub file, rectangle_ intersection.py, containing rect_intersection_area(rect1, rect), which arbitrarily returns None. An example of this code is shown as follows and is stored as rectangle_intersection.

py in the same folder. These names are based on the import statement at the beginning of the preceding test file code, as shown:

```
def rect_intersection_area(rect1, rect):
    return None
```

With the TDD process, we have encoded the requirements of the code as tests. The only missing piece is the actual implementation. Normally, we would iterate between writing the implementation and running the tests to ensure that the code functions as expected. Using GenAI, we can replace this process with a request to GenAI to iteratively write the code until it passes all the tests. We will discuss how this can be achieved using GitHub Copilot in both VS Code and PyCharm IDEs, and then show the TDD approach using ChatGPT.

TDD using GitHub Copilot within VS Code

The TDD approach within VS Code is arguably the most straightforward. First, we ensure that both rectangle_intersection.py and test_rectangle_intersection.py are open, then run the latter unit test file. Then, we can use this command in the Copilot chat window:

```
@terminal /fix rect_intersection_area according to the unit test failure
```

This produces an updated set of code in the same chat window that we copied and pasted as a replacement for the rectangle_intersection.py implementation. This is shown as follows:

```
def rect_intersection_area(rect1, rect2):
    """

    Calculate the area of intersection between two rectangles.
    Each rectangle is represented as a tuple (x1, y1, x2, y2):
    - (x1, y1): bottom-left corner
    - (x2, y2): top-right corner
    """

    # Calculate the overlapping region
    x_overlap = max(0, min(rect1[2], rect2[2]) - max(rect1[0], rect2[0]))
    y_overlap = max(0, min(rect1[3], rect2[3]) - max(rect1[1], rect2[1]))

    # If there is an overlap, calculate the area
    return x_overlap * y_overlap
```

Running the same unit tests against this new implementation reduced the number of tests that failed from 21 to 9. Most of the failures are caused by the lack of exceptions raised for invalid rectangles. These were included in the tests but ignored by the GenAI.

We repeated the process with the same /fix command to produce the next iteration of code implementation, but the errors persisted. In some cases, running the process two or three times resolved the errors. In other cases, we needed to manually revise the /fix command with more explicit instructions:

```
@workspace /fix rectangle_intersection_area according to the unit test
failure and be sure to raise ValueError for invalid rectangle dimensions
```

The generated implementation passed all the unit tests and is shown as follows:

```python
def rect_intersection_area(rect1, rect2):
    """

    Calculate the area of intersection between two rectangles.
    Each rectangle is represented as a tuple (x1, y1, x2, y2):
    - (x1, y1): bottom-left corner
    - (x2, y2): top-right corner
    """

    # Ensure the rectangles are valid
    if rect1[0] >= rect1[2] or rect1[1] >= rect1[3]:
        raise ValueError(f"Invalid rectangle dimensions for rect1:
{rect1}")
    if rect2[0] >= rect2[2] or rect2[1] >= rect2[3]:
        raise ValueError(f"Invalid rectangle dimensions for rect2:
{rect2}")

    # Calculate the overlapping region
    x_left = max(rect1[0], rect2[0])
    y_bottom = max(rect1[1], rect2[1])
    x_right = min(rect1[2], rect2[2])
    y_top = min(rect1[3], rect2[3])

    # Check if there is an actual overlap
    if x_left < x_right and y_bottom < y_top:
        return (x_right - x_left) * (y_top - y_bottom)
    else:
        return 0  # No overlap
```

In this section, we used a simple one-line command within the VS Code chat to create an implementation. It uses the implementation code, unit tests, and the output of the tests directly to write an improved version of the implementation code.

TDD using GitHub Copilot within PyCharm

Using the TDD approach within PyCharm is not quite as simple as with VS Code. As of January 2025, GitHub Copilot cannot access PyCharm's terminal window, which means it cannot access the failed unit tests directly. The output of failed tests informs Copilot what needs to be fixed in the implementation, and so this is a critical component. As a solution, we can paste the error message of the failed messages into the GitHub Copilot chat window:

```
CONTEXT: You will be given an error message enclosed in {{{ERROR}}}.
TASK: Fix the implementation of rectangle_intersection_area _mean so it
passes all tests.
ERROR: {{{ ... <omitted for brevity> ... }}}
FIXED CODE:
```

This prompt, whether used in an inline chat or a chat window, should generate a fully functional implementation that passes the unit tests.

For TDD with PyCharm, we need to use a more complete template call within the chat that passes the output of the failed unit tests. With this information, as well as the implementation and test code, a new version of the implementation code aims to solve the issues and pass the unit tests. A similar approach can be used with ChatGPT, which will be described next.

TDD using ChatGPT

As part of the TDD process, ChatGPT can also be used to generate improved implementation code based on the combination of the existing implementation code, unit test code, and the errors or results of the unit test execution. We use triple brackets to enclose each of these components:

```
CONTEXT: You are provided with
1. Python function enclosed with {{{ FUNCTION }}} that has a bug.
2. Test suite code enclosed with {{{ UNIT TESTS }}}.
3. Error message enclosed with {{{ ERROR }}}.
TASK: Fix the function implementation
FUNCTION: {{{def rect_intersection_area(rect1, rect2):
    return None
```

```
}}}
UNIT TESTS: {{{ ... omitted for brevity ... }}}
ERROR: {{{ ... omitted for brevity ... }}}
CODE:
```

In this instance, ChatGPT produced the following output code, which is similar but mildly different from the GitHub Copilot output. ChatGPT explained the implementation, and all the created tests passed in the first iteration.

```python
def rect_intersection_area(rect1, rect2):
    x1_1, y1_1, x2_1, y2_1 = rect1
    x1_2, y1_2, x2_2, y2_2 = rect2

    # Validate input rectangles
    def is_invalid_rect(x1, y1, x2, y2):
        return x1 >= x2 or y1 >= y2

    if is_invalid_rect(x1_1, y1_1, x2_1, y2_1) or is_invalid_rect(x1_2,
y1_2, x2_2, y2_2):
        raise ValueError("Invalid rectangle with non-positive width or
height")

    # Find intersection bounds
    inter_left = max(x1_1, x1_2)
    inter_right = min(x2_1, x2_2)
    inter_bottom = max(y1_1, y1_2)
    inter_top = min(y2_1, y2_2)

    # Check if rectangles intersect
    if inter_left >= inter_right or inter_bottom >= inter_top:
        return 0

    # Compute and return intersection area
    return (inter_right - inter_left) * (inter_top - inter_bottom)
```

If the tests had not passed, the new code would need to be copied and pasted into the IDE, replacing the previous version. The unit tests would need to be rerun against the new code. The revised implementation code and resulting unit test errors must be copied again into the ChatGPT template.

The advantage of the TDD approach is that it asserts that the implementation is correct based on the fact that the code passes the unit tests. The code produced in this simple example is quite reasonable, but more complex tasks may produce functional code of lower quality. In such cases, the code should be refactored. However, this is much easier with a full set of tests that continue to prove the code is meeting the functional requirements.

Whether TDD is the ideal strategy is still up for debate. Without TDD, the user focuses on the implementation, from which the GenAI can certainly create reasonable tests. As we observed, some of the tests may fail, and some may indicate limitations of the implementation. The software developer must then understand all the tests and provide enough logical coverage to be confident in the implementation. With TDD, the cognitive effort is in assuring the tests are sufficient, from which code can be generated. If the GenAI provides an implementation, the most the developer will have to do is refactor the code.

Whether the code or tests are written first, the tests often require meaningful datasets. The next section describes how GenAI can be used to create realistic data.

Sample data creation with GenAI

One aspect of testing is the availability of data that is representative of the kind you will encounter in the wild. If you have been involved in creating mock data in years past, you will certainly appreciate GenAI approaches to this problem. The new techniques can create a variety of types of data with as specific a prompt as you need. For example, the following prompt works in either ChatGPT or GitHub Copilot:

```
create a table with 10 rows and the following columns:
5 digit integer id called "ID"
first name
last name
address consisting of a number, street name, and whether it is a st., dr.
or ave.
city
country
disease
age
```

The resulting table output is shown in *Figure 13.13*, which includes typical names, address formats, diseases, and so on. This kind of data can be saved to a file and used for testing. Although such data could be generated on the fly, the purpose of unit testing is to create repeatable tests that achieve consistent results. Tests are usually added to a **regression test** package as part of the CI/CD methodology and rerun periodically to ensure that past errors do not recur as code versions evolve. Therefore, the data should be stored and reused.

🐙 GitHub Copilot

ID	First Name	Last Name	Address	City	Country	Disease	Age
10234	Alice	Smith	123 Maple St.	Boston	USA	Influenza	34
20458	Brian	Johnson	456 Oak Dr.	Toronto	Canada	Diabetes	45
31567	Carla	Lee	789 Pine Ave.	London	UK	Hypertension	52
42689	David	Kim	321 Cedar St.	Sydney	Australia	Asthma	28
53790	Emma	Patel	654 Birch Dr.	Mumbai	India	Malaria	41
64821	Frank	Müller	987 Elm Ave.	Berlin	Germany	Arthritis	60
75932	Grace	Rossi	159 Spruce St.	Rome	Italy	COVID-19	37
86043	Henry	Dubois	753 Willow Dr.	Paris	France	Tuberculosis	50
97154	Irene	Chen	852 Aspen Ave.	Beijing	China	Hepatitis	29
18265	Jack	Lopez	951 Walnut St.	Madrid	Spain	Dengue	33

Figure 13.13: Example table of mock data produced by GitHub Copilot

Of course, the data is not limited to addresses but can be more technical, such as the `Create a FASTA file with 3 sequences of length 15 to 25 nucleotides` prompt, which returns three bioinformatics DNA sequences as shown in *Figure 13.14*:

Here's the FASTA-formatted file with 3 randomly generated DNA sequences, each 15–25 nucleotides long:

```shell
>Sequence_1
GAAATTACCGACGGCCGGCC
>Sequence_2
TGAAAGGACCCGCTCCTTA
>Sequence_3
TTCAGACGGTCTACTT
```

Let me know if you'd like to download this as a `.fasta` file or generate more sequences. [?-]

Figure 13.14: A FASTA bioinformatics sequence file with three DNA sequences

As can be seen from the previous output, it suggests saving the file as a `.fasta` file. In fact, it can create and save data in any format, including tables, JSON, CSV, and so on.

Another use case that is often convenient when scripting is to create some temporary data for a function, perhaps in a Jupyter notebook. Consider the Euclidean distance method:

```python
def get_euclidean_dist(a: np.ndarray, b: np.ndarray) -> float:
    """Return the squared Euclidean (L2) distance between two arrays."""
    return np.sqrt(np.sum((a - b) ** 2))
```

GitHub Copilot used the `Create sample inputs for get_euclidean_distance()` prompt to produce a few samples of inputs that can be directly applied, as shown in *Figure 13.15*:

GitHub Copilot

Here are some sample inputs for `get_euclidean_dist()`:

```python
import numpy as np

# Example 1: 1D arrays
a = np.array([1, 2, 3])
b = np.array([4, 5, 6])

# Example 2: 2D arrays
a2 = np.array([[1, 2], [3, 4]])
b2 = np.array([[5, 6], [7, 8]])

# Example 3: Negative values
a3 = np.array([-1, -2, -3])
b3 = np.array([1, 2, 3])
```

You can call `get_euclidean_dist(a, b)`, `get_euclidean_dist(a2, b2)`, or `get_euclidean_dist(a3, b3)` with these inputs.

Figure 13.15: GitHub Copilot creates example inputs for functions for informal testing

In the TDD process, developers write the unit test code first, and the implementation code is written to pass the unit tests. The unit tests can be written by developers using standard GenAI approaches to verify that the implementation code will meet the requirements. From either VS Code or PyCharm, GitHub Copilot can iteratively create the implementation code from the unit test code alone. ChatGPT offers similar functionality through a prompt template. The next section provides recommendations on how GenAI approaches can best be used to complete the implementation and test code.

Practical insights

Testing has been a focus of technology from the templates of "vintage AI" to the present time with GenAI. There has always been a tendency to write the code and eventually write the tests to make it acceptable to your organization. These new GenAI tools can definitely increase the velocity of the coding process. The verification process to check the code should not be just a one-time visual inspection but should involve unit tests that can be applied repeatedly to assert the correctness of the code.

The different GenAI solutions produce slightly different results, but we generally prefer GitHub Copilot for creating tests since the close integration with the code and iterative approach is easier using the single tool within the IDE, whether VS Code or PyCharm. By keeping similar test code open in the browser, accuracy and style improve due to the extra context.

Regardless of the particular GenAI tool used, it is critical to check the implementation and test code. Using GenAI to create the test code from the implementation or vice versa helps minimize errors since the implementation code that passes unit tests achieves at least a first level of requirement verification. Failing unit tests provide a chance to rethink code requirements for the implementation and test code.

Summary

In this chapter, we explored various aspects of testing using GenAI. Although there are many types of tests and they are the topic of many books, the most common tests are unit tests. In unit testing, each test should test a single point of functionality and should be independent of other tests. Together, a complete set of unit tests proves that the code implementation functions as expected. If the code is refactored, augmented, or integrated in the future, the same unit tests assert the correctness of the functionality.

The chapter described a few approaches to creating tests from the implementation. GitHub Copilot and ChatGPT can both be used to easily write unit tests for a single method or an entire Python file. Both techniques have some variability in terms of the types of tests and coverage that they provide in a first pass. In some cases, the tests may not be correct and may need additional prompting or manual correction. In other scenarios, prompting may be useful to add further tests to improve the coverage of the edge cases. Developers must be cautious that the tests accurately capture the requirements and are sufficient to assert the correctness of the code.

TDD is a methodology from Extreme Programming where unit tests are written first and, by definition, fail. The implementation code is written to pass all the unit tests. GenAI can help suggest the test code, especially when descriptive method names are used. Using a set of tests, either GitHub Copilot or ChatGPT can iteratively generate the implementation code automatically. The process repeats until the unit tests pass. By writing the full set of tests first, the developer conveys the scope of the tests and behavior in various edge cases. The only required interaction with the generated implementation code is possibly refactoring it to improve quality, which is easier to achieve with the unit tests.

Two additional topics were covered in the chapter, which involved enriching data for tests. GenAI can create more elaborate tests by synthesizing different scenarios. Data-driven testing creates test pairs for inputs and outputs to test multiple scenarios. In addition, the technology can create realistic test sets applicable to a wide range of disciplines.

In the next chapter, we introduce ways that GenAI can identify capacity limits in terms of execution speed and memory management. We will also show how GenAI can optimize code to improve performance under these two constraints.

Quiz time

Before you proceed to the next chapter, make sure that you can confidently answer the following questions:

Question 1: What are the advantages of TDD?

Answer: TDD, or test-driven development, is a methodology where the tests are written first, and the implementation code follows. The tests cover the range of required functionality and edge cases to ensure they meet expectations. Using TDD ensures that the tests are written and that the code (written by humans or GenAI) functions correctly. Empirical results show that the implementations are generally structured better and are more amenable to tests.

Question 2: If software includes both implementation and unit tests, does it need to be manually verified?

Answer: Without question, a full set of unit tests and correct implementation help identify failures or misinterpretations of the requirements. A failed test is likely due to a flawed test or a flawed implementation and provides an opportunity to review the requirements. While testing helps identify such issues, we have observed many cases where the generated tests lack full coverage and may be incorrect. Similarly, there are numerous examples of incorrect implementations. The authors recommend manual verification in addition to complete unit tests.

Further reading

- Kent Beck's book on extreme programming. 2000. *Extreme Programming Explained: Embrace Change.*

- Kent Beck's book on test-driven development. 2002. *Test-Driven Development by Example.*

- *Effects of Test-Driven Development: A Comparative Analysis of Empirical Studies.* Simo Mäkinen & Jürgen Münch: https://link.springer.com/chapter/10.1007/978-3-319-03602-1_10

- *Leveraging Large Language Models for Python Unit Test.* Medlen Jiri, Bari Emese, Patrick Medlen. 2024: https://ieeexplore.ieee.org/document/10685204.

Unlock this book's exclusive benefits now

Scan this QR code or go to packtpub.com/ unlock, then search for this book by name.

Note: Keep your purchase invoice ready before you start.

14

GenAI for Runtime and Memory Management

In the age of big data, artificial intelligence, and intensive data processing, an essential characteristic of well written Python programs is their ability to efficiently manage both **memory usage** and **runtime performance**. As part of the **Software Development Life Cycle (SDLC)**, it is common practice to profile our programs, anticipate performance limitations and strive for efficiency in both aspects.

In addition to utilizing traditional tools for profiling program performance and addressing inefficiencies, we can leverage the **model mastery** of **Large Language Models (LLMs)** to code profile snippets, analyze maximal capacities, and optimize code to handle larger workloads.

In this chapter, we will examine two examples of inefficient implementations: a Fibonacci calculator with significant runtime overhead and a statistical analysis function that demands excessive memory for large matrices. By utilizing prompt precision best practices and **chaining** prompt engineering technique, we will demonstrate how GenAI applications can help profile performance metrics, estimate maximum capacities, and optimize the code to handle larger inputs effectively.

The topics covered in this chapter include:

- Introducing time and space complexity analysis
- Profiling runtime and memory consumption with GitHub Copilot
- Analyzing maximal capacity with ChatGPT
- Optimizing code with chained prompts

Technical requirements

To get the most out of this chapter, ensure you have the following:

- GitHub Copilot account
- IDE – either VS Code or Pycharm
- OpenAI account with access to ChatGPT and OpenAI API
- Access to the book's repository available at: `https://github.com/PacktPublishing/Supercharged-Coding-with-Gen-AI`
- Virtual environment set up in VS Code or PyCharm
- OpenAI API token

For assistance setting up a GitHub Copilot account, refer to *Chapter 3*. For instructions on setting up OpenAI API access and token generation, see *Chapter 2*. If you need help creating an OpenAI account or setting up a virtual environment in your IDE, refer to the *Appendix* for detailed guidance.

Introducing time and space analysis

In our current technology cycle, most companies are leveraging big data and artificial intelligence to improve their businesses. For example, videos on the YouTube and TikTok platforms are viewed over a billion times per day which generates recommendations and advertising value. In these cases, even 1% gains in efficiency for storage or computation may save millions of dollars.

According to *Lambda Labs*, training the generative pre-trained transformer model *GPT-3* involved about 700 gigabytes of **Random Access Memory (RAM)** and thousands of powerful Nvidia GPUs operating in parallel, with a cumulative compute time equivalent to 355 years. Even a minor inefficiency in implementing these models could lead to substantial costs or, in the worst case, create a bottleneck that would prevent the model from running effectively.

The runtime of a program

The runtime of a program refers to the time it takes to execute the tasks defined in the source code on a specific hardware configuration with a given input. The runtime duration of a program depends on factors such as the computational complexity (the number of operations required to complete the task) and the hardware such as the **central processing unit (CPU)**.

For example, consider an inefficient implementation of the Fibonacci number computation using recursion:

```
def fibonacci_recursive(n):
    if n <= 1:
        return n
    return fibonacci_recursive(n - 1) + fibonacci_recursive(n - 2)
```

In this implementation, each Fibonacci number computation involves two recursive calls: one for the previous number and another for the one before that. Each of these calls triggers two additional recursive calls, and so on, until the base condition n <= 1 is met.

To illustrate how quickly the runtime of this implementation grows, here are examples of recorded runtimes on a MacBook Pro with an M1 chip using this implementation:

Runtime for fibonacci_recursive(5): 0.000006 seconds

Runtime for fibonacci_recursive(35): 1.7051 seconds

Runtime of fibonacci_recursive(40): 19.5045 seconds

Computing the fibonacci_recursive(100) is estimated to take 15 trillion seconds, or approximately 475,000 years, making it completely impractical. This exponential growth represents one of the least desirable complexities in algorithm design as it remains inefficient regardless of the hardware used, as we will now explore.

Runtime complexity refresher

Since computers vary in speed, it is widespread practice to measure runtime complexity in general terms using **Big-O notation**, denoted as $O(...)$. This notation describes how the runtime scales relatively to the size of the input data.

For instance:

- Finding the minimum number in an unsorted array of length n has a runtime complexity of $O(n)$
- Printing all (i, j) combinations of elements in an array of length n has a runtime complexity of $O(n^2)$.

Retrieving the nth Fibonacci number using fibonacci_recursive has a runtime complexity of $O(2^n)$.

If you need a further refresher on Big-O notation or are unfamiliar with it, we recommend checking the *Further Reading* section at the end of this chapter. Big-O notation is an essential concept for developers, both in application design and day-to-day problem-solving.

The space consumption of a program

The RAM consumed by a program during execution reflects its memory space usage. For instance, a MacBook Pro with 16 **gigabytes (GB)** of RAM can hold about 2 billion float64 values where each `float64` occupies 8 bytes.

Consider the following inefficient function get_top_video that reads a **comma-separated values (CSV)** file into memory as a *Pandas DataFrame* and returns the video with the highest average watch percentage:

```
def get_top_video(path):
    interactions = pd.read_csv(path)
    avg_ratio = interactions.mean(axis=0, skipna=True)
    return avg_ratio.idxmax()
```

The input CSV file may represent a matrix as follows, where each cell indicates the percentage of a specific video watched by a user:

	video_1	video_2	video_3	video_4	video_5	video_6	...
user_1		0.5				1	
user_2	0.1			0.7		0.9	

If the input dataset contains 50,000 users (rows) and 50,000 videos (columns), this would involve loading 2.5 billion cells into memory. Such a large dataset exceeds the 16 GB RAM limit, leading to an **out-of-memory error** and causing the function to fail.

Space complexity

To assess memory usage, developers often use space complexity, expressed in Big-O notation, to describe how memory usage scales with the size of the data structure. For example, in get_top_video, the space complexity is $O(m \times n)$ for a CSV file with m rows and n columns, as the function loads the entire dataset into memory.

Balancing efficiency tradeoffs

When designing programs, it is common to encounter tradeoffs between memory usage and runtime efficiency. For instance, **caching** is the process of storing information such as a function's calculated output values in RAM rather than recomputing them. This can significantly improve the speed of repeated calculations but also increases memory consumption. In a program that calls `fibonacci_recursive` repeatedly with the same input, such as n=35 which previously took 1.7 seconds to run, caching the result could save 1.7 seconds for each subsequent call.

Another tradeoff is with the `get_top_video` we read the entire file into memory before starting the calculations. It may be more practical to read smaller batches of data from disk and compute the cumulative top videos for each batch sequentially rather than handling the entire dataset at once. Reading and processing smaller chunks of large CSV files might take more time but helps avoid exceeding RAM limitations.

Now that we grasp the importance of runtime and space efficiency, how to assess their complexity, and the trade-offs involved, we can move forward and explore how GenAI can assist with each step in managing and optimizing program efficiency.

Profiling runtime and memory consumption with GitHub Copilot

Profiling runtime and memory usage is a straightforward process. The built-in `time` module is useful for tracking runtime and the third-party `memory_profiler` library monitors memory usage. The next two sub-sections describe how GitHub Copilot can assist by either completing our implementation or generating the code from scratch for these two cases. At the end of this section, we will ask ChatGPT to predict runtimes and memory size constraints using these analyses as input.

Profiling runtime

Measuring the runtime of a function in Python helps evaluate whether the time taken to complete the tasks in the source code aligns with acceptable thresholds and identifies potential areas for improvement. This can be achieved using a script like the following:

```
start = time.process_time()
recursive_fibonacci(35)
end = time.process_time()
print(f"Time taken: {end - start:.3f} seconds")
```

By recording the time before and after execution, we can calculate the runtime as the difference between these times to compute the 35th Fibonacci number.

In *Chapter 15*, we will explore how to use **decorators** to log application performance. For now, we will simply use start and end times to measure program runtime.

Since the profiling code is short and straightforward, the authors mostly use GitHub Copilot for such tasks. The following example demonstrates how Copilot can understand the purpose of our file, *profile_runtime.py*, by applying the five S's for prompt precision as shown in *Figure 14.1*:

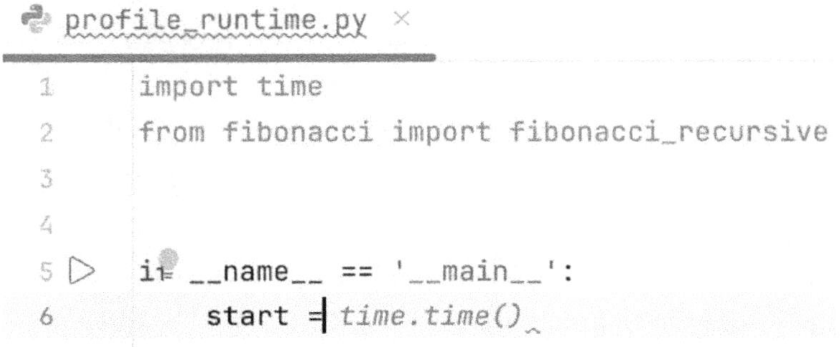

```
🐍 profile_runtime.py ×

1    import time
2    from fibonacci import fibonacci_recursive
3
4
5 ▷  if __name__ == '__main__':
6        start = time.time()
```

Figure 14.1: Copilot completion

In this example, we named the file *profile_runtime.py* and included the necessary imports for the time package and the fibonacci_recursive function to establish a clear context for Copilot. Based on these, Copilot is likely to identify our goal of profiling the fibonacci_recursive function and suggests a complete implementation for runtime profiling.

Alternatively, we can use chat, ChatGPT or OpenAI API to generate the profiling script from scratch. For example, we could use the following prompt in Copilot chat:

```
print the runtime of fibonacci_recursive for n=35
```

Below is a sample implementation provided by Copilot in PyCharm:

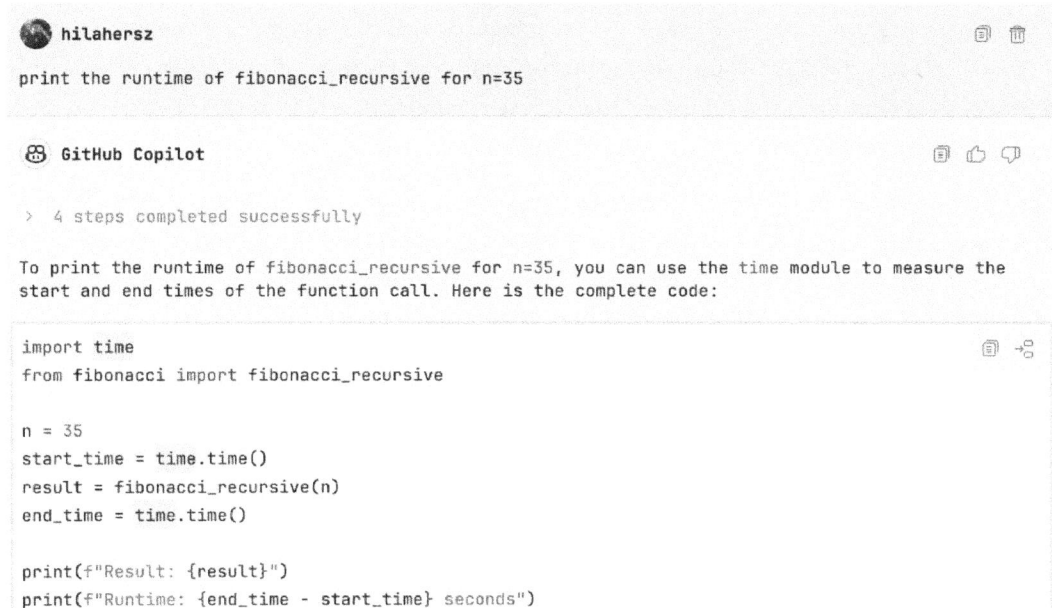

hilahersz

```
print the runtime of fibonacci_recursive for n=35
```

GitHub Copilot

> 4 steps completed successfully

To print the runtime of `fibonacci_recursive` for n=35, you can use the `time` module to measure the start and end times of the function call. Here is the complete code:

```python
import time
from fibonacci import fibonacci_recursive

n = 35
start_time = time.time()
result = fibonacci_recursive(n)
end_time = time.time()

print(f"Result: {result}")
print(f"Runtime: {end_time - start_time} seconds")
```

Figure 14.2: Copilot chat to write the full method from a profiling suggestion

This code can be used as-is to profile the runtime of the function. Alternatively, we can make slight modifications, such as rounding the runtime value for better readability.

Here is an output from running the suggested profiling script:

```
Result: 9227465
Runtime: 1.7093181610107422 seconds
```

While a runtime of 1.7 seconds for n=35 might seem reasonable, the runtime for larger inputs, such as 50 or 100, becomes impractical. Later in this chapter, we will explore techniques to identify and address these challenges.

Profiling space usage

Profiling a program's memory usage can be achieved with the `@profile` decorator from the `memory_profiler` package. This lightweight tool monitors memory usage for every line within a function. The package should be included in the *requirements.txt* file of this book's repository, so it should already be accessible in your virtual environment.

For example, to profile the function `get_top_video`, which retrieves the video with the highest average watch percentage, we can add the `@profile` decorator before the function definition. A call to the function with the file *interactions_10_000.csv* that records 10,000 users' watch percentages of 10,000 videos will log the memory consumption for each line:

```python
import pandas as pd
from memory_profiler import profile


@profile
def get_top_video(path):
    interactions = pd.read_csv(path)
    avg_ratio = interactions.mean(axis=0, skipna=True)
    return avg_ratio.idxmax()


get_top_video('interactions_10_000.csv')
```

The profiling output provides details such as line numbers, total memory usage, incremental memory usage, the number of times each statement was executed, and the content of those executions. For reference, *Figure 14.3* shows the output from the code above:

```
Line #    Mem usage    Increment   Occurrences   Line Contents
=============================================================
     5    130.7 MiB    130.7 MiB           1     @profile
     6                                            def get_top_video(path):
     7    1020.4 MiB    889.7 MiB           1         interactions = pd.read_csv(path)
     8    1113.4 MiB     93.0 MiB           1         avg_ratio = interactions.mean(axis=0, skipna=True)
     9    1113.4 MiB      0.0 MiB           1         return avg_ratio.idxmax()
```

Figure 14.3: Profiler output showing memory consumption by line

The file *interactions_10_000.csv* contains 10,000 x 10,000 cells of type float64, requiring 8 bytes each, and the expected memory usage is approximately:

$$10{,}000 \times 10{,}000 \times 8 \ \approx 800 \text{ MB}$$

This aligns closely with the memory consumption recorded at line 7, where loading the CSV file into a Pandas DataFrame consumed 889.7 MB. This includes both the memory required for the cell data and the overhead associated with the Pandas DataFrame object such as column and row names, metadata, and type.

Having learned how to use GitHub Copilot to simplify the creation of profiling scripts for runtime and space complexity, we can move forward and explore how to use Copilot to profile multiple runs and ChatGPT to estimate the maximum input capacity that our functions can manage.

Analyzing maximal capacity with ChatGPT

Identifying the maximal capacity of a function means determining the largest input beyond which it will fail due to either memory limitations or unacceptable runtime. One strategy for such predictions involves profiling its performance for a few input sizes, identifying the runtime or space growth, and then estimating the maximal capacity the function can handle. GenAI can assist in this two-step process by automating profiling for different inputs and using the results as supplementary data for a prompt to compute the maximal capacity.

Profiling runtime across multiple runs

Copilot can assist us in creating a profiling loop for `fibonacci_recursive` like we did for a single profile. For instance, if we want to profile the runtime of the function for inputs ranging from 10 to 40 in steps of 5, we can start by adding the following import statements to the file:

```
import time
from fibonacci import fibonacci_recursive
```

Then use a prompt in Copilot chat like this:

```
print the runtime of fibonacci_recursive for n=10:41:5
```

This prompt, along with the surrounding context of the import statements in the file, is likely to generate a code to profile runtimes for varying arguments:

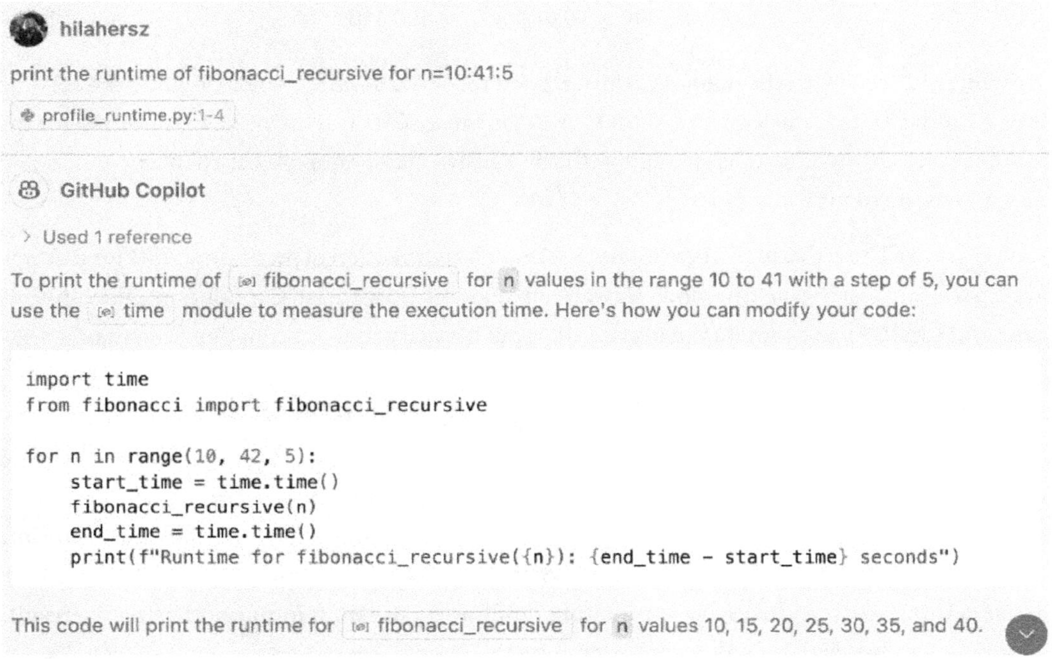

hilahersz

print the runtime of fibonacci_recursive for n=10:41:5

⊕ profile_runtime.py:1-4

GitHub Copilot

> Used 1 reference

To print the runtime of ⊙ fibonacci_recursive for n values in the range 10 to 41 with a step of 5, you can use the ⊙ time module to measure the execution time. Here's how you can modify your code:

```
import time
from fibonacci import fibonacci_recursive

for n in range(10, 42, 5):
    start_time = time.time()
    fibonacci_recursive(n)
    end_time = time.time()
    print(f"Runtime for fibonacci_recursive({n}): {end_time - start_time} seconds")
```

This code will print the runtime for ⊙ fibonacci_recursive for n values 10, 15, 20, 25, 30, 35, and 40. ⌄

Figure 14.4: Profiling suggestion for profiling multiple Fibonacci inputs

We can use the generated code as-is or make minor adjustments, such as rounding the recorded times to four decimal places or changing the range's stop value to 41. When executed on an M1 MacBook Pro with a 16GHz CPU, the following runtime profiling was recorded:

```
Runtime for fibonacci_recursive(10): 0.0000 seconds
Runtime for fibonacci_recursive(15): 0.0002 seconds
Runtime for fibonacci_recursive(20): 0.0013 seconds
Runtime for fibonacci_recursive(25): 0.0150 seconds
Runtime for fibonacci_recursive(30): 0.1571 seconds
Runtime for fibonacci_recursive(35): 1.7051 seconds
Runtime for fibonacci_recursive(40): 19.5045 seconds
```

This runtime profiling will be used as input for a GenAI application to analyze the function's complexity and determine the input size capacity.

Profiling memory consumption across multiple runs

Profiling the memory consumption across multiple runs of get_top_video function can be done with a straightforward approach:

```python
paths = ['interactions_100.csv',
         'interactions_1000.csv',
         'interactions_10_000.csv']
for p in paths:
    print("top video: ", get_top_video(p))
```

In this example, the files *interactions_100.csv, interactions_1000.csv*, and *interactions_10_000.csv* represent datasets of user-video interactions of row and column length corresponding to the numbers in their filenames.

Copilot can assist by completing the for loop, after including the filenames, as shown below:

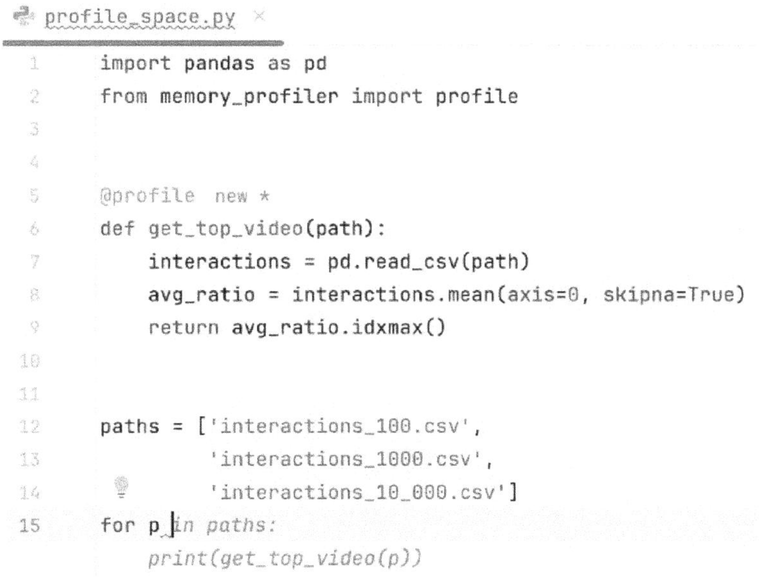

```python
profile_space.py  ×

1    import pandas as pd
2    from memory_profiler import profile
3
4
5    @profile  new *
6    def get_top_video(path):
7        interactions = pd.read_csv(path)
8        avg_ratio = interactions.mean(axis=0, skipna=True)
9        return avg_ratio.idxmax()
10
11
12   paths = ['interactions_100.csv',
13            'interactions_1000.csv',
14            'interactions_10_000.csv']
15   for p in paths:
        print(get_top_video(p))
```

Figure 14.5: Copilot code completion suggestion

The generated code can be used as-is or modified slightly, for instance, by enhancing the print statement to include information about the file size.

For reference, running this code produced the following profiling:

```
Filename: /Users/hila/PycharmProjects/private/supercharge/ch14/profile_space.py

Line #    Mem usage    Increment  Occurrences   Line Contents
=============================================================
     5     93.2 MiB     93.2 MiB           1   @profile
     6                                          def get_top_video(path):
     7     93.8 MiB      0.6 MiB           1       interactions = pd.read_csv(path)
     8     94.0 MiB      0.2 MiB           1       avg_ratio = interactions.mean(axis=0, skipna=True)
     9     94.0 MiB      0.0 MiB           1       return avg_ratio.idxmax()


top video:  video_82
Filename: /Users/hila/PycharmProjects/private/supercharge/ch14/profile_space.py

Line #    Mem usage    Increment  Occurrences   Line Contents
=============================================================
     5     94.0 MiB     94.0 MiB           1   @profile
     6                                          def get_top_video(path):
     7    124.0 MiB     29.9 MiB           1       interactions = pd.read_csv(path)
     8    131.6 MiB      7.6 MiB           1       avg_ratio = interactions.mean(axis=0, skipna=True)
     9    131.6 MiB      0.0 MiB           1       return avg_ratio.idxmax()


top video:  video_629
Filename: /Users/hila/PycharmProjects/private/supercharge/ch14/profile_space.py

Line #    Mem usage    Increment  Occurrences   Line Contents
=============================================================
     5    130.7 MiB    130.7 MiB           1   @profile
     6                                          def get_top_video(path):
     7   1020.4 MiB    889.7 MiB           1       interactions = pd.read_csv(path)
     8   1113.4 MiB     93.0 MiB           1       avg_ratio = interactions.mean(axis=0, skipna=True)
     9   1113.4 MiB      0.0 MiB           1       return avg_ratio.idxmax()


top video:  video_7238
```

Figure 14.6: profiling memory usage output

The memory usage for reading the CSV files grows as follows:

- 0.6 MB for a 100 x 100 matrix
- 29.9 MB for a 1,000 x 1,000 matrix
- 889 MB for a 10,000 x 10,000 matrix

This memory consumption data can be included as supplementary information in our prompts included as supplementary information in our prompts to estimate maximum matrix sizes that the function can handle, as we see next in this chapter.

Determining maximal capacity within runtime constraints

The *GPT-4o1* model is specifically designed to excel in chain-of-thought reasoning, making it highly effective for determining maximum capacities under runtime constraints. To leverage this capability, we can create precise prompts following the five S's, including the function's source code and associated profiling. An ideal structure for these prompts might look as follows:

```
CONTEXT: You are provided with:
1. Python function enclosed with {{{ FUNCTION }}}
2. Runtime profiling enclosed with {{{ PROFILING }}}.
3. Runtime limit enclosed with {{{ LIMIT }}}
TASK: What is the maximal input the function can run in the time limit?

FUNCTION: {{{ ... }}}
PROFILING: {{{ ... }}}
LIMIT: {{{ ... }}}

MAXIMAL INPUT:
```

For example, when using this prompt with a runtime limit of 100 seconds, the *GPTo1-mini* model in ChatGPT provided the following reasoning steps:

1. **Profiling Analysis**: Repeatedly reviewed the reported profiling.
2. **Observations**: Identified the exponential growth in runtime.
3. **Calculations**: Computed the largest input within the time limit.
4. **Conclusion**: Determined the maximum input to be 43.

These reasoning steps result in the final answer, the conclusion step, as illustrated in *Figure 14.7*:

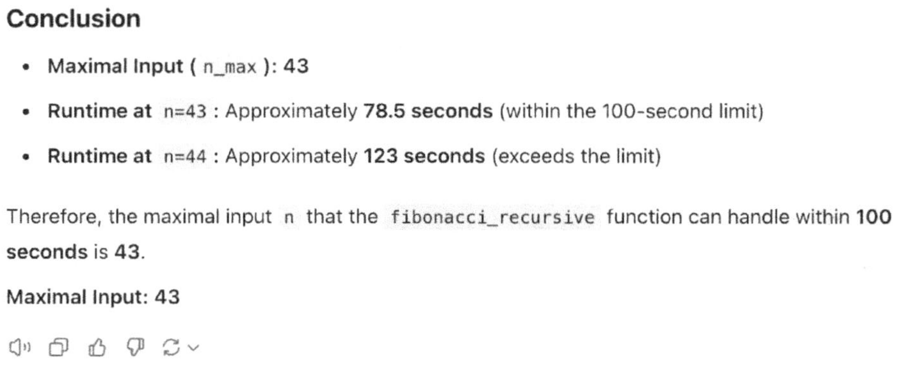
Conclusion
Maximal Input (n_max): 43
Runtime at n=43 : Approximately 78.5 seconds (within the 100-second limit)
Runtime at n=44 : Approximately 123 seconds (exceeds the limit)
Therefore, the maximal input n that the fibonacci_recursive function can handle within 100 seconds is 43.
Maximal Input: 43

Figure 14.7: GPT-4o1-mini maximal capacity conclusion

The model predicted a runtime of 78.5 seconds for n=43 and 123 seconds for n=44. When we measured the actual runtime using our script, it was 81.08 seconds and 129.07 seconds respectively, demonstrating a close match and correct identification of the maximal capacity:

```
Elapsed time for n=43: 81.08 seconds
Elapsed time for n=44: 129.07 seconds
```

For your reference, here is the full prompt used in this example:

```
CONTEXT: You are provided with:
1. Python function enclosed with {{{ FUNCTION }}}
2. Runtime profiling enclosed with {{{ PROFILING }}}.
3. Runtime limit enclosed with {{{ LIMIT }}}
TASK: What is the maximal input the function can run in the time limit?
FUNCTION: {{{
def fibonacci_recursive(n):
    if n <= 0:
        return 0
    if n == 1:
        return 1
    return fibonacci_recursive(n - 1) + fibonacci_recursive(n - 2)
}}}
PROFILING: {{{
Runtime for fibonacci_recursive(10): 0.0000 seconds
Runtime for fibonacci_recursive(15): 0.0002 seconds
Runtime for fibonacci_recursive(20): 0.0013 seconds
Runtime for fibonacci_recursive(25): 0.0150 seconds
Runtime for fibonacci_recursive(30): 0.1571 seconds
Runtime for fibonacci_recursive(35): 1.7051 seconds
Runtime for fibonacci_recursive(40): 19.5045 seconds
}}}
LIMIT: {{{ 100 seconds }}}
MAXIMAL INPUT:
```

In the upcoming chapters, we will explore how to intentionally collect data for integration with OpenAI API as part of SDLC automation.

Determining maximal capacity within memory constraints

A similar prompt structure to the one used for identifying maximum capacities under runtime constraints can also be applied to memory constraints:

```
CONTEXT: You are provided with:
1. Python function enclosed with {{{ FUNCTION }}}
2. RAM usage profiling enclosed with {{{ PROFILING }}}.
3. RAM usage limit enclosed with {{{ LIMIT }}}
TASK: What is the maximal input the function can run in the RAM limit?

FUNCTION: {{{ ... }}}
PROFILING: {{{ ... }}}
LIMIT: {{{ ... }}}

MAXIMAL ROWS / MAXIMAL COLUMNS:
```

Here, the cue in the prompt is adjusted slightly to MAXIMAL ROWS / MAXIMAL COLUMNS, to emphasize the 2D dimensions of the input.

For instance, when using this template for the get_top_video function in ChatGPT with the *GPT-4o1* model, along with recorded results from sparse matrices of sizes 100 x 100, 1,000 x 1,000, and 10,000 x 10,000, the model generated the following reasoning steps:

1. **Profiling Analysis**: Included an understanding of the memory usage data and its scaling behavior.
2. **Conclusion**: Estimated the largest input for a memory limit of 5GB.
3. **Final Recommendation**: Suggested a matrix size of 22,000 x 22,000 as the largest feasible input.

These reasoning steps result in the final answer, the final recommendation step, as illustrated in *Figure 14.8*:

ChatGPT o1-mini ⌄   ⬆ Share

Conclusion

The maximal input size that the `get_top_video` function can handle within a
5 GB RAM limit is approximately 22,000 rows by 22,000 columns.

Note: This estimation assumes a square matrix and linear scaling based on the
provided benchmarks. Actual memory usage may vary slightly due to factors like
data types, overhead, and system-specific memory management. To ensure
stability, it's advisable to use input sizes slightly below the estimated maximum,
such as **20,000 rows x 20,000 columns**.

Figure 14.8: GPT-4o1-mini reasoning for maximal capacity

When executing the script with a file containing a 22,000 x 22,000 matrix, the recorded memory
usage peak was 4.63 GB, closely aligning with the model's prediction.

```
Line #    Mem usage    Increment  Occurrences  Line Contents
================================================================
     5     93.1 MiB     93.1 MiB            1  @profile
     6                                         def get_top_video(path):
     7   3562.4 MiB   3469.3 MiB            1      interactions = pd.read_csv(path)
     8   4643.5 MiB   1081.1 MiB            1      avg_ratio = interactions.mean(axis=0, skipna=True)
     9   4643.7 MiB      0.2 MiB            1      return avg_ratio.idxmax()
```

Figure 14.9: Memory usage below 5GB

This memory usage aligns with ChatGPT's capacity assessment and is below the required 5GB
RAM limit.

For reference, here is the complete prompt used to generate this output:

```
CONTEXT: You are provided with:
1. Python function enclosed with {{{ FUNCTION }}}
2. RAM usage profiling enclosed with {{{ PROFILING }}}.
3. RAM usage limit enclosed with {{{ LIMIT }}}
TASK: What is the maximal input the function can run in the RAM limit?
FUNCTION: {{{ def get_top_video(path):
    interactions = pd.read_csv(path)
    avg_ratio = interactions.mean(axis=0, skipna=True)
```

```
        return avg_ratio.idxmax() }}}
  PROFILING: {{{...}}}
  LIMIT: {{{ 5 GB }}}
  MAXIMAL ROWS / MAXIMAL COLUMNS:
```

The profiling information was omitted due to brevity constraints and includes a direct copy-paste of the terminal output, as shown in *Figure 14.6*. The full prompt can be found at *ch14/code_samples/ chatgpt_maximum_input_prompt.txt*. This prompt successfully predicted a maximum input size of 22,000 rows and 22,000 columns.

In both these cases, ChatGPT is certainly extrapolating the input values to predict the runtime or maximum dimensions. It requires sufficient input values to make such a prediction and may not be as accurate as performing your own calculations, but it is a reasonable approximation.

Next in this chapter, we will explore how to use GenAI and increase the capacity of the functions such as algorithms with better runtime complexity and dealing with chunks.

Optimizing code with chained prompts

The previous examples depict the simple coding and estimation capability of LLMs. However, LLMs can do much more. They can create code for improved algorithms and even balance specific runtime and memory efficiency goals.

To effectively increase the input capacities, we will **chain** our optimization prompt to the results of the maximal capacity prompt. The initial prompt already provides essential details, such as the function, runtime or memory limits, and profiling various inputs. The optimization prompt should also include the following key information:

- **Optimization goal:** Clearly specify the primary goal, either on improving runtime complexity, reducing memory usage, or both. Detail the desired approach as much as possible, such as batching, or improving algorithm complexity.
- **Function docstring:** Provide a concise description of the function's purpose, along with any constraints or requirements.
- **Input requirements:** Define the new input goals under the runtime or memory constraints, such as computing the $1,000,000^{th}$ Fibonacci number or handling a matrix with 100,000 rows and 100,000 columns.

For more complex scenarios, additional details may be helpful, such as previous optimization attempts, dependencies on external functions or resources, frequency of function calls or concurrent usage patterns, and acceptable trade-offs, such as allowing longer runtimes in exchange for reduced memory usage.

This information will be integrated into a chained prompt, following the five S's for precision and clarity.

Runtime optimization

Let us examine a runtime optimization for the fibonacci_recursive function. Below is an example of a chained prompt, building on an initial prompt of maximal capacity as presented earlier in the chapter. This prompt requests an improved implementation with better runtime complexity to handle an input of 1,000,000:

```
CONTEXT: You are provided with the function's docstring enclosed with {{{
DOCSTRING }}} and the required input enclosed with {{{ REQUIRED_INPUT }}}.
TASK: Optimize the function to run in a better time complexity within the
runtime limit.
DOCSTRING: {{{ """
    Calculate the nth Fibonacci number using a recursive approach.
    Args:
        n (int): The position in the Fibonacci sequence.
    Returns:
        int: The nth Fibonacci number.
    """
}}}
REQUIRED_INPUT = {{{ 1,000,000 }}}
IMPROVED IMPLEMENTATION:
```

This prompt includes a docstring describing out specific task of optimizing runtime complexity to achieve the target input of 1,000,000. Providing different constraints, such as a smaller input size, will yield a different output from the model.

A typical approach for Fibonacci calculations has a $O(n)$ complexity, however *GPT-4o1* suggested a more efficient implementation for large inputs, achieving a runtime complexity of $O(\log n)$ through the fast-doubling recursive approach:

ChatGPT o1-mini ⌄

Why Fast Doubling?

The recursive method for calculating Fibonacci numbers has a significant drawback: it recalculates the same subproblems multiple times, leading to an exponential time complexity. Fast Doubling addresses this by computing Fibonacci numbers in pairs and utilizing previously calculated values to build up to the desired n , thereby avoiding redundant calculations.

Fast Doubling Algorithm Overview

The Fast Doubling method calculates two Fibonacci numbers at a time, specifically $F(n)$ and $F(n+1)$, using the following identities:

$$F(2k) = F(k) \times [2F(k+1) - F(k)]$$
$$F(2k+1) = F(k+1)^2 + F(k)^2$$

Figure 14.10: Fast-doubling approach for handling large inputs

And here is the code proposed by *GPT-4o1*:

```python
def fib_pair(n):
    if n == 0:
        return (0, 1)
    a, b = fib_pair(n // 2)
    c = a * ((2 * b) - a)
    d = a * a + b * b
    if n & 1:
        return (d, c + d)
    else:
        return (c, d)
```

While this implementation also uses recursion, it makes a call to $n//2$ ($n \div 2$ without remainder) reducing the number of function invocations to approximately $\log(n)$. To illustrate its efficiency, here are performance comparisons for calculating the 1,000,000[th] Fibonacci number:

```
Fast-doubling approach: 0.057893 seconds
Iterative (memoization) approach: 9.175633 seconds
```

As another benchmark, computing the 10,000,000[th] Fibonacci number with `fibonacci_fast_doubling` took 2.26 seconds, whereas the iterative approach did not complete within a 10-minute time limit.

This method leverages the mathematical identities:

$$F(2k) = F(k) \cdot \big(2F(k+1) - F(k)\big)$$

$$F(2k+1) = F(k+1)^2 + F(k)^2$$

Where $F(k)$ is the k-th Fibonacci number.

Using these identities, once $F(k)$ and $F(k+1)$ are calculated, $F(2k)$ and $F(2k+1)$ can be determined efficiently. This means we do not need to compute all Fibonacci numbers sequentially up to the 1,000,000[th] number but only focus on its halves, significantly reducing the required computations.

Space optimization

Like the runtime optimization prompt, we can chain a request to optimize a function to fit within RAM constraints. The prompt structure remains similar, but it describes a memory limit instead of a runtime limit, along with an optimization request to address memory usage.

For example, consider the following chained prompt requesting an optimization for the get_top_ video function to handle a matrix of 100,000 rows by 100,000 columns within a 5GB RAM limit:

```
CONTEXT: You are provided with the function's docstring enclosed with {{{
DOCSTRING }}} and the required input enclosed with {{{ REQUIRED_INPUT }}}.
TASK: Optimize the function to run in batches within the RAM limit.

DOCSTRING: {{{ """
    Reads a CSV file containing video interactions, calculates the average
watch ratio for each video,
    and returns the video with the highest average watch ratio.

    Args:
        path (str): The file path to the CSV file containing video
interactions.

    Returns:
        str: The identifier of the video with the highest average watch
ratio.
    """
}}}
```

```
REQUIRED_INPUT = {{{ 100,000 rows x 100,000 columns matrix}}}

IMPROVED IMPLEMENTATION:
```

This prompt specifies the size of the input matrix (100,000 rows by 100,000 columns) and builds upon the previously defined RAM limit of 5GB.

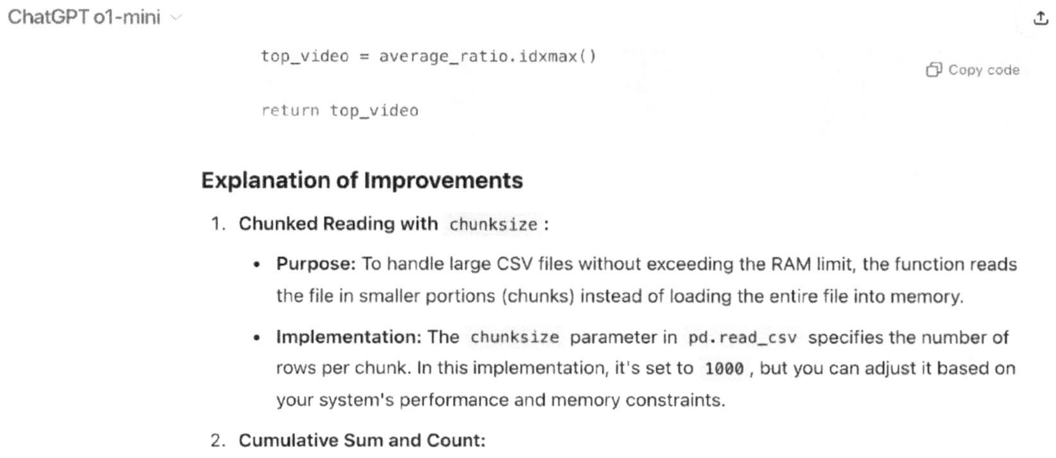

ChatGPT o1-mini ⌄   ⬆

```
                    top_video = average_ratio.idxmax()                      ⎘ Copy code

                    return top_video
```

Explanation of Improvements

1. **Chunked Reading with** `chunksize` :

   - **Purpose:** To handle large CSV files without exceeding the RAM limit, the function reads the file in smaller portions (chunks) instead of loading the entire file into memory.

   - **Implementation:** The `chunksize` parameter in `pd.read_csv` specifies the number of rows per chunk. In this implementation, it's set to `1000` , but you can adjust it based on your system's performance and memory constraints.

2. **Cumulative Sum and Count:**

Figure 14.11: ChatGPT suggestion for chunk-based processing

Based on this information, ChatGPT suggested processing the CSV file in batches of 1,000 rows, which is an appropriate solution for handling data of this size efficiently.

In this scenario, specifying the input requirements is vital. For larger matrices, working with a Pandas DataFrame may become impractical, necessitating an alternative solution. Conversely, for matrices with fewer columns, larger column chunks might be sufficient.

For your reference, here is the implementation for processing the matrix in chunks provided by ChatGPT with the prompt above:

```
def get_top_video(path):
    cumulative_sum = None
    cumulative_count = None
    chunksize = 1000
    for chunk in pd.read_csv(path, chunksize=chunksize):
        chunk_sum = chunk.sum(skipna=True)
        chunk_count = chunk.count()
```

```
        if cumulative_sum is None:
            cumulative_sum = chunk_sum
            cumulative_count = chunk_count
        else:
            cumulative_sum += chunk_sum
            cumulative_count += chunk_count


    average_ratio = cumulative_sum / cumulative_count
    top_video = average_ratio.idxmax()
    return top_video
```

When profiling the implementation with an input of 100,000 rows and 100,000 columns, the chunked implementation concluded with a memory usage of 4,326.1 GB:

```
Line #    Mem usage    Increment  Occurrences   Line Contents
================================================================
     5     93.1 MiB     93.1 MiB           1   @profile
     6                                          def find_top_watch_ratio_video(path):
     7     93.1 MiB      0.0 MiB           1       cumulative_sum = None
     8     93.1 MiB      0.0 MiB           1       cumulative_count = None
     9
    10     93.1 MiB      0.0 MiB           1       chunksize = 1000
    11
    12     93.1 MiB      0.0 MiB           1       i=0
    13   4326.1 MiB -25998.3 MiB         101       for chunk in pd.read_csv(path, index_col=0, chunksize=chunksize):
    14   4326.1 MiB  -9607.8 MiB         100           print(f"chunk {i}")
    15   4326.1 MiB  -9607.9 MiB         100           i+=1
    16   4420.9 MiB    162.9 MiB         100           chunk_sum = chunk.sum(skipna=True)
    17   4515.5 MiB    131.7 MiB         100           chunk_count = chunk.count()
    18
    19   4515.5 MiB  -9323.6 MiB         100           if cumulative_sum is None:
    20   2221.3 MiB      0.0 MiB           1               cumulative_sum = chunk_sum
    21   2221.3 MiB      0.0 MiB           1               cumulative_count = chunk_count
    22                                                 else:
    23   4515.5 MiB  -9303.6 MiB          99               cumulative_sum += chunk_sum
    24   4515.5 MiB  -9307.2 MiB          99               cumulative_count += chunk_count
    25
    26   2657.0 MiB  -1669.2 MiB           1       if cumulative_sum is None or cumulative_count is None:
    27                                                 raise ValueError("The provided CSV file is empty or only contains NaN values.")
    28
    29   2657.0 MiB      0.0 MiB           1       average_ratio = cumulative_sum / cumulative_count
    30
    31   2657.0 MiB      0.1 MiB           1       top_video = average_ratio.idxmax()
    32
    33   2657.0 MiB      0.0 MiB           1       return top_video
```

Figure 14.12: Improved memory utilization with chunking

In line 13, we can see that the matrix was processed in 100 chunks, with each chunk containing 1,000 columns.

The proposed solutions can be further refined to meet both memory and runtime requirements. It is always advisable to test new implementations against both criteria to ensure the solution is satisfactory in terms of both efficiency and performance.

Further runtime and space optimization

The previous optimizations focused on single CPU algorithms. GenAI can go beyond these and recommend additional techniques. For instance, it may be appropriate to use parallelization with threads, leverage **graphical processing units (GPUs)**, or adopt more efficient file formats like sparse matrices or *Apache Parquet*. In the function get_top_video, processing different videos can be performed in parallel by integrating threading. Further acceleration could be achieved by leveraging GPUs, as each column can be processed independently of others. Alternatively, converting the file format from CSV to a more efficient option could enhance performance. Formats like **compressed sparse row (CSR)** or **compressed sparse column (CSC)** from *SciPy* are well-suited for sparse data, while columnar storage formats like Apache Parquet are ideal for handling large datasets.

Summary

In this chapter, we explored how LLMs can assist in ensuring efficient applications by profiling runtime and memory usage, identifying maximal capacities, and suggesting optimized code to increase those capacities.

Using the recursive Fibonacci example, we saw how adopting a more efficient algorithm significantly reduces runtime. With the get_top_video function, we tackled large matrices under RAM constraints, assisting GenAI to optimize memory usage through chunking. GitHub Copilot assisted in profiling runtime and memory consumption and profiling runs across different inputs. ChatGPT estimated the maximal capacity within runtime and RAM constraints. Leveraging chained prompts, ChatGPT demonstrated the ability to vastly improve the implementation to achieve larger capacities and can do much more.

In the next chapter, we will further explore how to integrate GenAI into the SDLC, focusing on logging, monitoring applications, and error handling.

Quiz time

Before you proceed to the next chapter, make sure that you can confidently answer the following questions:

Question 1: How can Copilot assist in profiling the runtime and memory usage of a program?

Answer: Profiling runtime and memory usage in Python can be achieved using the built-in time module and the third-party memory-profiler package. Copilot can assist by either completing a starter code or generating that functionality from scratch based on a precise prompt.

Question 2: How can ChatGPT help identify maximal inputs under runtime or RAM constraints?

Answer: By crafting precise prompts that include the function's source code, runtime or RAM constraints, and profiling results, we can utilize the *GPT-4o1* model, designed for chain-of-thought reasoning, to calculate the largest input manageable within those constraints.

Question 3: How can chaining prompts help increase program input capacity?

Answer: After identifying the maximal input a function can handle without becoming a bottleneck, a chained prompt can include the desired input size and a specific optimization request. *GPT-4o1* can leverage this information to propose an optimized solution that follows the runtime and/or memory constraints.

Further reading

To learn more about the topics that were covered in this chapter, look at the following resources:

- Wikipedia, CPU: https://en.wikipedia.org/wiki/Central_processing_unit
- Geeks for geeks memory consumption: https://www.geeksforgeeks.org/how-to-get-current-cpu-and-ram-usage-in-python
- Introduction to memory profiling in Python: https://www.datacamp.com/tutorial/memory-profiling-python
- Big-o Python package: https://pypi.org/project/big-O-calculator/
- Lambda Labs on GPT-3 training costs: https://lambda.ai/blog/demystifying-gpt-3

Subscribe for a free eBook

New frameworks, evolving architectures, research drops, production breakdowns—*AI_Distilled* filters the noise into a weekly briefing for engineers and researchers working hands-on with LLMs and GenAI systems. Subscribe now and receive a free eBook, along with weekly insights that help you stay focused and informed.

Subscribe at `https://packt.link/TR05B` or scan the QR code below.

15

Going Live with GenAI: Logging, Monitoring, and Errors

Large Language Models (LLMs) can supercharge our going-live processes, which refers to deploying code to production. But if prompted incorrectly, they can also degrade code quality. In this chapter, we will examine how, even when following the five S's to prompt GenAI for logging, monitoring, and input validation, the resulting code can become cluttered, combining these elements with core functionality and violating the **single responsibility principle**. For instance, models sometimes suggest using `print` statements instead of proper logging, handling input validation within functions, or incrementing counters without reporting their values. This violates the single responsibility principle and reduces overall code quality.

To address this, we will apply the **Chain-of-Thought (CoT)** prompt engineering technique to GitHub Copilot to generate well-monitored code without interfering with the function's core functionality, leveraging **decorators** as a design pattern. We will also leverage **few-shot learning** to guide it toward following a coding style. While GitHub Copilot is well suited for these tasks, we will explore how similar results can be achieved using CoT with few-shot learning in ChatGPT and CoT with **fine-tuning** in OpenAI API.

The key topics covered in this chapter include the following:

- Introducing logging, monitoring, and raising errors
- Leveraging GenAI for higher-level coding patterns
- Applying inverse CoT with ChatGPT and OpenAI
- Utilizing few-shot learning and fine-tuning as style guides

Technical requirements

To get the most out of this chapter, ensure you have the following:

- A GitHub Copilot account
- An **integrated development environment (IDE)** – either VS Code or PyCharm
- An OpenAI account with access to ChatGPT and OpenAI API
- Access to the book's repository, available at `https://github.com/PacktPublishing/Supercharged-Coding-with-Gen-AI`
- A virtual environment set up in VS Code or PyCharm
- An OpenAI API token

For assistance with setting up a GitHub Copilot account, refer to *Chapter 3*. For instructions on setting up OpenAI API access and token generation, see *Chapter 2*. If you need help with creating an OpenAI account or setting up a virtual environment in your IDE, refer to the *Appendix* for detailed guidance.

Introducing logging, monitoring, and raising errors

When Python software goes live in the production stage and serves clients, it is important to verify that it is consistently working as expected in real-world use cases. If some problems are identified, understanding the behavior of these issues is critical. Thus, logging, monitoring, and raising errors for problematic inputs are an essential aspect of the **Software Development Life Cycle (SDLC)**. They involve tracking key checkpoints within internal processes, which are usually performed by loggers, and these facilitate debugging and other analyses. Recording performance statistics such as counting function calls is often used with profiling to improve performance. Lastly, handling unexpected scenarios, such as receiving arguments of an invalid type, is a process to ensure that the code is robust against the wide range of user inputs. These three aspects help maintain software quality, minimize unexpected issues, and simplify debugging when problems occur.

In this chapter, we will focus on these three fundamental practices since these are typically the first going-live initiatives in any project, and they are likely to be relevant to your software as well. As your strategy expands to additional metrics and error-handling techniques, these standard approaches using GenAI tools can easily be generalized and extended from what we introduce in this chapter.

The FizzBuzz use case

To explore how monitoring efforts can be integrated into our code, let us consider developing a program that generates the **FizzBuzz** sequence, a coding challenge introduced in *Chapter 2*. As part of the monitoring efforts for this program, we want to log each function call along with its arguments, maintain a counter of total function calls, and ensure inputs are positive integers less than 500.

As a starting point, a basic implementation of FizzBuzz can be generated from the function signature:

```
def print_fizzbuzz(limit: int) -> None:
```

Figure 15.1 shows an implementation suggested by GitHub Copilot in PyCharm:

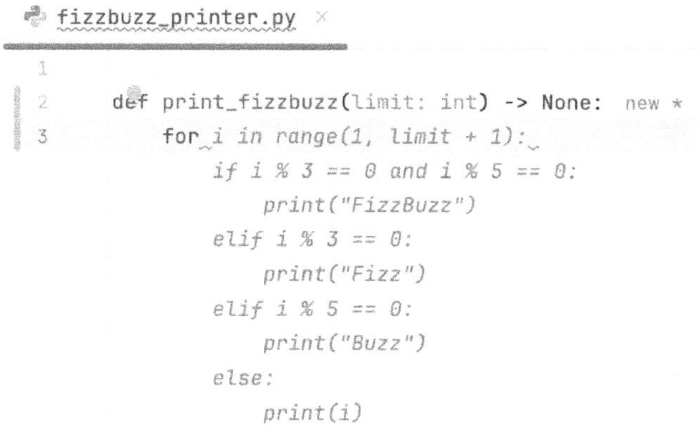

```
fizzbuzz_printer.py ×
1
2    def print_fizzbuzz(limit: int) -> None:  new *
3        for i in range(1, limit + 1):
            if i % 3 == 0 and i % 5 == 0:
                print("FizzBuzz")
            elif i % 3 == 0:
                print("Fizz")
            elif i % 5 == 0:
                print("Buzz")
            else:
                print(i)
```

Figure 15.1: Copilot's initial FizzBuzz implementation

This implementation serves as a foundation for incorporating going-live features. Before introducing best practices for monitoring with prompt engineering techniques, we will first explore how simply chaining logging, monitoring, and error-raising requests can degrade code quality. Adding GenAI implementation for these tasks results in a longer and more complex function. However, techniques such as CoT and few-shot learning can help add these functionalities yet maintain clean, well-structured code.

Logging

Logs are generated text records that serve as a diary of our program's execution. For example, at the start of the FizzBuzz sequence, we may want to log the call's arguments. While using a simple print statement is an option, the built-in logging library is a much better choice as it can write to the console but also provides more control over the output and where the logs can be written, such as files and remote servers. It enables the structured formatting of records and log-level management, which can report all outputs for debugging, or a subset of warnings based on importance.

To use the logging library, we typically define a logger instance with the module's name:

```
import logging


logger = logging.getLogger(__name__)
```

This creates a logger instance linked to the module name using the __name__ special attribute (also referred to as a **magic attribute**). This association allows better filtering and customization of log messages in that file.

When using GenAI for logging, it is essential to separate the logging task into its own prompt, rather than embedding it within the implementation prompt. This approach aligns with the **single-task** principle, one of the five S's best practices introduced earlier in the book.

For example, when working with Copilot in VS Code's **edits window**, we can select the print_fizzbuzz implementation and use the following prompt:

```
#selection log the function arguments
```

For your reference, here is the suggestion we got when using the *3o-mini* model as appears in *Figure 15.2*:

```
⬥ fizzbuzz_printer.py  ⬡  ●                         ▷ ⌄  ⌥  ▭  ⋯        ⬚ ⬚                      ⟲ ⟳  +  ✕
ch15 > application > ⬥ fizzbuzz_printer.py > ⬡ print_fizzbuzz
  1    import logging                                                            ⬤  hilahersz
  2
  3    logger = logging.getLogger(__name__)                                      #selection  log the function arguments
  4                                                                              ☰ Selection
  5
  6    def print_fizzbuzz(limit: int) -> None:                                   ☷  GitHub Copilot
  7        logger.debug("print_fizzbuzz called with limit: %s", ⟲ ⬚
           limit)  # Log function argument                                       ›  Used 1 reference
  8        for i in range(1, limit + 1):                                         Step-by-step:
  9            if i % 3 == 0 and i % 5 == 0:
 10                print("FizzBuzz")
 11            elif i % 3 == 0:
 12                print("Fizz")                                                 Working Set (1 file)  Accept  Discard  ⬚ ⬚
 13            elif i % 5 == 0:                                                   ⬥ fizzbuzz_printer.py  ch15/application
 14                print("Buzz")                                                  + Add Files...
 15            else:
 16                print(i)                                                      Edit files in your workspace

                           Accept  Discard  1 of 1  ↑  ↓  ⬚             📎  🎤              o3-mini (Preview) ⌄  ▷
```

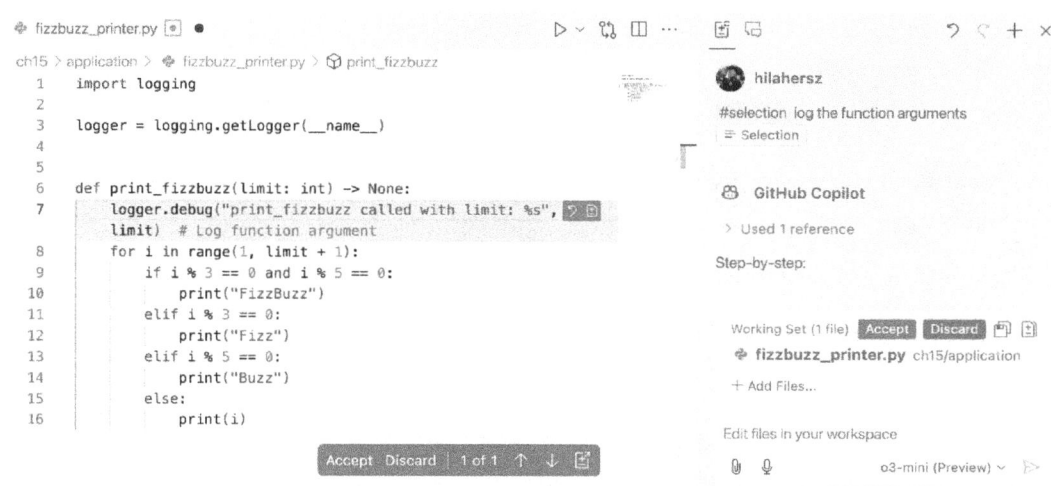

Figure 15.2: Log suggestion for FizzBuzz

In PyCharm, we can leverage the inline chat after selecting the function's code, and prompt the following to yield similar results:

```
Log the function arguments
```

While the generated log statement correctly logs the function's argument, it also introduces two lines of unnecessary code clutter within the function, which should remain focused on printing the FizzBuzz sequence. Later in the chapter, we will explore how to maintain cleaner code with prompt engineering techniques.

Handling unexpected input

When our program receives unexpected inputs at runtime, such as incorrect argument types (for example, float instead of int) or values that are beyond a manageable range for our program, we want to control the program's behavior by **raising errors** rather than failing or producing unpredictable results.

For instance, in the print_fizzbuzz function, the limit argument is expected to be a positive integer so that we can print numbers, fizz, or buzz from 0 up to that value. An additional constraint might be that the input should be less than 500 to ensure the output fits on the screen. To enforce both requirements with error handling, we can leverage Copilot.

When using Copilot in VS Code's edit window, we can select the `print_fizzbuzz` code and use the following prompt:

```
#selection validate limit type, and that it is in the range [0,500]
```

In PyCharm, we can use the inline chat by selecting the `print_fizzbuzz` function and entering the following prompt:

```
validate limit type, and that it is in the range [0,500]
```

For reference, here is the result obtained using Copilot for VS Code with the o3 mini model:

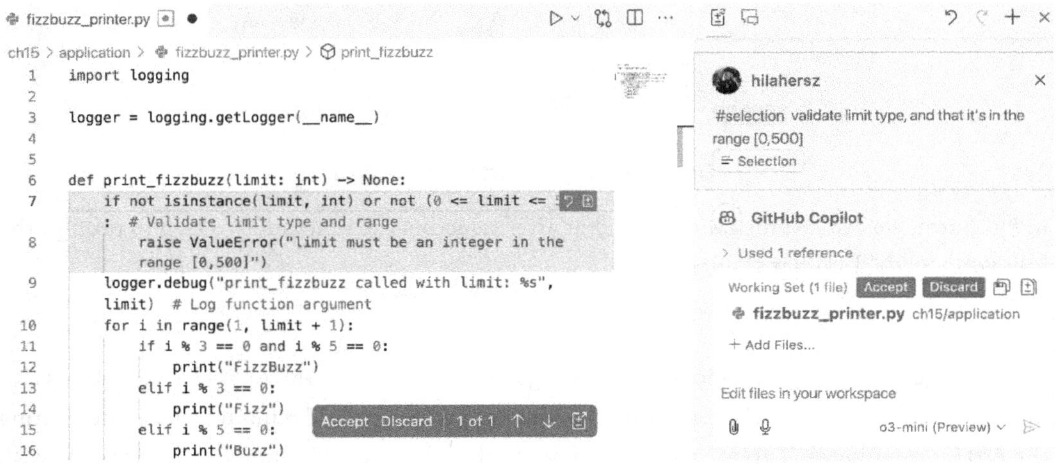

Figure 15.3: VS Code output correctly handles inputs but creates code clutter

This recommendation verifies both the argument's type and its range limits, as requested. However, like the logging prompt, it introduces an additional responsibility of validating inputs to the function. Later in this chapter, we will explore how prompt engineering can help generate higher-quality code.

Monitoring

Another key aspect of going live is tracking the usage of different functions. By recording metrics, we can collect valuable statistics on performance, call frequency, and execution rates.

A simple starting point is to track the number of function calls in our program. To do this with `print_fizzbuzz`, we can define a global counter variable, `FIZZBUZZ_COUNTER = 0`, and instruct Copilot to increment it before or after each successful execution. For example, when working with Copilot in VS Code's **edits window**, we can select the `print_fizzbuzz` implementation and use the following prompt:

```
#selection increment FIZZBUZZ_COUNTER after a successful execution.
```

Similarly, in PyCharm, we can select the code and use the inline chat to prompt the following:

```
Increment FIZZBUZZ_COUNTER after a successful execution.
```

Figure 15.4 illustrates a suggested completion for this prompt when using Copilot in VS Code with the o3 mini model:

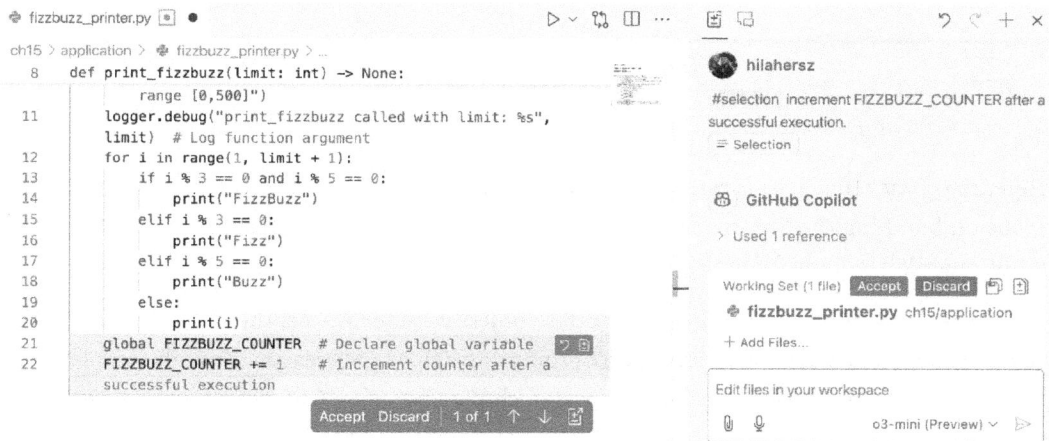

Figure 15.4: VS Code adds a record usage counter

At this point, our `print_fizzbuzz` function integrates multiple monitoring components: logging, handling invalid inputs, and counting calls. While these fulfill our monitoring needs, they lead to a lengthy and less readable function. This violates clean coding principles, particularly the **single responsibility principle**, which emphasizes that functions should focus on a single task.

Code created by GenAI using simple prompts tends to generate code and add it within existing methods which can lead to cluttered implementations. To maintain clean and structured code, we can leverage CoT prompting. This approach enables us to handle monitoring at a higher abstraction level, as we will explore next.

Leveraging GenAI for higher-level coding patterns

To balance clean code principles, such as the single responsibility principle, with the need for going-live requirements, a Pythonic approach is to use higher-level coding patterns such as decorators. Rather than embedding logging statements within a function, we delegate this responsibility to a decorator pattern:

```
def log_function_args(func: callable):
    # Logging logic here


@log_function_args
def print_fizzbuzz(limit: int) -> None:
    # main functionality here
```

Here, `log_function_args` is responsible for logging function calls, allowing `print_fizzbuzz` to focus on handling the FizzBuzz sequence. This approach ensures cleaner, more modular code while enabling logging for multiple functions.

GenAI applications may not suggest this pattern unless we actively steer them toward clean coding practices. As introduced in *Chapter 9*, CoT prompting helps LLMs reason through complex tasks. We can direct the model toward better design choices by using CoT prompting and explicitly writing a decorator call, such as `@log_function_args`, prior to implementing the actual decorator function. This will result in cleaner and more maintainable implementations.

Using decorators to separate responsibilities

A **decorator** is a structural design pattern that enables stacking tasks before and after a function call without altering the function's code. It is a specialized use case of a **closure**, where a function retains access to its associated arguments. A typical decorator implementation looks like this:

```
def sample_decorator(func: callable) -> callable:
    def wrapper(*args, **kwargs):
        print("Function is wrapped")
        return func(*args, **kwargs)

    return wrapper
```

A common usage involves applying the @ annotation, as shown here:

```
@sample_decorator
def foo(*num):
    return len(nums)
```

Here, the `sample_decorator` decorator accepts a function object and returns a wrapper function that takes the same arguments as the original function but prints `Function is wrapped` before execution.

LLMs can certainly include decorators in their generated code as their training data contains many common decorator implementations. For well-known use cases such as timers, loggers, argument validation, and retry mechanisms, the models can generate decent implementations based on the decorator's signature when prompted to.

Next, we will explore how to apply inverse CoT prompting to generate the desired implementation.

Inverse CoT for decorator implementation

In *Chapter 9*, we explored how defining a function that calls low-level implementations provides strong guidance for GitHub Copilot. With inverse CoT, we take a similar approach by referencing functions that have not yet been defined. We use the term *inverse* because we want the decorators to appear earlier in the file than the function that uses them. To achieve this, we place the cursor higher in the file, allowing Copilot to generate code above an existing implementation.

As a review, here is an example of CoT prompting used in *Chapter 9* to implement a variation of a geometric mean calculator, where Copilot successfully generated the missing low-level functions:

```python
get_geometric_mean.py ×

1    from typing import Union
2    import cmath
3
4
5    def get_geometric_mean(*args: float) -> Union[float, complex]:  new *
6        product = get_product(*args)
7        nth_root = len(args)
8        is_positive = is_product_positive(product)
9        is_nth_root_odd = is_odd(nth_root)
10       is_mean_real = is_geometric_mean_real(is_nth_root_odd, is_positive)
11       mean = get_mean(product, nth_root, is_mean_real)
12
13       return mean
```

Figure 15.5: CoT-driven implementation of a higher-level function with GitHub Copilot

In this approach, the function is broken into named functions that are intentionally called undefined. Copilot understands that its role is to generate these necessary implementations. Such an approach enables Copilot to implement the missing functions, producing structured and predictable code.

We can apply the same technique when implementing going-live functionality, by defining a decorator structure and allowing Copilot to generate the implementation. By merely adding calls to the required decorators, we guide Copilot to generate their corresponding implementations. For instance, in our FizzBuzz use case, we can layer three monitoring functionalities onto our function:

1. **Validate the input:** Define a decorator with parameters to enforce input bounds, that is, `@validate_args_types_and_limits(0, 500)`.

2. **Increment a global counter:**

3. `@increment_counter`.

4. **Log function calls:**

5. `@log_function_args`.

For reference, here is how stacking these decorators would appear before Copilot generates their implementations:

```
fizzbuzz_printer.py  ×

1    import logging
2
3    logger = logging.getLogger(__name__)
4
5    FIZZBUZZ_COUNTER = 0
6
7
8    @log_function_args   new *
9    @increment_counter
10   @validate_args_types_and_limits(0, 500)
11   def print_fizzbuzz(limit: int) -> None:
```

Figure 15.6: Inverse CoT approach

Here, as usual with the CoT technique, the IDE will correctly mark the decorators as undefined with the red underlines. After calling the decorators, we move the cursor to line 7 before the call to the first decorator, press *Enter* three times to create space for their implementations, then return to line 8 and type the following:

```
def l
```

This prompt is sufficient for Copilot to infer that it should generate the first decorator, interpreting 1 as a reference to log_function_args. Moving the cursor up and pressing *Enter* three times is all that is involved in **inverse CoT**, but it is very effective. As shown in *Figure 15.7*, this cue enables Copilot to generate a complete implementation of a logging mechanism, including the function's arguments.

```python
fizzbuzz_printer.py
1     import logging
2
3     logger = logging.getLogger(__name__)
4
5     FIZZBUZZ_COUNTER = 0
6
7
8     def log_function_args(func):  new *
          def wrapper(*args, **kwargs):
              logger.info(f"Function {func.__name__} called with args: {args}, kwargs: {kwargs}")
              return func(*args, **kwargs)

          return wrapper
9
10
11    @log_function_args  new *
12    @increment_counter
13    @validate_args_types_and_limits(0, 500)
14    def print_fizzbuzz(limit: int) -> None:
15        for i in range(1, limit + 1):
```

Figure 15.7: Copilot's decorator implementation

The suggested implementation of log_function_args correctly logs the function name and arguments as an info-level log statement.

After the initial def 1 prompt, pressing the *Enter* key twice is enough for Copilot to generate the next decorator, increment_counter, as shown in *Figure 15.8*:

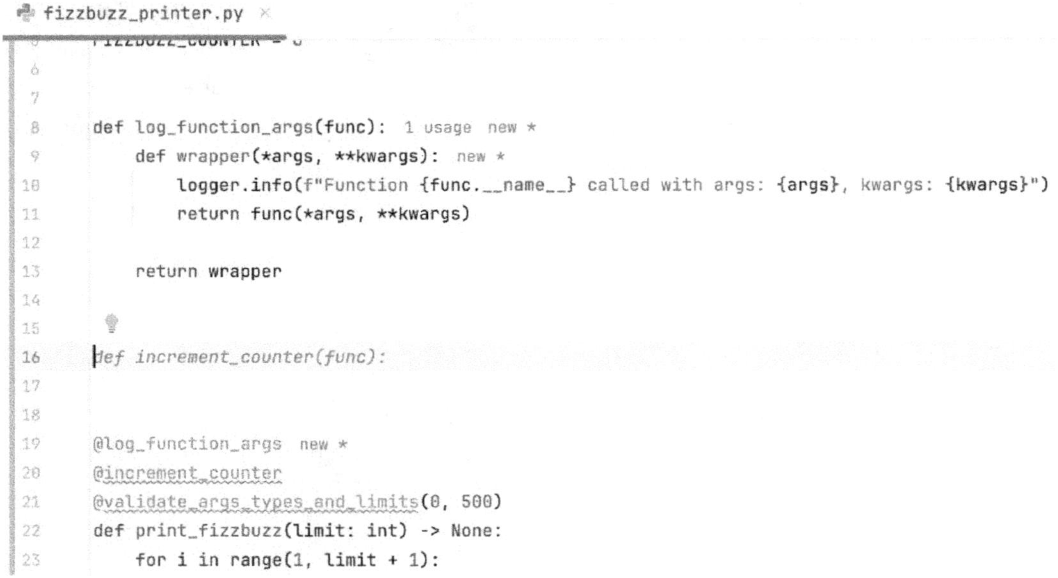

```
 fizzbuzz_printer.py  ×
     FIZZBUZZ_COUNTER = 0
6
7
8    def log_function_args(func):  1 usage  new *
9        def wrapper(*args, **kwargs):  new *
10           logger.info(f"Function {func.__name__} called with args: {args}, kwargs: {kwargs}")
11           return func(*args, **kwargs)
12
13       return wrapper
14
15       
16   def increment_counter(func):
17
18
19   @log_function_args  new *
20   @increment_counter
21   @validate_args_types_and_limits(0, 500)
22   def print_fizzbuzz(limit: int) -> None:
23       for i in range(1, limit + 1):
```

Figure 15.8: Enter key as a cue for Copilot to implement the next decorator

The *Enter* key serves as a sufficient cue for the next implementation. This highlights how Copilot can supercharge our workflow. For your reference, here is the suggested implementation of increment_counter by Copilot:

```
def increment_counter(func):
    def wrapper(*args, **kwargs):
        global FIZZBUZZ_COUNTER
        FIZZBUZZ_COUNTER += 1
        logger.info(f"Function {func.__name__} called {FIZZBUZZ_COUNTER}
times")
        return func(*args, **kwargs)

    return wrapper
```

This decorator correctly increments the previously initialized global variable, FIZZBUZZ_COUNTER, before the function call. If we prefer to increment it after execution, we could have used a different decorator's call, such as @increment_counter_after_call.

Finally, Copilot's suggested implementation for argument validation efficiently manages both type-checking and value constraints using a **parameterized decorator**. This type of decorator introduces an additional closure layer, allowing us to specify arguments, such as the minimum and maximum limits, in this case.

By calling @validate_args_types_and_limits(0, 500), we provide a clear cue for Copilot to recognize the need for a parameterized decorator with the given constraints. Here is the suggested implementation:

```python
def validate_args_types_and_limits(min_limit: int, max_limit: int):
    def decorator(func):
        def wrapper(limit: int):
            if not isinstance(limit, int):
                raise TypeError(f"Argument 'limit' must be of type int,
got {type(limit)}")
            if limit < min_limit or limit > max_limit:
                raise ValueError(f"Argument 'limit' must be between {min_
limit} and {max_limit}, got {limit}")
            return func(limit)

        return wrapper

    return decorator
```

Here, the parameterized decorator, validate_args_types_and_limits, ensures that the argument falls within the specified inclusive range before executing the function.

For reference, here is an example of calling print_fizzbuzz(-15), which should raise a value error due to the negative input:

```
File "supercharge/ch15/application/fizzbuzz_printer.py", line 32, in
wrapper
ValueError: Argument 'limit' must be between 0 and 500, got -15
```

validate_args_types_and_limits raised an error due to a bad input, preventing the function from being called with a negative limit. Similarly, if we had called print_fizbuzz(3.14), we would have received a TypeError error, indicating that it handles integers but not floating-point values.

To see how our `log_function_args` and `increment_counter` decorators operate, we will add a basic logging configuration at the beginning of the file, capturing INFO-level and higher logs, in a file named `fizzbuzz.log`:

```
logging.basicConfig(level=logging.INFO,
                    filename="fizzbuzz.log")
```

This ensures that the log messages are stored in `fizzbuzz.log`. In most software systems, print statements should not be used and should be replaced by logging that can direct output to the console or a file.

Next, we add two function calls with valid inputs:

```
print_fizzbuzz(5)
print_fizzbuzz(50)
```

For reference, the `fizzbuzz_printer.py` output is shown in *Figure 15.9*:

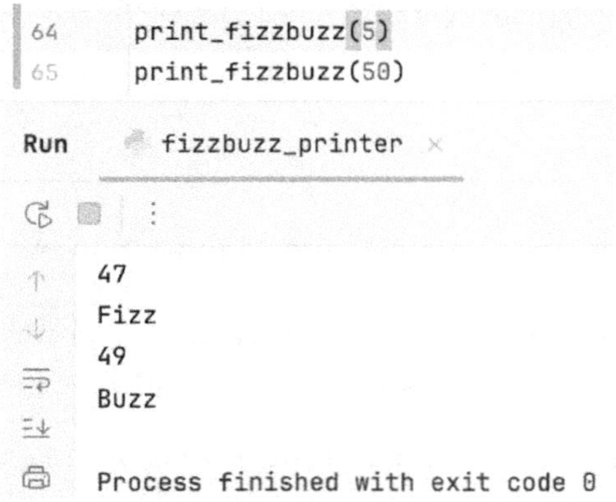

```
64        print_fizzbuzz(5)
65        print_fizzbuzz(50)
```

Run   fizzbuzz_printer ×

```
47
Fizz
49
Buzz

Process finished with exit code 0
```

Figure 15.9: Console output for the two function calls

This produces a clean output, containing the FizzBuzz results. Meanwhile, the `fizzbuzz.log` log file records log messages in the specified format, as illustrated in *Figure 15.10*:

```
≡ fizzbuzz.log  ×      🐍 fizzbuzz_printer.py

1      INFO:__main__:Function wrapper called with args: (5,), kwargs: {}
2      INFO:__main__:FizzBuzz function called 1 times.
3      INFO:__main__:Function wrapper called with args: (50,), kwargs: {}
4      INFO:__main__:FizzBuzz function called 2 times.
5
```

Figure 15.10: fizzbuzz.log output containing logs and counter messages

This implementation follows clean code principles, separating core functionality from monitoring while leveraging inverse CoT prompting in Copilot to generate neat and maintainable code. However, decorators can be styled in various ways. Later in the chapter, we will explore how few-shot learning can help refine their structure for even better results.

Next, we will apply the inverse CoT technique when prompting ChatGPT and OpenAI API.

Applying inverse CoT with ChatGPT and OpenAI

GitHub Copilot is the preferred tool for integrating going-live functionality, as it provides the fastest code completion experience. However, we will also demonstrate how to apply the same CoT prompting technique with ChatGPT and OpenAI API. To do this effectively, we will structure our prompts using the five S's best practices for prompt precision introduced earlier in this book.

Using ChatGPT to monitor decorators

Similar to our approach with GitHub Copilot, we can leverage ChatGPT to generate the required decorators for monitoring. Since we submit the full code rather than moving the cursor up in the file, this approach aligns with a standard CoT technique. The following is an example of a structured prompt that provides context about the incomplete Python implementation, focusing on a single task, with specific and short instructions, followed by a lead-in cue:

```
CONTEXT: You are provided with a partial Python script in {{{ FIZZBUZZ_
PRINTER }}}, where some of the code is missing.
TASK: Implement the decorators with the missing implementation in the
code.
FIZZBUZZ_PRINTER: {{{
import logging
logger = logging.getLogger(__name__)
```

```
FIZZBUZZ_COUNTER = 0

@log_function_args
@increment_counter
@validate_args_types_and_limits(0, 500)
def print_fizzbuzz(limit: int) -> None: ... full code implementation
omitted for brevity ... }}}
CODE:
```

When used in ChatGPT with the *o3-mini high* model (available to Plus subscribers as of April 2025), this prompt generated a complete script including the full implementation of the missing decorators, as follows:

```python
def log_function_args(func: callable) -> callable:
    def wrapper(*args, **kwargs):
        logger.info(
            f"Calling function '{func.__name__}' with args: {args} and
kwargs: {kwargs}"
        return func(*args, **kwargs)
    return wrapper

def increment_counter(func: callable) -> callable:
    def wrapper(*args, **kwargs):
        global FIZZBUZZ_COUNTER
        FIZZBUZZ_COUNTER += 1
        logger.info(f"FIZZBUZZ_COUNTER incremented to {FIZZBUZZ_COUNTER}")
        return func(*args, **kwargs)
    return wrapper

def validate_args_types_and_limits(min_limit: int, max_limit: int):
    def decorator(func: callable) -> callable:
        def wrapper(*args, **kwargs):
            # Use inspect to bind the arguments to the function's
signature
            sig = inspect.signature(func)
            bound_args = sig.bind(*args, **kwargs)
            bound_args.apply_defaults()
            # Expecting the argument to be named 'limit'
```

```
        if 'limit' not in bound_args.arguments:
            raise ValueError("Missing required argument 'limit'.")
        limit = bound_args.arguments['limit']
        if not isinstance(limit, int):
            raise TypeError("Argument 'limit' must be an integer.")
        if not (min_limit <= limit <= max_limit):
            raise ValueError(f"Argument 'limit' must be between {min_
limit} and {max_limit}.")
        return func(*args, **kwargs)
    return wrapper
return decorator
```

This implementation retains the same functionality as the decorators generated by Copilot but differs in style. It includes docstrings and the addition of the `@functools.wraps(func)` decorator, which helps preserve the original function's attributes. Later in the chapter, we will explore how to guide ChatGPT toward a more desirable implementation style using few-shot learning.

Using OpenAI API to monitor decorators

The approach for using OpenAI API closely mirrors the ChatGPT prompt structure. We construct a system prompt that provides context and a single task, as was done for ChatGPT. Additionally, we use a user prompt that includes the existing script along with a cue for code completion.

The system prompt should look as follows:

```
SURROUND = "You are provided with a partial Python script in {{{ FIZZBUZZ_
PRINTER }}}, where some of the code is missing."
SINGLE_TASK = "Implement the decorators with the missing implementation in
the code."
```

These prompt pieces serve the same role as the context and task definitions in the ChatGPT prompt. The user prompt should incorporate the incomplete implementation, for example, by reading the code from a file, as shown here:

```
def get_user_prompt(script_path: str) -> str:
    with open(script_path, 'r') as file:
        incomplete_code = file.read()

    return f"""
```

```
FIZZBUZZ_PRINTER: {{{{{{ {incomplete_code} }}}}}}


CODE:
"""
```

By providing the incomplete script alongside the `CODE:` cue, we can guide OpenAI API toward generating the missing decorator implementations. Calling OpenAI API with these prompts should yield a decorator implementation like the outputs from ChatGPT and GitHub Copilot. The full script is available for your reference at `ch15/inverse_cot_openai.py`.

Now that we have seen how to use GenAI tools to implement monitoring decorators, the next step is refining their style to better fit our needs. This can be achieved using few-shot learning to guide Copilot and ChatGPT with structured examples or by fine-tuning a model through OpenAI API GUI. We will explore both approaches in the next section.

Utilizing few-shot learning and fine-tuning as style guides

While the decorators generated by GenAI applications provide the desired functionality, we can further refine their style using few-shot learning techniques, as introduced in *Chapter 8*.

For instance, we might want to include the `@functools.wraps` decorator to preserve the original function's attributes and enforce a specific logging style with the `extra` parameters. Both objectives can be achieved by supplying few-shot examples to Copilot and ChatGPT or adding desired prompt outputs to our fine-tuning file to be used by OpenAI API.

Few-shot decorator style for GitHub Copilot

As introduced in *Chapter 8*, enforcing a specific style with GitHub Copilot requires a few examples, which can be provided as a style guide script. This few-shot example achieves the desired implementation.

To achieve this, we can create a `style_guide_decorator.py` file, which should be treated like another non-project file and is typically placed outside the `src` folder in a project repository.

This style guide should include all the elements we want Copilot to follow, such as log message formatting, type hints, and spacing. These examples guide Copilot and reduce the need for chained prompts or additional edits.

When creating a style guide for decorators, we suggest including a time_it decorator to log a function's runtime. The implementation should demonstrate the use of @functools.wraps to retain the decorated function's attributes, type hints for arguments and variables, and a hanging indent logging style with extra parameters:

```python
import logging
import time
from functools import wraps
from typing import Any


logger: logging.Logger = logging.getLogger(__name__)



def time_it(func: callable) -> callable:
    @wraps(func)
    def wrapper(*args, **kwargs):
        start_time: float = time.time()
        res: Any = func(*args, **kwargs)
        end_time: float = time.time()
        logger.info(
            "Function called.",
            extra={
                "function": func.__name__,
                "args": args,
                "kwargs": kwargs,
                "error": "",
                "timing": f"{end_time - start_time} sec"})
        return res


    return wrapper
```

In this case, the logger message combines static text with the extra parameter, resulting in a structured log message that is better suited for large-scale logging. For instance, to quickly identify all timing messages where execution exceeded five seconds, we could filter logs based on the timing parameter with a condition such as timing > 5.

To incorporate the style guide into the session, we open `decorators_style_guide.py`, then cut and paste the entire content of the file in place. This trick ensures that Copilot recognizes the code in the file as part of the active session and incorporates its style when making suggestions.

Next, we return to `print_fizzbuzz.py` and repeat the inverse CoT process. This time, Copilot's suggestions should align with the style guide defined in `style_guide_decorator.py`. As shown in *Figure 15.11*, Copilot includes the `@functools.wraps` decorator in its suggested implementation, while the logging indentation and extra parameters maintain the same formatting as specified in the style guide:

```
def log_function_args(func: callable) -> callable:  new *
    def wrapper(*args, **kwargs):
        message: str = "Function called."
        logger.info(message,
                    extra={"function": func.__name__,
                           "args": args,
                           "kwargs": kwargs,
                           "error": "",
                           "timing": ""})
        return func(*args, **kwargs)

    return wrapper


@log_function_args  2 usages  new *
@increment_counter
@validate_args_types_and_limits(0, 500)
def print_fizzbuzz(limit: int) -> None:
```

Figure 15.11: Decorator implementation using the style guide in GitHub Copilot

This implementation demonstrates that Copilot follows our preferred logging style, using a static log message and extra parameters to support a more structured logging format.

Next, we will explore how to apply the style guide when prompting with ChatGPT. We will then show how to incorporate it into a fine-tuning approach when working with OpenAI API.

Few-shot learning in ChatGPT

When using ChatGPT, we can apply a few-shot approach to deploying decorators, like that we explored in *Chapter 8*. For this task, we recommend the o3-mini high model since it is better at complex coding tasks.

We first enhance the prompt's surrounding context by including a reference example:

```
CONTEXT: You are provided with a partial Python script enclosed with
{{{FIZZBUZZ_PRINTER}}} where some of the code is missing, and examples of
a good implementation enclosed with {{{ EXAMPLES }}}.
TASK: Implement the decorators with the missing implementation in the code
while following the style guide.
```

For the few-shot example, we will label the input and output code snippets, with `INCOMPLETE_CODE` used for the input, indicating the missing `time_it` decorator, and `COMPLETE_CODE` for the fully implemented script. This distinction clearly highlights the intended transformation:

```python
INCOMPLETE_CODE: {{{
import logging


logger: logging.Logger = logging.getLogger(__name__)


@time_it
def my_func(a: int, b: int) -> int:
    return a + b
}}}
```

With this incomplete code snippet, we expect the model to generate a fully implemented decorator that follows a specific style. To guide the model, we will provide a fully implemented version of the desired code, as shown here:

```python
COMPLETE_CODE: {{{
import logging
import time
from functools import wraps
from typing import Any


logger: logging.Logger = logging.getLogger(__name__)


def time_it(func: callable) -> callable:
    @wraps(func)
        ...omitted for brevity but using "extra" parameter...
```

```
@time_it
def my_func(a: int, b: int) -> int:
    return a + b
}}}
```

Providing this example of the desired output helps guide ChatGPT toward generating the expected implementation. The following is the structure of the prompt, with previously introduced parts omitted for brevity:

```
CONTEXT: You are provided with a partial Python script enclosed with
{{{FIZZBUZZ_PRINTER}}} where some of the code is missing, and examples of
a good implementation enclosed with {{{ EXAMPLES }}}
TASK: Implement the decorators with the missing implementation in the code
while following the style guide.

EXAMPLES:
INCOMPLETE_CODE: {{{...omitted for brevity...}}}
COMPLETE_CODE: {{{...omitted for brevity...}}}
FIZZBUZZ_PRINTER: {{{...omitted for brevity...}}}


CODE:
```

The full prompt is available in the book's repository at `ch15/decorators_few_shot_chatgpt.txt`. For reference, the results generated using this prompt closely resemble Copilot's code completion, as shown in *Figure 15.12*:

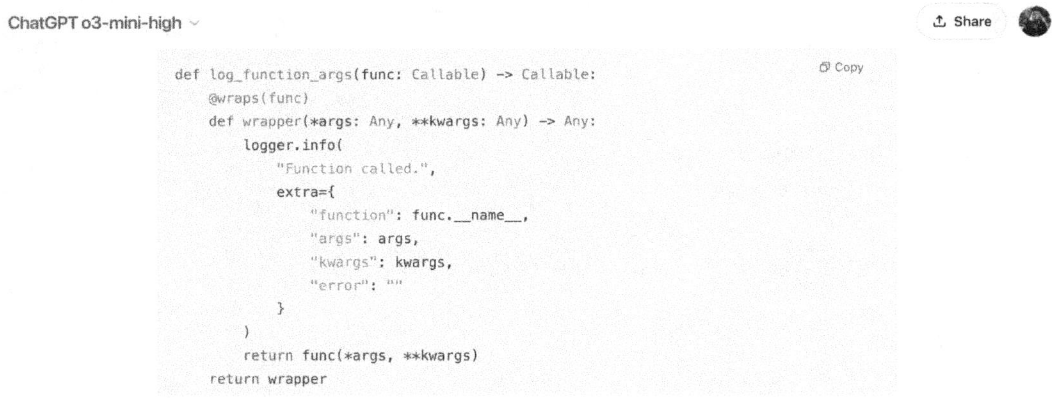

Figure 15.12: Few-shot learning using ChatGPT

In ChatGPT's implementation, we can see that the model followed the style guide from our example, incorporating the extra parameter alongside the static log message and using the @functools. wraps decorator to preserve the function's attributes. However, this is a relatively lengthy prompt to achieve a code completion that GitHub Copilot can generate much faster. Therefore, we recommend using Copilot whenever possible for a more efficient workflow.

Leveraging fine-tuning for OpenAI API

With OpenAI, we can either apply the few-shot technique, as in the ChatGPT input-output examples, or train a **fine-tuned model** by adding a few training samples in JSONL format, as introduced in *Chapter 11*. This approach would take even longer than ChatGPT to achieve what GitHub Copilot can generate almost instantly. Fine-tuning would be more practical for large-scale projects, such as scanning an entire repository to implement logging, monitoring, and error handling for all files automatically, at scale.

As we saw in *Chapter 11*, fine-tuning generally requires more examples than few-shot learning because of the differences in how models handle prompts versus how they update weights during fine-tuning. However, considering our starter fine-tuning file, fine_tuning.jsonl, from *Chapter 11*, which has already established the preferred logging style, indentation, and spacing, a single decorator may be sufficient to achieve the desired implementation.

For example, here is a time_it decorator added to ch13/fine_tuning.jsonl, structured with a system and user prompt as used in ChatGPT, along with a desirable assistant response assigned a weight of 1:

```
{"messages": [{"role": "system", "content": "You are provided with a
partial Python script enclosed with {{{ INCOMPLETE_CODE }}} where some of
the code is missing. Your task is to implement the decorators with the
missing implementation"}, {"role": "user", "content": "INCOMPLETE_CODE:
{{{import logging\nimport time\n\nlogger: logging.Logger = logging.
getLogger(__name__)\n\n@time_it\ndef my_func(a: int, b: int) -> int:\n
return a + b\n}}}\n COMPLETE_CODE:"}, {"role": "assistant", "content":
"...omitted for brevity...", "weight": 1}]}
```

We can then upload the fine-tuning file by going to platform.openai.com, selecting **Dashboard | Fine-tune**, and uploading the JSONL file, as shown in *Figure 15.13*:

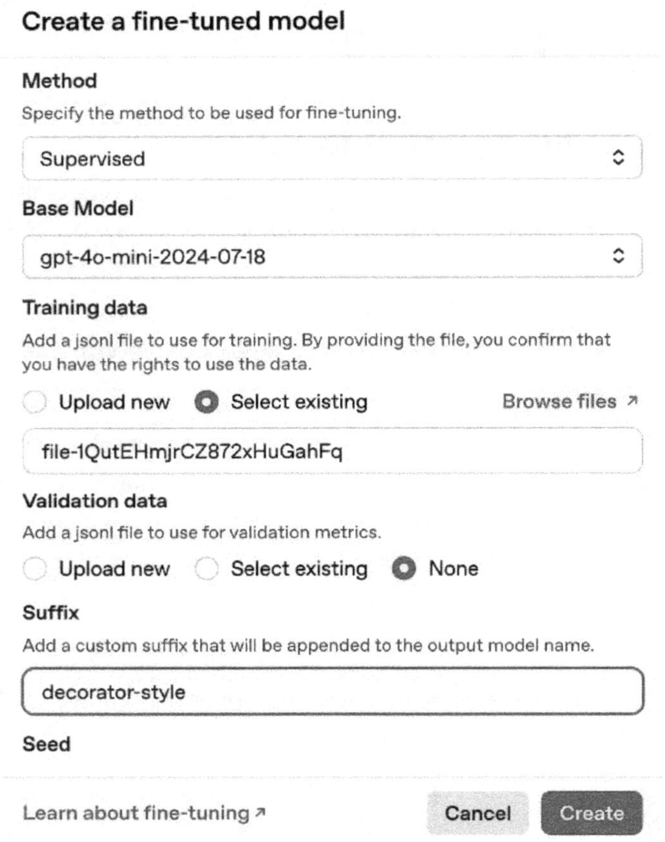

Create a fine-tuned model

Method

Specify the method to be used for fine-tuning.

Supervised	◇

Base Model

gpt-4o-mini-2024-07-18	◇

Training data

Add a jsonl file to use for training. By providing the file, you confirm that you have the rights to use the data.

◯ Upload new   ⦿ Select existing   Browse files ↗

file-1QutEHmjrCZ872xHuGahFq

Validation data

Add a jsonl file to use for validation metrics.

◯ Upload new   ◯ Select existing   ⦿ None

Suffix

Add a custom suffix that will be appended to the output model name.

decorator-style

Seed

Learn about fine-tuning ↗   [Cancel] [Create]

Figure 15.13: Upload the fine-tuned JSONL file

After the upload is complete, the fine-tuned model will be trained, which takes around 15 minutes. When done, a **Succeeded** icon will appear, as shown in *Figure 15.14*:

🖵 Learn more   + Create

MODEL

ft:gpt-4o-mini-2024-07-18:pazpaz-the-coder:decorator-style:AydMPYCg

◯ Status	⊘ Succeeded
ⓘ Job ID	`ftjob-zDa73ZywRRDInwOHngNeAfUy`
ⓘ Training Method	Supervised
🗁 Suffix	`decorator-style`
⊕ Base model	`gpt-4o-mini-2024-07-18`
⊕ Output model	`ft:gpt-4o-mini-2024-07-18:pazpaz-the-coder:decorator-style:AydMPYCg`
⊘ Created at	Feb 8, 2025, 1:24 PM

Figure 15.14: Successful fine-tuning job indicates the model has finished training

To compare the benefits of fine-tuning against the base GPT-4o mini model, we can use the **Playground** page. This allows us to compare the fine-tuned model's output against the baseline results, highlighting improvements. It is always recommended to validate these enhancements on key prompts once the fine-tuning process is complete.

We will select **gpt-4o-mini-2024-07-18** as the base model on the left and choose the fine-tuned model from the drop-down menu on the right, as shown in *Figure 15.15*:

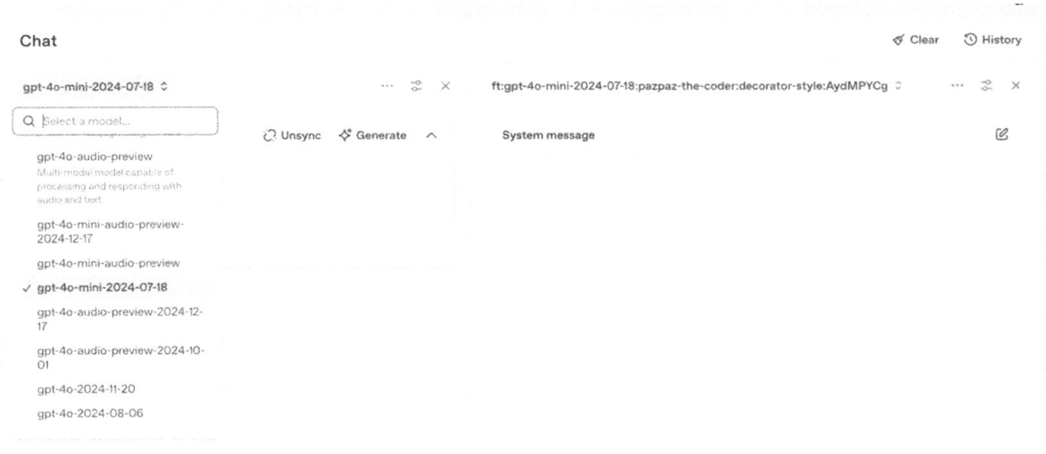

Figure 15.15: Base model and fine-tuned model comparison

This comparison allows us to assess the performance of both models. Next, we add the system instructions on both sides of the screen, mirroring the surrounding context and single-task approach used in ChatGPT:

```
You are provided with a partial Python script in {{{FIZZBUZZ_PRINTER}}},
where some of the code is missing. Your task is to implement the
decorators with the missing implementation in the code.
```

The user message follows a format like our ChatGPT prompt:

```
FIZZBUZZ_PRINTER: {{{ ...omitted for brevity... }}}
CODE:
```

At this stage, our prompt is ready to run, producing more precise results when using the fine-tuned model. Compared to **gpt-4o-mini-2024-07-18**, the fine-tuned model returns only the code with our preferred logging style, and including the `@functools.wraps` decorator, as shown in *Figure 15.16*:

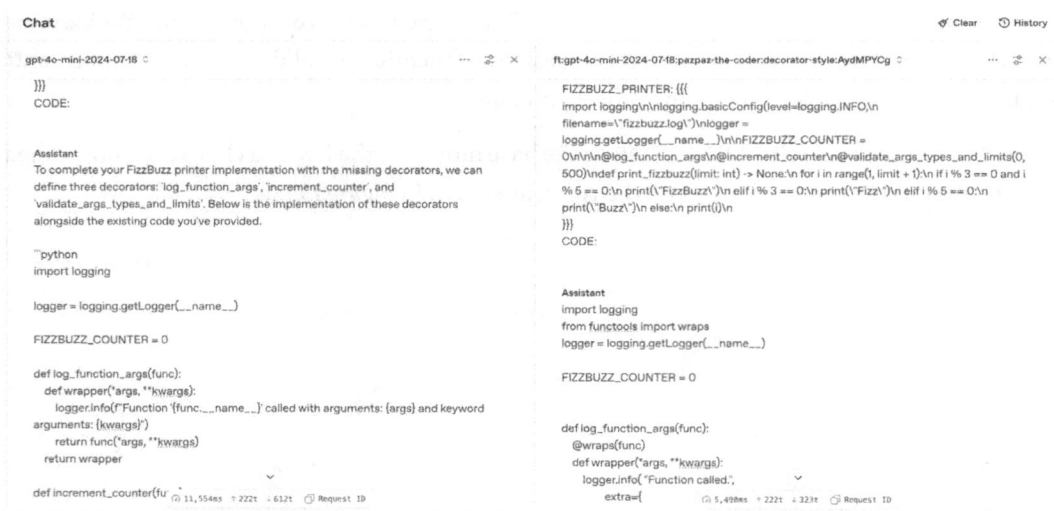

Figure 15.16: Comparison of the fine-tuned model and the base model

In this figure, we can see that the assistant's response begins directly with the code, reflecting the influence of the fine-tuned examples. Additionally, the preferred logging style is consistently applied, aligning with the provided sample.

While fine-tuning helps maintain the desired structure and style, it requires significantly more effort than using Copilot for going-live tasks related to code completion. For this reason, we recommend Copilot as your primary tool for such tasks. Fine-tuning may be a viable option if you're building a custom GenAI application for internal use and have dozens of training examples, such as scanning an entire repository for suggestions or developing a GenAI-powered solution to serve other customers. However, Copilot with few-shot learning tends to be a more efficient method of achieving results without having to invest time in finding many use cases.

Summary

In this chapter, we explored how going-live tasks, such as adding logs, monitoring usage, and handling bad input, can introduce unnecessary complexity to functions. GenAI does not inherently suggest using decorators to separate these objectives from the core functionality of the program, which can lead to lower-quality code.

The most effective way to leverage GenAI for these tasks is through CoT prompting with GitHub Copilot. This approach involves first implementing the core function and then specifying additional requirements for decorators to handle logging, metric recording, or argument validation.

To ensure that the decorator implementation follows our desired style, we can use few-shot learning with Copilot and ChatGPT or fine-tune a model for OpenAI API. This allows us to achieve more desirable results, minimizing the requirements for chained edits to the code.

In the final chapter of the book, we will summarize the key takeaways from the 15 chapters and explore how to enhance our coding efforts with GenAI tools.

Quiz time

Before you proceed to the next chapter, make sure that you can confidently answer the following questions:

Question 1: Do LLMs guarantee higher coding standards?

Answer: No, not necessarily. Simply asking GenAI applications to add monitoring responsibilities can lead to undesirable suggestions, such as merging monitoring tasks with core functionality instead of properly separating responsibilities.

Question 2: What is the inverse CoT for Copilot?

Answer: It involves defining higher-level coding structures, such as decorators, first and then moving the cursor up to let Copilot complete the implementation details.

Question 3: How can we guide GenAI applications to follow a style guide that aligns with our internal standards?

Answer: We can use a style guide file for Copilot, provide a few examples when prompting ChatGPT, and apply fine-tuning when working with OpenAI API.

Further reading

To learn more about the topics that were covered in this chapter, take a look at the following resources:

- Real Python on decorators: `https://realpython.com/primer-on-python-decorators/`
- Python's logging documentation: `https://docs.python.org/3/howto/logging.html`
- Metrics of code, Wikipedia: `http://en.wikipedia.org/wiki/Software_metric`
- Exception handling, Wikipedia: `https://en.wikipedia.org/wiki/Exception_handling_(programming)`

Unlock this book's exclusive benefits now

Scan this QR code or go to `packtpub.com/unlock`, then search for this book by name.

Note: Keep your purchase invoice ready before you start.

16

Architecture, Design, and the Future

It seems that every discussion about the future of **artificial intelligence** (**AI**) bears considering the famous quote of Niels Bohr: *"Prediction is very difficult, especially if it's about the future."* When it comes to AI, though, we already have ideas about what the future will bring. That is, we have read various science fiction books by Asimov and other authors. We have watched *The Terminator* and other futuristic movies and TV shows. Even cartoons across different generations embody different versions of the future, whether it's *The Jetsons*, *Futurama*, or various anime. We have conceptions of what the future looks like; the uncertainty rests on how long it will take to get there.

With the increasing investments in AI and their exponential growth, the fields of AI and GenAI continue to evolve and bring new capabilities faster than most practitioners expect, let alone can keep up with. The landscape of software engineering is changing as a result of the new capabilities brought about by AI and GenAI for coding. Before we can look forward and estimate the timeframes for advancements in the future, it is useful to look back and understand the major technological advances that have accelerated the transformation over the past 10 years. This chapter briefly reviews these major advances as a conceptual framework for what happens next.

This book enables readers to embrace these changes and gain the skills to effectively use them for not just coding but a range of software engineering skills. As we all continue to learn, it is useful to understand the impact of these advances on the industry. These include the impact on software engineers and their companies, as well as what the future might bring.

In this chapter, we explore the following topics:

- The rapid rise of GenAI
- The economics of faster software development
- The shifting landscape of software developers
- Will GenAI change programming languages?
- The future of GenAI in software engineering

The rapid rise of GenAI

It was only in late 2012 that Thomas Davenport and DJ Patil declared that data science is the *"sexiest job of the 21st century"* in their Harvard Business Review article (https://hbr.org/2012/10/data-scientist-the-sexiest-job-of-the-21st-century). Just over a decade later, the pace of transformation in the industry has been nothing short of remarkable.

In the same period of the last decade, neural networks were finally making their third resurgence after a couple of AI winters. Although neural network research started back in the 1950s, it faced difficulties in reaching its extremely hyped expectations, which resulted in periods of minimal funding and research known as the "AI winters." By 2012, new neural network architectures had emerged. AlexNet, a type of **convolutional neural network (CNN)**, drew widespread attention from the computer vision community after winning the **ImageNet Large Scale Visual Recognition Challenge (ILSVRC)** in 2012 by a wide margin. This changed the course of computer vision as all image understanding work quickly shifted to CNNs. The ensuing research over the next few years led to the ability of CNNs to extract information from images as accurately as humans by 2016, according to the ILSVRC competition, although human accuracy levels are still disputed.

While computer vision work was advancing through the CNN architecture, the **transformer architecture** was introduced through a 2017 paper from Google. This *Attention Is All You Need* paper (https://arxiv.org/abs/1706.03762) describes an **attention mechanism** and the transformer architecture. In the years since, this architecture has had a massive impact on neural networks and the field of AI. Although it has improved solutions for many diverse problems within AI, its primary beneficiary has been the subfield of **natural language processing (NLP)**. The work of this paper led to the adoption of **large language models (LLMs)**.

LLMs have had a profound impact on the public perception of AI, though the early generations of this technology were far less impressive. GPT-1 and GPT-2 were released by OpenAI in 2018 and 2019 and served as a step forward in LLMs. These models are essentially prediction models trained on large volumes of text to predict the next word. The transformer architecture learned the relationship between the words in a sentence to predict the next word. Empirical research found that the LLMs performed significantly well with ever larger models trained on ever more data. GPT-3 was released in 2020 with 175 billion parameters as compared to the 1.5 billion parameters of GPT-2. GPT-4, released in March 2023, scaled up to an estimated 1.76 trillion parameters, a 10-fold increase over GPT-3.

InstructGPT and ChatGPT were developed as new tools that utilize underlying GPT LLMs. InstructGPT was designed to generate text for specific tasks that follow user instructions. These tasks could be emails, summaries, or even code. InstructGPT included AI predictions based on training data as well as a **reinforcement learning** technique based on human feedback to adjust the next word predictions based on a human feedback mechanism. In contrast, the release of OpenAI's **ChatGPT** in November 2022 was based on GPT-3.5 and was arguably the first time an average user could interact with an LLM without having to program. It focused on conversations with users and general dialogue but also included the reinforcement learning method. These two tools developed many of the LLM methods that led to the **prompting techniques** field.

The LLM and ChatGPT methods focus on accurately predicting the next words across languages. The same models have opened other research avenues by training on other types of data. Instead of training on text, researchers in biology have found that the same results can be applied to genomes and protein sequence predictions. Chemists are using the technology to create new drugs and chemical substances with specialized properties. This book, of course, is based on the same idea of applying the same prediction techniques to code by training on public code bases.

A few years ago, AI was rarely discussed in the media. Today, the financial news seems to focus on the recent technology advances and their implications for the markets and the larger economy. The next section discusses some of the economic issues that GenAI coding may offer.

Economics of faster software development

Software development is one of the key enablers of technology and the digital economy. Software impacts many aspects of modern society, from governments to businesses. Most industries rely on software. Software is closely tied to the productivity of workers across the globe, making it a key economic measure.

The field of software economics researches and estimates the value provided by software against the costs associated with its development. Software platforms and tools are designed to provide incremental business/economic value to the organizations using them. The key decisions of buying **commercial off-the-shelf (COTS)** software, licensing software, customizing third-party software, or building it in-house are based on the estimated incremental value proposition.

With GenAI, software engineers can write quality code substantially faster. With the techniques described in this book, the efficiency in writing code should improve and the quality of the produced code should remain quite high. The ability to automate the testing and documentation further reduces the costs of software development. In financial terms, the use of GenAI by the same workforce would result in an increased supply of software. The current costs for the GenAI coding empowerment remain $25/month or under, which is arguably a bargain. The reduced cost will increase the demand for software, creating greater automation and adding value for businesses. There are always more problems to solve, and the lower development cost barrier will alter the economics of software engineering. To reap these benefits, software engineers need to begin using this technology, which is discussed in the next section.

Will GenAI be adopted by software engineers?

The improved efficiency, speed, and capability that GenAI brings for software engineers is at least a paradigm shift but may be a revolution in the way that software is being developed. As discussed in this book, the current capabilities of GenAI include many of the tasks that software engineers engage in daily. These include writing code and tests, generating documentation, refactoring, and optimizing code. GenAI aids with the cognitively complex tasks of code debugging down to the less mindful tasks of conforming to code style.

Gartner predicts that 50% of software engineers will use AI-powered coding tools by 2027, which is up from the 5% in 2023 when GenAI was at the peak of the hype cycle (`https://www.gartner.com/en/newsroom/press-releases/2023-11-28-gartner-hype-cycle-shows-ai-practices-and-platform-engineering-will-reach-mainstream-adoption-in-software-engineering-in-two-to-five-years`). Over the last two years, GenAI tools have rapidly shifted from marginally useful due to their many errors to widespread tools that software engineers and corporations find valuable. In this brief period, KPMG claims that GenAI has become a software engineer's most valuable coding partner (`https://kpmg.com/us/en/articles/2023/generative-artificial-intelligence.html`). Over the next few years, these tools will continue to evolve and produce ever higher quality code, test instances, docstrings, and documentation.

Given the improved accuracy and overall efficiency that GenAI coding provides, the effect may not be uniform across all ranks of developers. The next section examines how the tools may affect different classes of programmers.

Shifting landscape of software developers

At the current market pricing, GenAI tools are generally available to all developers. It is interesting to speculate how the software engineer landscape may change due to this recent technology. Some have suggested that GenAI tools will level the playing field since any developer will be able to program with increased efficiency in any language. They argue that junior developers may take over more roles and increase the volume of code delivered, and more senior developers will be pushed out of organizations. Others argue the opposite.

The rise of GenAI tools has also lowered the barrier for software development. Programming in each language has a steep learning curve since it includes syntax, algorithms, libraries, **integrated development environments (IDEs)**, compiler messages, and more. Printing the "hello world" message in any language is usually the first accomplishment. If coding a new language is like reading the front page of a foreign language newspaper, GenAI for coding is a tutor that shows the meaning of all words and explains the grammar upon request. For coding alone, a junior developer may quickly become productive in straightforward coding.

Tools such as ChatGPT and GitHub Copilot will empower developers to quickly learn and become productive in new programming languages. There are always new languages and frameworks that all software engineers must continually learn and apply to projects. The implication is that developers can more quickly get up to speed with new languages and frameworks and become productive in far less time. This has implications for not only new languages but also older languages such as COBOL, FORTRAN, and others that are still running in legacy systems, described later in this section.

Our perception is that the landscape will shift toward senior developers, and more junior developers may be displaced by the GenAI tools. If we consider a typical software engineering or computer science undergraduate curriculum, the primary technical courses include calculus, programming, data structures, algorithms, and maybe software engineering. The more advanced courses will include networking, compilers, operating systems, big data, AI, programming language theory, optimizations, cloud computing, and much more.

Junior developers tend to focus more on writing code, tests, and documentation, while the more senior developers focus on the complex interplay between the system requirements, stakeholders, architecture, design, and other aspects that tend to require more experience. The GenAI efficiencies clearly overlap the skillsets of the junior developers, but not the senior developers.

GenAI as related to the Software Engineering Body of Knowledge

Another viewpoint is that GenAI performs very well within a limited scope of coding within software engineering. The IEEE Computer Society produces a **Software Engineering Body of Knowledge (SWEBOK)**. The current version, developed in 2024, captures the collective skills, methodologies, knowledge, and so on for the software engineering profession. It has been curated by experts with the goal of reaching a consensus on the core body of knowledge. *Table 16.1* lists the 18 **knowledge areas (KAs)** found in the SWEBOK guide, available at `https://www.computer.org/education/bodies-of-knowledge/software-engineering`:

Software requirements	Software architecture	Software design
Software construction	Software testing	Software engineering operations
Software maintenance	Software configuration management	Software engineering management
Software engineering process	Software engineering models and methods	Software quality
Software security	Software engineering professional practice	Software engineering economics
Computing foundations	Mathematical foundations	Engineering foundations

Table 16.1: Software Engineering Body of Knowledge (SWEBOK) 2024 V4

Compared to the SWEBOK, GenAI enhances a few processes but only a fraction of the overall skillset currently. Specifically, it directly enhances software construction and software testing. Indirectly, it helps support software maintenance and software quality KAs.

Democratization of software engineers

The GenAI tools will help a wider audience than many people expect. We have discussed how junior software engineers and those getting up to speed in a new language can receive help with their programming. Senior developers can leverage their architectural, design, and other software systems experience. There is a wide class of former developers who have software experience but have shifted into other roles in computational biology, finance, business, or management.

Former programmers who have left the field to take on different responsibilities may return to coding in the near future with the GenAI tools. If they have been out of programming for several years, they would need to learn new languages, cloud computing, new IDEs, and so on. Normally, they would be unlikely to invest considerable time learning this multitude of new skills. However, with GenAI, they are now empowered to write niche applications within their specific roles that use their expertise. The implications are that part of software engineering may shift somewhat from being a domain-independent technical skill to an extra skill of domain experts. That is, rather than hiring expert software engineers who have traditionally applied their technical skills to write code for banking, healthcare, or other industries, these industries may turn to experienced practitioners in their field who can also program. We started to experience some of this with **robotic process automation (RPA)**, where the subject matter experts learned the tools and drove specific workflows. In the last couple of years, we have seen similar domain experts learning prompt engineering to leverage LLMs in their workflow pipelines. We see a similar shift in the democratization of AI, where subject matter experts may be replaced by subject matter experts with AI experience.

Legacy software and flexible teams

With the explainability and guidance of GenAI technology, software development will certainly change corporate and industry approaches to software, especially legacy systems. Many companies and industries rely on legacy software systems developed decades ago and continue to run. The systems may be decades old and written in a language that only one or two people in the company have ever learned. The software systems pose a significant risk to organizations. They may run on legacy hardware, but they are still part of existing workflows. Efforts to understand, let alone rewrite, such systems have been cost-prohibitive.

GenAI systems can now be trained on the code bases and both provide support for understanding the code and perhaps enable them to be quickly rewritten. Using similar technology to human language translation, the code can use GenAI techniques to efficiently rewrite the full code base, adhere to the more recent documentation and testing strategies, and eliminate the risk. In terms of staffing, this would reduce the need to keep developers with specialized language ability or experience with these legacy systems.

As the barriers with legacy systems decrease, software engineers may become empowered to work on a wider set of projects. While subject matter knowledge in the industry domain is critical, the coding implementation has become more accessible through GenAI.

With GenAI, coders can more quickly get up to speed with new code bases and become productive, but this has implications. The speed provided by GenAI increases the flexibility of developer teams. Developers can shift more quickly between projects and gear up for new projects. With agile project development practices and changing requirements, this is certainly a positive outcome. However, this flexibility would also presumably lead to increased outsourcing of code development since offshore teams could also quickly ramp up to tackle projects in a similar fashion. This is not a new trend, and many teams still rely on senior developers, designers, and business analysts who interact with customers.

This section focused on the people involved in software engineering and the impact of GenAI on the field. The next section discusses the potential opportunities for computer languages to change based on GenAI capabilities.

Will GenAI change programming languages?

The traditional art and science of writing software involves creating a set of instructions that a computer can follow. This communication currently occurs through a specific programming language. The instructions usually include combinations of data structures that store and manipulate data. The instructions may include algorithms that efficiently sort, manipulate, or transform data to add business value. Most programming languages can perform these operations, but their true power is only achieved when using added libraries or packages that enable user interfaces, networking, database interaction, and much more.

Our GenAI coding tools today focus on writing and modifying our code. That is, ChatGPT, OpenAI API, and GitHub Copilot serve as programming assistants that guess the specific programming language code lines from the method signature. While this speeds up our programming at the method level, it requires that the developer have knowledge of how the problem breaks down into multiple methods and the transmission of information between the methods as dictated by their signature.

We can draw parallels between writing a document using an LLM and writing code using GenAI. ChatGPT and other LLMs are remarkable at rephrasing text for technical audiences, doctors, or children. This is equivalent to refactoring code. To write a letter from scratch, it's not a single command but a series of prompts that map out the instructions and sequence. Similarly, one does not write the entire code file but must break it down into a series of commands that can each be developed into code. Throughout this book, we have provided many examples that illustrate that GenAI will usually write reasonable functional code. However, by breaking functions into smaller units, the GenAI will produce higher-quality and more readable code that is easier to maintain.

The next stage of GenAI software development is possibly a more natural language way of communicating with computers. While computer languages emphasize the precision of commands, they require an unnatural and more formal structure for communicating ideas. This requires a learning curve and arguably slows down development. Natural language could speed up the translation into computer-readable form and enable greater accessibility to software.

The rise of natural languages for computer instructions will likely require some time and face some hurdles that can be overcome with pseudocode. Three of the formal steps of computer languages are sequences, iterations, and selection (conditions). The interaction of these elements is the formal control flow of computer programs. Natural language can handle the sequences and conditional flows reasonably well, but the notion of iteration loops is arguably not commonly part of languages. Pseudocode represents a somewhat arbitrary syntax but captures the three formal steps well. General pseudocode that can be interpreted by LLMs to produce formal programming languages may further empower a wider set of developers.

The future of GenAI in software engineering

This section first discusses vibe coding and then breaks down the future of software engineering into two different horizons. The shorter term considers the next few years, and the longer term considers what the field might look like in five or more years.

Vibe coding

Vibe coding is a recent trend where the developer describes what they want to do in natural language and leaves the technical coding aspects up to the LLM. Using LLMs to write code is certainly a theme of this book, and vibe coding essentially takes this to an extreme. Essentially, vibe coding provides a form of rapid prototyping that is a valuable part of the overall software engineering process, particularly in defining requirements. We believe the software community will come to recognize its value as such. However, for larger projects, code quality is important since most of the costs associated with software are in its maintenance, such as adding new features. Many unhappy memes describe the difficulty of "vibe debugging" the relatively poor-quality code produced by vibe coding. we expect a future that lands somewhere between where we are now and vibe coding. We will describe the shorter- and longer-term expectations next.

Shorter term

Over the last year, the GenAI market has blossomed, and many developers are now working with this technology. It is available as a VSCode extension, Jetbrains products including PyCharm plugin, and other integrated development environments (IDEs) so it's readily available. In addition, new IDEs with built-in GenAI capabilities have entered the market, including Cursor, Windsurf, and Replit. Other tools, such as AWS CodeWhisperer and Tabnine, offer code suggestions for multiple languages. All of these are offered at a low price, compared to the potential savings of developer time. In the short term, all of these will increase their accuracy and lead to the creation of better software in less time.

Longer term

After many have adopted the GenAI coding approaches and can use them effectively, the technology push will focus on trying to move from formal requirements and specifications to code. As one of the first steps in the software development life cycle, requirements gathering is a formal process to understand the intended goals, the user interfaces, non-functional requirements, and so on. In many organizations, there are more formal diagrams, such as **Unified Markup Language** (**UML**), that describe the design. Others include sample user interface designs from **Balsamiq** and **Figma**. Efforts are underway to automatically convert these diagrams directly into code.

GenAI has not solved many of the other aspects of software development processes. The planning, designing, higher-level integration, DevOps, deployment, orchestration, and other aspects of software have had minimal impact from GenAI. We are excited about the long-term prospects, but do not have an opinion on when GenAI techniques will make meaningful strides in these areas.

Will AI replace software engineering?

The need for software engineering will continue for two reasons. First, we know that GenAI is much more effective at writing parts rather than full end-to-end content. For prose text, we don't expect GenAI to draft full reports, but we can break it down into sections and paragraphs and use prompt engineering. It's no surprise that some of the main use cases are web searches and summarization, which have weak parallels in software engineering and improving text, which is essentially refactoring. With software engineering, knowledge of software structure and supporting architectures is needed to break code into modules, files, and succinct methods. The need for human skills for these tasks will likely continue for several years, even though individual methods may be fully crafted using GenAI. Humans will shift to roles in architecture, design, and integration, and will still ultimately be responsible for validating the code.

The second reason is that GenAI is most effective when working with widely available code bases but often fails without such expansive sets of examples. Most software engineers need to learn a new language every 3–5 years on average. Certainly, some of this is due to switching jobs. However, new languages, frameworks, and new versions of both continue to emerge—none of which begin with sufficiently large code bases for training GenAI models. Domain-specific languages are another good example of limited training data. In addition, the newest technologies in databases, cybersecurity, quantum computing, and so on need software engineers since their respective code bases are still being written.

Risk and governance

Humans are currently ultimately responsible for the code that is produced, but the use of GenAI raises a number of challenges. In heavily regulated industries such as transportation, banking, and healthcare, the use of AI will undergo significant scrutiny. The ability to provide explainability and understanding of which programmers, agents, or AI created different sections of code will likely become standard. The risks, legal responsibilities, and ethical considerations will need to address responsibilities and safeguards for software. The ethical, moral, and legal issues around self-driving cars today provide a good example of some of the considerations. MIT's trolley problem (`https://en.wikipedia.org/wiki/Trolley_problem`) and the Moral Machine (`https://en.wikipedia.org/wiki/Moral_Machine`) provide further examples of the challenges.

Another challenge is the copyright issue of software. For regular texts, News Corp, the Financial Times, the Associated Press, and other media companies have negotiated agreements to license their text to OpenAI. Microsoft and Google have also negotiated with content providers to scale their training sets without violating copyright laws. For software code, the laws are less clear since it's a relatively new problem that has not yet been resolved. It is certainly possible that the GenAI could duplicate copyrighted code. Since the accuracy of the GenAI depends in part on the size of the training set, more code licensing may be required to improve performance.

The education in programming languages and the evaluation of skills must also adapt. Schools and universities have taught programming skills for decades. Just as spelling and grammar checkers are standard practice for writing reports, GenAI is likely to eventually not just be accepted but be a required part of software development. Universities have tended to focus more on the language nuances and syntax rather than the set of available tools, such as compilers, debuggers, and linters. However, ignoring GenAI will be difficult since it will be used extensively. Job interviewers have often used LeetCode forms of technical questions to weed out candidates, even though many of the questions are more academic than common industry practices. With GenAI, such low-level coding skills have become even less relevant, and we expect these forms of interview questions to evolve as well.

Summary

AI and GenAI capabilities have advanced rapidly over the past several years through a number of major technology innovations. With GenAI's boost in software engineering productivity at a low price point, it will increase the volume of code written and lower the overall costs. This will change the software engineer landscape, perhaps to favor more senior developers with more experience in architecture, design, and SWEBOK. It may also enable specialists with deep domain experience to develop more code. Legacy systems may be rewritten with GenAI support, which will free companies to use software developers across projects in a more agile manner.

There is a strong movement toward adopting GenAI for coding, and it has already been integrated into many IDEs. In the longer term, we will see how it surpasses the coding tasks and enters more aspects of software engineering. GenAI still requires the communication of commands to computers, and natural language may eventually supplement or replace programming languages, but pseudocode may be the next frontier. The world will still need software engineers for the foreseeable future. There are still many issues to manage, from risk to compliance, but GenAI has arrived and is already supercharging software engineering.

Further reading

To learn more about the topics that were covered in this chapter, take a look at the following resources:

- Thomas Davenport and DJ Patil. Harvard Business Review. `https://hbr.org/2012/10/data-scientist-the-sexiest-job-of-the-21st-century`

- AI winters: `https://www.historyofdatascience.com/ai-winter-the-highs-and-lows-of-artificial-intelligence/`

- Alex Krizhevsky, Ilya Sutskever, Geoffrey E. Hinton. *ImageNet Classification with Deep Convolutional Neural Networks*. NeurIPS 2012. `https://proceedings.neurips.cc/paper_files/paper/2012/file/c399862d3b9d6b76c8436e924a68c45b-Paper.pdf`

- ImageNet Large Scale Visual Recognition Challenge. https://arxiv.org/pdf/1409.0575

- *Attention Is All You Need.* https://en.wikipedia.org/wiki/Attention_Is_All_You_Need

- Gartner hype cycle for AI practices. https://www.gartner.com/en/newsroom/press-releases/2023-11-28-gartner-hype-cycle-shows-ai-practices-and-platform-engineering-will-reach-mainstream-adoption-in-software-engineering-in-two-to-five-years

- *The startling power generative AI is bringing to software development.* https://kpmg.com/us/en/articles/2023/generative-artificial-intelligence.html

- H. Washizaki, eds., *Guide to the Software Engineering Body of Knowledge (SWEBOK Guide), Version 4.0*, IEEE Computer Society, 2024. https://www.computer.org/education/bodies-of-knowledge/software-engineering

- Moral Machine. https://en.wikipedia.org/wiki/Moral_Machine

- Trolley problem. https://en.wikipedia.org/wiki/Trolley_problem

Subscribe for a free eBook

New frameworks, evolving architectures, research drops, production breakdowns—*AI_Distilled* filters the noise into a weekly briefing for engineers and researchers working hands-on with LLMs and GenAI systems. Subscribe now and receive a free eBook, along with weekly insights that help you stay focused and informed.

Subscribe at https://packt.link/TR05B or scan the QR code below.

Appendix

Set up an OpenAI Account

Here are the steps to create an OpenAI account:

1. Navigate to https://openai.com/. At the top left of the page, click on either ChatGPT or API Platform to start the account creation process, as shown in *Figure 1*:

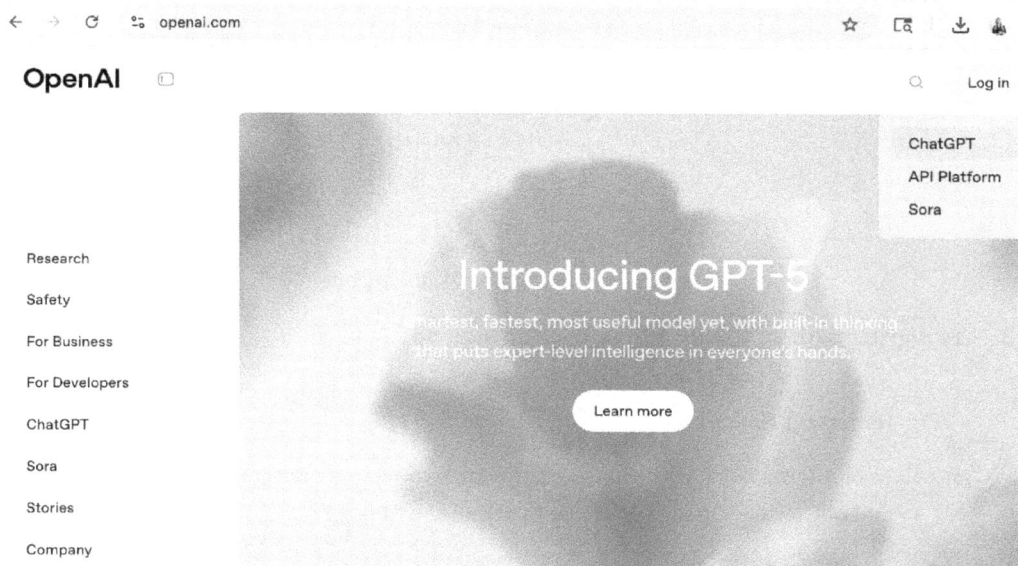

Figure 1: Access to ChatGPT and API Platform from OpenAI API

2. Each of these links will take you to an account creation page, where you can sign up using popular platforms such as Google, Microsoft, or Apple, or register with an email address, as shown in *Figure 2*:

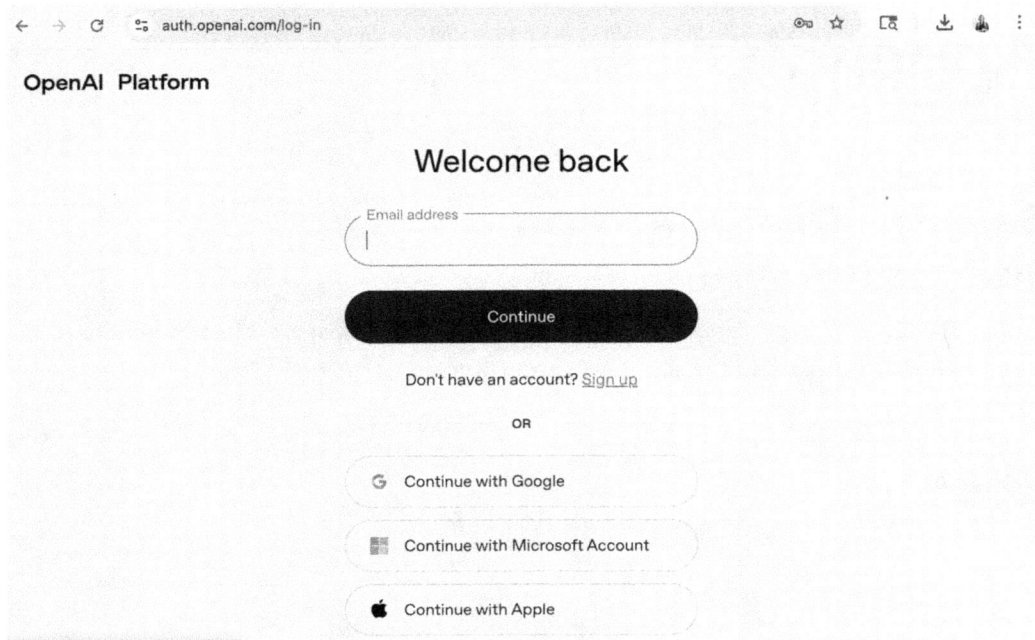

Figure 2: OpenAI platform sign-up page

3. To register with an email address, click on **Sign up**.

> **Important Note**
>
> As of August 2025, you will need to create two separate accounts: one for ChatGPT and one for the OpenAI platform to access the API.

In the next section, we will go through the setup of a virtual environment.

Creating a virtual environment

A **virtual environment** in Python is an isolated setup that ensures the reproducibility of dependencies, which are external libraries our project depends on.

For example, consider the following code:

```
import pandas as pd

df = pd.read_csv('df.csv')
df.to_markdown()
```

Here, we depend on Pandas, a third-party and open-source library available at: https://github.com/pandas-dev/pandas. Pandas provides the read_csv function, which returns a DataFrame. Since version 1.0.0, which can only run on Python 3.6.1 or higher, the DataFrame class also includes the to_markdown method. If we use earlier versions of Python or Pandas, this code may not run.

Generally, developers specify their required dependencies in a file named requirements.txt. In this book's repository, you will find a specification of the external libraries that we use in requirements.txt, as shown in *Figure 3*:

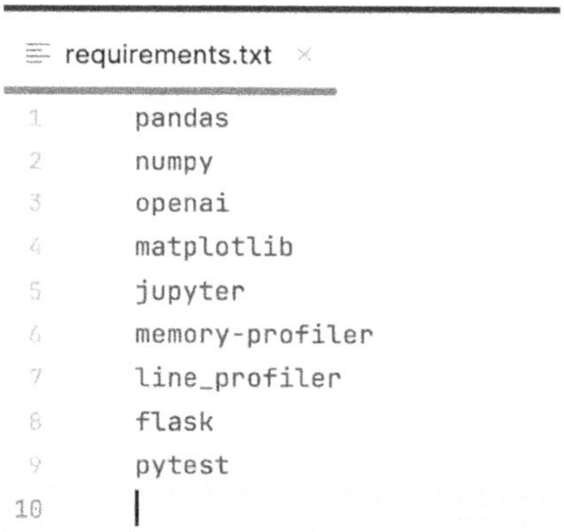

```
≡ requirements.txt   ×
1       pandas
2       numpy
3       openai
4       matplotlib
5       jupyter
6       memory-profiler
7       line_profiler
8       flask
9       pytest
10      |
```

Figure 3: Requirements.txt file for this book

In later chapters of the book, where we dive deeper into the **software development lifecycle (SDLC)** functions, the requirement files for these projects will include specific versions, as shown in *Figure 4*:

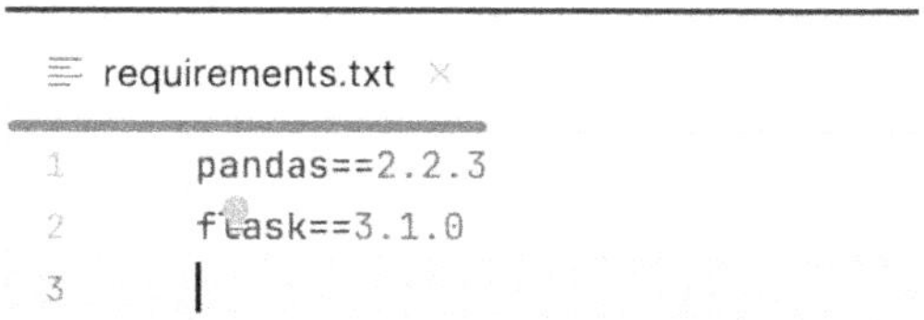

```
≡ requirements.txt   ×
1       pandas==2.2.3
2       flask==3.1.0
3       |
```

Figure 4: requirements.txt with versioning from Chapter 10

Just like in this figure, our production projects also include specific versioning. For the dependency versioning resolution, we leverage dependency and environment management tools such as *pipenv* that proposes dependency management for specific versioning resolution. Other developers may use *Conda*, *poetry*, or other tools. In this book, however, we will use Python's built-in *venv* tool for our environment setup.

Prompting virtual environment

In this book, we leveraged GenAI for every step of the SDLC, and installing a virtual environment is no exception. This task is a good candidate for using the **agent** mode within the GitHub Copilot chat window, with a prompt that follows the **Five S's** discussed in detail in *Chapter 4*.

A prompt to install our dependencies should include the following components:

1. **Python version**: Which version of Python should be used to run this project, in our case, it is *Python 3.11*.

2. **Environment tool**: Either *venv* or its alternatives.

3. **Requirements file**: The default is requirements.txt placed in the root of the project.

4. **Environment name**: A common practice is to name the environment .venv. We can also customize it to suit the project name with a prefix of a period, such as .supercharged.

5. **Environment location**: The library code is typically installed at the project root.

Considering these, here is an example of a prompt we can use with GitHub Copilot, either in PyCharm or VS Code:

```
CONTEXT: You are provided with:
1. Python version enclosed with {{{ VERSION }}}
2. Requirements file path enclosed with {{{ PATH }}}
3. Environment tool enclosed with {{{ TOOL }}}
4. Environment name enclosed with {{{ ENV NAME }}}
5. Location for the environment enclosed with {{{ Location }}}

TASK: Set up a virtual environment using the Python version, requirements
file path, using the provided name and location for this project.

VERSION: {{{ Python 3.11 }}
PATH: {{{ requirements.txt }}}
TOOL: {{{ venv }}}
```

```
ENV NAME: {{{ .supercharged }}}
LOCATION: {{{ project root }}}
```

For reference, the output of the setup using agent mode with GitHub Copilot and the underlying *Claude Sonnet 4.0* specifies the steps for setting up an environment, activating it, and installing its dependencies. *Figure 5* demonstrates creating the environment with our desired name and activating it:

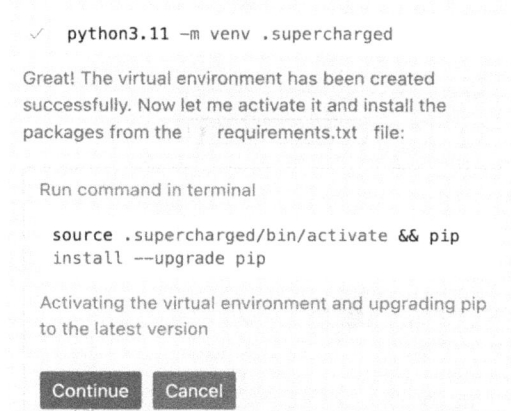

Figure 5: Activating the virtual environment

Figure 6 illustrates the installation of dependencies as specified in `requirements.txt`:

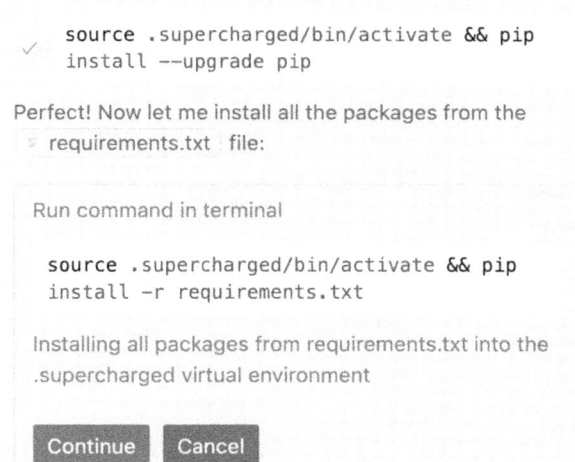

Figure 6: Installation of the dependencies

Once installation is complete, Copilot may propose some tests, such as validating the correct versioning of the packages, concluding with a success message as shown in *Figure 7*:

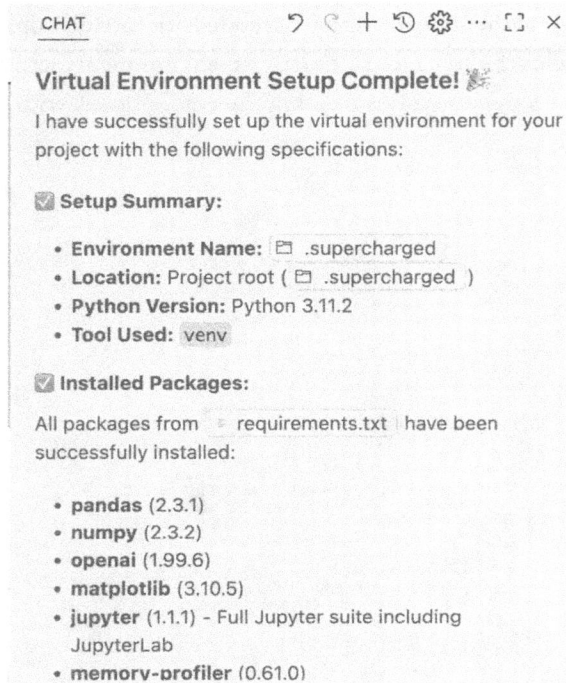

Figure 7: Successful installation message

After the setup is complete, we can see that a `.supercharged` folder is added to the repository, as shown in *Figure 8*:

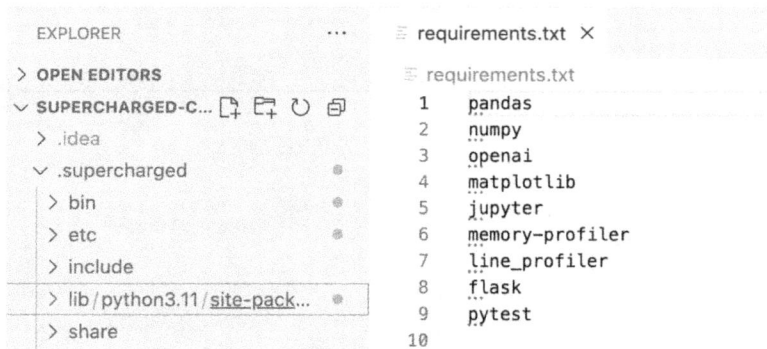

Figure 8: Added files to the repository

For reference, here are the typical three shell commands we can use to manually install the virtual environment:

```
python3.11 -m venv .supercharged
source .supercharged/bin/activate
pip install -r requirements.txt
```

Next, we will see how to instruct git to ignore the dependencies files.

Adding virtual environment to .gitignore

Since requirements.txt is sufficient for replicating the dependencies on any machine, there is no need to include the actual environment code in the repository. For that reason, it is best practice to ignore the installed dependencies. We can do this by adding the path of the installed requirements to the .gitignore file. We can chain another prompt in agent mode:

```
Add the environment path to .gitignore file.
```

This prompt successfully adds the path of the virtual environment to .gitignore, as shown in *Figure 9*.

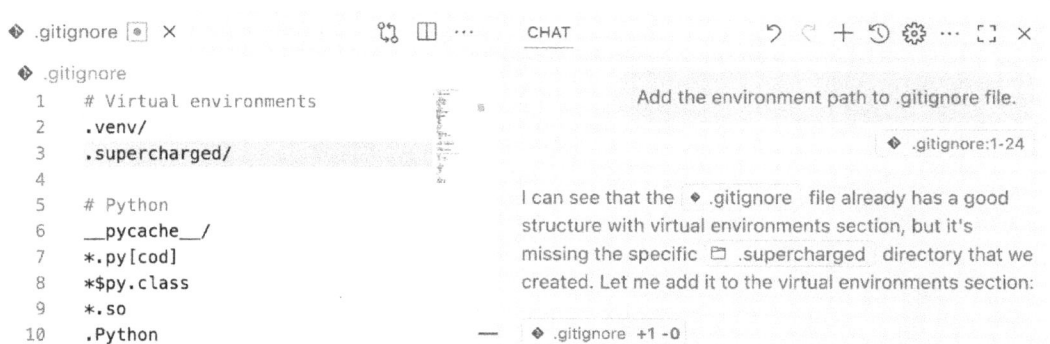

Figure 9: Adding the path to the .gitignore file

If you named your environment differently, Copilot would likely add the correct name to the file. If you used .supercharged or .venv, no changes are required because these names are already in our files.

> **Important Note**
>
> Now that you are a supercharged coder, we encourage you to help your colleagues use these prompts when setting up a new virtual environment. These can be adapted for different environment tools, environment names, and projects, reducing the chances of errors when working with Agent mode

Further reading

To learn more about the topics that were covered in this chapter, take a look at the following resources:

- Venv, virtual environment built-in: `https://docs.python.org/3/library/venv.html`
- Pipenv, dependency and environment management tools: `https://pipenv.pypa.io/en/latest/`
- Poetry, dependency and environment management tools: `https://python-poetry.org/docs/dependency-specification/`
- Conda, dependency and environment management tools: `https://anaconda.org/anaconda/conda`

‹packt›

packtpub.com

Subscribe to our online digital library for full access to over 7,000 books and videos, as well as industry leading tools to help you plan your personal development and advance your career. For more information, please visit our website.

Why subscribe?

- Spend less time learning and more time coding with practical eBooks and Videos from over 4,000 industry professionals
- Improve your learning with Skill Plans built especially for you
- Get a free eBook or video every month
- Fully searchable for easy access to vital information
- Copy and paste, print, and bookmark content

Did you know that Packt offers eBook versions of every book published, with PDF and ePub files available? You can upgrade to the eBook version at packtpub.com and as a print book customer, you are entitled to a discount on the eBook copy. Get in touch with us at customercare@packtpub.com for more details.

At www.packtpub.com, you can also read a collection of free technical articles, sign up for a range of free newsletters, and receive exclusive discounts and offers on Packt books and eBooks.

Other Books You May Enjoy

If you enjoyed this book, you may be interested in these other books by Packt:

Building Agentic AI Systems

Create intelligent, autonomous AI agents that can reason, plan, and adapt

Forewords by
Matthew R. Scott, Chief Technology Officer, Minset.ai
Dr. Alex Acero, member of the National Academy of Engineering, IEEE Fellow

Anjanava Biswas | Wrick Talukdar   <packt>

Building Agentic AI Systems

Anjanava Biswas, Wrick Talukdar

ISBN: 978-1-80323-875-3

- Master the core principles of GenAI and agentic systems
- Understand how AI agents operate, reason, and adapt in dynamic environments
- Enable AI agents to analyze their own actions and improvise
- Implement systems where AI agents can leverage external tools and plan complex tasks
- Apply methods to enhance transparency, accountability, and reliability in AI
- Explore real-world implementations of AI agents across industries

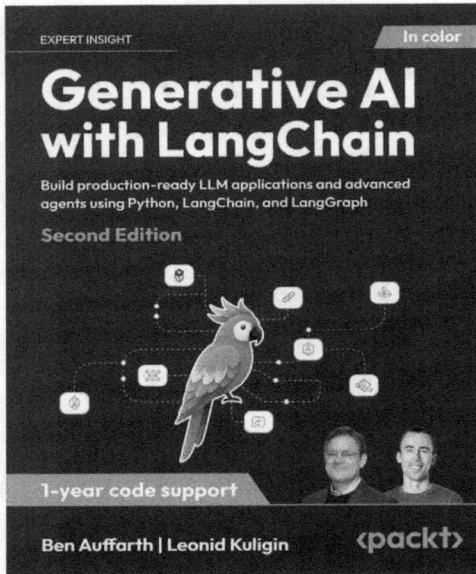

Generative AI with LangChain - Second Edition

Ben Auffarth, Leonid Kuligin

ISBN: 978-1-83702-201-4

- Design and implement multi-agent systems using LangGraph
- Implement testing strategies that identify issues before deployment
- Deploy observability and monitoring solutions for production environments
- Build agentic RAG systems with re-ranking capabilities
- Architect scalable, production-ready AI agents using LangGraph and MCP
- Work with the latest LLMs and providers like Google Gemini, Anthropic, Mistral, DeepSeek, and OpenAI's o3-mini
- Design secure, compliant AI systems aligned with modern ethical practices

Packt is searching for authors like you

If you're interested in becoming an author for Packt, please visit authors.packtpub.com and apply today. We have worked with thousands of developers and tech professionals, just like you, to help them share their insight with the global tech community. You can make a general application, apply for a specific hot topic that we are recruiting an author for, or submit your own idea.

Share Your Thoughts

Now you've finished *Supercharged Coding with GenAI*, we'd love to hear your thoughts! Scan the QR code below to go straight to the Amazon review page for this book and share your feedback or leave a review on the site that you purchased it from.

https://packt.link/r/1836645295

Your review is important to us and the tech community and will help us make sure we're delivering excellent quality content.

Join our Discord and Reddit spaces

You're not the only one navigating fragmented tools, constant updates, and unclear best practices. Join a growing community of professionals exchanging insights that don't make it into documentation.

Stay informed with updates, discussions, and behind-the-scenes insights from our authors. Join our Discord space at `https://packt.link/z8ivB` or scan the QR code below:	Connect with peers, share ideas, and discuss real-world GenAI challenges. Follow us on Reddit at `https://packt.link/0rExL` or scan the QR code below:

Index